Marie Dressler

MARIE DRESSLER

A Biography; With a Listing of Major Stage Performances, a Filmography and a Discography

by MATTHEW KENNEDY

McFarland & Company, Inc., Publishers
Jefferson, North Carolina, and London

For my mother

Frontispiece: Marie poses for photographer Ruth Harriet Louise, circa 1930. The oddly draped dress, shortened fur, cheap hat, and pigeon-toed feet contribute to Marie's uncanny tragicomic gifts. Courtesy of Eric D. Bernhoft.

The present work is a reprint of the library bound edition of Marie Dressler: A Biography; With a Listing of Major Stage Performances, a Filmography and a Discography, *first published in 1999 by McFarland.*

LIBRARY OF CONGRESS CATALOGUING-IN-PUBLICATION DATA

Kennedy, Matthew, 1957–
    Marie Dressler : a biography; with a listing of major stage performances, a filmography and a discography / by Matthew Kennedy.
      p. cm.
    Discography: p.
    Filmography: p.
    Includes bibliographical references and index.

    ISBN-13: 978-0-7864-2844-1
    ISBN-10: 0-7864-2844-9 (softcover : 50# alkaline paper) ∞

    1. Dressler, Marie, 1869–1934.   2. Actors—United States—Biography.   I. Title.
PN2287.D55K46   2006
792'.028'092—dc21
[b]   98-31206

British Library cataloguing data are available

©1999 Matthew Kennedy. All rights reserved

No part of this book may be reproduced or transmitted in any form or by any means, electronic or mechanical, including photocopying or recording, or by any information storage and retrieval system, without permission in writing from the publisher.

On the cover: Marie Dressler in *Dinner at Eight*, 1933 (MGM/Photofest)

Manufactured in the United States of America

McFarland & Company, Inc., Publishers
   Box 611, Jefferson, North Carolina 28640
      www.mcfarlandpub.com

Contents

Acknowledgments vii
Introduction 1

1. The Koerbers   9
2. The Apprentice   14
3. "Nothing to It but Dressler"   27
4. The London Ache   43
5. A Wretch Named Tillie   59
6. Mack Sennett's Grand Idea   76
7. Give Till It Hurts   93
8. Ghosts   106
9. The Undying Affection of Friends   121
10. The Raspberry Season   135
11. *Anna Christie*   147
12. Working   156
13. Queen Marie of Hollywood   171
14. "Careless Rapture"   187
15. Pacific   206

Epilogue   217
Appendix 1: Major Stage Appearances   229
Appendix 2: Filmography   233
Appendix 3: Discography   238
Notes   239
Bibliography   253
Source Institutions   257
Index   259

Acknowledgments

As I complete this, my first book, one cliché of authorship shines through: the debts to so many good people. This book could not have been written without the professionalism, guidance, enthusiasm, and good wishes of everyone listed below.

The conservators: My temptation is to effuse over the work of Sam Gill and the staff at the Academy of Motion Picture Arts and Sciences Margaret Herrick Library, for the job they do is truly remarkable. Hats off to Robert Cushman, Faye Thompson, David Marsh, Lisa Jackson, Jonathan Wahl, Grafton Harper, Sandra Archer, and Steve Garland. Ned Comstock of the USC Cinema-Television Library made available rare documents from the MGM production files and the Frances Marion Collection. Eric D. Bernhoft graciously shared his edifying collection of Dressler artifacts, including a wax cylinder recording, estate checkbook, financial ledger, photos, and sheet music.

Thanks, also, to Evelyn Ward at the Cleveland Public Library; Geraldine Duclow of the Free Library of Philadelphia; Bruce Sher and Michael T. Dumas at Harvard; Rosemary C. Hanes, Madeline Matz, and Edwin M. Matthias at the Library of Congress; Sally Dumaux at the Hollywood Branch of the Los Angeles Public Library; Marty Jacobs at the Museum of the City of New York; Maryann Chach, Reagan Fletcher, and Mark Swartz of the Shubert Archive; and Ann L. Wilkens of the Wisconsin Center for Film and Theater Research.

The Marie Dressler Foundation in Cobourg, Ontario, is kept by the most generous, most hospitable and warmest group of people imaginable. They cleared tables and hauled boxes from storage, giving me free rein in a trove of artifacts, clippings, photos, and recordings. Special affection and appreciation go to Joan Long, Barbara Garrick, Gael Moore, Cecilia Nasmith, and Ed Haynes, the ringleader of the effort to keep Marie's memory alive.

Hunting down Marie's rare films was as fun and rewarding as finding written sources. I am in debt to all those who helped in the quest: Larry Chadbourne, Don Koll, Randal Malone, Charles Lindsley, Earl Anderson, John Cavallo, Larry Quirk, William Schoell, and Dick May, vice president of Preservation and Distribution Services at Turner Entertainment Company. Kathleen MacRae and Ed Stratmann at the George Eastman House, Lou Ellen Kramer at the UCLA Film and Television Archive, and Charles Silver at the Museum of Modern Art Film Studies Center welcomed me to screenings with the courtesy of top-quality innkeepers. A special nod to Elliot Lavine of San Francisco's Roxie Theater for being agreeable to a mini Dressler tribute.

The detectives and literati: In tracking Marie's elusive family, help was ably supplied by Karen Franklin, Estelle and Bambi Sue Camerman, Arthur James, and Janice Slocum of the Family History Center at the Golden Gate–Bay Ward of the Church of Jesus Christ of Latter-Day Saints. Appreciation, too, to those who helped track down the Dalton clan: Anne Brewer of the Steuben County Historical Society, Susan Reynolds of the Corning–Painted Post Historical Society, and Eleanor Black of the Corning–Painted Post Roman Catholic Community. Experts at publishing helped dearly along the way, including Richard La Bonté, Lawrence Ganem, and Chris Minichino. In unraveling Marie's housing history, thanks go to Ken Hanke, Mark and Debbie Roper, Scarlett and Max Schumacher, Hunter Drohojowska-Philp, Maria Churchill, and Maria Herold of the Montecito History Committee.

The witnesses: I am deeply grateful for generously shared memories from those who knew Marie, including Sally Blane, Frank "Junior" Coghlan, Jackie Cooper, William Edmonson, Karen Morley Gough, Marion Shilling Cook, Joan Marsh Morrill, Maureen O'Sullivan, Anita Page, Dora Eastman, and "Major" Carl Roup. Valuable reflections were also supplied by Marcella Rabwin, Maurice Rapf, Marilyn Strickling Read, and Joseph J. O'Donohue IV. Special mention is due Grace Annable Ruthrruff, Joseph Newman, and Elaine St. Johns. Their personal and eloquent testimony helped me understand Marie's place in movies and in the hearts of Americans. Valuable information on the lives of Mamie and Jerry Cox was provided by Mr. W. W. Law, head of the Savannah branch of the Association for the Study of Afro-American Life and History, and by Sadie Davis Steele, Mamie's niece by marriage. Delores Bryant and John Phillip Law went above and beyond in their assistance with the history, career, and personality of Claire DuBrey. Sierra Pecheur performed minor miracles in shedding light on the life of this private woman.

The scholars: I have been fortunate to correspond with a number of excellent biographers, historians, and writers. Back in 1970, Roberta Raider earned her Ph.D. from the University of Michigan for her dissertation on the art of Marie's acting. Now she is Dr. Roberta Raider Sloan, chair of the Department of Theater Arts at the University of Central Oklahoma, and her exhaustive research made my job much easier. Great advice and ideas came from Michael G. Ankerich, Roi A. Uselton, Barbara Probst Solomon, Cari Beauchamp (biographer of Frances Marion), John R. Cocchi, Diane MacIntyre, Joanna Rapf, Margaret Tante Burk, Boze Hadleigh, Betty Lee, Linda Fresia, Charles Musser (an authority on Thomas Edison), Miles Kreuger, Anthony Slide, Mark Vieira (an authority on George Hurrell), Frank Thompson, and Armond Fields and L. Marc Fields (great-nephew and great-great-nephew of Lew Fields). David Stenn was a terrific help in locating interviewees. Doug McClelland is a faithful pen pal and has an encyclopedic knowledge of movies. And every first-time book author needs a James Robert Parish in their lives. No e-mail message was too trivial, no tantrum was too self-indulgent — he answered them all with humor, understanding, and patience.

Friends and family: Like Marie, I have been blessed. For loyalty, encouragement, and the occasional well-placed phone call, copious thanks go to Newton Butler, Nicole Smalley, Ralph Cole, Jr., James Kerr, Phyllis Grilikhes-Maxwell, Earl Jackson, Jr., Chris Culwell, Jerry Windley, David Moreno, Teresa Roberts, Peter Scheubel, Mary Redick, Tanja Orbeck, Antoine Garth, George Shardlow, Richard Jessup, Tom Schumacher, Jimmy Bangley, James Brown, and Tom McIntire. I miss Tom Hoonan a lot. This great wit did not live long enough to realize his dream of morphing Marie into *Lost in Space*, our favorite childhood television series. Then there's Mark Cromwell, whose great research, editing, and pithy conversations are exceeded only by his gift of abiding friendship.

The eager conversations and sincere interest from everyone in my family has meant more than I can say. Cousin Kacy Cook made the Meher Baba connection with the help of Karina Page. Brother James Kennedy did some Internet perusal. Sister Anne Peterson read raw versions of every chapter and went at them with a busy pencil. Stan Godin, companion and confidant extraordinaire, deserves some kind of award for never once saying, "Shut up about Marie Dressler already!" To all, "thank you" is inadequate.

Finally, to my mother, Carolyn Kennedy, an unconditional fan of everything that matters: movies, theater, and world travel. Her faith kept me at the computer and made this book happen.

*'Tis not a lip, or eye, we beauty call,
but the joint force and full result of all.*

— Alexander Pope

Introduction

Marie Dressler and I came together with *Dinner at Eight*. I first saw the sterling 1933 Metro-Goldwyn-Mayer comedy on commercial television in the 1960s. Two performances stood above the rest: Jean Harlow as status-seeking, two-timing golddigger Kitty Packard, and Marie Dressler as overripe, faded stage star Carlotta Vance.

The movie's final scene between the two women has become a permanent reference for sublime comedic exchange. It is the most famous moment for either actress, as Marie delivers one of the greatest double takes and line readings ever captured on film. Harlow attempts small talk by mentioning she "was reading a book the other day." Marie's enormous body lurches awkwardly in a double take as subtle as a foghorn. "Reading a book?" she asks incredulously. Oblivious to this insult, Harlow goes on to say that the author predicts "machinery is going to take the place of every profession." With that, Marie pauses a half-second, scans Harlow's revealed front side, takes her hand and assures her, "Oh, my dear, that's something *you* need never worry about."

I saw *Dinner at Eight* again, in college, but not until the third viewing did the movie and Marie Dressler take hold in my imagination. Circa 1989, three friends and I caught *Dinner at Eight* and *Grand Hotel* on a double bill in the old restored Crest Theater in Sacramento. We all agreed that Marie Dressler was a perfectly magical comedienne but that she had an undercurrent of sorrow and loss that made her moving and very human. Who was this large, unpretty woman who had top billing over Harlow, Wallace Beery, and two Barrymores?

Cursory research left me startled. Dressler starred with Charlie Chaplin in the first feature-length comedy, *Tillie's Punctured Romance,* in 1914. She later starred in famous movies such as *Min and Bill* and *Tugboat Annie,* the former winning her an Academy Award. Her partnership with Wallace Beery in those movies is considered one of the most uncanny pairings in screen history. She worked with or knew virtually every major star of her era, including Lillian Gish, Greta Garbo, Clark Gable, Marion Davies, Norma Shearer, Myrna Loy, Ramon Novarro, Mary Pickford, and Rudy Vallee. She knew several presidents and was more than once their private guest at the White House.

Before World War I, Dressler was hailed as America's finest comic in a 20-year string of Broadway, musical revue, and vaudeville successes such as *The Lady Slavey, Miss Prinnt, Higgledy Piggledy, The Man in the Moon, Roly Poly, A Mix Up*, and, most spectacularly, *Tillie's Nightmare*. Her popularity plummeted after the war. For several years she was a has-been, pitiable and broke. Her later success in talkies was all the more satisfying as she rose from middle-aged obscurity to become the world's top box-office draw.

Her work did not spawn any great or easily identifiable theatrical and cinematic traditions. Her early mentor Lillian Russell established the prototype for the larger-than-life Broadway diva. Joe Weber and Lew Fields, her frequent vaudeville and revue employers, had routines that now look like the blueprints for every subsequent male comedy duo, from Dean Martin and Jerry Lewis to Laurel and Hardy and the Smothers Brothers.

Dressler's legacy is much harder to trace because she remains an anomaly. How many times have I come across the sentiment that Marie was absolutely unique: humble, proud, bumbling, and noble all at the same time? There was nothing intellectual about Marie's comedy. Her low characters were salty and irritable, while her monied characters were stuffy and self-important but not well educated. Throughout her career she took delight in dismantling pomposity. During her stage years, she became a primary purveyor of reactive theater, or, in other words, staged entertainment based on the defamation of "legitimate" stars and productions. Even as late as the film *Anna Christie* in 1930, she was deflating overheated prose and injecting somber moments with humanity, grit, and humor. Comediennes and farceurs such as Beatrice Lillie, Hermione Gingold, Fanny Brice, Imogene Coca, Kaye Ballard, Lily Tomlin, Whoopi Goldberg, Phyllis Diller, Carol Burnett, Moms Mabley, and Totie Fields are indebted to Dressler because she was the first woman to make movie audiences laugh for more than 20 minutes. Without an obvious lineage she remains distinct, which may explain why she is too rarely listed among the great entertainers of the twentieth century. "There is only one Marie Dressler," noted critic Archie Bell.[1] "Perhaps there will never be another, because the world wheeled on some thousands of years before her species was evolved, and a casual glance over the horizon doesn't show any more Maries in the making."

She was a big woman, five feet, seven inches tall and weighing about 200 pounds. Perched atop a massive and ungainly body was what Marie called "the funniest face that the Lord had ever put on human shoulders."[2] The famous visage was described in 1932: "She has small twinkling eyes, alight with humor, tolerance and goodness — small and green they are, like little sparkling aquamarines. She has a short round nose, a full serious upper lip above her wide smiling, tender mouth. Several chins. A complexion soft as satin, and rose, with a few freckles above the nose."[3]

Dressler's expressive possibilities seemed limitless, but she was much more than an amusement with rubberized features. It is tempting to label her a great proletarian comedienne, filled as her comedy was with pratfalls, puns, malapropisms, and multiple references to her weight. But she was foremost a brilliant comedienne in body, timing, inflection, and reactions. She received pies in the face as well as anyone, but her talents far exceeded the expectations of slapstick. One interviewer[4] observed that "behind the humor of her characters there is rugged strength which comes from something deeper than frivolity. Hers is a humor which finds its roots deep in an understanding of human nature — where great acting always begins." On the occasion of seeing her stage hit *Tillie's Nightmare* in 1911, Montgomery Phister of the *Cincinnati Commercial* stated:[5] "She is absolutely unique, alone and unapproachable as a delineator of eccentric comedy; and such comedy, indescribable as it is irresistible. The realistic mixed with the grotesque and yet suddenly, unexpectedly, with a shadow of the pathetic thrown across it, a shading of the voice into some tender expression, a little emotional touch, an appeal to your sympathies, that fairly astonishes you in the midst of the wild fun of burlesque. It is an act that few possess."

She hated flappers, loved backgammon, needlepoint, croquet, card games, and roses. She read histories and biographies because[6] "I like to know about the people who messed up the world for us." She loathed smut, reveled in clean humor, and fought hard for the rights of women and actors when both were held in subservience. She smoked, and she tagged "dear" and "darling" on the end of sentences. She never flew. She loved animals and children but was childless. It is not well known that she had a very real talent at music. Her piano playing was fine, but she usually botched it to win a laugh. In her younger days, she had a fine contralto and a promising career in comic opera. Her parties often included sing-alongs around the piano, and she proudly counted soprano Luisa Tetrazzini, tenor Enrico Caruso, violinist Fritz Kreisler, and composers Irving Berlin and George Gershwin among her friends.

Dressler was an accomplished dressmaker and costume designer. The bizarre sartorial travesties she wore in *Tillie's Nightmare* were her own creations. She loved the mountains and gave a party for close friends at a Tujunga Canyon retreat shortly before she died. She was reputed to be a fine cook, but that reputation may have been manufactured by the publicity machine at MGM. She suffered horrible stage fright, forgot her lines, and could improvise brilliantly. She was a dreadful money manager and found herself at the distant ends of poverty and wealth more than once in her life.

At the time of her death in 1934, Dressler was the most beloved film star in America. According to an August 1933 *Time* magazine cover story, her films then earned an average of $800,000 each—a sum far exceeding the draw of all other stars. The honor of box-office champion was officially given to her in 1932 and 1933 by the Quigley Publication and the *Motion Picture Herald*'s nationwide poll, which asked 12,000 motion-picture exhibitors to name movie stars with superior earning power. Dressler topped Jean Harlow, Joan Crawford, Clark Gable, Greta Garbo, and Mickey Mouse.

There were Marie Dressler puppets, dresses, fan clubs, and commemorative flowers. Movie historian and collector Earl Anderson had a clear recollection of seeing the first-run engagement of Marie's 1930 stock market comedy *Caught Short*. He offered an account of her appeal:[7]

> She was the best loved star of her time. She occupied a role in public consciousness that was later taken over by Shirley Temple. I didn't understand this as a child, but I do now. Times were very, very hard and both of them provided something no one else could. There's something irrepressibly cheerful and hopeful about both of them. Marie was so comfortable with herself, so funny using all that old schtick. If people had ten cents to their names she made them feel better. She looked like your grandmother, or yourself. To hell with young love, to hell with getting rich. We had Marie. She became a national icon. It was a horrible shock when she died, but her fans used her courage to grieve. Public feeling ran to "the old lady's gone, but we have the future."

With her deeply set eyes, maternal smile, and highly skilled voice, Dressler melted the hearts of Depression-era audiences with an adroit mixture of robust humor and homily-infused sentiment. During her spectacular comeback in the early 1930s, audiences and reviewers marveled at her skill at playing lowlife drunks and haughty society matrons. Her secret was simple but effective—inject some humility into regal characters and some majesty into the downtrodden. Witness *Anna Christie*, *Min and Bill*, *Emma*, *Dinner at Eight*, or her queen travesty in *Hollywood Revue of 1929* for evidence of this successful formula. "A lady may stand on her head in a perfectly decent, self-respecting way," she once said.[8] Marie combined her basic "rules" with a constant awareness of the presence of an audience beyond the camera lens. She had a great gift for communication, but her characters were often made of little bits of business that obliterated whatever her costars were doing. Why did she suddenly bug her eyes or pout her lips? At her most self-indulgent, she seemed almost desperate for attention and approval. "Those wild facial reactions were all natural to her," said Marcella Rabwin,[9] David O. Selznick's assistant on *Dinner at Eight*. "She acted on her long stage experience. Her reactions weren't anything a director told her to do."

Dressler could get away with anything. First-rate directors such as George Hill and Clarence Brown succeeded in toning her down and guiding her to her best work, but they did so with a light touch. "One did not direct Marie Dressler at all," said Hill.[10] "One simply gave her the script, time to formulate her character and learn the lines, and then sit, inspired, at a magnificent, spontaneous performance. I think Marie Dressler was the greatest dramatic figure on the screen in the character field." Louis B. Mayer, studio head of MGM, shared Hill's esteem for Marie. He proclaimed her, Spencer Tracy, and Greta Garbo the three greatest actors his studio ever hired.[11]

Whatever shameless scene-stealing techniques she employed, accounts of Marie in her movie heyday are sprinkled with words like "triumphant," "humorous," "admired," and "inspirational." She was forgiven all excesses. "She makes the faces all right," wrote a reviewer[12] of *Christopher Bean*, her last film. "And she does a lot more than that too. She makes you howl and she makes your heart come right up to the point where you have to remove the false teeth to keep from biting it." Those who knew and worked with her maintained a lifelong reverence for her. "Marie was indeed a lady. She spoke well, dressed well and was beloved in all walks of society," wrote Maureen O'Sullivan,[13] who played her daughter-in-law in *Tugboat Annie*. "Marie stands out," said actress Anita Page,[14] who co-starred with her in three movies. "She was a delight to work with and she worked very hard. She was a very great actress." Joseph Newman,[15] assistant director of *Min and Bill* and *Dinner at Eight*, remembered that Marie was "a remarkable woman. She was revered by all at the MGM Studio. Everyone who worked with her loved and admired her. She was not only the ultimate trouper but, as the crews always referred to her, a regular fellow. I have never heard anyone say a disparaging word about her." Newman remembered above all that she had a "great respect for humanity and her graciousness and humor to all those who had the good fortune to know her and work with her, are as vivid as they were sixty-six years ago." Marcella Rabwin[16] said that "she was *the* most unusual star. Through the sheer magic of her ability as an actress, she became a favorite in American film history." George Cukor,[17] the young director of *Dinner at Eight*, said, "she acquired a kind of peculiar distinction, a magnificence. She was a law unto herself."

Joan Marsh Morrill met Dressler years before they appeared together in *Politics* in 1931. Marie watched Joan grow up as a child actress and daughter of acclaimed cinematographer Charles Rosher *(Sunrise)*. "Marie was one of the great ladies of the screen," said Morrill.[18] "To meet her you'd never know she was in show business. Very simple, gentle, loving human being. She was full of love and warmth and camaraderie. She was always interested in the other person. She was also a very good listener. I have a lovely autographed picture of her that I wouldn't give up for the world. I felt very close to her."

One writer on film[19] gave up on muckraking. "I wouldn't know where to go for spice to counteract the sweet, so I guess we will just have to admit that Marie is unusual and stands alone, which obviously accounts for the lack of jealousy in the film colony." Who would begrudge Marie her success when it was won against all conventions of stardom? Who would deny her fame and riches after years of mediocre material, typecasting, dishonest managers, ill health, romantic betrayals, and bankruptcy? She made the eternal demons of age and ugliness nothing to fear. She even celebrated them and by doing so gave everyone permission to let go of their vanity, seriousness, and self-doubt.

Fans devotedly paid five cents to enter a dark theater and watch a haggard but unbowed woman battle conformity, evil, and cruelty. Drawing on her personal tragedies, Dressler could play the sacrificing mother of *Min and Bill*, the loving domestic of *Emma*, the mayoral candidate of *Politics*, the waterfront denizen of *Tugboat Annie*, or the world-weary grand dame of *Dinner at Eight* with equal aplomb. The appeal of "the funniest woman in the world" often eluded precise definition. "There is something universal about her, something magnificent, something fine and altogether human," wrote one observer.[20] "I have seen her in good pictures and bad ones, but I never have seen her give a performance which I did not enjoy thoroughly." If success as a movie star is measured in love, then hers is one of the most wildly successful film careers.

At MGM, where Dressler made all but two of her talkies, her characters were most often gruff, impatient, inept, and morally correct in all matters of true importance. She often had lessons to teach, but she did it with such good humor that it never appeared preachy or self-righteous. In *Caught Short, Reducing, Politics,* and *Prosperity*— the low-budget comedies she made with fellow funny woman Polly Moran — Marie brought righteousness and rollicking humor to every role. In every feature there is a call to women's emancipation. Women are consistently victorious and strong in Marie's universe, while men are often humbled or sidelined. Chaplin was banished in *Tillie's Punctured Romance*, Jean Hersholt died in *Emma*, and Lionel Barrymore was chided for avarice and redeemed in *Christopher Bean*. Roscoe Ates was a stuttering nincompoop in *Politics*, and Beery hit the bottle in *Tugboat Annie*. Marie was always the suffering pillar of strength; she effectively replaced President Franklin D. Roosevelt for a rousing pep talk to the nation at the end of *Prosperity*.

Dressler does not reveal herself easily. Her two autobiographies, *The Life Story of an Ugly Duckling* and *My Own Story*, read like extended soliloquies full of wit and anecdotes, but they provide few revelations. Marie's silence and insistence on privacy are admirable qualities to carry through life, but they are rough on a biographer. The adoration she received was a problem for this writer: how to get past the gushing sentiment that accompanies so many recollections? What did she say confidentially to her closest friends about her private life or her working relationships with Louis B. Mayer, Wallace Beery, and Greta Garbo? What would they say, off the record, about her?

The greatest gaps were in her private life. Many assume Marie was a lesbian, but this may say more about sexual stereotypes than anything else. To see Marie maul Beery in *Min and Bill* is to see one seriously butch woman in action. But Marie was an actress, and the screen is an inappropriate place to draw conclusions about her sexuality. On the town she was a perfect lady in silk dresses, lilac perfume, soft furs, and jewelry around her wrists and throat. At home she collected knickknacks, had fresh flowers everywhere and was happiest playing bridge with her old friends. Sexual stereotypes are always as limiting as they are misleading.

It is certain Dressler loved men and women. In her memoirs, she made only vague references to the men she loved. She married briefly in 1894 and had a complicated and troubling affair with her manager from 1907 until his death in 1921. She made no reference to her romantic friendship with actress Claire DuBrey. Devotion to women dominated her life. Her many charities benefited women, and her closest friends were women. Whether she had ongoing sapphic relationships remains a matter of speculation. Raised in the age of Victorian discretion, Marie suffered years of sexual neglect. Even if she did have desires for starlets or Broadway chorus girls, what was a woman who built her career on being overweight and ugly supposed to do? The life of self-mockery made tatters of her self-image. Sex was more often unfulfilled, her options for physical intimacy remained limited, and she forever kept quiet. Her relationship with Claire DuBrey wasn't even well known inside the walls of the MGM studio. "She never talked about her private life," said Anita Page.[21] "She was devoted to her career. She took her comedy very seriously." Marie's marriage and love affairs ended bitterly.

Dressler was infinitely more successful at friendship, and no one was more influential than the brilliant and prolific screenwriter Frances Marion. Their 23-year friendship saw marriage, birth, offscreen contractual maneuvering, death, divorce, betrayal, financial ruin, war, and several successful screen collaborations. Most important, Frances reinvented Marie for the world. Without Frances, there would not be *Anna Christie, Min and Bill*, or *Emma*. Frances was the most important individual in Marie's career; her influence on Marie was far greater than that of any man.

Before her public and private makeover as an old softie, Dressler's relationships with men were filled with ambivalence. She was not always the robust grandmotherly type as seen in her most famous movies. Her childhood was tainted by a violent father whom she detested. When she started in theater, she found a profession ruled by men. To her credit and ruination, she claimed whatever power and authority she could. She entered protracted disputes with theater producers George Lederer and Abe Erlanger and film producers Gilbert ("Bronco Billy") Anderson and Mack Sennett. She once told William Randolph Hearst what to do with his newspapers. She won the wrath of every producer in New York when she headed the fabled actors' strike of 1919 and helped orchestrate the formation of the Actors' Equity Union.

Marie's first marriage, to George Hoppert, was short-lived. She found a more serious relationship with James Dalton, who managed to alienate their friends, lie to the press, and spend Marie's money on gambling and foolish business ventures. At the time of his death, Marie's life was nearly the stuff of Greek tragedy, and she devoted herself to forgetting. She once said, in her own defense,[22] "The thing is to regard life as a whole. Take it in a big sweep, take in the full scope of it. Remember the effect things had, what you learned from them, how you felt about them. But don't be fussy about the details." She explained that she purposely let the memories go. "You wouldn't go around burdening your friends with all the unpleasant things that ever happened to you. Well, why should you do it to yourself?"

The archaeology of Marie Dressler is challenging. Her legion of fans didn't write much, she kept no scrapbooks, and most letters and all diaries were destroyed or cannibalized many years ago. Theater history, at least to a biographer, is a delicate flower that disappears nightly, leaving nothing but yellowing clips, a souvenir program, and embellished memories.

As this book took shape, it became clear that a simple chronological account of Marie's life was inadequate. Too much has changed in American culture and entertainment, and she was changed too much by history. It is not possible to understand Marie's early successes without paying at least cursory attention to the freedom that the North American railroad system of the late nineteenth century brought. Likewise, her years on stage make sense only by reflecting on the cunning businessmen who used her. Her stage career is not just a succession of productions good and bad. It is a story of adversarial relationships with powerful men; it is a tale of combat against widespread assumptions that actors were eternal children to be bossed, manipulated, and enslaved. In an age before theater unions, actors had precious little control over their professional lives, and Marie's many rows during her years in theater were born from such conditions. As a stage actress, Marie could be unreasonable and throw her ego far and wide, but her complaints were not imaginary and her early legal battles were never mere sport. She believed in her causes and had no tolerance for exploitation. She made good on her outrage and paid dearly for it.

What strange confluence made Marie Dressler possible? She would attribute her final good fortune to fortuitous astrology, but I believe the answer is rooted in the earth and its people. It is not possible to write about Marie's prolonged career slump without accounting for the Great War, Prohibition, and women's suffrage. Especially Marie's comeback at the end of her life can be understood only in context of the Depression, the coming of sound to movies, and her friendship with Frances Marion. For her fans, Marie was nothing less than emotional salvation during an era of great uncertainty and fear. Her life and art were entwined in both historic moments and moving friendships. Without attention to them, this book would be incomplete.

Ultimately, it is her place as the grand, imperious dowager empress of early talkies that makes Dressler indelible. At that point, her art became a tonic for the masses. But she remains fresh and funny today; strength of character and superb comic instincts transcend history. For too short a time, she was a perfect and singular creation of the movies and was as loved as any star has ever been. This book explains how she came to be a great icon and artist.

Chapter 1

The Koerbers

The finest homes of Cobourg, Ontario, were east of Victoria Hall. The stately neo–Palladian building that dominates the old town center was built in 1860 when Cobourg aspired to be a rival of Toronto in commerce and political power. It was the undisputed center of civic life when Alexander and Annie Koerber and their daughter Bonita moved into a plain four-room brick cottage on King Street three blocks west of Victoria Hall.

Cobourg, population 5,000, was a full two-day stage coach ride along the north shore of Lake Ontario from Toronto. Gently rolling green farmland and orchards were between. Once an outpost for United Empire Loyalists who resisted the American Revolution, Cobourg was a busy port in the 1860s, conveniently situated across the lake from Rochester, New York. Victoria Hall was built with great confidence, but it nearly bankrupted the town as did the failure of the proposed Cobourg-Peterborough Railway line.

Cobourg was in the midst of a depression when the Koerbers' second daughter, Leila Marie, was born on a freezing day on November 9, 1868.* With the demands of 5-year-old Bonita and baby Leila, Alexander became ever more violent and moody. As Leila grew up, she remembered moving every few months when her father's bullying left his young music students in tears and the family without an income. "He could hate harder than any man I ever saw," wrote Leila[1] many years later. "He hated Canada, he hated privations and he hated his life as a music teacher. Sometimes I think he hated his children."

There is little on record about Alexander Rudolph Koerber. An Austrian immigrant born in the 1840s, he was a heavy smoker and a huge man said[2] to have resembled Kaiser Wilhelm. He may have served in the German army and fought for the British in the Crimean War. He was autocratic and domineering but also cultured and artistic. Leila's love and aptitude for music were born from her father's substantial talent at the piano and violin, but his

---

*Leila Koerber's conflicting birth dates range from 1860 to 1873. Most sources list 1869, but her baptismal record and 1894 marriage certificate indicate 1868. Her death certificate lists 1871. The most reliable date is 1868, since it was recorded close to her birth. Leila shaved one or more years off her age later in life.

temper frightened her away. He was equal parts musician, soldier, and tyrant. Patience and sympathy were in short supply; Leila watched in horror as he ejected one young pupil after another from the house. "I can't teach that stupid brat to play!" he bellowed.[3]

When she was 7 or 8, Leila began lessons with her father. She could feel his glare on her face and delicate hands as she struggled to play. Finally, he broke. "It is useless!" he told Annie.[4] "She will never learn." More than once Leila was whipped for her imperfections. "My father was all for accompanying me to the proverbial woodshed," she remembered. "But my ... dancing experience had taught me quick footwork and I nimbly skipped around the room just out of my father's reach. Objects fell wherever I went; books, vases, etc., all in the path of destruction. But the wicked never come to any good, so I ended the little episode by sprawling headlong on the highly polished hall floor. The fall must have been a scream, because my fond parents just stood there and laughed and laughed."

On one Sunday, in her best velveteen dress, the boys teased her:[5]

> Leila's in satin,
> Leila's in lace —
> Leila's afraid she'll get
> Mud on her face.

They dared her to jump across a muddy ditch. "My aim was free, wide and handsome; my skirt, alas, was narrow," she recalled. Leila landed smack in the ditch and then tried to sneak her muddied self home without notice. Alone in her room, she accidentally ripped the bed ticking, which sent goose feathers flying around the room. Once found, the newly feathered Leila got the switch from Alexander. As Leila got older, she fought back. The two mighty tempers exploded numerous times. "One thing I know," wrote Leila.[6] "My red hair is my own, but it was [my father] who bequeathed me the T.N.T. that goes with it."

Leila adored her mother and sister. "You will find," she once said,[7] "that it is seldom that both parents in a family measure up. Usually one is fine and the other is a washout. In my family my mother was a saint. A greater woman, in my opinion, than any I have known since." Annie was a blond, frail Irish Canadian with a genealogy as vague as Alexander's. According to one family source, Annie's father was James Henderson, a struggling harbormaster from Port Hope, Ontario. Another source[8] has Annie's father named George Henderson, Jr. Yet another[9] has Annie born on November 18, 1846, in Marshville, Ontario, as the daughter of Jane and Edward Henderson. Whatever her parentage, she married Alexander, her physical and temperamental opposite, when she was not much older than twenty. There had been a murder in the Henderson family. On September 23, 1856, Annie's uncle Thomas was shot dead on the wharf at Port Hope. George Brogdin, the first husband of Thomas Henderson's wife, was charged but was acquitted. Brogdin had an ace defense attorney and Henderson was not too popular in Port Hope, since "he had gone off to Australia in the early 1850s, made his pile of money and came back to swagger around."[10]

"I got my sense of fun from [my mother]," said Leila.[11] "Oh, I got everything from her. She was my life." When Leila began showing a penchant for clowning, her mother was her first audience. "When I was a kid around the house and I knew things were tough for her, I used to try to make her laugh," wrote Leila years later.[12] "Usually I could. No laughter I have ever won since, from Broadway openings or movie audiences, has ever been quite so precious to me."

Older sister Bonita had big, dreamy eyes and dusky golden curls. In childhood, she was described as a pink-and-white Dresden doll. When she and Leila were dressed in their Sunday finery, adults would pat Bonita's head and exclaim, "My, isn't she lovely!"[13] If Leila was patted on the head, she believed the compliment included her, too. Everyone in the family loved Bonita, but Leila didn't find her much fun to play with. There were assorted cousins in the area and they could be counted on to climb trees or throw rocks. She usually played with neighborhood boys or brought home stray dogs, which often got her another whipping from Alexander. "My troubles as an underdog fancier started early," she noted.[14]

As she grew, Leila realized that she was not a beauty.[15] "When I was a little girl my feelings were terribly hurt once because my sister and I had our pictures taken together. After they were finished, and I asked eagerly to see them, my face had been left out. Indeed, I had been carefully removed from the picture. Later, I said that any such possession as that face was an asset. I started in to build around it and capitalize on it."

Leila quickly grew to be a large girl, with green eyes and round cheeks spotted with freckles. "I was born homely," she sighed with some overstatement.[16] "No one ever exclaimed 'isn't she a beautiful child!'" she recalled.[17] "But I found it quite as delightful when they said 'isn't she funny?'" She was most noticeably big, robust, and ungainly. But her mass disguised and belied an extraordinary physical agility, flexibility, split-second coordination, and great strength. She would never be mistaken for conventionally beautiful, but if well dressed and poised she approached handsomeness. Her light brown wavy hair turned red in the light and she had incongruously feminine hands with slender fingers.

During her first 13 years, Leila and her family moved frequently from Cobourg and Lindsay, Ontario, to Saginaw and Bay City, Michigan, and Findlay, Ohio. After the family disembarked from the train, Leila would watch their few belongings, father would survey the piano, and mother would look for a house. Once resettled, the parlor belonged to father, but the sweet-smelling kitchen would be mother's and Leila's haven. Leila never saw a big city in that time and had no consistent schooling. Most everything academic she learned at home from her mother. "I never had any lessons in anything," said Leila.[18] "Perhaps it's just as well. I didn't have so much to unlearn and I had to figure things out for myself."

The cycle was miserably predictable. Each town had a Protestant Episcopal church with an organ. Sweet-faced Annie would offer Alexander's services as organist and piano teacher to prosperous townspeople. Once his reputation became known, pupils stopped coming to the house. Eventually, he alienated students, parents, and everyone else and the family would have to move on. Food was sometimes scarce. Alexander was a gifted musician and was bitter that he never flourished on concert stages. His talent did no good to a family forced into transcience. "My earliest memories are of packing and moving, catching trains, settling down briefly, packing again. Home was simply where my mother was," summarized Leila many years later.[19]

Though reserved, Annie had a flair for the dramatic. She arranged church entertainments[20] to benefit the poor and served as stage manager, author, star, costumer, and carpenter. She persuaded Alexander to orchestrate music and play the organ. Bonita and Leila participated with a great deal more enthusiasm than Alexander.

While living in Lindsay, Ontario, Leila made her stage debut in one of her mother's concoctions. She was five and given the pivotal role of Cupid, sans clothes but with the obligatory bow and arrow. Annie had carefully planned a tableau but it was ruined when Leila fell off her pedestal. The spectators roared with laughter and Leila never forgot the lesson. "Yes, I got my first laugh with a fall," she recalled.[21] "And I've been doing 'em ever since." She committed herself to others' amusement.[22] "I basked in the sunshine of the laughter and attention I drew ... it was lack of beauty that drove me." The young Leila was learning how to maintain her own well-being as Bonita grew more beautiful and Alexander grew more violent and sullen. "Life is full of compensations. If you can't get one thing, you can get another. If you haven't one asset, you have something else."[23]

For a brief time, the family lived in Findlay, Ohio, on West Front Street in a modest frame house near a gas well along the Blanchard River. As a devout Anglican, Annie insisted that they all attend the Protestant Episcopal church service held every Sunday in a vacant storeroom. Findlayites remembered[24] a "vivacious and extremely personable daughter of a music teacher ... restless to get away and do things." She led amateur plays and would bring down the house when she forgot her lines and made up much better ones. School meant nothing to her except when she had a part in a play. She was always the ringleader, recalled one alumnus of a Leila Koerber opus:[25] "She usually wrote, directed and starred in the productions and because she was so much fun we were always glad to let her. However, her mischievous nature sometimes led our parents to question the desirability of her influence."

Saginaw, Michigan, enjoyed great prosperity as a lumber boomtown in 1879, but that made little difference to the Koerbers' fortunes. A neighbor named Mrs. McCron[26] recalled the heated confrontations between Leila and her father: "She took part in numerous theatrical ventures ... and used to aggravate her father and mother at times with the declaration, 'all right, if you don't like it, I'll go over to Boardwell's Opera House and dance on a barrel.' ... In those days [Boardwell's] reputation left something to be desired." Leila avidly followed the exploits of leading stage stars, never seeing any but knowing them through magazines and newspapers. When she confessed her desire to go on the stage, a boyfriend named Jake said, "What chance would you have on the stage?" Leila "wasn't a pretty girl," said a childhood acquaintance from Findlay. "But [she] was always looking for a good time and she had all the boyfriends she wanted."

Because of Alexander's volatility, the burden of supporting the family often fell on Annie. In homes the family rented, she took in borders. She worked every day at the washtub, stove, and sewing machine. Leila knew that she had to go to work if her mother was ever going to enjoy any comfort. Her first paying job was behind the counter of a big department store.[27] Nervous and ready to please, she mistakenly wrapped a pair of men's red flannel drawers for Miss Jennie Thistlewaite, a gaunt and prim old woman. Miss Thistlewaite angrily returned the merchandise and saw to Leila's dismissal.

The first firing did not shatter Leila. She was more interested in making money as a chariot driver. She was enchanted by a visiting circus and meekly confided to the travelers that she wanted to join their troupe.[28] To compete, she had to display skills at horseback riding. "The boss won't take you," they announced to Leila, "unless you know how to ride." So Leila trained and improved her skills, but her circus ambitions were shortlived.

The booming war of tempers between Leila and her father intensified. When she was 14, it reached its climax. A family member retells the episode:[29] "One night ... and at the command of her father who was rather a tyrant, she was washing the dinner dishes and she rebelled, dried her hands and told him she did not intend to be a slave to any man as her mother had been to him." She was more like him in temperament than either would care to admit and it seemed living together grew more untenable as Leila matured. Ever unrepentant and defiant, she said "I never did like my father, and that's all there is to it."

Leila immediately made plans to work in the theater. Somewhere Leila had heard that the Nevada Stock Company recruited players as the company traveled the hinterlands. When she saw their ad, she composed a 20-page letter detailing her and Bonita's extensive stage experience. She neglected to mention that their distinguished careers came from neighborhood shows and Sunday school and that all casting decisions were made by her or her mother. The Nevada manager, by whatever process guided him while reading the letter, hired Leila and Bonita, sight unseen. Leila, then 14, wrote in the letter that she was 18 and Bonita was 19.

The horrible disclosure brought Alexander to another explosion. When he saw that there was no stopping his daughters, he insisted that his family name not be dragged through the mud by their showing off behind the footlights. Leila conceded and chose the name Marie Dressler, after an aunt whose name was apparently less valuable than Koerber. The woman lived in Germany and she and Leila had never met.

Annie was supportive, hopeful, and fearful of her daughters' plan. The night before they left, she stayed up late with the sisters. She had taught them to read and cried when she told them[30] to "make everything count. Fill your heads with knowledge and hold them high. If you can do nothing else for yourself, you can at least read the newspaper every morning. That alone will keep you from ignorance."

The young women's departure was something of an event in their small universe. Neighbors came to the house with small gifts and good wishes. Downtown the two girls boarded the coach amidst hugs, tears, and promises to write. As the coach pulled away, the Koerber parents watched their only two children leave home on the same day.

Chapter 2

The Apprentice

Years after Bonita and Leila left home, Marie Dressler felt compelled to mythologize and mystify her early years. Her ancestry took on rarefied and tragic circumstances. According to Marie's memoirs, Annie Henderson came from a family who owned a string of trading stores,[1] a fleet of sailing ships, and the finest racing stable in Ontario. Annie's father opposed her marriage to Alexander and withheld financial support from the struggling family as long as Annie stayed in the marriage. Grandfather Henderson might have relented, but Grandmother Henderson was killed suddenly in an accident involving a horse-drawn cart. He then married his housekeeper, who helped prevent any money from going to Annie and Alexander.

Marie inflated her pedigree and social position. The Hendersons were poor boat operators in Ontario, according to nonfamilial sources. She tacked a "von" in front of the Koerber surname to give it a touch of Old World class. When Marie writes that she and Bonita were heiresses until a fire destroyed most of the family fortunes, suspicions arise.

Marie and Bonita disembarked from the dusty day coach and were met by a Nevada Stock Company member. The first challenge was their freight. Alexander had made a huge trunk that was a cross between a tool chest and a summer house. "Everything we owned, except the kitchen stove, [was] stowed in the cavernous maw of that huge edifice," recalled Marie.[2] "If we had gotten stranded we could have lived in it. Frequently baggagemen absolutely balked at handling it and at last we allowed it to be split into kindling."[3]

The company manager was shocked that Marie was so young and so large. She was nearing her full height of five feet, seven inches and had already developed an hourglass figure with a tiny waist between enormous hips and breasts. At every opportunity she put on airs as if to reconcile her scant experience with her maturing body. To Bonita, she'd ask in a stage whisper,[4] "Where did I play Lady Macbeth first? Was it in Cobourg or that nice town just beyond Ottawa?"

With a salary of $6 a week, and half of that sent home, Marie was retained for bit parts and the chorus. After six months, she was given the pivotal role of Cigarette in *Under Two Flags*.

"Of course I thought that Madame Bernhardt, her predecessors and successors could not equal me," Marie said.[5] The play was based on Ouida's romantic 1867 novel of the French in Algiers and was adapted by Richard Ganthony, an aspiring 26-year-old British playwright, actor, and critic. After winning her first important role, she trudged upstairs to her dingy hotel bedroom with its cracked water pitcher, funny brass bed, and horrible wallpaper, in a state of despair. How was she going to meet the demands of *Under Two Flags*?

Cigarette would seem tailor-made to Marie's buoyant teenage energy, if not her looks. As Ouida envisioned her,[6] she was "pretty, she was insolent, she was intolerably coquettish, she was mischievous as a marmoset, she would swear if need be like a Zouave, she could fire galloping, she could toss off her brandy or her vermouth like a trouper ... she was an *enfant de Paris* and had all its wickedness at her fingers, she would sing you *guinguette* songs till you were suffocated with laughter and she would dance the cancan at the Salle de Mars. ... she was not wholly unsexed, with all that she had the delicious fragrance of youth, and she had not left a certain feminine grace behind her."

Dressler had bouts of forgotten lines and stage fright,[7] but she set about conquering her troubles alone in the hotel room. She wept, circled the room, and kicked the furniture until the man next door pounded on the wall.[8] She successfully learned her lines for opening night in a small Michigan town, but she was seized with stage fright just before going on. The anxiety did not overwhelm her. One patron[9] noted that Marie's first performance in *Under Two Flags* was "above average" and noticed that "she appeared in extra short skirts in a day when women were not supposed to have ankles, let alone legs. ... the costume caused comment." After her first success, Marie was given greater responsibilities. In typical stock company fashion, she might have a leading role in a matinee performance and a chorus role by night. If not on stage, she and the others were recruited for stage managing, costume supervision, set construction, or any number of backstage duties.

Marie recalled[10] that company members "had to play everything from a child to a doddering octogenarian."

There was the endless travel from one "dog" town to another. Trains were heated with coal stoves and lit with kerosene lamps. Pay was sporadic if the company was rejected from a theater because of poor attendance. Frequently, too, townspeople were inhospitable to the vagrants and sent them on their way. Hotels often refused their patronage. The company sometimes slept in cold, run-down opera houses when snow was too deep to get to a boarding house. Marie claimed[11] to have slept in haystacks more than once and received breakfast from milking a cow. Of the unladylike circumstances she said,[12] "I suppose the bones of some of my relatives and ancestors are still turning over in their respective and highly respectable graves."

Despite the rough conditions, Marie thrived. "Nevada's company proved a wonderful school in many ways," she said.[13]

> Often a bill was changed on an hour's notice or less. Every member of the cast had to be a quick study. I have gone on in a part which I had only read over hastily while dressing, more intensive study being pursued while I waited in the wings for my cue. ... If they had a sketchy outline of the plot and a rough idea of the characterization, a troupe of old hands could almost create a play as they went along. This was fun if everybody played ball. It was ghastly if somebody fumbled or "went dead."

Marie fell in love with fellow Nevada trouper Terrence,[14] though she forgot his last name over the years. She remembers a handsome young man of dark good looks. They often engaged in romantic partnerships on stage, which led to Marie's infatuation off stage. She and Bonita shared a boarding-house room while they traveled with the Nevada Stock Company, but at night she would dream of her theatrical romance with Terrence turning into something real.

With Terry, she also felt the first sting of romantic betrayal. When the company added a new young woman, Terry's affections veered away from Marie. She took the rejection well, continued with the Nevada troupe, and poured her heart out on stage to Terry even as their offstage relationship cooled. This, she felt, would demonstrate her professionalism as an actress. She was right. The company manager once told her that "you keep on working like this, kid, and you'll get there!"

Terry wasn't Marie's only would-be lover. "I fell in love with all the handsome leading men — madly and sleeplessly in love. I hung around, watching them with adoring eyes, and I suffered tortures when they paid attention to the good-looking girls in the company. No one took me seriously in a romantic way. At fifteen I wrote a poem on the horrors of unrequited love."[15]

It eventually came to her callow mind that the 11-member Nevada Stock Company was at best a mediocre troupe. Others there had no more experience than she and Bonita had when they joined. Still others were enfeebled. "The type of theatrical company which would engage a 14-year-old amateur for leading lady seems to have vanished from the face of the earth," Marie wrote.[16] "In those days there were hundreds of companies, composed of broken down professionals who had come down the ladder and eager amateurs on the way up. Nevada's collection ran the scale from has-beens to would-bes."

When she wrote of her youth, the Nevada years became a blur:[17]

> I have retained few memories, because youth lives in the passing moment and I did not take time to feel my pulse or set down reactions from any given incident. Today I remember few of the names of my very early associates — but then I am always getting into embarrassing situations because I cannot remember the names of charming people I met only yesterday.

Bonita's tenure with the Nevada Stock Company was short-lived. After only a few months on the road, she had left to marry Richard Ganthony,[18] the playwright who adapted *Under Two Flags* for the company. Bonita had quit before hard times hit the company. Marie was not so lucky. She found herself stranded in a small Michigan town in midwinter with a third-rate theater company dissolving around her. She was soon picked up as a chorus member of the Jules Grau Opera Company. For constant touring through the Midwest, Marie was to receive a salary of $8 a week.[19]

Dressler was positively quivering with excitement when she learned that the Grau Company had *The Mikado* in its repertory. Ever since she had seen a production of Gilbert and Sullivan's new comic opera, she was desperate to play the funny old hag Katisha. Of that role, Marie said,[20] "it was conceived in heaven especially for me." A reporter[21] later noted that she "saw in it a chance to make people laugh — just as she had by exploiting her own awkwardness as a child."

She practiced and memorized the role everywhere she could, in the tiny hotel rooms she shared with two other girls, on the street, and in empty theaters. Alas, Katisha was not hers. It was played more than adequately by company member Agnes Halleck and there was no indication that she would give up the part. Marie wasn't even Halleck's understudy, and so she perfected the role in solitude. One time[22] a stagehand, arriving early to a town opera house, heard a powerful voice shouting from a dimly lit stage, "I have a left shoulder blade that is a miracle of loveliness. People come miles to see it!"

He peered around a flat and found a tall, large young woman projecting to an empty house. When Marie saw him, she did not break character. "Observe this ear," she said.

"Huh?"

"Observe this ear!" She failed to alert the stagehand that she expected him to assume the role of Ko-Ko, Lord High Executioner of Titipu. She gave him a jab in the ribs. "Say 'large.'"

"Large," he echoed.

"Large?" she bellowed. "ENORMOUS! But think of its delicate internal mechanism. It is fraught with beauty! As for this tooth, it almost stands alone. Many have tried to draw it, but in vain."

A chain of events occurred that gave Marie a chance to play the role. While the company was in Philadelphia, Halleck sprained her ankle by stepping in a mudhole on Broad Street. The understudy was summoned but she did not know her lines adequately. "I have always felt a little guilty about that ankle," confessed Marie.[23] "I used to pray every night that something would happen to her. And when they called the understudy, I actually tried hypnotizing her so that she wouldn't know her lines!"

Marie seized the opportunity and came storming onto the scene at rehearsal. "I can play it! I can sing it! I know it! Please let me play it — please!" The manager relinquished and said, "The clothes fit her, anyway. Put her in."

The teenager convulsed the audiences in Philadelphia, but her memory of this engagement grew dim. Years later, she wasn't sure whether *The Mikado* played the theater on Broad Street or Columbia Avenue. Still, she knew that it was a broad street if not the Broad Street where she first played Katisha. The boulevard was "as wide as any I had ever seen before — as a matter of fact, it was the first street I ever found that fit me."[24]

Back on the road, Marie was ecstatic about playing Katisha, but Grau, a member of a well-known family of operatic managers, neglected to pay her salary. He had a rule that anybody in the company who drank was given 25 cents every night for beer. Marie didn't drink, and so she got nothing. It didn't seem fair to her and she said so.[25]

Grau found her tiresome and devised a way to be rid of her. Since her first "triumph" was in Philadelphia, why not deposit her there again? He had his brother send him a telegram that read: "Send Dressler to Philadelphia. Want to get her clothes for opening here." When she arrived at the station late at night,[26] no one was there to meet her and she owed 50 cents on her fare. A kindly cop directed her to the Continental Hotel.

"I want a room, but I have no money and no job," she told the clerk.

Through a miracle of kindness, the clerk gave her a room. The next morning she found an envelope that had been slipped under the door. In it was $2 with a note reading, "I got a kid of my own."

Grau actually did Marie a favor by sending her back to Philadelphia. It was a great show town in the mid–1880s. The Forepaugh Brothers exceeded Barnum in fame, while Nixon and Zimmerman's Chestnut Street Opera House, the Academy of Music, and the Arch Street Opera House were all thriving. Two actresses she knew from her touring, May Duryea and May Montford, were performing in town with the Starr Opera Company. Marie dropped in on them during rehearsal. Unhappy at how their fellow trouper had been treated by Grau, the two successfully talked the manager, Frank Deshon, into hiring her. Years later, Montford[27] recalled Marie's antics on the road with the Starr Company:

> In those early days, if she wasn't in trouble she was laughing herself to death. She adored practical jokes and she didn't care on whom she played them. We all adored her, but we never knew what was coming next. One April Fool's Day she put Epsom salt in the sugar bowl and we nearly didn't give a performance that night. Her clothes, which she made herself, were strung all over the state — and never, in all the time I knew her, did she succeed in getting her suitcase properly closed. It was always popping open. ... She could no more help singing than a bird and when we got into some little hotel at midnight she would charge down the hall singing at the top of her lungs. Doors would open and irate faces would appear, but the moment they saw Marie they began to laugh. We were all broke, of course, but Marie was always brokest. We only got $8 a week, and Marie sent half of that home. ... She had an enormous appetite. She wouldn't flirt with managers and she never noticed stage-door johnnies, as we called them then. But the eyes she would make at men behind lunch counters ... She always got twice as big an order as the rest of us.

High spirits hid a lingering sorrow. Marie was woefully homesick and wanted nothing more than to see her mother again.[28] "Most people in going home have a definite picture in mind—how the sun falls on the doorstep, in what room the folks are sitting, whether the furniture has been changed around. Some of these delicious flutters were denied me. ... But, thank God, it was always home where my mother was!"

Her parents were presently in Saginaw, and after a bittersweet reunion, Marie noticed that the Bennett-Moulton Opera Company, based in Cazenovia, New York, was coming to town. "Opera stock companies recruited as they moved from spot to spot," Marie stated[29] as a way of explaining her sudden association with the Bennett-Moulton Company. This company was fundamentally different from those of Nevada or Jules Grau. Its director and manager, George A. Baker, was a relatively shrewd impresario nicknamed "the choir snatcher" for his ongoing perusal of small town church singing groups in search of talent. Baker was driven and disciplined in ways that Marie found both unfamiliar and refreshing. She declared[30] her time with him "the three hardest years of my life, but they were the rock upon which my future was built."

The company's repertoire was taken fresh from the opera houses of Vienna and Paris. Imported Austrian and French *opéra bouffe* was immensely popular in the smaller cities of the United States, and Baker staged new productions as fast as composers and librettists could write them and get them translated. The music of Friedrich Zell, Franz von Suppé, Henri Chivot, Alfred Duru, Richard Genée, Henri Meilhac, Eugène Leterrier, and Jacques Offenbach posed few demands on highly trained singers. Someone of Marie's immature but pleasing contralto could fit right into the repertory.

Dressler, as the sturdiest and most buxom woman in the Bennett-Moulton Company, bypassed the ingénue phase altogether. Her roles fell into one of four types: chorus, old woman, royalty, or men. She went immediately to older characters. In *Said Pasha*, she played Balah Sojah, aunt to Alti, the queen of Altara. As Peronella, a grocer's sister in *Boccaccio*, she was expected to get away with such lyrics as "he tells me in his letter that he shall be here soon. What joy! I hope he will not delay. I hate to lose a minute at my time of life."

With restrictive binding under her costumes, Marie's cross-dressing assignments were nearly as varied as her women's roles. She played Vladimir Samoiloff, lieutenant of a Circassian Cavalry Regiment in *Fatinitza*, and Don Philippe of Aragon in *Three Black Cloaks*. She was the queen in *Three Black Cloaks* and *Bohemian Girl*, "except when the King was drunk, and then I played the King."[31] The diversity of roles meant Marie's emerging talent found discipline, but that fact was lost to the audience. With great predictability, the Bennett-Moulton comic operagoers could expect plots and characters to blur one into another. Guaranteed themes included mistaken identities, fictitious empires, illegitimacy, lost love letters, political exile, war, arranged marriages, maiden virtue, balcony serenades, and happy endings.

Marie's stage fright and bad memory could not be indulged in this company. She claimed[32] to have learned no less than 40 operas during her first year, sometimes a new one every week. "One night I'd be Barbara in *The Black Hussars*—what a part *that* was—and the next I'd be in the chorus. We didn't squawk about our parts, either, and whether it was an audience of three hundred in a tank town or three thousand in Chicago, we did our best."

Marie arrived in Cleveland on May 22, 1891, armed with a repertoire of choral and speaking roles. By May 25, she debuted as the Countess Palmatica in *The Beggar Student* at the Euclid Opera House. The production was heralded[33] "the most stupendous, colossal, musical extravaganza ever produced in Cleveland. Fifty people in elaborate costumes." Marie stood out as the Polish mother hellbent on marrying her daughter to high nobility. "Anyone beneath the rank of Count need not apply," she trilled. After *The Beggar Student* opening, Marie and company encamped for the summer and survived a punishing regimen. With seats going for 25 to 50 cents each, a new production debuted every week and after they were all unveiled they played in nightly rotation:[34]

June 1—*The Black Hussars*, as Barbara, a maid of all work and housekeeper to Hackenback, magistrate of Frautenfeld
June 7—*Boccaccio*, as Peronella
June 15—*Grand Duchess*, as the title role
June 22—*Chimes of Normandy*, as Serpolette, the good-for-nothing harum-scarum girl
June 29—*Fatinitza*, as Princess Lydia Imanovna
July 6—*Olivette*, as Bathilde, Countess of Roussillon
July 13—*Bohemian Girl*, as the king or queen
July 20—*Three Black Cloaks*, as the king or queen
August 3—*Fra Diavolo*, as Lady Alloash, the foolish wife
August 10—*The Mikado*, as Katisha
August 17—*Boccaccio*
August 18—*The Black Hussars*
August 19—*Chimes of Normandy*
August 20—*The Beggar Student*, as the Countess Palmatica
August 21—*Olivette*
August 22—*Bohemian Girl* (matinee)
August 22—*Madame Favart*, as Madame Favart

It would seem Marie had few of the physical or temperamental prerequisites for success in comic opera. "The young girl who played Barbara in *The Black Hussars* tried to hide herself in the chorus [of *La Mascotte*], but she has a shape which would well win the golden apple," wrote a reporter[35] from Minneapolis. Lewis Strang,[36] a leading theater commentator, declared that "the juvenile comedian in opera finds himself confronted by practically the same difficulties that beset the light comedian in drama. He, too, must closely approximate nature. When inspiration fails, he cannot, after the habit of the 'dog faced' comedian, fall back on ancient jokes and weird and astounding physical contortions; he must play his part 'straight,' and still he must be infinite in resource. Moreover, he must be pleasant to look upon and attractive in personality."

Dressler was hardly beautiful nor was she approximating nature in playing old women, men, and royalty. What made her an audience darling? The sheer magnitude of her body and personality were winning her loud applause. What Marie lacked in traditional graces she made up for in high energy and endless goodwill in front of an audience. She wanted nothing more than to put smiles on faces. Marie "has a mental quirk that keeps the incongruous side of life in her view practically all the time," noted Strang.[37] "She cannot help pricking constantly the bubble of mirth any more than she can help breathing."

Behind her farcical face was an emerging thoughtful mind. She was beginning to think like a real actress.[38] "It was not until Barbara in *The Black Hussars* that I realized that almost anyone could play *Nanon, Boccaccio, Olivette*, and the other operas, which, up to then, had been among my favorites," she wrote. "But the lines and especially the 'business' of Barbara were meat, drink and custard pie to me and I went at them like a famine sufferer. This was my first real opportunity really 'to get' an audience and I realized then that it was portraying a type more human than a grand duchess or a queen that gets one over the footlights and into the hearts of those on the other side."

Bennett-Moulton employment was seasonal, so Marie decided to make an inauspicious arrival in New York after her local success in Cleveland. Having apprenticed in so many nameless towns across America, she was eager to assume a career there but uncertain of the necessary means of success. She was, as is the case with many young artists, unsure of what she could give an audience. "I was too homely for a prima donna and too big for a soubrette," she sighed.[39]

Playwright and actor Maurice Barrymore guided Dressler toward important decisions during her first months in New York. He noted that Marie's gifts for comedy were developing faster than her singing. "You were born to make people laugh, Marie," he announced and encouraged her toward comedy and away from comic opera. He saw in her an immature but unmistakable talent and cast her in the show he had just written. She played the small role of the brigand Cunigonde in his premiere production of *The Robber of the Rhine*,[40] a musical spoof of Robin Hood to be staged at the newly refurbished and highly ornate Fifth Avenue Theater. Rehearsals went badly and the cast was not too discreetly unhappy with Marie. "I realized that I was the right person in the wrong pew," she wrote. "Nobody wanted me in the cast, and everybody did everything they could to get rid of me. I pretended that I was a rhinoceros and laughed gaily at barbed darts."

Marie was understandably petrified on opening night, May 28, 1892. Barrymore's faith and Marie's ingratiations had not won over the other cast members. For added anxiety, actors were flubbing their lines as Marie tried valiantly to save the production from calamity. From offstage, she prompted erring actors with their lines. When the first tension-filled performance was over, director Richard Barker came to Marie's rescue and praised her assistance. It was not enough. The show was a turkey and closed just five weeks later. "The fact cannot be concealed that Mr. Barrymore sadly disappointed his friends and bored the public," announced the *New York Dramatic Mirror*.[41] Marie consoled herself by boasting that her inaugural show in New York was penned by the esteemed Barrymore, who had hand-picked her to bring his work to life.

Out of the wreckage came new opportunity, though no offers were made immediately. The successful Broadway producer George Lederer happened to see *The Robber of the Rhine*.[42] At the intermission, he was approached by the show's producer.

"How'd you like the show?"

Lederer answered the question with a question. "Who's the big girl on the end of the opening chorus?"

After *The Robber of the Rhine* made its sniveling farewell in New York, Marie was back in Cleveland for a hasty reunion with the Bennett-Moulton Company. She had started in Cleveland one year earlier as a journeyman, but she returned a local star. The perfor-

2. The Apprentice

Marie in two contrasting personas from comic operas: the dignified matron (*opposite*) and the androgynous rogue. (Courtesy of the Marie Dressler Foundation/Cleveland Public Library Photograph Collection.)

est families] realized that an actress is a real human being and enjoys human company."

Marie was hungry to try melodrama and got her chance when the company performed *La Périchole* in Boston.[44] Unfortunately, the man playing a jailer was drunk and had to be dragged from behind sets and trunks and shoved on stage at his cue. Marie then rushed on, looked at the man behind bars and anxiously asked, "Jailer, is he violent?"

The scripted answer was, "No, if he makes a move strong men will come and chain him to the wall." The stewed actor instead blurted, "I don't give a damn if he is! I don't give a damn if the damn show closes!" The curtain came down prematurely on the scene and on Marie's first stab at anything halfway dramatic.

mance schedule for 1892 was no less grueling than it had been the previous year, with *The Black Hussars, Fatinitza, Beggar Student, The Grand Duchess, Chimes of Normandy, The Mikado,* and *Three Black Cloaks* offered again and *Erminie, Mascot,* and *Said Pasha* premiering.

When she appeared as the aged Princess de Granponeaux for a Fourth of July performance in *Erminie*, the company ad in the *Cleveland Plain Dealer* announced the "reappearance of Marie Dressler" and did not name any other performers. She reveled in the role of a rich woman who should have been wise to the deceptions of men but got fleeced instead. "Marie Dressler attracted people to the local theater who haven't been there much since," chimed Archie Bell,[43] a Cleveland reporter who would follow her entire career with singular devotion. "How they loved her! ... She was invited everywhere to dine. [Cleveland's old-

Despite drunken colleagues, Marie's tenure with the Bennett-Moulton Company remained forever amiable. She was happy and proud of three years of "good parts, pleasant associates and a manager who always paid salaries."[45] It matters little that the purveyed productions would look corny and amateurish today. What matters is that Baker's company was of high quality for its type, and its audiences were generally captivated by thespians and their "magic." But theatrical delights did not bring social acceptance. Much of America reasoned that anyone who submits to life on the road may be great fun at showtime but a horror at the family dinner table. While productions were cheered, very often their casts were banished to society's fringes. People everywhere assumed that troupers were wanton, reckless, and carefree. Even the *New York Dramatic Mirror*, the self-proclaimed "organ of the

American theatrical profession," was quick to fuel the image. It wrote[46] that "the general impression has prevailed for many years, not without cause, that variety performers are happy-go-lucky people who never give a thought to tomorrow, or future rainy days, or illness, or old age, or any of thousand and one things which suggest the necessity of saving money with which to meet and overcome as far as possible the troubles of life."

Marie came into her trouping life just as America learned how to go out at night. The nation was positively mad over theatrical entertainment in the 1890s. The *New York Dramatic Mirror* estimated that traveling road companies increased from 40 to more than 500 between 1880 and 1900. Virtually any medium-sized to large community could be counted on to offer local and visiting productions of Shakespeare in nightly competition with variety acts, roadshow comedy, minstrel shows, melodrama, orchestral concerts, recitations, the circus, and comic opera.

Abundance did not mean great productions or high living for theatrical personnel. Quality was spotty at best as road shows picked up and discarded eager young talent along their routes. There were not enough actors for the demand and troupes often promised more in promotion than they delivered on stage. With names like the "She, Him, Her Comedy Company," "Bottle's Baby Company," and the "Hands Across the Sea Company," they arrived in town by late afternoon, staged an evening show, and were gone by late night or early the next morning.[47]

Actor's hell was banishment to the American outback of small towns and shoddy lodgings. The local reception could be warm, with kindly people offering a place to stay for the actors and appreciative crowds milling around the stage door after a performance. Elsewhere shows were canceled because of indifference or hostility. New England boardinghouses were notorious for refusing to take thespians. "Of all the routes in those days I most dreaded the New England tour, because of the cheap hotels to which our salaries consigned us," Marie said.[48] "We wanted to go to boarding houses, but the weary rounds of them met always with a door banged in our faces and a sharp 'We don't want any troupers!'"

No surprise that New York was the promised land for the weary road actor. With its new rooftop gardens and theaters far above the street grime and choking summer heat, it seemed an eminently civilized place. The actor found no provincial attitudes, no need for explaining the rudiments of theater and, best of all, a population that took pride in ennobling the art of acting. The celebratory electric signs flashing one or another star began appearing on Broadway in the 1890s.

After a brief but pleasing tour with *The Tar and the Tartar*, the Harry B. Smith and Adam Itzel, Jr., comic opera of sultans, slaves and sailors, Marie returned to New York. Foremost on her thoughts was making money. Saving was difficult for three reasons: she was forever tempted to buy nice clothes she could not afford, she could not resist lending money to needy friends, and a full half of her earnings went home to her parents. If a pair of aged aunts or Bonita and her new husband Richard were having hard times, Marie would float them as well.

She found a gig singing two songs nightly at the old Atlantic Garden on the Bowery.[49] Her nightly take-home pay was $10. On Sundays, she sang at the dilapidated Koster and Bial's Music Hall on 23rd Street for $15.[50] Though the joint was famous and popular, it hardly ranked as a first-class engagement. Any theater stub was good for admission there, for Koster and Bial's was more a saloon than anything else. Performers had to contend with an orchestra section of chairs and tables, incessant chatter and the clink of glasses.

Marie lived in a boarding house in Brooklyn, which was substantially cheaper than equivalent accommodations in Manhattan. If money was extra tight, she saved the fare by walking home from the Bowery across the new Brooklyn Bridge. "What a grueling period it was!" Marie said. "For the first time in my life I was job hunting and nearly crazy lest my family starve to death before I could get more money to them."[51]

The pressures mounted as Annie not too subtly wrote about her heartache. "Your father and I sit alone at night with our babies gone. I wish we could see you occasionally! If we could only live in New York."[52] Marie reasoned that money could be better saved living together and set about moving her parents. After she found a simple frame house on Van Alst Avenue in Long Island City,[53] she wired her mother a one-word message: "Come!"*

Marie was not daunted by needy kin, the commute to Manhattan or meeting the rent. "I simply could not imagine that my flaming red mop would ever grow dull or my splendid energy diminish," she wrote. "Happy, full of irrepressible spirits, bursting with fun, I played as hard off the stage as on. My fun was that of a boisterous, undisciplined puppy."[54] She once played her piano in the middle of busy Van Alst Avenue much to the astonishment and amusement of wagon drivers, bicyclists and pedestrians. At home, she and her father learned to tolerate each other out of mutual adoration of Annie. Marie loved the time with her mother, relaxing on Sundays and attracting various urban animals to the backyard. Marie lured a squirrel by hiding nuts in the "creases of my fat middle and [I tried] to sit still while my favorite foraged for his dinner."[55]

While Marie lolled at home, George Lederer, the producer who inquired about the "big girl" in *The Robber of the Rhine*, was putting together a show. He was potentate at the Casino Theater at Broadway and 39th Street in nominal partnership with Thomas Canary. The Casino was a fantastic showplace, with a Moorish-inspired exterior and lavish roof garden, but the real attraction was Lederer's leading lady. His new show was *Princess Nicotine* and the star was Lillian Russell. Marie was given the supporting role of the duchess.

The pedestrian story of a love triangle between a pretty cigarette maker (Russell), a rich tobacco planter (Perry Averill), and a governor (Digby Bell) opened on November 20, 1893. The plot, the music, the theater and the costars were all rendered irrelevant by the presence of Russell.[56] At that moment in her career, she was supreme among musical comedy stars, the "Queen of Comic Opera" commanding $700 a week plus half the profits. In 1893 she made more money than President Grover Cleveland.

Marie's weekly salary for *Princess Nicotine* was just $40, but that was less important than her introduction to Russell. Marie was spellbound and rhapsodic[57]: "She was as beautiful inside as she was out. Her nature was like sunshine. When she came on to the stage for rehearsals and tossed into my lap the great bunch of violets which she always wore, I was in heaven. From her I learned what courtesy meant, how kindliness could glorify everyday existence. From her I learned to keep my troubles and my corns and my toothaches to myself and just pass on the pleasant things. She was a great lady and made me long to know people who were cultured and fine and gentle."

Lillian Russell was born in Clinton, Iowa, in 1861, the daughter of a newspaper editor and an early suffragette. The family moved to Chicago when she was very young and she was educated at the School of the Sacred Heart. She later moved to New York with her mother after her parents divorced. Under the guidance of pioneering vaudeville showman Tony Pastor, her christened name of Helen Louise Leonard was dropped for the more ephemeral Lillian Russell. Pastor cultivated her stage image and singing voice as her stardom rose steadily under the affectionate nickname "Airy Fairy Lillian." Lewis Strang[58] wrote that "her voice, a brilliant soprano, was rich, full, and complete, liquid in tone, pure and musical."

Marie and Lillian grew to be protective friends. During the run of *Princess Nicotine*, when Lillian learned of Marie's paltry salary, she asked Marie what she thought she was worth. "A hundred a week," was Marie's reply.[59]

"You certainly are. You have made a hit in this play. Will you be guided by me?"

Marie nodded yes.

"Then go tell George Lederer that you

---

*Marie recalled moving to Long Island City in 1896, but public records indicate she lived there by 1894.

"Airy Fairy" Lillian Russell, circa 1895.

"Oh, no!" said Lillian. "We can't have a new woman tonight. I am not going to have my performance ruined completely. You must get Miss Dressler back somehow, otherwise I can't play, and remember, my contract states you cannot discharge anyone without my permission." Marie got her raise.

On stage, the two women created whole new situations nightly. Marie would "go up" in her lines. Then Lillian, who found Marie exceedingly amusing, would get to laughing and forget her own lines. Soon the audience and other cast members were laughing bystanders as Marie and Lillian made hash of entire scenes. The chemistry was as genuinely funny and caring offstage as on and observers dubbed their friendship a coming together of "the Beauty and the Beastie."

The women had entirely different public images to cultivate. Russell was a comedienne and singer who delighted audiences in performances of sexual suggestiveness. She was an exquisite beauty with pale blue eyes, perfect complexion, and golden hair. Dressler was a robust near-vulgarian who made her name as an accomplice to her own demoralization. Lillian extolled glamour and Marie deflated swollen self-importance. The contrast was startling on stage, as few women welcomed so much mockery as Marie. Even fewer had Lillian's combination of fine comedic impulses and radiant beauty. Friend and critic Mollie Merrick wrote, "I could never forget the hush which followed Lillian's first gorgeous appearance ... that hush of sheer admiration of her beauty."

Merrick claimed[60] that Marie was never jealous of Lillian's beauty, but one episode

must have a hundred dollars a week from now on, or you will not appear tonight," instructed Lillian. Marie nervously left to perform her assignment.

Lederer made a booming entrance to Lillian's dressing room a few minutes later. "What do you think of that?" he asked. "Marie Dressler wants a hundred dollars and says she won't play tonight unless I give it to her."

"Are you going to do it?" asked Lillian.

"I am not," he answered. "She can stay away from the theater forever. I will have a new woman tonight."

could be interpreted otherwise. When they were playing a small town, Marie decided to pull a major stunt. Instead of preparing to play Lillian's mother, she tried to pass as Lillian herself. Pulling on a blonde wig and the necessary finery, she made her entrance to wild applause. Many were fooled, but when the applause died down, one woman shouted, "Who says she's beautiful? I think she's a sight!"

Marie worshiped Lillian. Though just eight years older, Lillian had substantially more theatrical experience and found something wonderfully fresh and naive in Marie. One day Marie sighed to her mentor[61] that "it must be wonderful to be famous." Lillian was quick to reply: "La, no, child. You ought to try to eat raw oysters in a restaurant with every eye focused on you. It makes you feel as if the creatures were whales, your fork a derrick and your mouth the Mammoth Cave."

They could be seen riding bicycles through Central Park as their none-too-successful method of weight reduction. Lillian also introduced Marie to a crowd of people who fulfilled Marie's notions of upper-class breeding. Lillian was one of the rare birds who had broken through the glass ceiling of New York's lobster palace society, and she took a grateful young Marie with her. Marie watched agape as Lillian's platonic companion, Diamond Jim Brady, made obscene amounts of money selling railroad equipment all over North America. His spending habits are legendary. The famous bicycle[62] he bought for Lillian was reported to cost $10,000, with mother-of-pearl handlebars and spokes encrusted with diamonds, emeralds, rubies and sapphires that caught the sunlight so as to mimic fireworks.

Above all else, Diamond Jim and Lillian loved to eat.[63] They dined at New York's premier eating places, including Rector's, the Waldorf-Astoria, Delmonico's, and Sherry's. From Lillian, Marie learned that to be classy was to gorge. Ten- to twelve-course meals hosted by Diamond Jim and Lillian included oysters on the half-shell, fowl, fish, roast meat, apple pie à la mode, and plenty of champagne. At the United States Hotel in Saratoga, "Lillian Russell and Diamond Jim engaged in an eating competition [that] must have been vaguely reminiscent of Henry VIII entertaining Cardinal Wolsey at luncheon while the dogs under the royal table disputed among the rushes for the discarded carcasses of swans, geese and venison."[64]

Marie was a close observer to Lillian's star temperament and tantrums. Lillian knew how to break contracts and walk out without notice if something or someone was not to her liking. Directors were easy targets, since they were regarded as little more than traffic officers, moving chorus lines effectively and pacifying star egos. Their control was limited, since ad libbing, encores, and spontaneous inspiration could change everything. Marie was inclined to follow Lillian's example and resist the meddling of directors. Even in her twenties, Marie discovered how to avoid taking orders. As she explained it:[65]

> The stage director picked me out as one who needed instruction. He started to tell me how to play a certain difficult role. ... He tried a dozen times or more to make me do something which I felt was wrong and awkward and I finally broke down and cried. The manager, George Lederer, was out in front of the house and cried out to the stage director: "Oh, let her do it her own way; she's funny!" ... After that, it was an unwritten law with all stage producers that Marie Dressler was to have the privilege of interpreting her own part as she saw fit.

Marie was in awe of Lillian's beauty and success, but she was realistic on one account. She gently noted[66] that Lillian was "none too clever about men." Lillian was a teenager when she married her first husband, orchestra leader Harry Braham. Eight years later, she divorced Braham to marry Edward "Teddy" Solomon, another orchestra leader. They had a daughter, Dorothy, born in 1884, but Lillian hated Solomon's stinginess and they fought bitterly. The end of that marriage came when he was arrested for bigamy.

Signor Don Giovanni Perugini,[67] a tenor of notable vanity, assumed the role of the tobacco planter during the run of *Princess*

Nicotine. Lillian's trademark bad judgment in men appeared yet again and she quickly formed an offstage romance with Perugini to accompany the hot reviews they got on stage. "The way in which the tenor and prima donna made love to each other on stage astonished even the most cash-hardened critics," noted one onlooker.

Marie made no secret of hating Perugini. For starters, he was a fraud, not an Italian tenor bred at La Scala but a Michigan hick né Jack Chatterton. Many said he was homosexual, but others said he was too self-absorbed to have relations with anything but a mirror. His effeminacy drove Marie to imitations and one night backstage before a performance she said[68] to Lillian, "I just passed Perugini's door and she had on the loveliest pink robe — blue bows and everything."

When Lillian asked Marie to stop teasing because she and Perugini were engaged, Marie was stupefied. They were married on January 24, 1894, but work kept them from a honeymoon. *Princess Nicotine* played at the Casino for a hearty three months and then toured with the newlyweds and Marie to Baltimore, Washington, Pittsburgh, Philadelphia, New Haven, and Boston.

Trouble on the road started immediately. Lillian did not use her matrimonial status to get Perugini's name alongside hers on the marquee as he had hoped. Their relationship soon degenerated into a gross public spectacle as he muttered obscenities to Lillian on stage and then played to his young women swooners as the misunderstood groom. Marie found the groupies and their delusion disgusting and wasted no time in telling them so. She claimed, "The nearest I ever came to murder ... on the stage [was when] one night he said something to her that made me see red, and I was going to throw him into the bass drum."[69] Instead, she chased him out of the theater while brandishing a stage brace, a potentially deadly weapon of hardwood and iron. He subsequently refused to go on until the management gave him a bodyguard. In the basement bar of the Hotel Normandie, a favorite watering hole less than a block from the Casino Theater, gossip circulated and sympathies were reevaluated. Due in part to Marie's revelations, Perugini's former fans were now calling him nothing but a "superfluous larynx on legs."[70]

The uneasy trio, Lillian, Perugini, and Marie, managed to rehearse and perform another production. In March 1894 the popular comic opera *Giroflé-Girofla* returned as a vehicle Lillian first performed a year earlier to tremendous success at Chicago's Columbian Exhibition. Twenty-four-year-old Marie was cast as thirty-three-year-old Lillian's mother and got away with the chronological illusion to everyone's satisfaction. But the sunshine generated on the stage in *Giroflé-Girofla* was all fake. Friends considered the nuptials of Lillian and Perugini a marriage of convenience — his. He grew evermore churlish over reviews proclaiming that he "was more interesting from mere juxtaposition ... than he was effective either vocally or in acting."[71] The status of the marriage was common knowledge by then and audiences squealed in amusement when the groom said, "I think it is a proper plan to take a business view of marriage."

Perugini continued to brutalize his wife. A crisis was reached when he attempted to throw Lillian out a seventh-story window of Philadelphia's Hotel Stenton.[72] On return from the tour by June, Perugini promptly sued for divorce and Lillian reportedly had an abortion. They weren't legally divorced until 1898. In telling his side of the story, Perugini said, "Do you know what she did to me? Why, sir, when we had to share apartments, she took all my pillows; she used my rouge; she misplaced my manicure set; she used my special handkerchief perfume for her bath; she always wanted the best mirror when we were making our toilets, whether for the theater or street, and she usually got it. She's a desperate character."[73]

One might hope Marie had learned a lesson from Lillian on the dangers of hasty marriages. She hadn't.

Chapter 3

"Nothing to It but Dressler"

As Russell and Dressler continued their tremendous stage repartee, Marie was seeing a young theater employee named George Francis Hoppert.[1] Born into German and French ancestry, he had dashing good looks. His handsomeness and easy manner made him much in demand as cashier of the Atlantic Garden on the Bowery, where Marie sang on cash-strapped days. He later worked for George Lederer, who promoted him to assistant treasurer. Though he had none of Marie's fast wit, they were great pals who would tickle, grab, and crack up without any apparent provocation. They "were always rough-housing and having fun and laughing together," recalled Lederer.[2] "We used to see them at Martin's — which was the smart place to be in those days — and they were always cutting up like two kids." They were an odd pair visually. "He was maybe the handsomest man I ever saw," recalled producer-actor Joe Weber.[3] "Like a Greek god, we used to say. All right, I guess every woman has a right to a romance with a big handsome dummy, like gentlemen from time to time prefer dumb blondes. And Hoppert was a big handsome dummy."

On May 6, 1894, Marie and George took a ferry from New York to Jersey City just across the Hudson River. There, in the shadow of the eight-year-old Statue of Liberty, they were married in a ceremony witnessed by father Alexander and brother-in-law Richard.[4] Annie had hoped to attend, but ill health kept her at home. It was George's first marriage; he was 34 and Marie was 25. It is not clear whether the newlyweds lived with Marie's parents in Long Island City or they kept George's apartment at 41st and Broadway. Perhaps it didn't much matter, since Marie was on the road through most of their marriage.

There was no time for a substantial honeymoon. After *Giroflé-Girofla* ended its acrimony-filled tour, Marie was traveling again. She appeared with Baker's company again in *Chimes of Normandy*, *Boccaccio*, and *The Black Hussars*. She then joined Camille D'Arville's company playing Mary Doodle, a sextuple widow, in *Madeleine; Or, the Magic Kiss* for the rest of 1894 and for 80 performances on Broadway in early 1895.

She had a more important assignment waiting for her at Chicago's Schiller Theater in the spring of 1895. Much anticipation was made over the production of a lavish new Harry B. Smith concoction called *Little Robinson Crusoe*. Set at "the anti-fat Summer Hotel," the story hung on a love triangle involving the mariner Crusoe, lovely Polly Perkins, and an amateur pirate played by Eddie Foy. Marie, as landlady Ophelia Crusoe, and Foy won most of the show's praise. After running for a week, opinion[5] was "fairly divided as to who is the star, Eddie Foy or Marie Dressler. Both are doing very clever work."

Foy was one of the nation's top funnymen and Marie wanted to know his secrets. She closely watched her more seasoned costar at work and noted[6] that "he was invariably hunting funny accessories for business. Perhaps it was because of his continual trouble in locating and keeping them at hand, always getting fussed if one were missing, that unconsciously developed my own aversion to their use. At any rate, I have never used a prop of any sort. This has inconvenienced me at times, since this eccentricity excludes even a handkerchief, that delightful pièce de résistance of most actresses."

Little Robinson Crusoe enjoyed a healthy run in Chicago through the summer. In early September, Marie defected when the show headed for Cleveland. Next up was a stint as Queen Isabella in *1492*, which first opened in 1892 for the quadricentennial of Columbus's arrival in the New World. Coming into the show almost three years later, Marie replaced female impersonator Richard Harlow as the Queen of Spain.* The show and the role did little to advance her career, but it kept the bills paid for a time.

She soon announced to producer Edward E. Rice that she was leaving *1492* and was headed back to Chicago for an out-of-town tryout of the new play *A Stag Party*. The broken contract led to bravado about legal action, but nothing happened. Marie was excited about her inflated salary of $150 a week and happy to get to Chicago and see Lillian, who was performing there on tour.

Many in the theater were trying to find some consistency and equity in business negotiations. The breaking of contracts and canceling of performances was common, and loyalty between actors and managers was rare. Albert Palmer, the large, muttonchopped producer of *A Stag Party*, saw no breech of ethics in luring Marie away from a fellow producer. By the standards of 1895, Marie was reasonable in hastily leaving *1492* for a more lucrative situation. Palmer[7] remarked that "the present contract between actor and manager is perfectly equitable. It says distinctly that if, at any time, either party wishes the engagement to come to an end he can close it by giving two weeks' notice. This cuts both ways."

After the stint in Chicago, Marie opened as Georgia Vest in *A Stag Party* on December 17 at the Garden Theater in New York. Directed by *The Robber of the Rhine*'s Richard Barker, the paper-thin story of deer hunting, according to the *New York Times*,[8] was "extremely silly and some of it is deplorably vulgar." Marie was "buxom and energetic. Her singing is capable. Her dancing is vigorous if scarcely graceful. She acts all she can and is particularly impressive when she imitates now a hen, now a cat."[9]

Present at opening night was M. B. Curtis, who received an unwelcome shock. Curtis was an actor who had bought the rights to bring the English musical *Gentleman Joe* to New York and, while seated in the Garden Theater, he heard familiar melodies from *Gentleman Joe* arising from the orchestra pit. The stage setting was also more than evocative of *Gentleman Joe*. Curtis interrupted the performance and "began to hiss like a steam-engine."[10]

Mrs. Curtis[11] explained the situation to a reporter:

> We had heard that Richard Barker, who put on the *Stag Party*, proposed to take

---

*Cross-dressers were rife in 1890s American theater, from beautiful Hal Johnson and Frances Leon to boyish Vesta Tilley and Beatrice. Unlike Johnson, Leon, Tilley, and Beatrice, the decidedly curvaceous Marie never made transvestism her specialty.

musical numbers from *Gentleman Joe*. My husband met with Mr. [Paul] Potter, one of the authors of the play, and warned him against such a theft. Mr. Potter gave his word of honor that none of *Gentleman Joe*'s songs or business would be introduced in the *Stag Party*. ... Imagine our surprise [on opening night]. Between the acts my husband met Mr. Potter and told him he was a plagiarist. He could not deny the accusation.

"How much of *Gentleman Joe* was incorporated in *A Stag Party*?" the reporter asked. Mrs. Curtis replied, "The opening chorus, a song called 'Go to Paree' and another called 'Gate Ajar.' Some of the words and business were stolen, too." With lawsuits pending, *A Stag Party* was yanked from the Garden Theater less than two weeks after its premiere. *Gentleman Joe* opened in January and managed ten performances.

Amidst an unyielding schedule, Dressler found time to divorce George Hoppert. The marriage was perhaps the grossest and most ill-conceived miming of Lillian imaginable. George was no better suited to Marie than Signor Perugini was to Lillian, though he had a far sweeter disposition. He wasn't physically or verbally abusive, and he did not have a preening and belligerent attitude, but he was lacking in mental horsepower. He was good natured, but incompatible with Marie. "I guess [good looks] was all there was to him, because it didn't last long," said Lederer[12] years later. "He wasn't up to Marie's caliber."

During the breakup, she bunked at Lillian's elegant home near Central Park on West 77th Street. There, the two had time to reflect on the similarities of their matrimonial travails. Marie married George less than four months after Lillian married Perugini and both couples lived together less than a year. Both tried to keep the dynamics of their marriages a secret from the public, though Marie was decidedly more successful at privacy. Perugini's lust for notoriety and Lillian's fame kept their marriage on the front pages, while Marie was not yet a major star getting major attention and George had no apparent desire for scandal and gossip.

The silence from all parties could fuel miles of speculation. Marie's marriage to George remains one of the most underreported events of her life. She is characteristically vague; she didn't even remember how long the marriage lasted.[13] "I married ... for thrills. It didn't work out. The thrill soon vanished and after a year or two we realized there was no basis for companionship." Documents and recollections are sketchy and inconsistent, but explanations can be ventured. It is possible that she married him to gain United States citizenship and continue to perform without threat of censure. The marriage made her an American citizen and she used that fact many years later as evidence of her patriotism and legal residence. It was also rumored that they had a daughter who died in infancy, but Marie wrote not a single word on the subject — and when did she have time to be pregnant? The great unspoken sin of the time, homosexuality, may have motivated both Marie and George. Was Marie in love with Lillian? Was her marriage to George some payback for Lillian's "betrayal" by marrying Perugini? Could Marie and George end speculation about their private lives by conducting themselves as respectable heterosexuals?

Whatever their motives, he didn't last long. Lederer recalled George's death, and one account has him in a wheelchair after an accident.[14] Others have him quietly divorcing Marie and leaving their circle of friends and business associates. Whatever the fate of George Hoppert, he achieved a permanent and complete exit from Marie's life.

He was out of the picture when *The Lady Slavey*, the greatest hit of Marie's early theatrical career, opened on February 3, 1896. Even though she substantially contributed to the success of *Princess Nicotine* and *Giroflé-Girofla*, Lederer did not originally want her on the *Lady Slavey* payroll as Flo Honeydew of the Music Halls. "I didn't want her for it a bit," he said.[15] "I wanted a big star name." He tried out a dozen more prominent actresses, but once Marie began rehearsing, he spoke what would become an axiom of future productions: "there was nothing to it but Dressler."

The Lady Slavey first tried out for a run of

less than one week in Chicago at the Lafayette Opera House. It was one of many English musical imports doing big business across the United States. The *Stag Party* plagiarism of *Gentleman Joe* was motivated by the assured success of English music-hall confections that were then the rage. Housed at the Casino, *The Lady Slavey* was the eighth English musical of the season, but Lederer instructed writer George Dance to liberally "Americanize" the property. With a revamped book and score, Dan Daly was the lazy sheriff who must reclaim the estate of a bankrupt Englishman. The bankrupt man tried to marry one of his daughters (the lady slavey — house servant — Virginia Earle) to a wealthy young heir with the help of Flo (Marie).

When *The Lady Slavey* opened in New York, the *Times* proclaimed[16] "Miss Dressler an utterly preposterous musical hall performer." Lewis Strang noted that "It was hardly a case of acting. Better call it a case of letting herself go ... She seemed a big, overgrown girl and a thoroughly mischievous romp with the agility of a circus performer and the physical elasticity of a professional contortionist. ... Her comic resource was inexhaustible, her animal spirits were irrepressible and her audacity approached the sublime." One publicity photo of *The Lady Slavey* had her costars each in a conservative pose while Marie is on the floor in an evening gown doing a back bend. She "panoram'd a smile ... large and dental. ... [S]he exuded magnetism from all her pores."[18]

The only setback of *The Lady Slavey* was the temperament of thin, graceful star Daly. "Dance with that elephant of a Dressler?" blurted Daly during rehearsals.[19] Lederer was there to pacify Daly, who ultimately consented. His dance with Marie, dubbed "The Human Fly," became the topic of the town. "I threw myself into it like a tornado," Marie wrote about that infamous dance on opening night.[20] "Daly was a hard worker and quick to catch a situation. In order to keep up with me, he had to dance as he had never danced before. As we started off stage, I whispered, 'jump on my hip and I'll carry you off!' He hesitated a second, then did as I told him and we went off in a whirlwind of applause. As we stood panting in the wings, listening to the deafening clap-clap of the many hands, which told us we were a hit, Daly said worriedly, 'My God, what'll we do for an encore?' Sweet music, that, after his witticisms at rehearsals."

The *New York Times*[21] reported that "Several members of the company declare she weighs 240, but to funny Dan Daly that makes not the slightest difference when it is a question of dancing. ... He circles around her, watching for a chance to rush in; then, quick as a flash, he has her, and both begin to fly about the stage. Up she shoots in the air and down to the stage come 240 pounds with a crash that shakes the theater." Throughout *The Lady Slavey*, Marie practiced the planned spontaneity she learned so well from Lillian. On one occasion, she accidentally struck her hat on stage and it spun around and landed back on her head. The results won so much laughter that she perfected the "mistake" into a nightly routine. At another point she perfected the "accident" of bumping into the scenery.

The Lady Slavey was Marie's first production to get her a star's attention and salary. Shopping sprees for clothes, jewels, and animals followed. After years of promises, she gave her mother a fur coat and a horse and carriage. After surveying dozens of horses, Marie settled on a kindly beast living in a small New Jersey town and renamed him Teddy Roosevelt.[22] He was unusually cheap and on his first ride with his new family, Marie discovered why. Without warning, Teddy stopped abruptly after about 100 yards. He wouldn't budge. Then he moved again, only to stop in another hundred yards. Marie inquired to his former owner about this peculiar behavior. Seems he previously pulled a milk wagon on its daily rounds. When Annie took her friends riding, she explained that "Teddy is a very superior animal. He knows just where the best scenery is and he always stops without being told!"

Marie lived in Long Island City with her parents for four years, taking the ferry nightly across the East River. She became pals with the ferryman and the train hands that met the boat

Marie's favorite cartoon of herself. Hoisting her is Dan Daly, partner for the famous "Human Fly" dance from *The Lady Slavey*.

at Long Island. On cold nights, they would huddle around the potbellied stove on board for friendly small talk.[23]

In the olden days of Broadway, a hit lasted just a few months at its original theater. *The Lady Slavey* closed at the Casino in May. The cast scattered, with Marie finding herself as Mrs. Malaprop in a revival of Richard Brinsley Sheridan's 1775 comedy *The Rivals* at the Hearld Square Theater. The production came and went quickly, but Marie remained proud of this rare plundering of a classic.

When *The Lady Slavey* came to Washington in September of 1896, opening-night guests included Chauncey Depew, president of the New York Central & Hudson River Railroad, Buffalo Bill Cody in all his Western finery, and President Grover Cleveland.[24] While in Washington, Marie employed a maid named Jenny,[25] who was so happy to get the position that she broke off an engagement to work for Marie.

Marie quickly grew to like Jenny's self-confidence and wit. While waiting for a train, Marie recalls an exchange between Jenny and a drunk young man. He was encouraging her to become inebriated as well, but she ignored his crude invitation. "Oh, come on now, you know you coons never refuse a drink."

Jenny chose to say nothing, but instead shot him a withering glance. He grew more uncomfortable.

"My mistake. You'll excuse me, won't you, Jenny?"

"Yes, sir," said Jenny. "You got a standin' excuse with me."

She and Marie got along exceedingly well. Before the company had left Washington, Jenny was escorting Marie to her tour stops. They took the train to engagements at the Chestnut Street Theater in Philadelphia and the Euclid Avenue Opera House in Cleveland, later a site for past Bennett-Moulton comic opera successes.

At her mother's insistence, Marie took a vacation at the exclusive Marion House on Lake George after a year in *The Lady Slavey*.[26] Traveling alone, she was snubbed by the society types, who asked in a stage whisper whether Marie was "the *actress* who twirled that funny hat?" When the guests confirmed that an actress was in their midst, "even dogs were instructed not to wag their tails," Marie noted.[27]

She found a piano in an empty dance hall and began playing and singing. Evergreen garlands from an ancient party were dry against the walls and pieces of cigars and bunting were on the floor. A voice came to her from nearby. "Delightful. I wonder if you sing 'Believe Me, If All Those Endearing Young Charms?'" Marie saw a gray-haired old woman in the window. "It's one of my favorites, too," said Marie. "Won't you come in?"

She came in and continued. "I live at the cottage above here. I was passing and heard your voice." After much singing, the woman said, "Won't you come home with me for a cup of tea? I should like my daughter to meet you." The two were walking to the cottage when Marie felt obligated to tell her new companion the truth. The woman was not at all concerned that Marie was an actress, nor was the woman's daughter.

Dressler returned to the hotel and reluctantly dressed for dinner and the familiar snubs. But guests nearly shoved each other aside to gain her attention. "Do come over here, Miss Dressler," invited one dowager. "We've been saving a place for you," said a plump gentleman. What was this sudden change in attitude all about? Marie did not learn the answer until the next morning. The gracious old woman who introduced herself merely as Mrs. Grant was Julia Dent, wife of Ulysses S. Grant and former first lady of the United States.

Marie continued to perform *The Lady Slavey* for several seasons after its opening in 1896. In between *Slavey* engagements, however, she no longer spent her summer months with the Bennett-Moulton Company. Marie made the deliberate decision, with no apparent regret, to turn away from comic opera. She repeatedly stated her desire to wash customers free of sorrow and misery by telling jokes, singing songs, and dancing. The most effective way to do that was give them a great big dose of the Dressler personality via vaudeville and musical revues. Comic opera was too organized, the canon too set, and it left Marie little room to fly through the inspired antics that were becoming her trademark.

In February 1897, she went into her first burlesque engagement at Proctor's Pleasure Palace on East 58th Street. This was not a bump-and-grind strip show. Marie would never allow such vulgarity and she could never pull it off unless it was in jest. Her show was burlesque as satire or travesty of notable personalities and plays. The opus was billed as "Miss Marie Dressler and Her Supporting Company, in the Musical and Farcical Spasm, In One Act, by A. R. Phillips, entitled *Tess of the Vaudevilles*." This was an obvious attack on the hit *Tess of the D'Urbervilles*, and on Minnie Maddern Fiske, its current star known by all as Mrs. Fiske. Marie hungrily went after Thomas Hardy's heroine, getting good reviews and strong attendance. She "is a burlesquer in thought, word and deed," noted theater writer Lewis Strang.[28] "Being a burlesquer she is of necessity absolutely without illusions. ... Choosing to do this through the force of her own personality rather than by infusing her personality into a dramatist's conception, she became a droll, a professional jester."

Accompanying *Tess of the Vaudevilles* was the "scientific marvel" of the Lumière Cinematograph,[29] "The Most Perfect Device Yet Invented for the Photographic Portrayal of Life in Motion." Featured were various scenes such as a fish market in Marseilles, an electrical carriage race from Paris to Bordeaux, and the baths of Minerva at Milan, which ended with "a droll effect obtained by reversing the film." Marie thought the novelty amusing but hardly revolutionary.

More noteworthy was her unexpected friendship with fortyish society doyenne Marion Graves Anthon Fish. Known as Mrs. Stuyvesant Fish, or Mamie to her friends, she was the high-profile wife of the president of the Illinois Central Railroad. She happened to see *Tess of the Vaudevilles* just as Marie developed a new routine that involved throwing food at music director Maurice Levi. One night a grocery item flew past Levi and into the audience, where it struck Mrs. Fish's well-coiffed head by mistake. By varying reports, contact was made by an onion, an eel, or a bunch of leeks. Whatever the foodstuff, Mrs. Fish and her friends were most amused. And from that amusement, a friendship was born.

"I always admired her first for her brains and then because under her somewhat gruff exterior there was a protective instinct," recalled Marie.[30] "She always tried to hide her soft spot, but it was there. Early in our acquaintance, she sent for me to entertain one of her parties and asked what I would charge. I was making good money then and told her I wouldn't charge anything. 'Very well,' said she decisively. 'You may come to my party, but I won't let you appear.'"

Mrs. Fish's parties were by all accounts lavish and by some accounts infantile. She had guests dress as flowers for her "Flower Ball" and as Mother Goose characters for her "Mother Goose Ball." The most famous Fish affair had invitations going out to all her friends for a gathering at Crossways, her Newport estate, to honor some Prince so-and-so.[31] New York's elite was easily cowed by titled royalty and upon arriving, guests discovered that the prince was a monkey. Mrs. Fish wasn't alone in her eccentric partygiving. Hardcore equestrian Cornelius K. Billings hosted a

"Horseback Dinner" at Sherry's at which guests ate none too comfortably from the saddle atop an animal.³²

The gestures of friendship made by Fish toward Marie were altogether remarkable and bring to light a fundamental change in social attitudes toward actors. Both women found humor in satire and joy in exposing pompousness. Like Marie, Fish was imperious, brilliant, and generous and had no patience for dullness. Marie maintained a "just plain folks" attitude with Fish and her multimillionaire friends. She was moved by Fish's lavish gifts but found sentimental moments to be the most memorable. When Marie told her that she would boast to her mother of their friendship, Mrs. Fish responded by saying that she would be "proud to tell my children that Marie Dressler dined with me."³³

Once the obsolete wall separating performer from rich patron came down, Dressler was a popular guest in a world made lavish by banks, mines, and railroads. She and other performers went from the status of social pariahs to celebrities as the press began paying attention to them. The lives of actors, not the lives of the rich, were interpreted by press and public as endlessly interesting. The rise of well-publicized theatrical entertainment was simultaneous with the rise of widely known stars, and Marie was at center stage for this huge cultural change.

The financial and industrial elite began courting her, not as a peer but as a wildly amusing party trophy. With Mrs. Fish as her guide, Marie found herself a satellite member of New York's powerful Four Hundred. Her male friends included horseman Cornelius Billings, Major Dangerfield, and wine salesman

Marie at 28 in costume and character as *Tess of the Vaudevilles* (1897).

Freddy Gebhard. She was also friendly with banker Oliver Hazard Perry Belmont, architect Stanford White, dandy clotheshorse E. Berry Wall, and Harry Lehr, the gay and flamboyant "court jester" of Mrs. Fish's inner circle. Freddy Townsend Martin, a quiet but grand philanthropist who kept a shelter in the Bowery for down-and-outers, was another friend.³⁴ Grand opera diva Lillian Nordica and Marie sang and dined at the shelter during one Thanksgiving.

Marie cultivated a folksy charm on stage that endeared her to audiences of many social and financial stations, but she infiltrated the Four Hundred with singular determination. Even a case of tonsillitis and exhaustion didn't

Programme Continued.

7   **JAMES BALLARD, THE BARD**
Of Red Oak, Montgomery County, Iowa, U. S. A.
The Poetical Lecturer, and Only Living Rival of the Charming Cherry Sisters, who holds the World's Record for having written 44,678 lines of poetry (?), and has thus far escaped with his life. The Cherry Sisters are very envious since Mr. Ballard has broken loose in New York.

1. An Eloquent Ode to New York.
2. Gestures, with Rhymes and Tones.
3. The Mind.
4. A Word to the Critics.
5. "Look Out!" (Tune—"Oh, Do!").
6. "Spirit of Progress."
7. "The Bachelor's Consolation."
8. "The Cuckoo" (and it is).
9. "Squeak Ta-a-a It."—Marvelous Bird Imitation.
10. "Chirwain Tit-tit-tit" (another bird of a song).

(This is Mr. Ballard's first engagement in the Effete East.)

8   **THE ROGERS BROTHERS**
The Famous German Comedians
(Their first engagement at the Pleasure Palace).

9   **MISS MARIE DRESSLER**
And her Supporting Company, in the Musical and Farcical Spasm, in One Act, by A. R. Phillips, entitled

TESS OF THE VAUDEVILLES
(With apologies to "Tess of the D'Urbervilles").
Music by Frederick Clifton.   Words by Frederick Backus.

THE CHARACTERS.
SALLY, alias Tess of the Vaudevilles............................Miss MARIE DRESSLER
MR. SMITH, alias Angel Food...................................FREDERICK BACKUS
MR. BROWN, alias Alec Stoughtenbottle..........................FREDERICK CLIFTON
SCENE—A swell apartment on Cherry Hill.

Sixth week of the Scientific Marvel,
10   **THE LUMIÈRE CINEMATOGRAPH**
The Most Perfect Device yet Invented for the Photographic Portrayal of Life in Motion.

1. The Baby's First Lesson in Walking.
2. The Electrical Carriage Race from Paris to Bordeaux.
3. A Gondola Scene in Venice.
4. The Charge of the Austrian Lancers.
5. Fifty-Ninth Street, opposite Central Park.
6. A Scene near South Kensington, London.
7. The Fish Market at Marseilles, France.
8. German Dragoons Leaping the Hurdles
(Also a reverse view of this picture).
9. A Snow Battle at Lyons, France.
10. Negro Minstrels Dancing in the London Streets.
11. A Sack Race Between Employees of Lumiere & Son's Factory, Lyons.
12. The Baths of Minerva, at Milan, Italy
(Also a droll effect obtained by reversing the film).

As evidence of her growing popularity, Marie's *Tess of the Vaudevilles* was billed as the last live act of an evening at Proctor's Pleasure Palace. The finale was a showing of the brand new invention of moving pictures.

stop her. She was forever being invited to fancy luncheons and afternoon teas. In a confessional moment, she soliloquized on the machinations of social climbing to a newspaperman:[35] "Suppose that I, Marie Dressler, with blue, green or yellow blood in my veins — whatever it is — should go to Newport next summer for my vacation, would anything happen? ... I wouldn't make even a dent in the armor of the Four Hundred. Of course this is not right. ... The members of the Four Hundred come to see me act. ... They ask me to their home to sing songs and treat me with the same cordiality that they would one of their own but I am paid for it. When people of their own set amuse them they are not paid for it. That's the difference."

When she wasn't getting friendly with the Four Hundred, Marie was winning admirers in classical music. Tenor Enrico Caruso, pianist Leopold Godowsky, and violinist Fritz Kreisler spent late nights singing, playing the piano and laughing in Marie's Manhattan pied-à-terre. Caruso was an especially close friend. "The greatest person and the greatest personality I have known was Marie Dressler," he said.[36] "With Marie, it was impossible not to enjoy life. What more can you ask of a human being?"

She was back on the road with *The Lady Slavey* when producer Abe Erlanger bought into the production with George Lederer. This was unfortunate for Marie — she was fond of Lederer but took an instant dislike to Erlanger. Most everyone else did as well. Erlanger, with the ironic given names Abraham Lincoln, was arguably the most despised producer of the era. Described as squat, bull-faced, arrogant, heartless, and Napoleonic, he set himself the laudable goal of organizing the hundreds of companies moving in and out of thousands of theaters nationwide. In 1895 he had entered a partnership with lawyer Marc Klaw to form the Theatrical Syndicate, better known as the Trust. Theaters were grouped into regional circuits and booking agencies, while the Trust became the New York–based overseer of the vast network.

Without owning any property or theaters, or ever producing a play, the Trust took efficient control and acquired a roster of prestigious clients. Before long, abuses of talent became commonplace. The Trust collected from theaters and producers, but its fees and tributes were not consistent. Anyone not directly affiliated with the Syndicate or Klaw and Erlanger paid dearly. The celebrated Mrs. Fiske and Sarah Bernhardt were performing in tents in defiance to the Trust's bullying control, while the cooperation and loyalty of powerful showmen George M. Cohan, Florenz Ziegfeld, and Charles Dillingham strengthened the Trust's grip. Critics were bribed, uncooperative actors found themselves relieved of employment, and control by the Trust reached the level of near-absolute monopoly. The facts "make it impossible to avoid the conclusion that the Syndicate is chargeable with very serious economic abuses — unfair competition, restraint of trade, discrimination, ruthless commercialism,"[37] while operating on the outer fringes of the law.

Unlike Erlanger and other Trust businessmen, Lederer had only warm regard for Marie. He had produced her in *Princess Nicotine, Giroflé-Girofla*, and *The Lady Slavey* and knew firsthand of her growing talent.[38]

> I have been in show business a good many years. In all that time Marie Dressler is the only artist I ever knew whom you couldn't replace. Once Marie had played a part, that was the end of it. You folded it up and threw it away. I tried lots of good troupers to follow her ... but it was no use. There is only one Marie Dressler!

When Marie took ill during a run of *The Lady Slavey* in Denver, Lederer's new partner Erlanger thought that she was faking. He reasoned that she was just sick of playing small towns and was trying to find her way back to New York. But she was also going broke supporting her family, so she had little incentive to leave a steady gig. Erlanger would have none of her excuses, and Lederer's efforts to pacify him were unsuccessful. When Marie heard on reliable authority that Erlanger intended to fire her, she quit first.

Erlanger was wrong about Marie. She returned to New York truly ill and furthermore did not appreciate his suspicions. In one of her lapses of diplomacy, she chided him openly. On another occasion she brandished a stage brace and chased him out of his own theater, screaming, "Simon Legree!"[39] He had gotten around a six-day-a-week clause in actor's contracts by calling Sunday night performances "concerts."

Marie was on Erlanger's hit list and he had the power to keep her off Broadway stages for more than a year. Proving that she never turned down honest employment, and wishing to drum up publicity during her hiatus, Marie sold peanuts and hotdogs on Coney Island. She had no shame: "Those were *good* hot dogs! I cooked them exactly right — toasted brown and served sizzling, with snappy mustard on fresh rolls! Umm ... you can bet Marie Dressler's wienies were remembered by the Coney Island crowds!"[40]

She wasn't selling wienies for long. Though Erlanger barred her from New York, he knew that she made money and so exiled her to an indefinite round of touring engagements. This was common practice for erring performers who broke contracts or stood up to the strongarming of the Trust, but it seems particularly callous considering Marie's fluctuating health. She opened as Dottie Dimple in *Courted into Court* for a short-lived engagement at the Lyceum Theater in Cleveland. Perhaps to garner attention or perhaps from real need, she took time off to recover from "nervous prostration." She and Jenny boarded a train to San Francisco and were there, fully recovered, for a January opening of *Courted into Court* at the downtown California Theater.

As usual, Marie was not burdened by a plot. Instead, *Courted into Court* featured specialty dance numbers, including the cakewalk and the buck and wing. For many, seeing Marie maneuver her large body with surprising nimbleness was enough for a night's entertainment. Peter Robertson at the *San Francisco Chronicle* wrote[41] "she is a genuine woman comedian, as distinguished from a soubrette. She acts with intelligence and with a clear insight into the comic propositions. She contorts her face until it looks like the wattles of a turkey gobbler in a rage and she sways her huge frame about until it falls into all sorts of awkwardness; but she has magnetism and she is a comedian. She is unafraid to be unattractive; that makes her the comedienne unusual." Erlanger was still determined to teach Marie a lesson. She never played *Courted into Court* in New York. When it opened there, Erlanger arranged to have the popular May Irwin replace her.

Dressler was finally allowed back in New York, but the April 26, 1898, revival opening of *The Lady Slavey* was not as fresh and funny as the original.[42] Back at the Casino, Marie was the only holdover from the original cast, with Richard Cowle taking over Dan Daly's role. All was not forgiven; Marie was punished with another tour in May and was back on the road with *The Lady Slavey* in Philadelphia.

She found some relief with new material if not a reprieve from constant travel. *Hotel Topsy Turvey* had its happy world premiere in Washington at the Lafayette Square Opera House on September 20, 1898. It opened in New York on October 3 at the Herald Square Theater with Eddie Foy, the man who so impressed Marie in *Little Robinson Crusoe*. By January, she was back in Philadelphia with the new show.

Hotel Topsy Turvey (*L'Auberge Tohu Bohu*) was first a French original musical farce. It was an absurd and boisterous hit "vaudeville operetta" in London and Paris before reaching New York. As Flora, the proprietress of Cluny's Colossal Combination, Marie contributed more than her share to the merriment. After all the others are off the stage, she struck a tragic attitude and said solemnly, "End of the first act!" She "has never had a better opportunity to exhibit her versatility than as the proprietress of Cluny's Colossal Combination. She filled the air with her voice and feet alternately." It helped the proceedings to have Edgar Smith adapt the original material. Lillian Russell held the opinion that he was "the most clever burlesque writer of the day."[43]

During a brief time in New York, Marie decided to start a regimen of physical conditioning and weight reduction. She thought swimming would help accomplish her goal. Accepting the position of president of the Theatrical Women's Athletic Club, she also felt some responsibility to set a good example. The club was without a pool, so Marie planned to meet her fellow club members at a nearby private pool for women. At poolside, Marie observed that the old-fashioned society ladies who patronized the institution were shocked when they learned that the crowd was made up of women who were identified with the stage and that some of them belonged to the chorus. The management of the fashionable institution on 45th Street politely told the theatrical women they could not be accommodated and then not so politely told them again on a return visit. Marie defended her tribe[44] and announced that "we swim like perfect ladies. Perhaps our conversation was a bit more brilliant than that indulged by the other ladies, but it was entirely proper."

While Marie was now routinely being called the funniest woman in America, she came to the attention of producer-director Augustin Daly. The prospect of employment with Daly was enticing, since he was a dramatist and producer of the first rank. He made a hit from S. H. von Mosenthal's *Deborah*, renaming it *Leah, the Forsaken*. He had similar luck with an original play, *Under the Gaslight*, and a succession of Shakespearean offerings. Was this Marie's ticket into a whole new career in drama? What did he see in her that eluded everyone else? A reporter with the *New York Sunday Telegraph* delivered the news and made a suggestion:[45] "After interviews and great inducements, Miss Dressler agreed to tempt fate and say good-by to broad comedy. To do what? I want you, Miss Dressler, to alternate with Miss Rehan.* That is, to play here when she plays abroad, and to play abroad when she plays here."

Daly died on June 7, 1899, before any contract was signed. The entire proposition quickly disappeared. Marie insists that the

Mrs. Mamie Fish, hostess non-pareil of fin de siècle New York. (Courtesy of Joseph J. O'Donohue IV.)

negotiations had begun and offered a stoic analysis of the missed opportunity.[46] "It is better to make the world smile and give them something they wish than to go broke peddling Shakespeare. But still I do wonder what I would have been like if I played Ophelia. ... I might have been the greatest tragedienne the world has ever known. And then again, I might not have been."

Soon enough, Dressler was back at musical comedy. After yet another tour, she appeared in *The Man in the Moon*, "a spectacle of

---

*Ada Rehan was the most popular actress among Daly's players.

wondrous pageantry" produced and staged by George Lederer.[47] Opening in the spring at the New York Theater, it was filled with big stars, including Sam Bernard, but it was just a gag- and gimmick-filled revue. It featured Orchid and Pony Ballets and characters from Sherlock Holmes mysteries. The Temple of Freedom, the Shrine of Liberty, the New Proteges of the Republic and the Golden Halls of Columbia were among the awe-inspiring set pieces. Marie played the eternally angry Viola Alum and had her emotions expressed by a violinist who followed her around the stage. The revue format allowed her to metamorphosize into multiple characters, though one reviewer found her humor too coarse. Nearly a month after opening, the company added some gender play. The destruction of the balcony scene from *Romeo and Juliet* was complete with Bernard as Juliet in white silk robes and flowing brown hair and Marie as Romeo in black tights, purple cloak and doublet.[48] With general admission at 50 cents, *The Man in the Moon* did exceedingly well and ran for 160 performances. At final tally, it was the fifth longest running show among 92 productions opening in New York during the 1899-1900 season. As the ultimate markers of success, it was lampooned as *The Maid in the Moon* and inspired a Marieless sequel, *The Man in the Moon, Junior*.

During the run of *The Man in the Moon*, Marie moved to a comfortable apartment on Broadway at 46th Street, saw her parents on Long Island on days off and added another maid and servant to her staff.[49] She was also reported to take part in a public spectacle of world class gluttony. A newspaper reporter caught Marie having lunch at the Hotel Metropole[50] dining room on 42nd Street, where her meal consisted of a porterhouse steak, lobster, chops, green peas, succotash lyonnaise, French fried potatoes, mushrooms, sauerkraut, broiled onions, lettuce salad, Brussels sprouts, charlotte russe, lady fingers, macaroons, Roquefort cheese, Bent crackers, *café noir*, nuts, and raisins. Actresses Beulah Coolidge and May Duryea were seated beside Marie.

"What a great, coarse creature she is," said Coolidge.

"Hush, Beulah. She can lick anyone in the profession but Maggie Cline."

"Well, she can't lick me, May, and I want her to know it."

Marie swallowed a pound of steak, gulped down a schoppen of the best California claret, kicked aside her chair, and went to Coolidge's table.

"Can't lick you, eh? ... Trying to bluff me, are you? Take that." Coolidge was expecting the blow. She countered with a blow to Marie's solar plexus. Marie cried foul when Duryea delivered a blow below the belt and broke one of her corset ribs. Duryea appointed herself referee and dismissed Marie's complaint. The headwaiter implored Duryea to end the match, which was fine with Marie, the unofficial loser.

After this episode, Marie was expected to be amusing whenever a reporter was present. A rumor was circulating that she was engaged to Jack Stavordale,[51] the business manager of Miles Stavordale Quintette. "Who am I to marry?" Marie asked a reporter who was visiting her at home.

"Mr. Stavordale, leader of the quintette that plays in the concert room at the theater."

"Why, he's an Englishman!" she shrieked.

"You don't like Englishmen?"

"No Englishman for me, even if they were the only men left alive. ... No man can ever have the grand privilege of supporting me."

She was much happier to take Jenny out on the town than she was to contemplate marriage to a Brit. On a hot August night, they went to the theater in company with May Duryea, once Marie's roommate and recent referee for the lunchtime brawl with Coolidge. "The sight of two women in a box accompanied by a maid is a novel one, even in New York, but when the maid has a heightened color and is invisible in a dark room, and is also permitted to sip beverages, the sight becomes not only novel but unprecedented," gasped an onlooker.[52] Southern cities threatened a boycott of Marie's touring shows when photos circulated of her and Jenny side by side. Others were more accommodating: "Those who observed Miss Dressler and her maid reached the conclusion, after deep and cogent thought, that her action was inspired by a large and throbbing heart and a love for the household picture of Abraham Lincoln striking the fetters from the wrists and ankles of the negro race in America."

This woman of "large and throbbing heart" became one of the foremost performers of the popular "coon songs."[53] Sung until the 1920s, they came from Tin Pan Alley and were similar to ragtime. They were upbeat, affected, and sung by black or white entertainers in blackface. Using cultural dialect and black vernacular, coon songs were a stepchild of minstrel songs. Popular titles included "All Coons Look Alike to Me," "I Never Like a Nigger with a Beard," "Nobody's Lookin' but de Owl and de Moon," and "Coon! Coon! Coon!"

For many whites of the time, African Americans were not bad, just inferior. In an age of legal segregation, there was no psychological conflict in white entertainers singing coon songs and being friends to African Americans. Boulevardier Joseph J. O'Donohue IV of the high-ranking ferry magnate family remembers hearing coon songs as a child.[54] "I used to go to Harlem to see friends of mine. They used to do coon songs from shows like *Shuffle Along* and *Blackbirds*. Nobody found it offensive that I know of. Minstrel shows were still around and all the people were in black face. Black people were singing these songs for me in their apartments. And the terrible jokes! Even as a small child sitting at the Palace Theater, I would say 'no—dreadful!' after a punchline. But the coon songs were innocent—in the spirit of 'Ta-Ra-Ra-Boom-De-Aye.' I don't suppose they would be considered innocent today, but people didn't

Marie in a rare subdued moment from *The Man in the Moon* (1899).

think then the way they do now." Open criticism for coon songs was minimal for many years, but Robert Cole wrote in the Indianapolis-based African American newspaper *Freeman* in 1905 that "the word 'coon' is very insulting" while maintaining that "there is no harm in the words Negro, Darkey, Colored or Afro-American."[55] Marie's foremost contribution to the genre was "Every Race Has a Flag but the Coon!"

America was still entertainment-happy at the turn of the century. After a serious economic depression beginning in 1896, the new century was greeted with nicknames such as "The Age of Optimism," "The Age of Confidence," and "The Age of Innocence." Marie had lived in her apartment on Broadway for just a year but moved into a flat formerly occupied by Bonita and Richard Ganthony at the Louella Apartments[56] at 159 West 45th Street. She filled it with pillows and insisted on steam heat, hot water, two gas logs, and a 24-hour janitor. At home she liked nothing more than to "sit down at the piano and croon over sentimental ballads and quiet, tender things."[57] Her parents relocated to an upscale home in Bayside, Long Island, as part of Marie's continued benevolence. As she had done when they lived in Long Island City, she often took a late ferry and train to Bayside rather than sleep in Manhattan.

In late October 1900, Marie was back touring in *The Lady Slavey* once more in Cleveland. By early November, she was in Albany starting an out-of-town run of George Hobart's farce *Miss Prinnt* in which she did an imitation of Lillian Russell that was rewarded with numerous floral gifts handed to her over the footlights.[58] By the following week, *Miss Prinnt* moved to Boston, where it was under the management of Joseph Immerman, a businesslike gentleman known affectionately as "Immy" to theater folks. His practical approach to money was exactly what she needed, especially since *Miss Prinnt* was largely funded by Marie.

The *Miss Prinnt* road schedule was enough to leave anyone in a state of nervous exhaustion and certainly left no time to properly stage a new production. *Miss Prinnt* opened on Christmas day at Oscar Hammerstein's new Victoria Theater, where it was soundly flattened by the critics. The plot and dialogue were uninspired. The songs and lyrics could not keep it afloat, although the coon song "I'm Lookin' for an Angel (Without Wings)" was well rendered by Marie. As Helen Prinnt, a small-town newspaper editor, she assumed an engaging caterwaul for lyrics such as "I'm lookin' for a nice young man to buy me lotsa things." She was "as nearly funny as anybody could be in such a very hopeless muddle," wrote the influential and intimidating Alan Dale of the *New York Journal*. "Every time she went away to change her dress I felt suicidal."[59]

Miss Prinnt played Toledo's Valentine Theater, then billed as "the greatest showplace west of the Alleghenies."[60] Toledo was only a 45-minute horseless carriage ride from Findlay, Ohio, where Marie spent some time growing up. Many folks from Findlay went to see *Miss Prinnt*, not knowing the star's origins. When the curtain rose on her, they gasped and whispered "that's either Leila Koerber or her ghost." Confirming that Marie Dressler and Leila Koerber were the same person, *Miss Prinnt* was booked in Findlay to turnaway business.[61] The town's upper crust was at the train station to greet her with a reception committee. She gave them a grand dame routine. Marie was interested only in Jake, a girlhood flame. "He's the only reception committee I want," she said. By the time *Miss Prinnt* hit the Chestnut Street Opera House in Philadelphia for a week's run, Marie told the press that she was desperately tired and wanted nothing more than to retire from the stage and run a hotel. She even considered buying "Kid" McCoy's place in Saratoga,[62] but it needed too much work.

Dressler next appeared in *The King's Carnival*, a burlesque revue that opened in New York in May 1901 and lasted for 80 performances. Marie did a bit as Queen Anne of Spain rocking the *Infanta*, played by an adult in a giant crib. Another high point was Marie's anthem to a new musical genre, "Ragtime Will Be Mah Finish." There was only a vague storyline resembling *The Prince and the Pauper*, inspiring Louis Harrison as King Philip of Spain to proclaim that "the plot grows thinner." Marie made an unusually dangerous commitment to physical comedy. In a dance she did with Harrison and Dan McAvoy as Bombastes Furloso, they fell backward into three chairs and then fell heels over head backward.

The King's Carnival was under the management of the Sire Brothers, with lawyer sibling Albert at the helm.[63] "They were an odd combination," Marie wrote.[64] "Any woman could go to them with a hard luck story and get $200, yet it would take her two months to collect $50 if they owed it to her. Their chief claim to fame is that they did know how to select good companies. [*The King's Carnival*] proved that there was more poetry than truth in the popular adage, 'Sired by the Sires and damned by the public.'" Trouble started when Marie's personal manager, Joseph "Immy" Immerman and the Sires had no luck persuading Marie to control her lending and spending. She was bringing in up to $1,000 a week but had been spending far more for years. By June 1901 she owed various individuals $12,000.[65] The tour of *Miss Prinnt* was not successful enough to bail her out, and so she kept working to the limits of her ability, sometimes rehearsing a new show by day and charging into a performance of a current show by night. She was back on the road in November, taking *The King's Carnival* to Boston, Hartford, and Philadelphia.

By February 1902 she was at the New York Theater in new fluffery called *The Hall of Fame*.[66] When the Goddess Fame (Amelia Summerville) informs a fame-starved actor (Louis Harrison) that there is no real glory until after death, he plays a trick. He announces that he will go over Niagara Falls in a barrel, but said barrel is empty. He gains the fame he wanted so desperately but is nabbed and hauled away by Marie as Lady Oblivion. She sings of one man's moment of glory, describing what happens "When Charlie Plays the Slide Trombone." The production was panned, but Marie saved the day. "If Marie Dressler hadn't been on hand last night to unbosom herself to her audience in a heart-to-heart talk now and then, the proceedings would have frequently proved funereal," wrote one observer.[67]

Plots were materializing in comedy productions by 1902, but they were preposterous, otherworldly, and convoluted. *The Hall of Fame* is but one example of a trend toward occult-influenced entertainment in early twentieth century American theater. Audiences did not take these excursions seriously, especially with hucksters like Marie and Louis Harrison along for the ride. *King High Ball* was another in this strange genre.[68] The plot involved Martians and Earthlings who wanted to be royalty. To impart a suitably unearthly aura, the chorus danced on a darkened stage lit only by tiny light bulbs twinkling on costumes. "A fearsome, direful hodge-podge of old fashioned construction, baleful attempts at humor and the weakest sort of script," moaned a first-nighter from the *New York Dramatic Mirror*.[69] Marie played the former Queen Tarantula, the 46th wife of the king of Mars. She stole the comic honors once again and was found to be "always offensive to any sense of the delicate."[70]

Still the bills were not paid and nonstop stage work was becoming intolerable. Marie labored under the grind until she announced[71] that "it cannot be next season but it will certainly be the season after that I will retire never to play again." She continued to search out hotel investments when a reporter asked what she would do with a million dollars. "Well, you can bet all of that sum, if you have it, I would not put one cent of it in theatricals," she informed him.[72] "Me to the country, if you please. I'd love to live in the country, just far enough to come in town occasionally, very occasionally." Marie's deep fatigue and money crisis came just as the world was officially falling in love with her. One newspaperman[73] dubbed her "the most popular woman in the theater" and a woman of "expansive wit, a broad, tolerant, receptive mind [and] a heart that enfolds mankind."[74]

While returning from a tour to Detroit, Marie complained of fatigue and went to the Bayside home for rest. On October 5, 1902, she fainted during a performance at the Orpheum Theater in Brooklyn. She collapsed again on October 20 while singing "I'm Lookin' for an Angel" but managed to complete the performance. Since the displays were so public, rumors began immediately that Marie had caught the epidemic of typhoid running through the Bayside area. "So they have me down with typhoid, eh?" she responded, ever combative.[75] "Well, I'm just about the sauciest, liveliest case of typhoid fever you ever saw."

Whatever the malady, something was terribly wrong. After the October 20 performance, she was taking a carriage ride when she became delirious and attempted to climb from her car and jump into the Hudson River. She insisted that electric cars were flaming carriages trying to attack her. She was restrained by Joseph

Immerman, who canceled all upcoming engagements,[76] including 20 weeks of coveted Orpheum Circuit vaudeville bookings of $800 to $900 guaranteed a week.

She was diagnosed with typhoid by Doctor Henry Frauenthal, and by late October was bedridden in her flat on West 45th Street. With doctors and nurses in constant attendance, Marie suffered severe deliriums, diarrhea, vomiting, headaches, and skin rashes. Her father Alexander arrived to help, but her mother Annie had taken ill with a weak heart and was resting in Bayside. Marie's temperature rose to 105, her weight fell from 210 to 130 pounds, and her luxuriant red-brown hair fell out. After a minor improvement, she suffered a relapse in mid–November. Frauenthal prescribed a liquid diet and plenty of ice bags, but in an age before modern antibiotics, typhoid was often deadly.

In December she continued to decline and Frauenthal predicted her death within days. When her mother died on Sunday, December 7, Marie was too lost in a sweat-drenched delirium to comprehend. Alexander was inconsolable and the burden of funeral arrangements fell on Immerman. He, Frauenthal, and friends agreed that to tell Marie of her mother's death would assuredly kill her, and so the decision was made to withhold the news. A small obituary appeared in the *New York Times* announcing the death of Marie Dressler's mother. Her death was known by strangers throughout the English-speaking world before it was known by her daughter.

Marie's finances were exhausted and money was needed for mounting doctors' bills and rent. Inspired by comedian Charles Ross, friends decided to produce a benefit. "If ever a woman earned the right to a theatrical benefit in her hour of need, big-hearted Marie Dressler, who in the ten years of her stage career has helped more of her fellow associates out of financial holes than almost any other woman in the theatrical profession, is that person," opined a New York newspaper.[77] "Now that typhoid fever has laid her low, and the sudden death of her mother, when it is broken to her, promises to prove a serious setback to her recovery, her friends are rallying to her rescue, and at the Victoria Theater, on January 4, a monster benefit is to be tendered her."

With Oscar Hammerstein donating his Victoria Theater, the sold-out benefit was a potpourri of snippets from Marie's shows and starred the theater's brightest comic stars, including May Irwin, Harry Bulger, William Collier, Dan McAvoy, Joseph Cawthorne, Louise Allen, Peter F. Daly, Eddie Foy, George Fuller Golden, Fay Templeton, and Sam Bernard. "Everyone seemed to be a personal friend of the merry actress," noted an observer.[78] When the till was counted, $7,682 was raised for Marie's rent and medical expenses. Immerman rushed to her flat to tell her the benefit was a wild success and broke a previous Broadway fundraising record.[79]

Heartened by the demonstration, Marie slowly regained strength and more regular consciousness. Eventually she was coherent and announced,[80] "Well, here I am again, you see. They can't kill off old Marie, unless they take an ax to her." No one dared tell her about Annie, but Marie's inquiries about her mother could not be avoided forever. Late at night, during her recovery in January, she awoke screaming and sat up in bed. As a nurse arrived, Marie instructed her to turn on all the lights.[81]

"Come here and look me in the face. I want to ask you something." The nurse obeyed. "There's no use trying to lie to me. I know what's happened. Mother is dead."

"How did you guess, Miss Dressler?"

"I didn't guess. I dreamed it just now. [In my dream] I went down to the house at Bayside. It was all boarded up and deserted. I broke into the house. It was empty except for a sofa lying in a corner of the sitting room. Something was lying on the sofa covered with a cloth. I rushed over to it and tried to wrench the covering off it. I couldn't for a long time. Then finally I uncovered the face. It was mother."

Chapter 4

The London Ache

Recovery from typhoid and grief was not swift. The new widower Alexander Koerber set sail for a brief stay in England, where daughter and son-in-law Bonita and Richard Ganthony had relocated. Left behind in her fragile condition, Dressler was without close family. Alone, she suffered paralysis in her left arm and her legs wobbled whenever she walked.[1] Outside on the streets of New York she was frequently surrounded by well-wishers. Their hope for her recovery made a huge difference, as did Marie's restored faith in God. She didn't rush off to church every Sunday, but she once said that life knocks you to your knees because that is the position that leads you to prayer.[2]

By February she felt strong enough to get back on stage. Though exhausted, Marie took off again like a racehorse. Her vaudeville act at Brooklyn's Orpheum Theater grew into a three-month stint that took her as far west as Detroit. Percy Williams, manager of a dozen theaters in greater New York City, negotiated her $1,000-a-week salary. Rival Benjamin Franklin Keith complained to the Vaudeville Managers Association, accusing Williams of trying to bankrupt the business with Marie's swollen salary. He succeeded in having Williams temporarily expelled,[3] just as Abe Erlanger had exiled Marie to months of touring in the late 1890s. Marie was prone to view all theater managers as sharks, but she granted an exception to Williams. She maintained a lofty opinion of him, and she wasn't alone. Most everyone found him unerringly fairminded and generous. He and Marie had an easygoing relationship;[4] she was forever bringing him untried talent. When tried, the results were mixed.

In Brooklyn or on the road, she was nowhere near her previous frenetic energy. Her legs were still weak and her knees buckled easily. Her acrobatics were curtailed, but audiences didn't seem to care. Upon her return in April, everyone in the New York Theater jumped to their feet and shouted "Hurrah for our Marie!" when she came on stage. Overcome and crying,[5] she pulled Maurice Levi over the footlights and gave him a kiss. When there was nothing else to do, she pulled off her wig to reveal a bald head. The crowd went crazy. Women cried and men threw their hats into the air.

She played one week in May at Percy Williams's Circle Theater, accompanied by a talented teenager on the piano named Jerome Kern.[6] Then she left town, hoping to make a final and complete recovery. She met her father in Toronto and headed for the forests of Canada for relaxation.[7] They reconciled in mutual grief, but he never won the unconditional love Marie gave her mother. The craggy, stooped, and white-bearded Alexander was frankly too old to be combative anymore. They grew closer, at least in the bucolic weeks of tennis and croquet in Canada. By June Marie was up to 190 pounds, nearly her full bulk, but her hair was no more than one inch long. By October she was rested enough to appear for another week at the Circle Theater. During her time off, she found sanctuary at her Long Island home, where cronies such as librettist Edgar Smith, actress Georgia Caine, and vaudevillian Tony Pastor were regularly lolling around.[8] They were seen leading "the simple unwholesome lives of vaudeville farmers. Up at eleven in the morning, water the milk [sic] and cutting jokes out of the Sunday newspapers."

She was back headlining in vaudeville by March 1904 in *Sweet Kitty Swellairs*, a parody sketch of *Sweet Kitty Bellairs*.[9] Sharing the bill was Adgie and her lion and "the poor man's amusement," a short film from the Vitagraph production company. In *Sweet Kitty Swellairs*, Marie used her girth to maximum comic effect yet again. She climbed into a cradle and of course it collapsed. Playing Kitty, she gives a farewell to visiting troops as she "stands in a doorway with a raised umbrella that has seen better, if not rainier days, while a weird hand holding a watering pot does the rest." Marie "labored like a Trojan, but the burlesque was distinctly absent," noted a critic.[10] Another felt she was off her mark from her recent illness.

The money was rolling in fairly steadily these days. By April, Marie endorsed not one but two products simultaneously. She declared that she owed her life to "Old Doctor Gaxadub's Marvelous Liver Root." She posed for a photograph surrounded by vines and dressed in a flowing gown with a full head of hair for another endorsement and to share her secret of recovery:[11] "I lost flesh from the consuming fever and my nervous system was almost a wreck, so that when I commenced to recover it became necessary for me to take a strong tonic stimulant.... At this time a friend told me of the great healing and vitalizing powers of TO-NI-TA, the new and wonderful Mucous Membrane Bitters discovered by Dr. Lorenz."

For all her recent success, Dressler was uncertain and anxious about her future. With a life on the road, she was more likely to suffer compromised health and be struck down again by one malady or another. She became a bit desperate in seeking other options. She was unqualified for most everything but comedy while newspapers delighted in joking about her various get-rich schemes. When she announced her intention to sell peanuts, her plans were far more ambitious than they were when Abe Erlanger blackballed her and she sold hotdogs at Coney Island.[12]

"But why peanuts?" asked a reporter.

"But why not peanuts?" retorted the new businesswoman.

"Where?"

"Sshh! Soft now. Promise not to breathe it and I'll tell you. Promise!"

"Yes, yes. Tell me where."

"Coney Island," she confessed.

What does a reporter say to this revelation? He paused, then asked, "In — er — tights or —?"

"Oh, I'm not going to be one of the sights of Coney Island ... just a — a feature, I may say. I suppose I'd better tell you that I've just refused an offer of $1,000 a week to sell peanuts at five cents a bag."

"Give up $1,000 a week to sell peanuts at five cents a bag!"

"Sure. ... Listen." Marie explained how she'd get in on the ground floor of the mammoth Dreamland park project by buying a peanut concession. "Isn't it a grand idea? I'm so happy to get away from the footlights. ... don't you think pink-striped paper bags would be the nicest?"

Marie hired a fleet of young boys, dressed them in caps with devils' horns, and gave them each a wicker basket loaded with "Marie

Dressler's Peanuts." She explained her theme: "It has been suggested that a lady wearing horns and a lot of little cash boys made up as demons might do very well. There's millions in it! Millions!"

If anyone doubted Marie's veracity, they were soon convinced. She charged forward in the investment, undaunted by an attack of the measles. She expanded the inventory to include popcorn and even rented a home in Bensonhurst to be nearer her little red devils.[13]

Snacks did not keep Marie off the stage, they only provided a diversion so that her life would not be consumed by the theater. In August she announced a new working relationship with Joe Weber, one of the leading funnymen of the day. He had previously made an indelible name for himself as the partner of childhood friend Lew Fields. When they debuted in 1896 at their intimate Weber & Fields Music Hall on 29th Street, they were an instant sensation. Together they pioneered a whole new style of comedy. Fields was tall and lanky, Weber was short and made round by a pillowed middle. Inspired by the "burlesque" genre of Lydia Thompson and her British Blondes, Weber and Fields took the "leg shows" and cleaned them up. Under their vision, burlesque moved from raunchy to respectable with the interjection of satire, puns, silly jokes, and first-rate showmanship. Among their inventions were custard-pie-in-the-face routines and "that was no lady" jokes. New York was ravenous for travesty, and soon the Music Hall was where anyone went to be amused by well-executed topical humor, with the deflating of Jews, the Irish, New York's Four Hundred, and the legitimate theater. *Cyranose de Bric-a-Brac*, the title of a Weber and Fields' travesty, sums up their good-natured style, as do their musical titles *Fiddle-Dee-Dee*, *Hoity Toity*, and *Whoop-Dee-Doo*.

They perfected the "Dutch" comic duo of Mike and Myer.[14] The Dutch comedian was a "stupid, clumsy, blundering fellow, to be laughed at rather than laughed with, more often than not the unconscious butt for cheap wit and senseless practical jokes. ... He is without subtlety, refinement or intellectuality."

Spoken in a peculiar and unique German-Yiddish dialect, repartee included such exchanges as

> FIELDS: He says he will give $10,000 to the man who captures that bear.
> WEBER: He ain't got the money.
> FIELDS: I know, but ain't it a good offer?[15]

and

> WEBER: I am delightfulness to meet you.
> FIELDS: Der disgust is all mine.[16]

The men's relationship, on stage and off, can be summarized by their oft-repeated "choking scene":

> FIELDS: You look like a furnished room.
> WEBER: Why do you go with me, then?
> FIELDS: Why? Why? Because I *like* you! Mike, when I look at you—I have such a—a—oo-oo-oo-oo! (Chokes him, then turns to audience.) Why do I go with him? (Pointing at Weber.) When I look at him my heart goes out to him. (To Weber.) When you are away from me, I can't keep my mind off you. When you are with me I can't keep my hands off you! (Chokes him.) But sometimes I think you do not return my affection. You do not feel that—something that—oo-oo-oo-oo! (Chokes him again, etc.)

Between 1895 and 1903, Weber and Fields began their season on the first Thursday of every September to high anticipation. Opening night tickets were auctioned at outrageous sums. The two men were "lavish in expenditure, generous in the treatment of the public, faithful to promises, anxious to get the best and willing to make sacrifices, if necessary, for it."[17] Assembled around them were excellent performers, including beautiful chorines who could actually sing. By 1899 their product was so fine that company members included major stars Lillian Russell, Fay Templeton, David Warfield, Sam Bernard, and De Wolf Hopper,

Relaxing in a continental café: Joe Weber, Marie, and Harry Morris in the 1904 hit *Higgledy-Piggledy*. Blackface and padding were ordinary elements of comedy in the first years of the twentieth century. (Courtesy of the Academy of Motion Picture Arts and Sciences.)

collectively called the Weberfields. If the Music Hall fare was not for the most highbrow of tastes, it redefined burlesque and was light years beyond what Broadway comedy and musicals had ever been.

In 1903 Weber had his most damaging battle with Lew Fields over the future of their empire. The result was a split partnership, with Weber holding onto the Music Hall in partnership with Florenz Ziegfeld. They were optimistic and splurged on renovations, giving the small theater an elegantly appointed new interior of white, gold, and red. New chairs "that are comfortable even for a fat man to sit in" replaced narrow ones.[18] And the soon-to-open subway system would make theater more accessible than ever.

Marie came to Weber's attention via Joseph Immerman, who stood by horrified while she toiled in the peanut business. Immerman spoke to Weber about hiring his client.[19]

"I heard she walked out on Erlanger," mentioned Weber.

"You know Marie never walked out on anybody," Immerman said.

"Probably wants a lot of money," said Weber.

"Five hundred," said Immerman.

With a compromise of $400, Marie joined the cast of Weber's new *Higgledy-Piggledy*. There was much excitement with this union:[20] "It is a real hope that when the Weber Music Hall opens, Marie Dressler will gain the praise and recognition she deserves. Marie Dressler is an artist who has, for years, proved her worth. ... she has the art and ability to make her a great actress; only for some seasons now,

Marie's favorite stage photograph: As Philopoena to Joe Weber's Adolph Schnitz making their grand entrance in *Higgledy-Piggledy*.

Miss Dressler has not had the opportunity — which means the part — given to her."

Heading the show was Ziegfeld's wife Anna Held as Mimi De Chartreuse, patron saint of Parisian Bohemia. The French-Polish Held was one of the most celebrated beauties of her time, widely known for her expressive brown eyes, tiny waist, and lilting French accent. To stir up publicity, a Brooklyn milkman was hired to sue her for not paying the bill on 40 gallons of milk. When asked for an explanation, she said, "Eet eez for zee beauty bath."[21] Held is remembered as much for the alleged milk baths as she is for her gifts as an actress and singer.

Billed as "A Rigmarole of Fun, Fancy and Foolishness in One Exhibit," *Higgledy-Piggledy* was a hit with reviewers and audiences, first in Rochester and Buffalo and then at its New York opening, where tickets were sold at an auction that brought in over $8,000. As Philopoena Schnitz, heiress to her father's mustard millions, Marie displayed her ever-growing knack for on-stage thievery. Held had beauty on her side, but she could not match Marie for attention. "Without [Marie], the evening would have been a frost, and whatever success the new hall may have with its present show it must attribute to the ample Miss Dressler," gushed the *New York Telegraph*.[22]

Held was to suffer more direct insults. Lillian Russell was seen yawning[23] when Held gave a libidinous smirk to the men in the audience and queried, "Won't you come and play weeth me?" The rhetorical question was first posed eight years prior in *A Parisian Model*, and audiences were growing tired. To end any ambiguity, one critic[24] chimed that "if the electric sign in front of the almost new Weber Music Hall knows its business it will blaze forth the name of Marie Dressler in place of that of Anna Held." Held left the show by January 1905, but without bitterness:[25] "I told Flo Ziegfeld if he didn't put [Marie] under contract for ten years he would make zee mistake of hees life."

Though her role was not large, *Higgledy-Piggledy* did much to advance Marie's reputation. She had fully rebounded from typhoid and was better than ever. She costumed herself with a huge diamond pickle breastpin and a leopardskin contraption fastened on the left shoulder with a leopard head. She sang "A Great Big Girl Like Me," which became a much-requested standard in subsequent years. For her improvisations and acrobatics, she was dubbed "the greatest low comedienne of the world."[26]

Marie knew how to respond to split-

The first incarnation of Tillie: Marie in *The College Widower* (1905).

a rehearsed setup. Weber came to the footlights and shouted "I'll gif her to you, olt man, right after der performance. She's more den I can menach!" Everyone but Alexander broke out laughing. As the audience continued to guffaw en masse, the increasingly senile Alexander walked up the aisle and out the theater. It was the first time he had seen Marie work as a professional actress.[27]

Higgledy-Piggledy was billed alongside *The College Widower*, a parody of *The College Widow*. Marie was perfectly cast as shy, muscular Tillie Buttin, halfback of a girls' football team. The reviews were splendid and included one proclamation[28] that Marie is "probably the best in this particular line now on the American stage." Even with Weber showing up in drag, Marie stole the show, doing "some great work of hobble-dehoy and clumsy sort and her songs, both of them, were begged for furiously until she had repeated them a dozen times."[29]

In the spring of 1905, Weber and company hit the road with a double bill of *Higgledy-Piggledy* and *The College Widower*. Though Flo Ziegfeld was still a producing partner, Anna Held was long gone. She was replaced not by another sylph, but by Trixie Friganza, a comedienne even more corporeal than Marie. The show played twice in Philadelphia, in April and again in October, but it bore little resemblance to itself from one go around to the next. The show was "such a rigmarole of nonsense and jovial fun-making that it never seems twice the same. In fact, Marie Dressler injected so many unscheduled jokes that she quite brought down the house."[30] In battling performance ennui, she improvised all over the place and only skillful stars such as Friganza and Weber could keep up. "I never play two nights alike," she said slyly.

For a time, everyone was happy. *Higgledy-Piggledy* played an impressive 23 weeks. The gleaming new Weber Music Hall, like its predecessor, was a favorite roost for high society, attracting the Vanderbilts, Astors, Goulds, Fishes, Goelets, Mackays, Belmonts, and Roosevelts. Weber was thrilled that Marie joined his team to give his post–Lew Fields career a boost. It was hard to make a profit,

second changes on stage, but one performance was saved by Weber's cleverness. He played Philopoena's father, the pickle baron Adolph Schnitz, and in one scene he is dangling over a cliff in the Swiss Alps. Two guides hold onto him while Marie pleads:

> I pray you, spare my father,
> Ye hardy mountaineers!
> Ah! Let your hearts be tender
> And heed a daughter's tears!
> I know you will not send him
> To meet a fate so sad,
> When I have told you he's the only
> Pa I ever had!

A large figure rose from the third-row orchestra and boomed "What about me, Marie?"

"It's Father," she whispered to Weber.

The orchestra stopped while the audience stared at Marie, wondering how she would respond to what they no doubt assumed to be

Marie was proud of her good-looking chorus in *The College Widower*.

since tickets ranged from 50 cents to $2 and Marie's salary ate a good portion of the box office, but Weber's solo reputation was enhanced by Marie, and the payroll was met by leasing out adjacent stores and touring less expensive shows.

"They used to say Marie was temperamental," Weber recalled years later.[31] "Guess she was pretty quick on the trigger. But I only had one trouble with her. She wanted to run everything. Just her big heart, that's all. She always wanted to do something and sometimes it wasn't the thing for her to do. She cost me an awful good costumer one time. After he had the chorus all dressed right, Marie would go round and fix 'em up a little — tip their hats or fuss with their dresses. Miss Fixit — that was Marie." He tapped a slender finger on his desk. "One of the greatest things about Marie was that she loved being a clown. ... She worked for laughs as nobody else ever did. ... [A]t heart Marie wanted above everything else to make people laugh. That is why she was the greatest comedienne the theater ever saw."

When Dressler arrived in Cleveland for touring performances, she ran off to inspect a new amusement park on the shores of Lake Erie called White City. "I think that Cleveland's big new amusement resort should prove as successful in its way as the great Dreamland in Coney Island," she said.[32] "The bump-the-bumps naturally appeals to me, because it is a comedy hit of the most ludicrous kind." With income to spare, she made her new investment and then sailed off to Berlin, London, and Paris for a summer vacation with actress friend May Montford. A fall tour of *Higgledy-Piggledy* followed.

Twiddle-Twaddle, the next Weber silliness, debuted in January 1906. *Twiddle-Twaddle* differed little from *Higgledy-Piggledy*. Marie played Matilda Grabfelder, the social-climbing daughter of a rude and zaftig German sausage maker played by Weber. Marie and "father" Weber search Europe for a suitable nobleman husband for Marie. Marie "picked up her parent by the nape of his neck, tucked him under her arm, threw him over her shoulder and laid him across her lap for a spanking. When she swung her massive hips in a Spanish Fandango and hit Weber and Charley Bigelow, they flew right and left from her sides like rubber balls batted with a sledgehammer."[33] Once again it was her show. Marie carried "nine-tenths of the comedy burden. ... [W]ithout her, *Twiddle-Twaddle* would be naught."[34] During the 169 performances of *Twiddle-Twaddle*, Marie "plunged through her scenes like a wildcat locomotive or a star fullback."[35]

In addition to the popular singing comedy lament "It's Hard to Be a Lady in a Case Like That," she perfected a musical number called "Hats." Alan Dale, in the *New York American*, described the scene[36]: "Twelve pretty milliners brought on twelve hat boxes and Miss Dressler, seated in the middle of the stage, tried the hats on. This was a real good, novel idea and we clamored for more hats. But Miss Dressler probably thought that she had paid all the compliments necessary to her mutinous loveliness when she donned a little monkey-cap and locked the elastic under her nose. Nature never made her nose classic and that bit of elastic was a whole chapter in favor of the Darwinian theory."

To liven things up, she began plucking real fruit from one of the hats every night and throwing it at Maurice Levi in the orchestra pit as she had for her 1897 vaudeville routine at Proctor's Pleasure Palace.[37] Sometimes her aim was off and once she winged a banana at some poor woman in the third row, but it wasn't Mrs. Stuyvesant Fish this time. Marie and the rest of the cast also began showing up at the finale in clinging silk tights. She danced a "Little Buttercup" routine as the audience "demanded encore after encore until she was breathless as well as verseless."[38]

As was her growing custom, Marie gave a speech to the audience at the conclusion of opening night in New York and on tour. She claimed to be unhappy with the performance because she is a "timid and sensitive little thing."[39] The motives and sincerity of Marie's speech remained a mystery: "Seeing her downcast, her friends shouted words of reassurance, but she was unconsoled. The next day the critics ... were unanimous in the opinion that she alone had saved a generally dull occasion from disaster. In all probability, Miss Dressler felt that her performance lacked artistic reserve."[40] Audiences seemed to believe she was joking, but the newspapers weren't sure. Sincerely discontent or not, the public screamed its approval of "Hats" and everything else she did in *Twiddle-Twaddle*.

The Squaw Man's Girl of the Golden West opened on February 26, 1906, and played alongside *Twiddle-Twaddle*, necessitating condensation of the latter into a fast-paced second act. The new first act was a sendup of both *The Squaw Man* and *The Girl of the Golden West*, two atmospheric melodramas ready to be skewered. "Isn't all burlesque that has any point to it a keen analytical criticism in disguise?" Marie asked.[41] As keeper of the Polka Ice Cream Saloon, she wore a red blouse, top boots, and five bright green hair ribbons, making her look "like a third-alarm fire on St. Patrick's Day."[42] Marie lightened any occasion. She made merry on April 23, 1906, when she gave a benefit performance for San Francisco earthquake and fire relief, but something else was lurking in her performances. A *New York Times* writer noted,[43] "The ability to hold the attention of her audiences by her more serious utterances and by-play until she is ready to add the unexpected touch that produces laughter indicates something more of resourcefulness on Miss Dressler's part than the mere possession of a sense of humor."

Joseph Immerman made a quiet trip to London to meet with George Edwardes, the influential British producer who had caught Marie's act in New York. He was a leading impresario and had an almost unblemished record of burlesque, operetta, and comedy hits at London's Gaiety Theater. He and Immerman planned to fashion a stupendous British debut for Marie. "If I hit 'em hard, I can stay in London forever and live on Easy Street," she announced.[44] "If I don't hit 'em a fatal blow, I mean to stay in London anyway ... with little flyers to Paris and Berlin rather than Broadway and tours on the road."

When word got out that Marie was

contemplating a move to London, her fans were dismayed. The news drove one desperate soul to poetry:

> Without you Pa Weber would be lost.
> Don't go, Marie! Don't go!
> None can take your place at any cost
> Don't go, Marie! Don't go!
> ...Just think of all the frolics you've had.
> None left the place ever feeling sad;
> And it certainly would make us feel awfully bad,
> If you should go, Marie, should go.[45]

Marie was determined to do just that. *Twiddle-Twaddle* and the other shows were successes in New York and on tour, but she was tired of the Music Hall material. She had little patience for the high-strung and difficult Charley Bigelow, who appeared in *Higgledy-Piggledy* and *Twiddle-Twaddle*.[46] He forgot his lines easily and Marie needed no more memory deficient costars to muddy her own ability at recall. In addition, some in the audience were saying that a bit of the old magic was gone with the absence of Lew Fields, Lillian Russell, and others from the earlier ensemble.

On May 19, 1906, in the middle of a vaudeville stint, Dressler announced that she was leaving the Weber Music Hall with one week's notice.[47] The rumors of her export to London were buzzing through theater crowds, and some were compelled to bring down her display of ego. "Why is it that playerfolk the moment they attain success lose their equilibrium and topple over under the weight of an exaggerated cranial development?" pondered Rennold Wolf of the *New York Telegraph*.[48]

Weber decided to respond to the brewing fuss by giving Marie a raise to $550 a week and tightening her obligations to him. "My Music Hall will continue without Miss Dressler, but I consider it a duty I owe the management fraternity to see to it that the value of a contract is maintained," he announced.[49] "In other words, Miss Dressler will play nowhere unless it be under my management or with my permission."

While coping with a betrayed public and press, Marie's concessions investment in Cleveland was destroyed in a fire. Immerman was there to report home. "Yes, I have heard about it," Marie told a reporter backstage.[50] "I received a telegram from Mr. Immerman, my manager, and he said we were losers. We had $67,000 worth of stock in the White City, and I don't know whether there was any insurance or not, as he attended to that. ... It seems that I am always losing something. There is no use crying over spilt milk. Excuse me, I hate to run away, but I must go on. Good-by." Marie marched to the stage. Under bright lights and a full house, with no hints of power struggles and investment losses, she and Weber entertained. They were all sunshine and smiles in a routine of Marie as a clairvoyant. With a lace curtain over her head, she answered every carefully planned question from the audience except one: "How old is Marie Dressler?"[51]

Weber's contract did not deter Marie or Immerman from planning a new career in London. She had broken her deal with Weber and announced her intentions to remain in England for a year while Edwardes played an increasingly important role in her international management. There were many farewell parties in May, and on June 9, 1906, she left on the steamer *Minnetonka* with several trunks and her tiny puppy Jags. Described as "a drowsy little ball of wool," Jags was "a queer little fellow. ... [W]e can't tell whether he is going to turn out a poodle, a daschund or a Sam Bernard."[52]

"I've left a few friends in New York, so that if I go broke I can get ransom," she said.[53] More seriously, she added, "If they think I'm coming back to go on the road — the hateful road — with the Weber company, they are mistaken. ... I'll stay here. I'll divide my time between London and Paris and study music and French. I can be tough; I can be hard shell; I can be consistently common, but I hated all that business. My soul revolted at it." As for London, she chimed, "I love it! I simply love it. It makes me feel — er — respectable." She was rapturous in the courtly elegance of Edwardian England but got a shock at her long awaited meeting with Edwardes. He had failed to secure her engagements and upbraided her for breaking her contract with Weber. After a visit with

Bonita and Richard in Surrey, she headed back to the United States on August 24, 1906, contrite and embarrassed but resolved to play England someday.

A victorious Weber took her back and gave her a second raise to $600 per week. She begrudgingly rejoined his company as "Joe Weber's Amazon" in Chicago for early fall performances of *Twiddle-Twaddle*. By late 1906, she was again free of Weber and doing smashing business on her own in vaudeville at the Colonial Theater. Ignoring friends who said that going alone in vaudeville was a disastrous career choice and a big drop in prestige, Marie performed in *Oh! Mr. Belasco*, the title in reference to mighty theater producer David Belasco. In this, her first post–Weber outing, she broke the house records for New Year's attendance. Her standard "A Great Big Girl Like Me" and her imitations of legitimate actresses Mrs. Leslie Carter and Blanche Bates were greeted with cheers. As *Oh! Mr. Belasco* demonstrated, Marie thrived when left alone on stage. She exercised rare good instincts for the Colonial gig. In addition to the joyous freedom she experienced in doing her own show, the theater was under the highly ethical and accommodating management of her friend Percy Williams.

Marie followed up the Colonial engagement with a successful ten week stint at Proctor's 58th Street Theater. Despite so many protestations that Marie was foolish to leave the security of Weber, critics and audiences came around to her point of view.* The sentiments rendered in collective breast-beating and sorrowful poetry had disappeared. While she was on tour in Boston, one writer[54] noted that "Marie Dressler has at last escaped from Weber. ... So long she was identified with the little New York home of superior frolicsomeness and comic burlesque as to bring despair to the hearts of those who desired to see her twinkle in her own merry way by herself."

Still there was the gnawing desire to try London. Edwardes wanted Marie only when he wouldn't betray a fellow producer, and regularly wrote announcing that backers were being secured for a proper debut. She was on the road as negotiations in London continued and she still labored under reoccurring ill health. She suffered a throat abscess in Boston and had to cancel performances. By the time she arrived in Philadelphia in April 1907 for a two-week engagement, she suffered "greatly reduced avoirdupois."[55] For a change, it was nothing serious.

On a train from New York to Philadelphia, Marie met a mustached, rotund man three years her junior named Jim Dalton.[56] He had seen and admired Marie on stage. He also professed various accomplishments of his own at one time or another, including millionaire, Harvard law-school graduate, asbestos business executive, grocery store owner, and partner in a large brokerage house in Manhattan. This much is certain: James Henry Dalton was born on Christmas Eve 1871 just ten months after his parents Benjamin and Hannah were married. Both his parents were Irish; Benjamin made his living as a glassblower. Jim was born, baptized, and spent his early years in Corning, a small town south of the Finger Lakes of New York.[57] He was tall with thinning red hair, a red face, and bushy eyebrows over deepset eyes. "Never in my life have I seen a face that reminded me so much of a cherub," remarked journalist J. Lawrence Toole.[58] "It was round, good-humored and shone with the complexion they advertise with some massage creams."

Faithful Joseph Immerman had been eclipsed by George Edwardes in London and he was now quickly fading from Marie's business dealings. When Jim entered the scene, Immerman disappeared. When Marie met Mr. Dalton, "he was in financial straits, and I took him with me to manage my affairs," said Marie.[59] She soon learned that he was a heavy drinker and gambler, but he worked Marie more shrewdly and lovingly than any man ever had.

Marie demanded absolute devotion from those nearest her. She got it in Jim, who took on the role of emotional benefactor and obse-

---

Weber closed his Music Hall in 1907 after dwindling box-office and the final performance of Hip! Hip! Hooray!

quious companion. If Marie did one of her dramatic readings, he was moved to tears. He waited on her for dinner, toted her bags, and massaged her neck, shoulders or feet after a tiring performance. When Jim left Marie's dressing room while a reporter was interviewing her, she asked[60] "Isn't he a delight? He's been busy all afternoon having a duck and sauerkraut fixed up for my dinner. He's got just the right kind of a fowl and he's been superintending the preparation of it."

He sought a life of excess. According to film director and producer Mack Sennett,[61] Jim was "a bottleman of great prowess. He knew many people everywhere and had important political connections." Jim liked to tell the possibly make-believe story of his visit to the White House when Teddy Roosevelt was president.[62] Jim was entertaining Roosevelt with "tall and funny stories" when the president ordered the butler to open a bottle of champagne. After the men had done some libating, Roosevelt's secretary came in to remind the president that he was past due to meet the Women's Christian Temperance Union. Roosevelt excused Jim, hid the bottle, conducted his meeting, and pledged his support to the cause. When the women had left, Jim returned and they broke out the bottle again. "I was dry all the time they were here," Roosevelt gasped with disbelief.

Marie had her own Teddy Roosevelt story to tell.[63] When visiting the president, she was waiting in the anteroom near his office. He swept into a full room and pressed the flesh with an exclamation of "Dee-lighted! Dee-lighted!" When he came to Marie, he said, "Well, well, Miss Dressler, now that we meet, what do you think of me?" Marie blurted out, "I think you have the strongest-looking neck I ever saw!" With that Roosevelt started laughing.

Nothing would deter her London dream, which Jim wholeheartedly supported. She took a brief trip back to England and found a cottage to rent at Maidenhead on the Thames near London. To Edwardes delight, she then returned to the States to collect her belongings and furniture. The *New York Telegraph* printed

A newspaper rendering of "cherub" Jim Dalton and a winged, authoritative Marie.

that "one night about three years ago George Edwardes, the London manager, remarked that Marie Dressler was one of the funniest women he had ever seen. Then Marie Dressler's real troubles began. From that moment she was possessed of one mighty ambition — to appear before a London audience."[64]

The London obsession finally did Marie some good. The grind of touring, familiar cities, and derivative material was taking the fun out of work. London gave her a chance to win over a whole new nation. Her aged father was likewise happy for the change and accompanied her overseas. Edwardes had booked her at the important 1,400-seat Palace Theater in the West End district, five blocks up Shaftesbury Avenue from Piccadilly Circus. With songs, poems, and "musical interruptions" by the orchestra, Marie said that she "just put my best foot forward and let myself loose. ... I found some notes in [my voice] I didn't know I had in me."[65]

How would she translate across the Atlantic? Would her style bridge the many different ways Americans and British discover humor? Combining the freedom of her solo shows with the thrill of facing an alien audience, Marie was incandescent at the Palace Theater on a lightly windy opening night on Monday, October 28, 1907. Loyal American fan and critic Archie Bell recalled the evening:[66] "When she made her first entrance she sat down to the piano to sing a ditty. The house was still and reserved. There was a large concert grand piano and she sat back too far to reach it. Instead of moving the stool toward the piano, she leaned forward and jerked the big instrument forward to where she wanted it. The English men yelled as they had never yelled before. Marie Dressler had scored a triumph." An English admirer wrote,[67] "it is not easy to describe Marie Dressler. The obvious, and perhaps the truest, thing to say about her is that she is characteristically American. She has a magnitude and a volume almost terrifying to the Old World."

The suspense was over. Within a few days, Marie was on her way to unprecedented success in England. King Edward VII, the son of Queen Victoria who shared Marie's birthday of November 9, saw her performance and invited her to be his palace guest.[68] The two were delighted to note that he was on hand to open Victoria Hall in Marie's hometown of Cobourg when he was the 18-year-old Prince of Wales. To Marie, meeting the king of England was a singular thrill. The robust, elegant monarch "was the most magnetic and attractive man I ever had the pleasure of meeting."

At the Palace Theater she sang the favorite "A Great Big Girl Like Me" while the London press kept on chiming. "Her success was instantaneous. The theater rang with the vociferous applause of an audience that would fain have heard and seen still more of her."[69] Reporting from back home, the *New York Telegraph*[70] wrote, "There is no diversity of opinion regarding her merit. She is hailed as the most delightful comedienne ever sent to London by America." With turnaway business, Marie settled into the Palace for an astonishing four months.[71]

There were health problems as always. Unaccustomed to London weather, and under the strain of nonstop performing, she caught a severe cold that developed into bronchitis. In December 1907 she had a potentially catastrophic larynx operation. Cared for by her father, she recovered and "emerged from the ordeal with a great and triumphant access of contralto notes of much value."[72] Back on the job after a few weeks' rest, Marie was even better. She sang a new song, "The Bonnet Store-y," in which each new verse was performed with a new bonnet. Into early 1908, her act was still standing room only.

Marie excelled in London in part because the one-woman material let her have absolute control and free reign over the performance. There were others on the bill, but when Marie was on stage, it was hers alone. She succeeded by the overwhelming force of her personality unencumbered by a standard script or mediocre costars. She tore loose with her standard songs and jokes but also left the crowd spellbound when accompanying herself on the piano for a sad coon song such as "Why Adam Sinned."[73]

Hundreds were turned away when she closed the Palace on March 4, 1908. It was said[74] that "at her last appearance she was given an ovation that has never been exceeded in the history of theater." A three-year contract she signed with Edwardes seemed too much of a good thing, and she was amicably released. Exhausted from adrenaline, hard work, and surgery, she and Jim sneaked away for rest and gaming at Monte Carlo.[75] She breathlessly noted that "vaudeville is all right, but good gracious, my dear, did you ever think how hard it is to walk on a stage all by yourself and start in to make people laugh?"[76]

Marie and Jim boarded the *Lusitania* and sailed home for New York. Even before the ship docked on April 10, 1908, she was again under contract to Percy Williams' New York vaudeville house, the Colonial Theater, for a four-week stint. It was the first theatrical contract sealed by wireless telegraph and completed by sea after Marie had sailed from England.[77]

The Colonial engagement was another triumph of solo inspiration. Among her laugh getters was a song called "Girls, Keep Your Figure," in which she explained to all how she maintained her svelte curvatures. "All things that have a suspicion of pose or pretense are fair marks for Miss Dressler's keen satire," began *Variety*.[78] She incorporated a curly hairpiece she had bought in London for a routine that received much notice. "When I take off those curls during the piece I recite it is always a knock-out," she said.[79] "Many of the people in the audience want me to do it again. It is one of the loveliest pieces that was ever handed to me and I doped it out myself." Unfortunately, the curls were lost during the Colonial engagement, possibly through theft.[80] Through Williams' publicity office, she placed a "Lost and Found" ad and promised box seats to her show as a reward. It was not reported whether they were ever recovered or replaced.

Though she was on stage for just 16 minutes, the demands were great. Vaudeville acts, whether top-of-the-line shows at the Palace in New York or local efforts in small towns, typically went on from early afternoon to midnight. A brief appearance would play several times in one day. Headliners such as Marie were under great demands and expectations. By the time she finished a song or two, jokes, recitations, a burlesque of a sacred cow dramatic actress such as Sarah Bernhardt or Mrs. Fiske, and an ending speech, Marie said, "I put every bit of myself into it. ... The strain is terrible, and when I have finished, I am played right out."[81]

She made time to contemplate her relationship with Jim Dalton. She said that they grew "to care a great deal for each other and decided we would like to be married."[82] They faced a major obstacle, for Jim finally confessed that he was already married. In 1900 he had married a woman named Elizabeth in Jersey City, New Jersey. She was still his wife and she lived with their four-year-old daughter Dorothy in Brookline, a suburb of Boston.[83] While he was visiting England in 1905, he offered her divorce papers, but she refused. Jim tried again when he became involved with Marie. Together they went to Elizabeth, accompanied by Jim's brother Christopher, and begged for a divorce. Again she refused. The "great love" of Marie's life remained just out of the reach of marriage.

The wild success of London pulled Dressler across the Atlantic again. Her new plans included a September return to London and then retirement with Jim at "a little place near Monte Carlo right on the Mediterranean, with a garden full of roses and sunsets and silver moons that no scenic artist ever dreamed of."[84] Sure enough, after more vaudeville in the States, she was back in London by October 1908 and getting $2,500 a week at the Palace to tell stories, sing coon songs, and dance. Hers was the highest salary in the history of London music halls and "storms of applause greeted everything."[85]

George Edwardes had been at work trying to find a suitable nonmusical play to feature Marie, rather than a vaudeville show. When nothing materialized, plans were underway to take over London's Aldwych Theater for the musical *Little Minna*, based loosely on *Higgledy-Piggledy*. The Aldwych was an ornate three-year-old theater on Drury Lane, where extensive slum housing had been razed to make way for a huge urban restoration project. Near Waterloo Bridge and the Thames, it was situated in territory of equal prestige to the Palace. Marie served as manager and star and was responsible for casting the show with American and English entertainers. She enlisted two stalwart colleagues, writer Edgar Smith and composer-conductor Maurice Levi, to collaborate on the project. When Smith and Levi arrived in London in February, they were upset to learn that Marie had not yet secured any local talent. She in fact had made very little progress toward the scheduled February 27 premiere.

A normal person would be in a terrified panic. She had leased the Aldwych for seven years, renamed it "Marie Dressler's Aldwych Theater," and declared herself resident manager, choreographer, and producer. She then hired a chorus of 65 but had yet to secure a score, script, or costars.

Somehow it all came together on the rain and sleet-soaked night of February 27, 1909. *Philopoena* and *The Collegettes* opened as a retooling of *Higgledy-Piggledy* with warm enough reviews, but soon everything started unraveling. Audiences stayed away from the 1,000-seat Aldwych and this time Marie was financially responsible. She was shortly taken ill with an ulcerated throat. In order to pay the company, she pawned jewelry and furniture and borrowed $5,000 from an English lender. After her throat recovered, she learned that bills had

Marie in 1909, a year of financial, professional, and physical catastrophes.

not been paid and money was mysteriously missing. She and Jim never nabbed the culprit.

Not quite willing to take full responsibility for her rotten judgment, Marie philosophized that[86]

> all sorts of persons prey on professionals — they are in the limelight — their lives are by necessity unsettled and they are easy targets for the unscrupulous. That is why they so often go into bankruptcy. They are frequently accused of owing bills they never contracted, gross overcharges, etc. and bankruptcy is simpler than going to court and paying lawyer's fees to prove that some outrageous amount is not owed. Actors cannot afford the time away from their work to drag through a long suit. ... I gathered from my own experience that the law seems to be made for thieves.

London had meanwhile soured on the Yankee import. *The Evening Standard*[87] ventured a reason for the sudden absence of affection:

> They bring to London a very American play and expect London to welcome it by laughing at jokes which require special knowledge for their appreciation. Dan Leno's cockney humor was a complete failure in New York, simply because it was not understood. For the same reason the boisterous fun which appears to delight a certain section of American playgoers cannot appeal to Englishmen. ... It is rather sad to find that the comedy of our cousins, who speak our language and are so nearly related in many other respects, is Greek or algebra to us. But the fact cannot be denied and for their own sakes American managers ought to look it in the face. Wit and humor are delicate plants.

After the first signs of disaster, Marie drastically pruned *Philopoena* and axed *The Collegettes* altogether. She then invited the critics back for another look. No one took much notice and Marie was out of alternatives. On March 12, 1909, she wrote a letter to the company:[88] "I am unable to continue the fight. Fate is against me. I am too ill to explain as I would like to, but I want you, my company, to know that I mortgaged everything I had in the world to pay you your last week's salary." In all, the company rehearsed five weeks without pay and performed one week with pay. *Philopoena* logged in 12 performances, *The Collegettes* eleven. "We're the ghosts of a troupe that was stranded in Peoria," said Smith,[89] paraphrasing a song of the era. "Miss Dressler couldn't carry the whole thing herself. It was about the poorest company that I have ever seen."

"I put on *Philopoena* entirely at my own risk," Marie announced.[90] "I have no syndicate, no backer. Play producing costs more in London than in New York and there is between $35,000 and $40,000 of my own money in this venture. They are all my savings and if they go I shall begin again." With this proclamation, Marie left London a virtual pauper with losses at $25,000. Back in the United States on March 15, her liabilities were totaled at $10,000 and her assets at $3,000.[91]

Almost immediately, there was much speculation on Marie's departure from both sides of the Atlantic. Gossip had her deceiving her cast and creditors and leaving town in absolute disgrace. She had her own interpretation of the events.[92] "As an individual an American may make as much of a hit as one wishes in London. But an American star in an American play has no chance there. ... I am no fool. I know when I am beaten. ... I knew they needed a funny show. Heaven knows they haven't got three funny people in all England, outside of Parliament." She vowed never to play London again, then continued spewing sour grapes five days later.[93] "Any people that are so narrow, so prejudiced, jealous and vain in their own surroundings, show to me so clearly their lack of education, that it is only a question of time when it will deteriorate so much that it will cease to be a nation."

She was back doing vaudeville. It would take years to pay her debts, but she began financial recovery with a well-received turn in *Little Nemo*, a rehash of *Philopoena,* at the Colonial Theater in Chicago. But new bills kept piling up on top of old ones. Throat trouble returned; she now had two large growths, one from each tonsil. She was operated on in Chicago while rehearsing a new project called *The Boy and the Girl*.[94] The growths were removed successfully by surgery and she rested for a week; physicians were confident that she would regain her normal voice. A subsequent case of blood poisoning[95] landed her in the hospital with a $2,000 bill.

Jim was with her through her many ordeals. He proved indispensable with low-grade management and high-grade tender loving care. He counted the tickets and presided over local management when Marie was on tour. The two were so tight that in interviews and casual conversation, they introduced the deceit of being husband and wife. The lie worked for a while, and Marie was confident that Elizabeth would stay quiet and eventually honor Jim's wish for a divorce. It was easier in the meanwhile to pretend to the world that they were married, avoid the hassles of separate hotel rooms, and wait for the right time to make it legal.

The Boy and the Girl was mildly success-

Marie wandered into a Chicago studio in 1909 for this studio shot during the run of *The Boy and the Girl*. Her millinery skills and aversion to everything subtle are on full display.

ful at its Chicago opening. Marie, recovered from the latest assault on her throat, played "the girl" and sang "I'm in a Position to Know," "Seductive Caroline," and "Yoo-La (The Irish Spanish 'Sit Down!' Song)." More complications arose from the United States customs office when someone tried to sneak three extra trunks into the country labeled "Mr. Dressler." Two trunks in her name were already waiting, and after she assured customs by long-distance phone that she owned two trunks only, she said, "I wonder if they will arrest me. Troubles seem to be coming in bunches."[96]

While *The Boy and the Girl* played the Garrick Theater in Philadelphia, Marie came up with another harebrained idea to make money. She bought 50 Alabama opossums, equipped them with collars and bells, and raised them over two acres of borrowed land. "The 'possum is going to be the emblem of the Republican party for the next four years and I figure that I can raise as many bushels of 'possums as I could of turnips. They will bring a fancy price as household pets. Aside from this, I can find a ready New York market for my crop, which as everybody knows, when served on a hot plate, garnished with sweet potatoes, is about as dainty a delicacy as the most exacting gourmand could wish to sink his teeth into."[97] Marie was trying anything as an alternative to vaudeville, which she found more exhausting than musical revue of the Joe Weber or George Lederer type. She wrote that it was "really too hard a game anyhow twice a day over and over again and on some circuits so many performances that one is reminded of the tired vaudevillian who demanded of the manager: 'What do you think we are—fillums?'"[98]

The opossums did not make Marie rich again, and neither did *The Boy and the Girl*.[99] The show opened in New York on the roof garden of the New Amsterdam Theater and lasted a pitiful 24 performances. No reporter was specific about the plot, if there was one, but the star was boisterous as always. "If Marie Dressler returns to London, or Saginaw or St. Petersburg or any other foreign city ever again, she will go wantonly and with knowledge that she does so in face of stern protest from New York City. We have her here again and we want to keep her," wrote one unusually generous spectator.[100] Since *The Boy and the Girl* effort didn't provide steady income, Marie returned to the vaudeville circuit, where she claimed $2,000 a week.[101] She spent a muggy July at the Music Hall in Brighton Beach and Young's Pier in Atlantic City doing a 13-minute satire of showgirls and understudies called *In the Chorus*.[102]

Not even the fantastic summer vaudeville salary was enough to get Marie out of financial crisis. Reassessing her accounts in September, she had no choice but to file bankruptcy with liabilities totaling $24,886.32. Among her debts was the $2,000 medical bill encumbered during the rehearsals of *The Boy and the Girl* in Chicago. With remarkable naiveté and gall, she adjusted the bill to $250 and paid no more.[103] Her only declared assets were necessary clothing totaling $100. Fifty-nine creditors were listed, and all debts, except $4,000 from Paris, were from London.[104] She said that bankruptcy "doesn't feel any different, except that you have an exuberant feeling of responsibility."[105] Marie was working to the limits of her strength in trying to meet that new overwhelming responsibility. "When people say 'it's easy for you to be funny,' I long for an ax," she moaned.[106] "Don't you ever try [vaudeville] until you've got to your last chance. You may put it down that when you catch me in vaudeville it is because I need the money!"[107] Destitute or solvent, Marie found comfort in the continued loyalty of not just Jim but maid Jenny as well, who stayed on even after Marie's precipitous drop in fortune. She "looked out for me in every possible way," Marie recalled.[108]

"I suppose I ought to have a coat," said Marie as cold weather approached.

"Yes, missie, you ought, but get you a good one, darling. Just remember nothing's cheap that's cheap."

"But I can't afford a good coat," said the woman who could bring home $2,000 a week.

"Indeed you can, honey. I been saving out on you. I got $40 saved up you don't know nothing about."

A major break came to Dressler in September, when she began a contract with Lew Fields for three years of 30-week seasons.[109] Since splitting with Joe Weber, Fields had gone on to a successful career as producer and actor on his own or in collaboration with the young hot shot Shubert brothers. By Fields' agreement, Marie was to get 10 percent of gross receipts from ticket sales up to $10,000 each week and 15 percent over $10,000 each week. She had a minimum guarantee of $500 per week. But theater contracts had a way of sounding spectacular, getting shuffled aside, and disappearing when circumstances and scheduling of shows and stars changed. This contract didn't exactly disappear, but it did have a tortured history that ended in something altogether jubilant.

Chapter 5

A Wretch Named Tillie

Lew Fields once told Dressler that the only Shakespeare role she could muster was Lady Macbeth.[1] Yearning for some drama, she approached producer Lee Shubert with the idea, telling him she wanted a theater for such a purpose.

Shubert appeared to listen intently, waited for her to finish the brainstorm, and then sighed. "I've got a great comedy for you called *Tillie's Nightmare*," he explained.[2] "You play a poor drudge of a New England servant who goes to sleep and dreams she is an actress. ... [M]aybe I can get [composer] Harry B. Smith to rewrite Lady Macbeth for you next season."

"But Mr. Shubert," Marie declared. "Lady Macbeth is not a musical comedy."

"It would be if you played it," he answered.

Born to Lithuanian Jewish peasants, the Shubert brothers — Lee, Jacob, and Sam — began a modest theater circuit for stock companies and road shows in Syracuse, Rochester, and Troy, New York. They and the syndicate were cordial until 1905, when they gained control of the Casino in New York and other first-class theaters in Philadelphia, Buffalo, Baltimore, and St. Louis. The violent death of Sam in a train wreck that same year did not stop Lee and Jacob from challenging the Abe Erlanger–Marc Klaw monopoly and by 1909 the surviving brothers were lording over America's premiere theatrical empire. Erlanger continued in business for many years, but he never again had omnipotent control.

The Shuberts were businessmen first, notoriously tightfisted and often accused of crass and inhumane policies. But they brought American theater to a level of professionalism it had not seen before. They could also be generous. For every hasty firing there was the subsidizing of profitless theaters to aid friends or encourage promising talent. Lee, the eldest, had a passionate love for theater that set him apart from so many other businessmen who dominated the industry. Jacob, or Jake, was less adept at business and preferred to stage his favorite operettas. They were each smart enough to know their productions would not sell tickets without top actors, directors, and designers. The Sam S. Shubert Booking Agency assumed control of stars such as Jefferson

De Angelis, Lillian Russell, De Wolf Hopper, Eddie Foy, Lew Fields, and Mrs. Fiske.

Fields was especially valuable, since he was a gifted director as well as an actor. As gentlemanly immigrant Old World Jews, slightly embarrassed by their lack of formal education, Lee Shubert and Lew Fields formed a strong professional union. Fields admired Shubert's business head and Shubert admired Fields' showmanship. By the fall of 1909, Fields was ridiculously busy as director of Shubert-backed productions on various stages around the country. "Mr. Fields is a wonderfully sympathetic man because he is an actor," noted Lillian Russell.[3] "He has a greater talent than he has ever had the opportunity to express because the public always expects him to be funny." In one season, he expressed that talent as the exhausted director of *The Rose of Algeria, Old Dutch, When Sweet Sixteen, The Prince of Bohemia,* and *The Jolly Bachelors.*

Lee Shubert indeed planned to showcase Marie in a project originally called *Tillie's Dream.* Renaming it *Tillie's Nightmare,* the production was to be an expansion on the life of Tillie Buttin, the character Edgar Smith wrote for Marie in *The College Widower.* She was not a football player this time, but rather a miserable wallflower imprisoned by drudgery in her mother's boardinghouse. Smith was writing the story. A. Baldwin Sloane, who had a Broadway hit with *The Wizard of Oz* in 1903 and composed music for Marie's shows *The King's Carnival* and *The Hall of Fame,* was writing the songs. For this new production, Marie was happily reunited with May Montford, the trouper friend who helped her get a job with the Starr Opera Company back in the 1880s. Now Marie was the leading attraction, the once and future Tillie, while Montford assumed the supporting role of Peroxia Snow, excess baggage with the Frost and Snow vaudeville team.

Early rehearsals went badly. Marie was in an ill temper and walked out because of a disagreement with management. Fields owned a share of the production and checked in as his schedule allowed, but he had neither time nor interest in Marie's tantrums. He was responsible for too many productions and was constantly dodging conflicting demands. Lee Shubert began to voice his concern when *Tillie's Nightmare* failed to preview on tour by mid-December 1909. The company had visited the town where the show was set, Skaneateles, New York, amidst much coverage and praise from the locals, but there was still no income.

In December, Marie laid down her sword and was put on moving film for the first time through the auspices of the Thomas Edison Studio,[4] who registered a copyright on *Marie Dressler* on December 24. Surrounded by pillowy set pieces in front of a closed curtain, extant frames show Marie extending her right leg in what is likely a dance during a dream sequence of *Tillie's Nightmare.* Such live-action film prompted theater writer Robert Grau[5] to ask "is the moving picture crowding out the old-time stage? Is science and mechanical art, by the production of miles upon miles of fascinating films, encroaching on the 'legitimate' drama — in fact, revolutionizing the theatrical business?" He had reason to wonder. In addition to *Tillie's Nightmare,* productions of *Quo Vadis, H. M. S. Pinafore, The Mikado,* and *Chimes of Normandy* had been photoplayed with dialogue recorded on phonograph.

Marie's work with new technology didn't end there. She was among a number of top-drawer entertainers recruited by famed composer Victor Herbert for exclusive short-term recording contracts with Edison.[6] On wax cylinders she recorded her coon song favorites, including "Rastus Take Me Back," in which a transgressive wench admits to "gin-drinking, chicken-stealing, policy-playing and husband-beating." She reworked "I'm Lookin' for an Angel (Without Wings)" from *Miss Prinnt,* in which she bemoans her man who has run away "wid a chuckle-headed coon" and left her "flat broke." Her flirtation with recording ended as quickly as it began and she was soon back trying to pump life into *Tillie.*

Back on the road, *Tillie's Nightmare* finally opened in an out-of-town tryout on December 24 in Albany.[7] With an enormous company of 87, the production was a resounding flop at the Harmanus Theater. The below-par supporting cast got most of the blame.

Marie decided that the problem was in the writing and retooled much of Edgar Smith's script. Smith, a proud alumnus of Weber and Fields, was livid over Marie's changes and wanted to close the show. Half the cast was dismissed, and Fields fought with the Shuberts to keep the show open. Marie was collecting $1,500 a week and Fields reasoned that such an investment should not be abandoned prematurely.

Tillie's Nightmare continued its unsteady short engagements around the Northeast, opening in Rochester at the New National Theater on December 27 and in Buffalo on New Year's Eve. Tour manager Henry Winchell was making the home office nervous when he ran up a $500 bill in production expenses in Rochester. In January, the Shuberts were downright irate when he drew $3,000 on the company account in Chicago. When was *Tillie* going to start making money?

From New York, the Shuberts assigned the loyal Sam P. Gerson as point man on the road and press liaison for *Tillie's Nightmare*. Morale was low, notices were bad, expenses were high, and Marie was on her worst behavior. When Gerson met her and Jim in Chicago, she fired off with, "Oh, you're a Shubert man" and then proceeded to trash Jake and Lee "in outrageous fashion."[8] Gerson told her that she would be well advised to avoid insulting them. This incited both Marie and Jim to roast the Shuberts not just to Gerson but to journalists as well.

The situation grew dire when the Chicago reviews of *Tillie's Nightmare* began appearing. No longer were problems attributed to the script or the chorus. Local critics went gunning for Marie: "We have observed the lady in many grotesque manifestations, but in *Tillie's Nightmare* we think she reaches the heights of homeliness. Occasionally she looks like an amiable sea serpent and again her resemblance is to something prehistoric and unclassified."[9] She "is absolutely the ugliest woman on the American stage," blurted one.[10] Amy Leslie, who had written glowingly of Marie when she previously came through Chicago, was even harsher.[11] "The show is dominated by an actress whose sole aim is to make herself a monstrosity that she may use ugliness as a bludgeon to wallop the ignorant into blithering and painful laughter." Leslie was so unnerved by the spectacle that she left soon after the curtain rose on Act 2.

Gerson relayed the Chicago reactions back to Jake.[12] "As you will see for yourself [the reviews] are not very good. ... I guess the show must be pretty bad to get these notices, although I can not help but think that it has got a chance, with proper pruning and stage management to be a knockout." Despite Gerson's optimism, *Tillie's Nightmare* continued to do slow business in Chicago and the production remained in the red.

Ill will flowed in all directions. Though Marie and Jim remained uncooperative, she was not the only star to complain of the cold rigors of the Shuberts' theatrical machine. Alla Nazimova, Louis Mann, Eddie Foy, Thomas A. Wise, and Lulu Glaser went similar routes. Despite star temperaments, the complaints were largely valid. Cast members were unceremoniously dumped from the program in midtour with no severance pay. Road managers were threatened with dismissal if they gave away any free tickets. Rules of conduct, payment, and work hours were enforced with absolute resolve and no deviations were tolerated. Shubert cronies such as Sam Gerson responded to this working climate with complicity, and so won the affection of the brothers along with the disdain of self-centered stars such as Marie.

In the nonstop hostile confrontations Dressler had with management during this time, it is difficult to know who is most deserving of righteous indignation. Marie learned early to stand up to the male taskmasters who dominated early twentieth century American theater. Unions and binding contracts for actors were still a decade away; Marie's apparent fearlessness in the face of unemployment and litigation must have been intimidating. Jim encouraged this, consciously or not, by continuously telling her she was wonderful. He abetted her at every turn — siding with her as the lone man watching out for a woman who dared talk back. It's no wonder she hung onto him, supported him, and tolerated him, even as he helped to destroy her career.

By all appearances they were a belligerent and demanding pair. Jim incited Marie just enough to convince her to fight the bosses. When her act brought in cash, the demands were met. If her popularity waned, and it seemed to yo-yo with the seasons, Jim was an unadulterated liability. Without any major effort, he could be unwielding, overly ambitious, and demanding in the extreme. He and Marie gave reasons for the Shuberts to hate them and wish for their misfortune. At least in 1909 everyone was working toward the same goal of turning *Tillie's Nightmare* into a hit.

For *Tillie's Nightmare*, fortunes changed after the company left Chicago. Good reviews followed the Kansas City opening on January 16, 1910.[13] Everyone was happy except original author Edgar Smith, who was still stewing over the changes Marie had made to his script. He wanted to close the show, but Fields intervened and refused under threat of litigation by Marie and the others.

Positive momentum continued at the Garrick Theater in St. Louis. Though it had nothing to do with the already thin story, Marie couldn't resist adding an imitation of the sensational Italian soprano Luisa Tetrazzini in *La Traviata*.[14] Tetrazzini happened to be singing in St. Louis and caught Marie's act. She "fairly exploded with laughter as the imitation proceeded. Tetrazzini ... refused" to see Miss Dressler in that scene again, for she says that ever since, she has an irresistible impulse to try and do the same things whenever she sings the role of Violetta.[15]

To prove no rancor, Tetrazzini invited Marie to dinner at the Jefferson Hotel. Jim was there, too, but he was so drunk that he was having trouble walking. The two women proceeded to join Jim in inebriation and downed copious amounts of champagne. According to Tetrazzini's accompanist, they grew confessional. With the aid of a translator, they proceeded to make hysterical laughter by sharing tales of their husbands' sexual inadequacies. Jim had by then either passed out or was too incoherent to catch the repartee. Marie and Tetrazzini, meanwhile, came away as fast friends.

There was never any consensus on the merits of the early performances of *Tillie's Nightmare*. For every rave there was a pan. From the Lyric Theater in Cincinnati on January 25, Gerson fired off a letter to Jake articulating his concerns. Complacency on the road could bring catastrophe, he warned.[16] "I don't think [*Tillie's Nightmare*] would stand a chance in New York as it is now. Dressler is absolutely all there is to the show. ... The chorus is bad, there is no singing at all and absolutely no stage management. All the principals are bad. ... Mr. Winchell is a very fine man but I really believe that the job is a little too big for him. There is absolutely no discipline in the company." Jake shot back with a note the very next day.[17] "If the woman wasn't so impossible, she would be a good proposition to handle, but evidently she wants advice from no one save Mr. Fields, therefore nobody can show her anything or tell her where she is wrong."

As some sort of purgative therapy, Gerson maintained frequent correspondence with Jake:[18] "I really wish that ... someone could get on to see this show for there certainly is an enormous waste of money going on. ... Louisville does not look very good for us, although am exhausting every means of getting people here." In Cincinnati, the Shuberts finally decided to relieve the freespending Winchell of managing the production. They replaced him with Adolphe Mayer, who had served *The Rose of Algeria* on the road. The decision prompted Gerson to write[19] "am glad Mr. Mayer has taken Winchell's place with the Dressler show and Mayer should bring a little order out of the present chaos as he appears to be a competent man. Matters certainly were in a terrible mess when Winchell left." Lee told Mayer to cut the company down to 16 and discard the human flotsam at one or another tank town far from New York.[20]

As the production arrived in Louisville, Mayer sat down in his room at the Seelbach Hotel on Fourth and Walnut streets and wrote a letter to the Shuberts that is equal parts progress report and self-promotion. *Tillie's Nightmare* does not just need tighter management, he believed, it needs a shot of artistic inspiration from a fine director such as Ned Wayburn:[21]

> I have looked over this show carefully and have come to the conclusion it is the best of the season. It is a laugh from start to finish and I don't see how it could fail to do the same in New York. ... I have had no serious trouble with the stars and I have them pretty well in hand. They are anxious to get into the cities and I think will do a great deal to get it right. Ten days attention by a man like Wayburn will, I honestly think, give you a splendid property. ... I do *not* say that Miss Dressler and her husband are easy to get along with but I think the proposition can be handled successfully. They will be satisfied with any improvements in the right direction. I need a stage manager badly here who can also play a few small parts. ... The star is in a receptive mood now in spite of one-night stands and much can be done by me now, with a little encouragement held out to her as to improvements. ... I found a bad tangle on my arrival in Cincinnati, but a good spirit prevails now. I repeat again *Tillie's Nightmare* is the best laugh-maker of the season I'm sure.
>
> Yours Truly, Adolphe Mayer.
> P. S. ...Miss D. and her husband respect my authority *absolutely*.

Despite Mayer's rosy forecast, there was little relief for Marie's tormented psyche. Winchell, Gerson, and Mayer had nothing but disdain for her beloved Jim. Gerson reported to the New York office that Jim was engaged in "a continual stream of abuse and fault-finding" throughout the tour and was "the unofficial heavy of the troupe."[22] One erring electrician "bore [Jim's] marks of combat."[23] Communication must have been limited. Despite the proximity of continuous touring, Gerson was never clear on the marital status of Marie and Jim, noting him as her "husband (?)" in a letter to Jake.[24]

After successful runs in Baltimore and Toledo, the company settled briefly in Pittsburgh. Wayburn, known primarily as a choreographer, arrived and tried to whip the production into something exciting. He knew how to coddle Marie to get results, as he did directing her in *The Hall of Fame* in 1902. Guidance of her required one-on-one visits to the stage, rather than shouting orders from the auditorium floor. Marie hated being directed at all but especially detested it in the presence of other actors.

Simultaneous with Wayburn's arrival to the beleaguered troupe was a letter from Lee Shubert to Adolphe Mayer:[25] "We want the Dressler Company down to twenty-four girls or possibly thirty at the outside, and we do not want more than twelve or possibly sixteen men ... if you want better looking girls, I will try and send them to you ... Mr. Wayburn is doubtless there and he will go over this matter with you." As newly assigned director of the production, Wayburn most certainly was there, and from the Fort Pitt Hotel he composed a 12-page diatribe to the Shuberts about the shoddy production that had been knocking around the Midwest and Northeast without a captain. The creative punctuation and underlines are Wayburn's:[26]

> Dressler is the show—<u>she</u> make them <u>laugh</u>—at times coarse and disgusting—especially in "seasick" and "drunken" scenes—but she "gets over" herself in great shape and is very funny, <u>in spots</u>.
>
> The music, lyrics, costumes, etc. are worse than anything I have ever seen in <u>burlesque</u>—not one song hit in the show—nor any where near one—not one costume <u>effect</u> of any kind—just a <u>motley conglomeration of rags</u> ... whoever did this show should be <u>electrocuted</u> ... Of all the "<u>train wreckers</u>" I ever saw this chorus are the champions ... it woefully lacks class, not only in the <u>personalities</u> of the <u>cast, chorus</u> and <u>staff</u> but in "scenery," "effects," "props"—lyrics—music and everything else. ... Mayer means all right but he is <u>rough—ungentlemanly</u> and uses sort of bullying methods not becoming of a manager. Please be kind enough to inform him that I am taking charge....

Now the audience filing out say — "<u>She is the whole show</u>" — "There is nothing to the show but Dressler" — "<u>She certainly is funny</u>" "<u>I don't like the music</u>," "neither do I," "<u>Not a good song in the show</u>" "homliest chorus I ever saw" "Cheap company" "Cheap company," "Cheap" — "Cheap" "Cheap," but "she is great, isn't she?" That is the verdict and I saw for myself. When she is off the stage it is <u>pitiful</u> — would make your heart ache....

Yours Cordially, Ned Wayburn.

Lew Fields saw the production in Pittsburgh for the first time since the woeful opening in Albany. He did not share Wayburn's assessment and was said to be "insane with delight"[27] over the improved quality. Whatever the merits of *Tillie's Nightmare*, the *Pittsburgh Leader* ran some of the bons mots that the show would be famous for by the time it hit New York:[28]

The average woman acts as if a man ought to apologize for doing her a favor.

A scientist claims that hogs have souls, but he probably doesn't mean those who occupy two seats in a crowded street car.

What a noisy world this would be if we all preached what we practiced.

We are seldom content until we cease to care whether we are or not.

Much to Wayburn's pleasure, the entire cast received new costumes upon arrival in Philadelphia on February 26. Wayburn made his changes, but according to Marie,[29] the show "seemed to lose ginger. The audience went lukewarm on us." And always there were problems with Jim. Gerson wrote to Jake from Philadelphia:[30] "Don't like to bother you but must take up this matter of Dalton, Dressler's husband. He has been fussing and fighting ever since the first day I met him in Chicago. He announced last night that I purposely kept stuff out of the papers about Dressler in order to please the 'New York office' and that he 'would see that somebody took the show who could get and would get newspaper stuff and wasn't so fresh.'"

The show went on to Atlantic City and Washington, D.C. Marie's morale was improving, particularly since her suggestions had been incorporated into the show, as had Wayburn's. She gave a newspaperman predictions of Gotham success and said,[31] "I think we have got a genuine knockout. Edgar Smith knows my style from Dan to Beersheba and from Alpha to Omaha; that [Sloane] can certainly toss off the melodies like a farmer pitching hay at 6 p.m. with a husking bee due at 8, and Lew Fields is — well, he never stops when the block signal says 'gid-dap.' The story reads right and while I don't care to say that I have actually located the North Pole. ... If my play, *Tillie's Nightmare*, doesn't run three seasons then I will refuse the decoration which the King of Denmark has offered me."

Everyone was happy to be back in New York. With tremendous relief, the company no longer lived in big hotels in small cities. No more continuous forced intimacy that frayed nerves and brought fistfights. On May 5, 1910, *Tillie* was due to replace another Fields hit, *The Yankee Girl* with Blanche Ring, at the red-satined Herald Square Theater at the corner of Broadway and 35th Street.

No one much cared that *Tillie's Nightmare* was nearly plotless and most closely resembled a musical revue. No one much cared that the songs were largely forgettable. Miraculously, Marie's rewrites, Wayburn's doctoring, and cast changes resulted in the biggest hit New York had yet seen. Subtitled "A Mélange of Mirth and Melody in Three Acts," *Tillie* had the audience cheering and on its feet for the opening night final ovation.

The cast and crew cried backstage. Marie remembered that[32] "Jack [a stagehand] came up to me with tears in his eyes and said, 'Marie, you're a hell of a hit!' 'May I never see my kids again if you ain't put Bernhardt in the Old Ladies' Home,' cried the poor old wardrobe woman." New York reviews were glowing.[33] "Almost from the first minute to the last — that is to say, when the stage was not given over to dancers and singers in the lavishly provided musical and spectacular part of the production — she was doing stunts. And doing them with such amazing cleverness and with such an injection of rich humor and unflagging spirit that her appeal was irresistible."

As the play began, Tillie Blobbs dreamt of escaping to a better life, while her beautiful sister Maude (Octavia Broske) was idle. Maude was "too strong to work" and as this was a Cinderella story, the mother favored Maude, not Tillie. In dream sequences, Tillie was free of kitchen drudgery. She gleefully doffed her gingham and donned silk and velvet to become the toast of New York. Later she was aboard her own yacht and then hoisted into the clouds and onto an airplane. The well-received yacht scene included Marie attempting to quell her seasickness with a magnum of champagne.

One of Sloane's songs sealed Marie's lasting fame on stage. Early in the show, accompanying herself on a badly played piano and with surprising high doses of sadness and introspection, she sang "Heaven Will Protect the Working Girl."[34] The ditty was strikingly similar to the popular 1901 English tune "I'm a Respectable Working Girl" and began appearing in early versions during Marie's 1908 vaudeville stints. In all its forms, the song confronted the public's ambivalence toward women outside the duties of wife and mother. "Heaven Will Protect the Working Girl" was a sensation in America, and once New Yorkers had memorized its lyrics, the sheet music sales took off around the country. Audiences kept talking about the many other clever lines sprinkled throughout the play, many again in topical reference to women's changing roles at work and in education.

Marie in one of her homemade costumes as the irrepressible Tillie Blobbs in *Tillie's Nightmare*. (Courtesy of the Academy of Motion Picture Arts and Sciences.)

> Tillie: Calling me is getting to be a habit with Ma. She does it unconscious. Yesterday I was standing right alongside of her in the kitchen when she was talking to the guinea vegetable man and she said — 'Give me two bunches of beets — *Tillee!* and a peck of — *Tillee!* and a dozen ears of *Tillee!* and six turnips and....'"[35]
>
> Tillie: I ain't educated like Maude. Ma never let me go to school much. She said foolosopy and physiognomy and Parlee vous Francis ruined many a good dish washer. I don't believe I could ever mingle with the hoi polloi and the demi-monde.[36]
>
> Tillie: Ma hasn't been out of the kitchen except to go to bed for ten years. She did get outdoors — to a funeral — but she smelled so of fried onions she spoiled everybody's pleasure.[37]

Dressler loved doing *Tillie's Nightmare* as it was her show entirely. The rest of the cast was there to service her comedy, and for two and a half hours she supplied enough humor to keep the audiences rolling. "Irony is too fragile a tool for her to use when she desires to take a crack at anything or anybody; she employs the open palm of her hand. There is usually a resounding detonation when it strikes. But her vocabulary contains more kind words than ugly, and her heart appears to have developed in proportion to her body," concluded one reporter.[38] "No deft touches of comedy inspire the comedienne's portrayal of Tillie ... but the character is made excruciatingly funny by the very broadness of the illustrations," wrote another.[39]

Tillie was perfectly suited to Marie's heartfelt physical comedy and audiences' growing desire for recognizable people on stage. Tillie was not a cardboard character to be laughed at from afar. Everyone had met a Tillie. She was a real person who was "gawky, simpering, bellowing, rushing and bumping."[40] *Theatre* magazine identified the fantastic merging of character and actress:[41]

> Marie Dressler has a certain virility in her humor. Feminine enough by natural limitations, her grip of the comic is masculine in its strength. She has a clearness of mentality that is remarkable for its precision and vigor. ... Both vociferous and muscular, she goes through contortions of the most violent kind, which are amusing because they are her means of expression. ... If she has taken too much wine and misses her support, her recovery is made with as delicate an exercise of art as may be imagined. If she falls into the sea with her lover, seated on the gunnel, she does it effectively, artistically and with a response from the audience that thinks more of her exhibition as an acrobat.

Nothing good in Marie's life lasted very long, except her friendships. Less than one month after the New York opening of *Tillie's Nightmare*, she had a throat operation at the Roosevelt Hospital. Then she got ptomaine poisoning, necessitating a six-day cancellation of *Tillie*. In July, the company took an additional three-week hiatus. Most devastating was the death of Jenny, her tart-tongued and steadfast

"Something prehistoric and unclassified": Marie was made to look as repellent as possible for *Tillie's Nightmare*.

maid of 14 years. "Dear Jenny!" cried Marie.[42] "All her life she looked forward to a handsome funeral. And when she died, I saw to it that she got it. I took her body to Washington in a private car. I filled the church with flowers and I hired a colored choir to sing her beloved spirituals. All the colored elite of Washington turned out to do her honor." Mamie Steele, a young domestic from a prominent black Episcopalian family in Savannah, was later hired, and she grew to adore Marie as Jenny had.

Even with the setbacks, Marie was highly visible in New York in 1910. Socializing with great gusto, she was filmed by Vitagraph Company in "Actors' Fund/Field Day at the Polo Grounds."[43] She is preceded by a large banner with her name held by three men. The hot and humid outdoor benefit also included American Indians, blackface entertainers, baseball

Opposite: Title program page for *Tillie's Nightmare* after the 1910 summer vacation and Marie's hospitalization. (Courtesy of Theater Collection, Free Library of Philadelphia.)

LEW FIELDS HERALD SQUARE THEATRE

SAM S. and LEE SHUBERT (INC) & LEW FIELDS Lessees & Mgrs
HARRY M. HYAMS, Manager.

RESUMING THURSDAY EVENING, AUGUST 11, 1910.
Matinee Saturday.

LEW FIELDS Presents
MARIE DRESSLER
In
"TILLIE'S NIGHTMARE"

A Mixture of Mirth and Melody, in Two Acts.

Book and Lyrics by EDGAR SMITH. Music by A. BALDWIN SLOANE.

The Entire Production Staged by
NED WAYBURN.

Characters.

Tillie Blobbs, a boarding house drudge..........Miss Marie Dressler
Her Mother, a voice only.......................Miss Lottie Uart
Maude Blobbs, her sister.....................Miss Octavia Broske
Peroxia Snow, excess baggage with "Frost and Snow"
　　　　　　　　　　　　　　　　　　　　Miss May Montford
Sim Pettingill, a small town genius, with metropolitan aspirations,
　　　　　　　　　　　　　　　　　　　　Mr. Horace Newman
Harvey Tinker, an unappreciated inventor......Mr. Clarence Harvey
Smiley Bragg, a New York commercial drummer,
　　　　　　　　　　　　　　　　　　　　Mr. Charles H. Bowers
Harry Frost, of the vaudeville team of "Frost and Snow"
　　　　　　　　　　　　　　　　　　　　Mr. George Gorman
A Broadway Policeman.....................Mr. George Gorman
Metropole Bill, a pickpocket..................Mr. John E. Gorman
A Taxi Chauffeur..............................Mr. Sim Pulen
A Newsboy.................................Mr. Harry Wilcox, Jr.
Dorset Walkingly, head floorwalker at Pettingill's.....Mr. Lew Quinn
Dr. Rudolf Salve, of Bargain Ambulance Corps, at Pettingill's,
　　　　　　　　　　　　　　　　　　　　Mr. Barry Delaney
Miss Johnson, in charge of ribbon counter at Pettingill's,
　　　　　　　　　　　　　　　　　　　　Miss Lenora Novasio
Miss Johnson, in charge of perfume counter at Pettingill's,
　　　　　　　　　　　　　　　　　　　　Miss Nellie De Grasse
Mrs. Grouch, shopping for pink ribbon..............Miss Lottie Uart
Mrs. Jeffries Wolgast Rush, in search of a bargain..Miss May Brennan

PROGRAM CONTINUED ON SECOND PAGE FOLLOWING.

Egyptian **Deities**

"The Utmost in CIGARETTES"

As near perfect as mother nature
and human skill can make them.

Cork Tips or Plain

players, animal mascots, American revolutionaries, clowns, wild men of Borneo, a chorus girls race, and a greased pig chase.

The New York run of *Tillie's Nightmare* ended in November 1910, with the final performances taking place at the Majestic Theater in Brooklyn. To honor the occasion, Marie hosted a huge party for the cast, crew, and critics. Outside the restaurant dining room, a bare apple tree was aglow with hundreds of tiny lanterns. One present for each cast member was in the tree, but the recipient had to climb the tree to retrieve the gift. The "gifts for the ladies"[44] were hung on the lower branches and tree scrambling was followed inside by a hearty turkey dinner.

Tillie wasn't dormant for long. Another Shubert-sponsored tour was about to commence. Just one month after closing in New York, the Tillie company took its newly polished production to Providence, New Haven, Cleveland, St. Louis, Philadelphia, Boston, Toronto, Chicago, Minneapolis, Denver, and Seattle. It was a hit in every city.

Marie was excited to be coming as far west as San Francisco in her first visit there since *Courted into Court* in 1898. Accompanied by a Seattle-born laughing parrot named Toby,[45] Marie and Jim played at being the world's happiest couple for the waiting press. From her high-rise suite in the new St. Francis Hotel, Marie told a reporter[46] that "seven years ago, while I lay flat on my back with typhoid fever, my mother [died]. ... Then I recovered and had no one to go to. My mother went somewhere where she can watch me and think of my happiness. And I believe, too, that she selected my husband for me. He is a reward for all I've suffered. He just lives for me."

At that moment, Jim entered the room and interjected: "My dear, I've just been downstairs and I ordered a duck for you."

Marion de Lappe was a young-looking 22-year-old neophyte reporter with the William Randolph Hearst–owned *Examiner* newspaper when Marie's show came to San Francisco.[47] Freshly divorced from visual artist Wesley de Lappe, she was a woman of pale skin in striking contrast to dark hair. Brilliant and warm but steely, she had already tried other competitive professions, including advertising and modeling, before landing at the *Examiner*.

Marion was happily relieved from her duties writing obituaries to cover the opening night of the star Marie Dressler. It was a major break for the young woman. "You've been given the chance of a lifetime," said a top feature writer, not bothering to tell her that she was being set up for disaster. All Marion knew was that she was sent to interview a famous actress. Since she had gone to work to support a once patrician family that had lost everything in the earthquake and fire of 1906, she was all the more nervous.

The opening night of *Tillie's Nightmare* in San Francisco was a glittering affair on a rainy night, with men in their tuxedos and women in their best bibs-and-tuckers. Horse-drawn carriages crowded the wet streets. The newly built downtown Savoy Theater was overflowing with ermine, sable, and jewels. The press, far less ostentatious than the paying audience, scurried down the alleyway before the curtain rose. They went to the stage entrance and into the theater for question sessions with Marie.

Backstage at her door hung a huge gold star. After hearing a knock by a reporter, she answered wearing a typically ridiculous homemade costume drawing attention to all of her 200-plus pounds.

"Greetings, pals!" she exclaimed. "Make your interviews snappy. The circus is waiting for its elephant!" The seasoned professionals volleyed their questions as flashbulbs went off and a din of chatter rose. The inexperienced and shy Marion was overwhelmed until Marie spotted her in the back of the crowd. "I can see her this moment — a slim, big-eyed girl of seventeen [sic], shy as an antelope and just as graceful," recalled Marie.

"Hello, little girl. Where'd you come from?" asked Marie in a gentle voice.

Marion made the mistake of telling Marie what newspaper she worked for. By 1911 Hearst was something of a joke, albeit an exceptionally powerful one. He had run unsuccessfully for mayor of New York City, governor of New York state, and president, earning himself the title William Also Randolph Hearst. He had collected numerous enemies through the brutish, violent, take-no-prisoners journalism of his newspaper chain. One of those enemies was Marie.

With the Hearst name uttered, an awkward silence was followed by an explosion. "Get out!" boomed Marie. "You know better than to pull a trick like this. Get right out of here or I'll have you thrown out!"

The reporters were dismissed and left to watch the performance, but Marion remained backstage, immobilized by anxiety. Marie made her exits and entrances avoiding eye contact with her. After the laughter, applause, and curtain calls ended, Marie headed back toward her dressing room. Still Marion waited as minutes passed and "lights began to blink out in the theater before [Marie] emerged from her dressing room in street garb, looking exceedingly handsome in a plumed hat and fur coat."[48] Marion approached once again: "Miss Dressler, if I don't get an interview with you I'll lose my job. And I need it! I really need it!"

Marie at last saw her as something of a victim rather than conspirator. "Is that what those sons of ..."

Cutting her off, Marion ended "... bitches."

"Yes, bitches." Marie now warmed considerably. "Aw, you poor little kid, don't you realize that gang on the paper has played a practical joke on you? They knew I wouldn't let a Hearst reporter get within ten miles of me. Neither would W. R. give me an inch of space in any of his papers. We had a blowup, he and I, and you can take my word for it that when I blow I can outmatch Moby Dick." She placed her hand on Marion's shoulder. "You poor little kid," she repeated. "Come on into my dressing room for a cup of java. I'll send my maid out for an oyster loaf."

They spent an hour in Marie's dressing room, which was already festooned with telegrams and flowers. Marion did not need to ask any of the standard questions. "Marie Dressler reminded me of a Scottish bagpipe," recalled Marion.[49] "She filled up her chest with wind and never tuned off until the last gasp had been expelled."

Marie explained her lifelong predicament:[50] "Not able to wear a mask, I decided to make my face even funnier than nature's original design. Said I to myself, 'You're going to become the biggest ape outside of a zoo, Dressler, and make the whole world laugh at you.'" Marion was amused at the soliloquy, but she "caught an undertone of sadness running through it, like a drab thread in a cloth of gold, and wondered if she really were gay at heart."

It was after midnight when they left the theater. A carriage was waiting to take Marie to the St. Francis Hotel. "Hop in," she said. "I'll drive you home first." But Marion insisted on being left at the newspaper office. Once there, Marie looked at the young woman and said "Child, you're sweet," and then gave her a kiss. "I'll see you again."

Marion was not well when she visited Marie. Heavy rain and wind were merciless that night and she arrived without any wrap. The gargantuan Marie had given the diminutive young woman her coat and watched as the tiny figure struggled on Market Street against the elements. The affection was already there as Marie realized that Marion was "the daughter I should have had."[51]

Because of the London fiasco of 1909 and her many medical bills, Dressler was broke at the onset of *Tillie*. By 1911 she was rich again. After the return trip to New York, and for reasons only she will ever understand, she decided to buy a farm. "While on a motor trip, I passed by a big white house in Windsor, Vermont, and, well, I just had to own it!" she wrote.[52] The farm was tucked away in the White Mountains near the Connecticut River. Neighbors included American novelist Winston Churchill and *Collier's Weekly* editor Norman Hapgood. President Woodrow Wilson's Summer White House was across the street.

The Dressler spread began as a rundown 28 room, three-story colonial mansion, but Marie and Jim soon spent huge sums in restoration.[53] The grounds had an orchard, swimming pool, tennis courts, and a stable of 16 Shetland ponies and 30 Jersey cows intended to pay for it all with milk, cheese, and butter. Inside the main house was a grand piano and a fully stocked cellar. Despite the distance from New York, friends used to drop in and soon the large house wasn't large enough to support the army of guests. Marie and Jim had two guesthouses built in the backyard to accommodate everyone. Marie dove into her role as a bucolic by sporting Mother Hubbard clothes, including sunbonnet, boots, plaid shirts, and overalls. Guests saw her rise when the rooster called, take in huge gulps of country air, and exclaim,[54] "Never felt better in my life. Haven't missed Broadway for five minutes."

Financial problems began soon after they moved in.[55] Each of the bossies had "the appetite of a starved boa constrictor." The others of her menagerie, including horses named Brandy and Soda, a goose named Mutt, and a duck named Jeff, were similarly unprofitable. Marie was a champion when taking on powerful men, but she was a pushover with animals or hard-luck cases. When the cook delivered Jeff as dinner, Marie was mortified. "Take him away, we can't eat Jeff," she cried.[56]

Bills mounted, and the place went to seed when Marie was touring or performing in New York. "I no sooner get settled in one spot than I am whisked off to Oshkosh or Africa," she explained.[57] She was unprepared for and ignorant of rural life, planting flowers in the wrong season and expecting her cows to support the lavish estate. It slowly dawned on her that she had no business keeping a farm. But her love of the country life compelled her to hold on too long. When she finally sat down with a budget, the fortune was already far gone.

During the workweek, Marie stayed at 15 West 68th Street near Central Park, where she and Lillian Russell had taken their well-reported bike rides together. The neighborhood and building were stately and dignified, with "no less than three gentlemen of color in livery on guard around the portals."[58] For an interview there, Marie assumed the title "Mrs. Dalton"[59] and

> sat serenely, not to say solemnly, in a French gilt tapestry-upholstered chair, sewing on something or other. Around her was more gilt and tapestry furniture in a room so large and high-ceilinged that it resembled a French salon, a resemblance further heightened by canvasses which fairly concealed the walls. Modern impressionistic oils they were, for the most part, with below them low bookcases with odd bits of china atop them. Not a sign of a piano, covered with ragtime; no theatrical photographs draping walls and desk and falling over mantlepieces and bookcases; nothing to suggest either stage or comedy.

"I reserve my funmaking for the 'foundry,'" explained Marie. "There isn't anyone who can be funny all the time ... yet there are people who expect to roar the minute they see you. ... Only the other day I was invited to the home of some well-to-do and otherwise seemingly sensible people and when I was introduced it was like this: 'This is Marie Dressler.' Then, turning to me, my hostess said, 'Now say something funny.'"

Jim continued to attempt greater authority over *Tillie's Nightmare* than the Shuberts would give. When comptroller J. W. Jacobs noticed a bookkeeping discrepancy on the road, the brothers concluded that Jim had dipped into the till. They blasted him as a liar, crook, and blackmailer in numerous memos bouncing between New York and the show on tour. Matters grew stickier when Marie announced that she didn't want to tour anymore and was content to milk her cows. Then Edgar Smith and A. Baldwin Sloane claimed that they had not been paid and were threatening legal action. Everyone, it seemed, was in an ongoing battle over who owned what part of the play and who owed what to whom. With or without the accounting problems, the Shuberts weren't about to retire a profitable production like *Tillie's Nightmare* if Marie was contractually obligated to tour. And everyone knew the show was nothing without her.

Lew Fields and the Shuberts had ongoing disagreements of their own, but all three hated Jim in equal measure. Fields grew impatient when "Mr. Dressler" was remiss in paying expenses incurred during *Tillie* rehearsals. In seeking payment on his loan, Fields brought a suit against Jim, who was informed and actually arrested at home in Windsor.[60] Some backstage peacemaking kept them from court, and Marie could be counted on to return to work when her cash flow slowed down. The vitriolic memos and threats more often ended in a truce, with all parties agreeing on a settlement until another accusation sent them into a new round of name calling and ultimatums.

By the fall of 1911, as Vermont turned frosty, Marie was begrudgingly back at rehearsals for yet another tour of *Tillie's Nightmare*. No disagreements had been settled, but Marie and Jim insisted on final authority over the production. The Shuberts maintained all the control they could and Fields was distracted with new projects. Relations between Marie, Jim, Fields, and the Shuberts were so strained that the Shuberts accepted a $7,500 cash buyout of *Tillie's Nightmare* from Jim. On October 16, the stockholders of Fields Producing Company, Lee and Jake Shubert, William Klein, and Fields signed a bill of sale.[61] The scenery, costumes, props, effects, and playing rights were now exclusively owned by Jim, but he did not deliver cash on the spot. That was supplied by Fields to the Shuberts. Jim, in effect, made off like a bandit and never paid Fields a cent of his loan. Despite their apparent generosity, Fields and the Shuberts knew *Tillie's Nightmare* was running out of steam and would soon be retired.

Jim wasted no time clucking in his newfound autonomy as producer. Three days after the sale of *Tillie's Nightmare*, he wrote Klein telling him that he would be held "personally liable for the action you commenced against me in the name of Lew Fields at Windsor, Vermont, as it was unauthorized by Mr. Fields and he has notified you to that effect."[62] Klein gave the letter to Lee Shubert with the note "just see what a dirty dog [Dalton] is."[63]

Free from the bitter Shubert-Fields union, Marie and company returned their own *Tillie's Nightmare* to Philadelphia and Pittsburgh in November 1911. Back in New York before Christmas, they gave a performance at the huge Manhattan Opera House to benefit poor orphaned children. "Those youngsters almost made a riot over her," noted one observer.[64] "Their little hands clapped, some of them waved their crutches and their shrill voices rose high in repeated calls for 'Tille-e-e! Tille-e-e!'" Back on the dreaded road, with the farm in wintertime neglect, Cleveland once again welcomed *Tillie's Nightmare* at the Colonial Theater for an end-of-the-year engagement.

Despite the lucre of *Tillie's Nightmare*, Marie still had major unpaid bills. She had not settled her London debts[65] and the farm continued to be a money pit. Earnings dropped as *Tillie* had no more commercial potential. The show was looking threadbare by 1912. The cast and crew were profoundly weary, much to the unhappiness of their audiences. *Tillie* had appeared three times at the Lyric Theater in Cincinnati and the Columbus coverage[66] announced that she had become "a poor old broken down 'show'—scenery and costumes disgustingly dirty, a spiritless lot of mediocre actors and singers filling the parts. And worst of all Miss Dressler herself had ... so broadened and coarsened her comedy that it was disgusting." On March 16, 1912, just five months after Jim purchased *Tillie's Nightmare*, the show closed in Rochester after 753 performances.[67] No future bookings were scheduled.

Marie was unemployed, and Tillie was retired, when the *Titanic* smashed against an iceberg in the north Atlantic and sank in the early hours of April 15. Broadway theaters experienced decimated box-office returns as the full horror of 1,523 casualties came to be known. It seemed as though everyone knew someone who didn't survive; among the dead was Henry B. Harris, producer of Marie's 1897 production *Courted into Court*. No one was hiring for vaudeville and Marie was left with little to do for several months except tend the farm.

Demand for her services persisted. She was paid $1,500 for a single night's performance in Toronto, but a project of Tillie proportions was nowhere to be found. She managed steady income in November when she appeared in the highly anticipated reunion of Weber and Fields at the new Shubert-funded Music Hall on 44th Street.[68] This was a major event; the theater was an ornate and spacious auditorium seating 2,000. Choice seats were snatched up by Mamie Fish and her society cadre for $60. Diamond Jim Brady and William Randolph Hearst, great fans of Weber and Fields, paid $940 for a box through an auction. On opening night, gawkers crowded the new arcade on the east side of the theater and were crushed all the way to nearby Hotel Astor.

Marie was backstage terrified beyond consolation. She clung to a stage brace for comfort, nausea closing in and sweat ruining her makeup. Weber noticed her pitiful condition and approached.[69] "I can't do it, Joe," she breathed in a tremored voice. "I can't go out there and face 'em. My legs won't move." At Marie's cue, Weber put his knee on her back and pushed her onto the stage in an awkward Dressler-like spin. The crowd applauded and she was on her way to another popular performance.

The evening followed Weber and Fields' traditional two-part structure as written by long-term collaborator Edgar Smith. The first act was called *Roly-Poly* and opened with Meyer Talzmann (Fields) and Mike Schmaltz (Weber) taking the waters at Raatenbad Spa. Bijou Fitzsimmons (Marie) pursues Schmaltz, who plays dead to escape her advances. Much of the humor pointed to her heft. When she was hit by a miniature jalopy driven by Weber, she stopped it dead and barely acknowledged the impact. The second half of the evening was a travesty of Bayard Veiller's thriller *Within the Law* called *Without the Law*. Marie once again took her share of laughs when she entered handcuffed to diminutive Weber and proceeded to raise him off the ground and swing him around.

The usually staid *New York Times*[70] let loose with a screaming headline for their *Roly-Poly* review: "Gags, Girls, Glare; Oh! Such a Gladness!" The company was fully up to the task of properly inaugurating the new Music Hall, "the girls were never prettier, never, it seems, so gorgeously caparisoned.... Marie Dressler['s] talent is in direct ratio to her size—and that is saying something for her talent." Many onlookers were disappointed that her role was secondary to the veteran male team. "There might have been more of Miss Dressler," huffed the *New York Evening Sun*.[71]

Despite the glowing reception, full houses, and superb new theater, the players were discontent. Fields was none too pleased that Jim had yet to pay back his *Tillie's Nightmare* buy-out loan. Weber and Fields were trying to soothe other festering animosities, but cast members were slowly leaving the show. "I never enjoyed this engagement as I did my work with Weber alone," Marie remembered.[72] "Fields and I, unfortunately, never got along very well together." She accused him of jealousy when she stole laughs from him on stage. She even claimed that he excised popular routines that she invented. The protracted history of strained relations made *Roly-Poly* stressful for everyone.

What happened next is open to interpretation. Dressler wrote that she was fired from the company by being slowly starved of material. "Every time rehearsal was called they cut one of my scenes," she wrote.[73] When critic Charles Darnton stopped by the theater for a visit, she flippantly remarked that she expected to be cut out entirely in two weeks. Darnton turned that into a formal printed statement of her departure from the company. Fields was livid and carried the newspaper to her. "Did you say this?"

"Let's not talk now," she returned. "You are excited."

"You get out of my theater," he screamed. Fields was so angry that he suggested she leave his employ immediately (December 21) and avoid the standard two weeks' notice. Weber and Fields then issued a terse statement: "Miss Marie Dressler has severed her connections with the Weber & Fields all-star stock company." Her $1,500-per-week 20-week contract was effectively nullified when she announced to the press that she was given poor material and no songs. Tiring of the feud, she said, "I feel that I have a mission in life. I believe I was put on earth for a definite purpose. I am the outlet for the tired man's brains. He finds relaxation in seeing me make a fool of myself." With one nasty miscommunication, Weber and Fields no longer fulfilled Marie's proclaimed purpose in life. She invited the world to laugh at her looks, but she went searching for sympathy and respect when she wrote that "I have a certain dignity that is sacred to me and that I will not allow to be abused."[74]

Weber and Fields did not agree with Marie's spin on the breakup. After four weeks, "she left our employ of her own accord and has never come back," said Weber.[75] He did not mention Marie's dwindling exposure on stage, nor his own ongoing conflicts with Fields. "If there is any breach of contract, I think the responsibility rests with Miss Dressler, not with us." Marie responded by suing them for $24,000 in unpaid salary. Her attorneys claimed that she was discharged from the company without just cause. Weber shot back that she "sought to disorganize and undermine the company by circulating statements and reports derogatory to the efficiency of the other members of the company."[76] Her suit went nowhere, since she had quit in full earshot of several cast members and Jim still owed Fields money. Marie left, and the *Roly-Poly* New York box-office revenue collapsed. Weber and Fields had better luck when they took the Marieless production on a hastily planned six-week tour in early 1913. After that, the Weber & Fields Music Hall was once again put to rest.

There was still money to earn and debts to pay. In an effort to right wrongs, Marie and Fields negotiated a new production agreement. This time she wanted more stage time and more control. With Fields producing, Marie directed and starred in *All Star Gambol*,[77] a revue with the newly christened "Marie Dressler Players." She proved to be less than a first rate director. One observer of *All Star*

Weber and Fields in 1912.

Gambol implored Marie to forbid her supporting cast from sticking their heads through the curtain to watch the show in full view of the audience.

In this latest outing, she staged a burlesque of the Alexandre Dumas *fils*' romantic tragedy *Camille*, renamed it *Clamille*, and solicited the help of acrobatic actor Jefferson De Angelis as her leading man. "The dying coughs of the rotund Marie are very destructive to the furniture and when she finally collapses into Almond's arms, Almond collapses, too," reported the *New York Dramatic Mirror*.[78] Marie veered from her standard routine in doing a full dramatic restaging of Acts 4 and 5 from *Camille*. She and Fields hired Madame Yorska, a costar of Sarah Bernhardt, to play Camille. Marie played Madame Prudence, her shallow and self-centered friend. Critics were puzzled by her handling of Prudence as she thickly laid on the Music Hall style of comedy and merriment. Even more troubling was the sudden imposition of a dramatic story in the midst of revue entertainment. The package did not work any too well. It was in fact a complete bust and lasted for eight performances in New York.

Marie and Fields were understandably disappointed, but they avoided publicly laying blame on each other. Marie rebounded quickly, got on the train, and did a vaudeville tour almost immediately. She was back in top form on a swing through Cleveland, where Archie Bell[79] noted that he believed "some day Marie Dressler will wear a crown with many stars in it because she has done as much to make the people of the world forget themselves, their little prejudices and troubles, hates and dislikes, as any woman of our generation."

By April, Marie was once again in difficult negotiations with the Shuberts for a new production. She owed the organization $5,000, and the brothers were less forgiving of loans than Lew Fields. She opted to pay them back through another vaudeville tour of the brothers' theaters. The pain of being separated from the farm and back on the road was placated by fantastic press and ticket sales. "At the Majestic reigns the immortal Marie Dressler," wrote one critic.[80] "There absolutely is nobody on earth like Marie Dressler. She is a house on fire, (a) great big house; She is a tornado of fun and splendid originality."

In the spirit of Augustin Daly's offer of Shakespearean tragedy, Marie continued to explore serious material. Alone, beyond the control of directors or classic literature, she delivered the recitation "When Baby Souls Sail Away" that left audiences blubbering in their hankies. One onlooker at the Majestic recorded the occasion:[81]

> She came close to the footlights, brushed the grimace out of her face, assumed an attitude of dignity—nay, of stateliness—began a musing little poem about a child that died and had to fare away into the unknown without its mother. The whole woman changed. She stood regally—like a tragedy queen in meditation—but her face was touched with a soft tenderness. Her voice was rich, subdued, not tremulous, for that would have cheapened the inflection. The woman who had them guffawing thirty seconds before, and who guffawed with them, now made them listen with sympathy not unmixed with awe. She did not wring pathos from the little poem nor do any tactless, tasteless, excessive thing to bring out its wistfulness, seeming rather to take it close to her arms and caress it and sigh and muse over it—not obviously nor painstakingly, but in soft rapture. ... Miss Dressler never erred by a hair's breadth. She created her effect in a matter of seconds and she sustained it beautifully, reposefully, feelingly. ... The woman-buffoon became maternal and grand.

Windsor, Vermont, was hopping in mid-1913. As Woodrow Wilson settled into the summer White House, so, too, did a presidential press corps. Wan and bewildered far from Washington, the writers needed some tender loving care. Marie decided to practice her benevolence. "Come right home to mother," she told them.[82] They had free use of the pool, ice chest, and pool table. With a brand new "welcome" doormat, Jim acquired the nickname "What'll-You-Have" Dalton as the farm became known as "the Oasis."

The generosity could not be maintained, particularly since the productive end of the farm was losing money. Jim was inept at farming, and those 30 Jersey cows had produced $200 worth of cream in their first week but cost $250 in feed. After months of losses, Marie "gave the cows their two weeks' notice" and sold them to an impoverished man who gave her a $50 down payment on a $500 sale.[83] Marie never saw another penny for her cows. She had no better luck with poultry. Converting the backyard into a beer garden was temporarily lucrative, but the Oasis kept sucking up huge amounts of money.

Brilliant on stage, unpredictable off, Dressler continued to be regarded as a viable actress by audiences who declared her the funniest woman in America. She scores no points for seeing changes in public tastes. As for advancing the cause of women at work, she was more laudable as an example than as a visionary. "Heaven Will Protect the Working Girl" was hardly an anthem to self-determination. She stood up to the most powerful men in entertainment, yet saw no point in seeking increased authority for women through federal law. Nine states out of 48 had already granted suffrage when Marie said,[84] "I feel very keenly on this subject, for I believe there is something radically wrong with our womanhood when so many are clamoring to take man's place in the management of public affairs. Personally, I am a staunch believer in woman's equality with man, but I believe it is a mental quality, not a physical one, and that womankind was never devised to steer the ship of state or to go to the polls and cast their ballot with the men." As if to defend her own existence, she went on to explain that women's place is at home except "in certain individual cases where the expression of some talent, artistic or otherwise, seems to justify a professional career."[85]

Marie and Jim laid low for most of the rest of 1913. After another bout of ptomaine poisoning, Marie boarded a train to Nevada to see her latest investment.[86] Jim had urged her to visit the asbestos mine of the Yulida Copper Company in the Cocomough district, where they held controlling interest. Marie traveled into the desert by auto from the tiny towns of Goldfield and Lida to the camp, where she inspected the tunnels dug on the vein.

At each closing of each show, Marie had to reinvent her professional life. She was a jumble of contradictions — longing for the security of the farm and needing steady work but rarely staying anywhere long enough to make it happen. She spent years detesting the conditions of the theater, however generous they were to her financially. She openly disliked many of her employers and maintained an ultimately fatal we/them mentality when negotiating contracts. She frequently announced her impending retirement or a need to break free and succeed at something else. It didn't happen in Nevada or anywhere else; being funny was Marie's curse and blessing. The theater was driving her a little bit crazy by 1913 and she was quickly spending her second great fortune as if, yet again, heaven would protect this working girl.

Chapter 6

Mack Sennett's Grand Idea

In the ever-evolving world of revue theater, shows can appear, die, and reappear significantly altered in cast, director, script, and venue. Dressler was convinced that with proper restaging, *All Star Gambol* could be a hit. At the onset of 1914, she sought no backing from Lew Fields or the Shuberts and financed the new production with her own money. Her artistic decisions included scrapping the serious *Camille* diversion and rehiring her popular costar Jefferson De Angelis. The biggest problem was settling on a name. The Lambs Club, a male-only association of New York thespians, objected that they had been using "All Star Gambol" as the exclusive title of their annual entertainment.[1] Marie was stubborn as ever and the matter went to court. A judge decided to let them both use the name, suggesting that anyone confusing the Lambs Club with Marie Dressler must have much more serious problems as well. Marie still toyed with a number of titles, and the opus was alternately labeled *Merry Gambol, The Marie Dressler Players, The Banqueteers,* and the original *All Star Gambol.*

Marie's hodge-podge played well in several cities, including New Haven, Cleveland, Toledo, Baltimore, Detroit, Toronto, and Denver, but its run at the new Gaiety Theater in downtown San Francisco was particularly memorable. *Merry Gambol* had brief stints in Stockton and Sacramento and, according to Gilbert Anderson, owner of the Gaiety,[2] "it was not strong enough to be a San Francisco success. There is going to be a production of *Merry Gambol,* with Dressler if possible, and without her if necessary." Anderson postponed the opening.

From their sunny 12th-story flower-filled room at the St. Francis Hotel in downtown San Francisco, Marie and Jim voiced their ire. "We had a show that was certain to be a success," she told reporters.[3] "The reason for [the postponement] was purely personal. Mr. J. J. Rosenthal, the manager, has been angry because I would not permit his wife, Katherine Osterman, to take part in the play." Marie further complained that costumes and wigs had been seized and held by the management.

By January 28, Anderson, Rosenthal, Marie, and Jim had made up, and "it appeared that the only trouble was caused by theatrical

As advertised in the January 29, 1914, *San Francisco Bulletin*, all is well (momentarily) as *Traffic in Souls* plays the Gaiety and awaits replacing *Undying Story of Capt. Scott* at the Savoy when *The Merry Gambol* opens at the Gaiety on February 2.

temperaments. Miss Dressler is virtually to have her own way."[4] Then just as suddenly, Anderson confessed to losing as much as $15,000 in musical comedy ventures. He was the movie's Bronco Billy and the producer-director of popular westerns as well as Gaiety's owner. He was frankly terrified of more losses from Marie's expensive production and had booked the theater for the movie *Traffic in Souls* in replacement of *Merry Gambol*. Anderson was stuck with two obligations and so moved *Traffic in Souls* over to the Savoy Theater on short notice.[5] To appease the Savoy manager, he attached a $1,500 bond to the deal. With his *Merry Gambol* contract close at hand, Anderson reluctantly announced to the press that the play would open at the Gaiety on February 2.

To everyone's relief, the San Francisco production was a roaring success. Audiences loved "Symposium of Terpsichore — The Evolution of Dancing," a holdover routine from the original production staged by Marie.[6] With the full company in tow, Marie and De Angelis led program sections called Ancient Greek Dancing, Old-Fashioned Step Dancing, Original Spanish Dancing, Classic Toe Dancing, and Lightning Turkey Trot. Multiple curtain calls and a rocketing of flowers up over the footlights accompanied opening-night cheers. Celebrating backstage, the chorus attempted, and failed, to hoist Marie onto two of the stouter pair of shoulders in the cast. They settled for shrieking cheers of approval for their leading lady.

Problems with this production were not over. *Merry Gambol* was settling in for a long run when Marie suffered a week-long "nervous breakdown."[7] Martha Golden had the unenviable task of understudying to half-empty houses. Marie was back to packed houses by February 17, but by March, the war between star and house staff had resumed.[8] Marie complained that management dismissed 12 chorus members without her or Jim's approval. In retaliation, Marie refused to perform and Golden once again filled in. "I'm through," blasted Jim, "and I don't mind telling you that you are a bunch of pikers." In response, a Gaiety spokesman told Jim that "we are not going to let you or any other interloper run this enterprise" and had him ejected from the theater when he appeared at the stage door to escort Marie to their hotel. Rosenthal had open disdain for Jim and referred to him as a charter member of the "Only Their Husbands Club."

The Gaiety slapped Marie and Jim with a $35,000 breach-of-contract lawsuit. Marie and Jim filed a countersuit, likewise citing the Gaiety for breach of contract. The more shocking battle was launched against Jim. William M. Gorman of the Gaiety Theater and his attorney, Robert Chonynski, attempted to indict him for fraud, claiming that he was not legally married to Marie.[9] Gorman and Chonynski brought messages, letters, and an affidavit to the United States district attorney swearing that Jim had a wife and family on the East Coast. This made him a bigamist or a "white slave trader" by the Mann Act, which prohibited the interstate transportation of a female for any "immorality." His marriage to Marie, they concluded, was bogus and he ought to be jailed.

District Attorney John Preston, after hearing Marie and Jim's adamant denial of a faux marriage, declared that he saw no basis for the allegations. "Until further evidence is produced, I will not take any steps to bring an indictment against Dalton," he declared.[10] Jim stated that he believed that "it is a case to get me to help the Gaiety Theater in its fight between the management and the star." Gorman was shocked at Preston's decision. "The affidavits we have submitted to the United States Attorney include a sworn statement from Jim's wife that he was never divorced from her," he told the *Los Angeles Times*.[11]

"There is not a word of truth in the whole thing," declared Marie to the *San Francisco Daily News*.[12] She believed the problem came from a feud with the management, whom Jim, as Marie's representative, had alienated. Gaiety representatives say it began when Jim gave away four sets of box seats for a matinee performance without permission. Jim was not in the habit of asking anything from anyone, except Marie. He went crazy when they slapped him with a $32 charge.

Marie remained loyal to Jim and publicly lashed out at the Gaiety personnel. "In a way it's ridiculous; then again, it is a contemptible thing," she said.[13] "I'm glad to be through with the management, glad I don't have to associate with them any more. But this is certainly shocking treatment to get in chivalrous California." The suits were eventually dropped.

The episode highlights Marie's blind devotion to Jim, whom she alternately called "Daddy," "The Captain," or "Friend Husband." He was openly worshipful of the star, massaging her feet after a tiring performance and making sure her meals were just right. He appeared to be an exceedingly kind and attentive husband. With new stages, press, and audiences constantly, the demands on Marie were immense and his doting was more than welcome. She so desired affection and guidance that she tolerated his muddy-headed management, drinking, gambling, unsatisfying sexual performance, and expensive shopping habits.

Others in their circle disliked him and found him to be opportunistic, but Marie did not waver. If she doubted his good intentions, she did not reveal her suspicions. The San Francisco episode, marring an otherwise successful and extended engagement, was best ignored and forgotten. A few years later, when Jim told her the truth on a steamer from London to New York, the professional and emotional betrayal were nearly unbearable.

The nonstop performing and touring schedule of *Tillie,* followed immediately by *Merry Gambol* and the legal traumas, drove Marie to exhaustion. After *Gambol*'s March close in San Francisco, she took her doctor's orders and retreated to Los Angeles for sunshine and rest. Jim stayed in San Francisco to settle the ongoing Gaiety wrangle.

Mack Sennett had first met Marie in 1898, when she was touring *The Lady Slavey*.[14] He was an 18-year-old ironworker when she appeared at the Academy Theater in Northampton, Massachusetts. He wanted desperately to break into show business and thought a letter from a prominent local attorney would get him the attention of Marie. His letter read: "Dear Miss Dressler: This boy wants to go on the stage. CALVIN COOLIDGE."

Young Sennett accompanied his mother backstage and it was she who asked Marie how her strapping son might get into show business. Marie turned to her guests and said, "I have to tell you the truth. The theatrical profession is very uncertain. Only a very few ever reach anything like the top, even when they have great talent. I know — all this looks very fine and rich and easy, but you never have a home, you're out of work a great deal of the time. ... I can't be too emphatic about this. Anything you do with show business is hard work."

Sennett broke in. "Lady, talk about hard work, have you ever driven hot rivets all day long?"

Marie grinned. "I guess you ought to have a chance, Rivets. I'll write you a note — and make it a mite longer than this lawyer feller's letter to me. You take this to David Belasco in New York and God help you."

Sennett went to Belasco, then on to burlesque and vaudeville before becoming a promising film producer and director. From 1908 to 1912, Sennett apprenticed at the American Biograph Company, where David Wark Griffith was establishing principles of moviemaking, storytelling, and camera action. From there, Sennett joined the infant Keystone Film Company in 1912. With the financial support of New York bookies Adam Kessel and Charles Bauman, Sennett set up shop in Los Angeles, where he began directing half-reel comedies. Included in the cast of his early efforts was a teenager named Mabel Normand. Sennett saw in her an actress of rare comic abilities and radiant beauty; he fell in love with her. With Normand and others supplying laughs, Sennett's Keystone Film Company made money, and he was soon wanting to enlarge his turf. While Griffith was defining cinematic drama (*The Birth of a Nation* was released in 1915), Sennett was perfecting buffoonery and silliness.

Before going to work, Sennett informed his newly signed funnyman Charlie Chaplin of the environment on a Keystone set: there is no scenario, but a sequence of events always leads to a chase. The emerging Keystone trademarks, slapstick antics of pratfalls, hurling pies, and lampooning of everything stuffy and dignified, were to be expected in any movie from the studio. Chaplin held a low opinion of the product. Even before he created his tramp character, he exhibited a haughty attitude openly aimed at Sennett and the Keystone Film Company. In *My Autobiography*, he wrote, "I thought [Keystone comedies] were a crude mélange of rough-and-tumble. However, a pretty, dark-eyed girl named Mabel Normand, who was quite charming, weaved in and out of them and justified their existence."[15]

Though they had no story to deliver, Sennett and Bauman approached Marie during her rest in Los Angeles.[16] Their idea, they explained, was to play first-rate movie theaters; Marie's name on a project would guarantee success. And with the growing reputations of Mabel Normand and Charlie Chaplin, the film was sure to make money. In addition, Sennett was dreaming of a landmark undertaking: the first six-reel comedy.

Originally, Marie was not very keen on the idea. Movies were not taken seriously by most stage veterans. The "flickers" often played in sleazy makeshift theaters patronized by the great unwashed who could not afford tickets to live performances. Worse, Los Angeles at the time was considered a backwater with a strong conservative element attempting to block further growth of the infant film industry. Los Angeles' leading theater producer, Oliver Morosco,[17] expressed the sentiments of many in the early days of movies: "Those locusts are swarming into Los Angeles, building ramshackle studios from the beach to the mountains. Literally, thousands are trekking west and this is resented by large groups of people, mostly churchgoers, who are forming committees to keep these ragtags and bobtails off the streets and out of our parks. Those damn flicker outfits have even built more nickelodeons!"

Any film deal would have to be sweet in order to secure Dressler's involvement and keep her in that sleepy town. Sennett and Bauman agreed to give her a salary of $2,500 a week. The deal they struck, according to Marie, was a guarantee that the movie would be leased but never sold and they as producers would send her weekly statements. More important, she had half ownership in the movie and Jim was named publicist representative for Keystone. Since Marie had no stage offers, and she needed the money after her *Merry Gambol* losses, the negotiations were all the more attractive. She was finally seeing the possibility of monetary rewards in moviemaking. She wrote that "one hundred prints were made of each film and between ninety and ninety-five of these strips were running every day at $125 each, thus making the earning power of each individual film about $2,250 per day or about three quarters of a million per year."[18]

Marie claims in her autobiography to have selected Chaplin and Normand for *Tillie's Punctured Romance* and to have played a part in discovering Chaplin, but at the time of shooting he and Normand were already part of the Keystone ensemble. Chaplin's first year of making movies was 1914 and he was ridiculously prolific, turning out 32 one- and two-reelers for Keystone before starting *Tillie's Punctured Romance* in April. Any funny routine, it seemed, became a short movie, including early favorites such as *Twenty Minutes of Love, Dough and Dynamite,* and *Laughing Gas.*

Tillie's Punctured Romance was to have an unprecedented fourteen week shooting and editing schedule, rather than the typical one or two weeks. The movie posed a substantial financial risk to the young studio; several buildings were erected on the Keystone lot for the production and Marie's gargantuan salary commenced when she disembarked the train in Pasadena to begin shooting. The project was folly. Would audiences show up? Could people sit and laugh at moving images for almost 90 minutes? Would so much time watching "the flickers" harm the eyes?

Sennett was growing increasingly anxious, since his expensive star was drawing salary and his writers had yet to create a story for her. In a production meeting that went into the wee hours, scenario editor Craig Hutchison arrived at the inspiration of using the story line from *Tillie's Nightmare.* Sennett loved the idea and threw his best talent into the project, including writer Hampton Del Ruth, comics Mack Swain and Chester Conklin, and the entire lovable squad of Keystone Kops. Thanks to the efforts of his stage mother, six-year-old Milton Berle was cast as a newspaper seller.

World War I was unfolding through Europe during the planning and production of *Tillie's Punctured Romance.* Following the assassination of Franz Ferdinand and his wife in Saravejo, Austria-Hungary mistakenly believed the death was planned by the Serbian government. Tightly knit alliances designed to prevent war did just the opposite as Austria declared war on Serbia on July 28, Germany declared war on France on August 3, and Japan declared war on Germany on August 23. The first bomb fell on London on October 4. Americans watched the descent of Europe into chaos with detached horror. President Woodrow Wilson officially declared U.S. neutrality, a position supported by most Americans.

Marion de Lappe, the inexperienced *San Francisco Examiner* reporter who had interviewed Marie in 1911, had moved to Los Angeles in 1912 to do art work for Oliver Morosco. She had since married Robert Pike, a wealthy steel executive, and changed her nom de plume to Frances Marion.

She spent one casual Sunday sketching children at play in the old Mission district of Los Angeles.[19] Enjoying the shade of pepper and oleander trees, she noticed a large woman exiting a store with a bag of popcorn. The woman was soon using her stash to feed a swarm of pigeons. "Don't be so damned greedy!" she scolded. "Remember you're pigeons, not pigs."

On a second look, Frances saw that it was Marie. She was momentarily thrilled but concluded that Marie would not recognize her. Marie approached and struck up conversation as she would with a stranger. "I'm not really off my trolley," she said, glancing out from under a wide-brimmed hat. "I like birds. I talk to them. I have an old parrot, a regular scuzmullion — Say, aren't you the girl who interviewed me in San Francisco four or five years ago?"

Frances got up and said, "Yes, Miss Dressler, but I didn't dream you'd remember me."

"I'm not the forgetting type, I've often wondered what became of you. Hate to lose track of anybody I take a fancy to." Marie was hungry and suggested they go into "one of these little Mexican joints and have a tamale." They wound up at the intimate Señora Martinez's El Pajaro, where they caught up on each other's lives over spicy fare. "Now let's get down to cases," said Marie. "What are you doing in Los Angeles? Still reporting?"

"No, I flunked at that job. I'm a commercial artist."

"Sounds interesting," Marie interjected. "Not too exciting. Personally, I like excitement. I like a business where you're sitting in the middle of a cement mixer; noise, confusion and a nip of danger. The movies, for instance.... I've been kicked by a mule, tossed into a mudhole and had more pies aimed at my face than a bakery could sell in a month. The public expects that from comics like me and 'Fatty' Arbuckle and a little cross-eyed actor named Chester Conklin. Of course that young fellow you might have seen on the flicks, Charlie Chaplin, also comes in for some rough stuff. But he has his own particular style of comedy. He's a genius. ... A pretty young girl has an easier time of it, unless she is playing in a razzle-dazzle picture like the one we're making for Mack Sennett, then she also becomes a pie dodger. Mabel Normand's the girl I'm referring to. ... Whew! Who do you suppose invented this food, Satan? Next time I'll bring a fire extinguisher. Ever thought about going into the movies?"

Frances responded while Marie inhaled. "Do they use artists?" she asked.

"I mean to play in them. Be an actress. You've got the looks."

"Act!" Frances said. "I couldn't act if Svengali hypnotized me."

"Did you write up that interview I gave you?" Marie asked.

"I did, and it was wonderful material. ... but the editor said — because of the feud between you and Mr. Hearst that..."

"Isn't life a kick in the derrière?" Marie chortled. "Six months later I couldn't remember what the row was about. Neither could W. R. We've been the closest friends ever since. Believe me, that experience taught me a lesson; not to let yourself be eaten into by hate and anger. If you quietly close the door on folks you don't like, you can concentrate on those you love. Saves wear and tear on the human spirit. Fact is, if my heart gets any softer, I'll end up being kind to cockroaches."

Marie and Frances left the restaurant at dusk. They heard guitars strumming and the mission bell tolling as Marie urged Frances to stop by the Keystone studio. Perhaps she could help Frances land a job there.

Shooting of the movie took place agreeably under the working title *Dressler #1*. All three stars worked well together, though Dressler and Mabel Normand reportedly exchanged hot words over occupation of dressing room Number 1. Marie had few problems with her male costar but did take Sennett aside for one complaint about Chaplin's sartorial choices.[20] "I don't mind the same celluloid collar sixteen days in succession," she informed Sennett. "But I'm a mite squeamish about that same piece of decaying banana on the same collar for the past sixteen days. As a matter of fact, Mr. Sennett, if the banana is not removed, I shall enact you the goddamndest vomiting scene in the annals of the drammer."

At every turn, she exercised overwhelming authority and her acceptance of guidance from Sennett was limited. Since this was a screen treatment of her play, she had strong opinions on how the action should unfold. She had refused the casting suggestion of rotund comedian "Fatty" Arbuckle in the Chaplin role, fearing his bulk would compete with hers.[21] On the set, Sennett watched control of *Tillie's Punctured Romance* slip from his grasp. Later he wrote, "No matter that this was her first motion picture, she was a great star, this was her story, and she was inclined to remember me as an awkward boiler maker from Northampton."[22]

If Sennett was ineffectual and Marie was overbearing, Chaplin took an altogether different approach. He was not following the script and was leaving out many kicks, punches, and pratfalls.[23] "We can be funny without being punished too much," was his comment to Marie. She recalled the episode years later. "He was right. The picture was a scream largely because this solemn young clown, Charlie Chaplin, moved through it with sad mien and inexpressibly comic evolutions."

After the long shooting and editing, *Tillie's Punctured Romance* was repeatedly turned down for release. Its length was frightening both distributors and exhibitors, and it passed from one rejection to the next for months. In addition, financial backers Adam Kessel and Charlie Bauman grew mighty nervous when they realized that their distribution income would not even cover Marie's salary. *Tillie's* savior was early movie mogul Alexander Lichtman, former righthand man to exhibitor and Paramount Pictures founder Adolph Zukor. Lichtman observed that many producers such as Sennett were exploited when their films were sold to distributors. His opinion was that distributors and exhibitors should defer to the producers who, after all, keep the whole business going. Lichtman suggested that some of the country's leading movie theater owners form an organization that would partially finance the work of promising but cash-poor producers.[24] The theater owners in return would receive a steady flow of good pictures and a share of the producers' profit. Lichtman approached several of the nation's biggest names in the film business. All were interested, including former scrap-metal dealer Louis B. Mayer of Boston, who was looking to expand his young Louis B. Mayer Film Company. All accepted partnership immediately.

Lichtman called his organization Alco, short for Al's Company. He initially collected $150,000 from the founders and parceled it out in $15,000 bites to participating producers. One of those producers was Mack Sennett, and *Tillie's Punctured Romance* was sold to Alco.* The quality of Alco's first releases was uneven, but they made money. Alco might have enjoyed a long and profitable life, but poor management and a dubious financier sent the company into bankruptcy just a few months after it was formed. A dejected Lichtman returned to Zukor.

Despite the fate of Alco, its original members remained loyal to the idea and came together to salvage their business partnerships. In early 1915, several Alco founders met in New York and formed a new organization named Metro. Louis B. Mayer, the most influential man in Marie's later film career, was elected secretary. Alco, the company that sank despite its profitable features, would reassemble itself yet again in 1924 as Metro-Goldwyn-Mayer.

The plot of *Tillie's Punctured Romance* is silly enough, but it shows little resemblance to *Tillie's Nightmare*. Marie played Tillie Banks, an "innocent" Yokeltown farm girl "built like a battleship." She is corrupted by Chaplin's character, "the City Guy," a shameless gold-digger. He persuades Tillie to take her father's money and accompany him to the city, where an exciting new life awaits. At a nightclub, Tillie gets drunk while Charlie steals Tillie's money and leaves with "the Other Girl" (Normand). After time in jail for her drunken conduct, Tillie arrives at the mansion of her millionaire uncle Douglas Banks. She is ejected from his house and finds work as a waitress. Meanwhile, the uncle is presumed to have died in a mountain-climbing accident. Charlie and Mabel happened upon Tillie waitressing and

---

Among Alco's first releases were The Nightingale, *Ethel Barrymore's first film,* Michael Strogoff *with Yiddish theater star Jacob Adler,* The Vampire *with Olga Petrova,* Salomy Jane, *and* Tillie's Punctured Romance.

Entertaining at her uncle's mansion, Tillie is suspicious of the City Guy (Charlie Chaplin) and the Other Girl (Mabel Normand) in *Tillie's Punctured Romance*. (Courtesy of the Marie Dressler Foundation.)

soon after learn that Tillie is sole heir to Banks' estate. Charlie sneaks away from Mabel, courts Tillie all over again, and they are married immediately. Only then does Tillie learn of her inheritance. Occupying the mansion, the newlyweds throw a lavish party, but Mabel arrives disguised as a maid and, even more disruptive, Banks returns very much alive. Charlie and Mabel escape together, while Tillie, her uncle, and the Keystone Kops are on their trail for the last reel chase. The Kops and Tillie are thrown off a pier, and Mabel comes to Tillie's rescue. Charlie is rejected by both women, who embrace at the end and agree that life was better without him.

Tillie's Punctured Romance, ultratheatrical and wildly physical, was hailed "not without reason, as the funniest comedy ever filmed."[25] At every juncture, Marie earned her salary. Her costume for the elopement with Chaplin was one of her own creations: a modified adaptation of a clown's outfit, with low waist, huge buttons, and a hat resembling a chamber pot topped with a flower and bird. With her pachydermous behind forever getting in the way, one thrust in the wrong direction sent several mere mortals tumbling to the ground like bowling pins. When she learned that she was the inheritor of her uncle's $3 million estate, her face performed a phantasmagoria of expressions from shock to skepticism at Chaplin's sudden interest. Later, dressed in her "dancing frock" that resembled a slip over a Christmas tree, Tillie gyrated with startling abandon. When catching Charlie and Mabel in an embrace, she went on a pistol-wielding rampage through the mansion and out to the street. The *New York Dramatic Mirror*,[26] now reviewing movies to keep up with the times, chimed that Marie "is a brand new and extraordinary treat for picture audiences."

Tillie's Punctured Romance was finally released by the distribution company State Rights to record business in November of 1914. Normally staid critics joined in the fun. *Moving Picture World* wrote that "it is six thousand feet of undiluted joy. There is a 'laugh in every flicker,' not to mention a scream in every third one. If laughing really does put fat on the population of the United States, it will take on several tons in weight when this picture goes the rounds." *Variety* was very succinct, no more than a lengthy paragraph, but much of the praise was aimed at Marie:[27]

> Everything Miss Dressler does for public amusement runs to comedy. ... She is splendidly supported by the Keystone Company, including Charles Chaplin, Mabel Normand, Mack Sennett, Mack Swain and others. Miss Dressler is the central figure, but Chaplin's camera antics are an essential feature in putting the picture over. Mack Sennett directed the picture and right well has he done the job. Miss Dressler wears clothes that make her appear ridiculous. Furthermore she makes gestures and distorts her face in all directions, which help all the more. The picture runs a trifle too long, but the hilarious, hip-hurrah comedy finale is worth waiting for.

Even Thomas O'Day, an embittered business manager from the *Merry Gambol*–Gaiety Theater battle, enjoyed *Tillie's Punctured Romance* and agreed to screen it at his theater. "I'll tell you the reason I am letting this belligerent lady in my theater again," he said.[28] "The comedian [Chaplin] in the motion picture plot is continually kicking her. I am so ungallant as to enjoy the episodes."

While *Tillie's Punctured Romance* was doing impressive business in movie theaters and a war was being fought in Europe, Marie was back on stage. Her latest farce was alternately called *Angela's Substitute* or *The Sub* during its first rehearsals and it was warmly received in early performances in Cleveland. By the time it hit the 39th Street Theater in New York, Marie had two songs and the show was titled *A Mix Up*.

This was another Shubert production and past experience made the management nervous. The Shuberts wanted to avoid ambiguity and wrote two terse letters of agreement: Miss Dressler "is to receive a sum equal to fifteen percent of the gross receipts of the said play, should the gross receipts not exceed Five Thousand Dollars a week. ... Should the gross receipts per week exceed the sum of Five Thousand Dollars, then you shall receive a sum equal to twenty percent." To Jim they wrote, "We are to have sole charge of the management of the play and of the booking and you are to have no voice whatsoever in the management, control, operation or booking thereof." The couple signed both letters.[29]

A Mix Up, written by Parker A. Hord but substantially modified by Marie, was a modest hit.[30] It was filled with mistaken identity, plot complications, and broad farce designed to delight the most hardened audiences. As Gladys Lorraine, Marie proclaimed that her audiences should "smile awhile; and while you smile, others smile, and soon there'll be miles and miles and miles of smiles." *A Mix Up* also offered Marie the opportunity to show off her piano playing, though she sighed that "there isn't one person out of five hundred in the audience who believes that I am really playing the piano. They think that my piano is a dummy and that I have a confederate out in the wings during my musical work."[31] She dazzled audiences with her song "Sister Susie's Sewing Shirts for Soldiers" and its tongue-defying lyrics.

After delivering the song straight up, she then brought down the house by repeating it with a lisp. To conclude, Marie gave a curtain speech that foretold her imminent decline. One version of her delivery was printed in the *New York Herald*:[32] "Thank you for the success. We need it. I need it. You know, last summer I had a good think, during which I said to myself 'Marie, you've done this a lot of times. Can you do it again? Do you dare do it again? Do you know that there will be alot of gray heads out front that first saw you when you were knee high?' But I dared, after all, and that's the

An early ad for Marie's stage production *A Mix Up*. (Courtesy of the Shubert Archive.)

reason I thank you for this applause." The cast was just as affectionate to Marie, presenting her with a Persian gold bracelet at a dinner party at the Hotel Astor.[33]

With Marie's script doctoring and multiple tricks, *A Mix Up* did solid business on tour to Washington, Detroit, Pittsburgh, Buffalo, and Rochester with some onlookers proclaiming it funnier than *Tillie's Nightmare*. Though the material was decidedly stale, one reviewer[34] noted that "apparently her audiences will never tire of her antics and her popularity is everlasting." The comment proved to be a cruel irony in retrospect, considering that *A Mix Up* was Marie's last starring Broadway appearance.

A Mix Up toured in early 1915 while Marie was avidly pursuing more film work. Jim proved to be as ill equipped for farm living as Marie and both decided to scale back their Vermont empire. They had already sold the cows and taken a loss, and next went the Shetland ponies.[35] Marie told the newspapers that she had left the Oasis in the trust of a caretaker and was looking for less draining accommodations closer to New York, perhaps something in Westchester County.

Outside in Betzwood, Pennsylvania, for the shooting of *Tillie's Tomato Surprise* in 1915, director Howell Hansel supervises the hoisting of Marie over a fence as the cameraman awaits instructions.

Marie's attention was now on the movies. Before *Tillie's Punctured Romance*, her attitude to moviemaking had been more aligned with Oliver Morosco's ("those damn flicker outfits"). It was quite different after. She was a convert to "the flickers" by the completion of her first *Tillie* movie. She wrote warmly of the making of *Tillie's Punctured Romance* and of Chaplin, Normand, and Sennett. The film taught her a lesson in the power of moving pictures, their ability to preserve a performance forever and their simultaneous effect on far-flung audiences.

By 1914 the movies had grown into a medium challenging vaudeville. *Tillie's Punctured Romance* demonstrated that audiences could sit and laugh at a movie for more than one hour. Employment for comedy players, with fans who might never see actors in person, added to the new medium's attraction. Real stories could be told at full length, and for an actress of Marie's fortitude, the possibilities were enticing.

Marie and Jim agreed that another avenue for future success was giving the public more of Tillie. "How she loves that name!" chimed Cleveland critic and perennial fan Archie Bell.[36] In June and July of 1915, this time with the Sigmund Lubin Manufacturing Company rather than Keystone, Marie made the six-reel *Tillie's Tomato Surprise*. She and Jim fashioned a contract more comfortable than the one negotiated with the Shuberts for *A Mix Up*.[37] Transportation costs for Marie and her maid Mamie in first class-drawing rooms were to be covered by Lubin. Marie's name was to appear three times as large as any other in all advertising. With Jim named as manager, the books of accounting were to be kept in his office, with profits split down the middle between Lubin and "the Daltons." This was agreeable to both parties, at least for a time. A few months later, in a move no doubt exasperating to Lubin, Marie sent a letter to him detailing method of payment and voiding all previous contracts as "discharged and considered of no effect."[38]

The plot of *Tillie's Tomato Surprise* was even loopier than that of *Tillie's Punctured Romance*.[39] Tomboy Tillie Toddles gives her rich Aunt Sally a cheap tomato pincushion for her birthday, announcing that she made it by hand. Cousin Percy knows it was storebought and tells Aunt Sally, hoping to win a sizable portion of the eccentric lady's estate. Aunt Sally meanwhile takes flight in a newly invented contraption and disappears. She is declared dead and her estate goes largely to her pet monkey, James, and upon his death to Percy. So Percy plans to frame Tillie for James' untimely death. The police go after Tillie, and Aunt Sally returns from the dead. The ugly tomato pincushion is in Tillie's possession and upon ripping it open she discovers $1 million inside. Along the way, Marie manages entanglements with a turnstile at a football stadium. She sits on a bass drum and falls through it. On the way home, she falls off a donkey cart. She even dons a uniform and proceeds to play football, reducing her opponents to "hors de combat." *Tillie's Tomato Surprise* also required Marie to ride horseback, which she took up "with an enthusiasm which can only be estimated by the inverse ratio of gloom in the horse kingdom."⁴⁰ Additional scenes had her falling downstairs, sent airborne, hoisted over a fence by a derrick, shot at by guns and bows and arrows, dipped in molasses, and pushed through a brick wall. "I have been baked, fried and stewed — not the kind of stew you think I mean — and all in the cause of art."⁴¹

When shooting was completed on the Lubin ranch in Betzwood, Pennsylvania, Marie took her bruises to the rambling Gedney Farms Hotel in White Plains, New York, for a respite.⁴² She was still there when a final edited copy of the movie was ready and arranged for a screening. Surrounded by admiring vacationers, Marie endured the utterly novel and eerie experience of watching herself move in black and white.

Marie with her untutored opinions had undergone another transformation. No more did she believe women were meant to stay at home while men attended to duties requiring haler constitutions. Perhaps to stay in favor with high society's liberal women, she was now a bonafide champion of women's suffrage and made impassioned arguments to the men trying to relax at Gedney Farms. "As for women

Frances Marion, circa 1915. (Courtesy of Cari Beauchamp.)

holding office — most assuredly," she proclaimed.⁴³ "I believe not so much in one sex in advance of another as in their standing shoulder to shoulder. I would like to see this country have a man president and a woman vice-president, a man governor and a woman lieutenant governor, a man mayor and a woman president of the board." She predicted women's vote would triumph in the New York state elections of November 1915, but victory was not to happen for another two years.

Frances didn't make it to Keystone and the *Tillie's Punctured Romance* set to visit Marie, but she did land an excellent job in the movies. She was writing scenarios for the New Jersey–based World Pictures when she and Marie met for dinner at the Algonquin Hotel. Carrying on like old friends catching up, they were settling into a lobby couch when Marie said,⁴⁴ "Now start from the beginning and if I interrupt like I always do, just step on my foot to shut me up. I got a bunion that hurts if an ant walks on it." As Frances began, Marie broke in and regaled her with tales from *Tillie's Tomato*

Surprise. Then, overcome with a need for attention, Marie honked out a verse of "Heaven Will Protect the Working Girl" at full volume. She was soon surrounded by autograph seekers and when they left, Marie thrust her foot closer to Frances and said, "Now concentrate on my bunion and don't let me interrupt again." Frances finally spoke of her rising fortunes and of an imminent deal with Fox Studios. "I'm going over tomorrow to sign on the dotted line," she said.

"Soak them for it," advised Marie. "The more they pay for anything, the better they think it is."

"I might lose the deal," said a still modest Frances.

"Sissybritches," countered Marie. "Have you forgotten already how you landed the World Film job? Pull the trigger the moment you step into the office. They're used to being fired on." Frances took Marie's advice and was handed a $5,000 contract.

Tillie's Tomato Surprise did not enjoy the great business or critical response given to *Tillie's Punctured Romance,* but Dressler was praised. *Motion Picture World*[45] declared that "Miss Dressler is, as far as I know, without a peer anywhere. The picture is a litany of laughs." Another reviewer[46] marveled that "for a woman as large as she is and one who has lost the resiliency of youth she takes some risks that are thrilling and nerve wracking to say the least. Such little things as being thrown head foremost from an automobile into a thicket of underbrush, jumping from a bridge on to a moving freight train and then jumping off from the train into a bin filled with goose feathers, she executes with the nonchalance of an athletic young school girl ... and she is laughably funny." In the days when movie comedy was being invented, clichés came early and Marie was proud that her new project avoided policemen, telephones, and seltzer bottles and gave "the public something new in the line of vegetables, if not of photoplays."[47]

No matter Marie's assessment, *Variety*[48] stated that the movie contained "about the most conventional plot ever employed. [There is] no photography of note and absolutely no 'class' to the picture." The scenario for these not-too-well received shenanigans was written by Acton Davies, known primarily as author and theater critic for the *New York Evening Sun.* Film farce was new territory for him. The absence of the great comic pair of Charlie Chaplin and Mabel Normand, and Davies' inexperience at comedy, contributed to a dwindling of on-screen charm.

By 1915 Chaplin had abandoned Keystone and signed with Essanay Studios. He was perfecting the tramp and beginning his great ascent to celluloid immortality. In contrast, Marie was mired in legal and financial problems with few accompanying professional rewards. The Keystone-Alco negotiations for *Tillie's Punctured Romance* left her out in the cold, and she sued the Keystone Film Company for its accounting of the film's revenue.[49] She was additionally ired that Jim's involvement in distribution was neutered when Kessel and Bauman sold the film to Alco. Where was all the money she was promised? She testified that her contract provided her with half the film's profits and that owner company Alco announced a profit of $122,000 while she had seen not a penny of it. She further claimed that Alco devised a plan to sell the film without her consent. Not so, claimed attorneys for the now-bankrupt company. The case went to the New York State Supreme Court for a nine-day trial. The jury found something less than fraud in Keystone's bookkeeping but decided that Marie and Jim were entitled to half of the net profits based on accounting by Keystone to be approved by the court. Marie and Jim won a $50,000 settlement, but relations remained strained.[50] She even sued Nathan Goldberger, the lawyer who represented her in the case, for $5,000. With the financial rights of *Tillie's Punctured Romance* hopelessly convoluted, Marie never again worked at Keystone or with Mack Sennett.

In the spring of 1916, Marie had a small role on stage in *Sweet Genevieve* as a nurse from the psychopathic ward of Bellevue Hospital. She treats a wealthy patient at a health farm in the country and sang one ballad that closed the first act. Yet again, stage business expected her to exemplify the funny fat lady. She brought laughs to the scene that called for a tree to topple under her weight, but the show closed quickly. The fat lady jokes were getting old, and *Sweet Genevieve*, written by Marie's good friend James Forbes, didn't last long.

In August Marie announced that she was forming a production company for the purpose of cranking out two-reel comedies starring herself.[51] With Marie, Jim, and thick-skinned, churlish World Pictures producer William A. Brady as officers, the Marie Dressler Motion Picture Company filed its papers of incorporation and was born in Albany. Beginning with $10,000 in capital, 12 movies were to be produced by the company and distributed by Mutual Film Corporation. Charlie Chaplin's brilliant movies were being distributed by Mutual in 1916 and one headline wondered if Marie would rise to his accomplishments. Marie's first short films for Mutual, *Tillie's Day Off*, *Tillie's Divorce Case*, and *Elopement*, were released in 1916 and failed to generate much excitement. More would appear over the following two years, but they did little to spur interest in the aging comedienne. The security of a long-term contract and widespread public popularity on the scale of a Charlie Chaplin or a Mary Pickford were to elude her.

World Pictures was willing to go another round with Tillie in *Tillie's Night Out*, Marie's third full-length film. With Frances as the scenarist, Marie was delighted to be working on a project with her for the first time. The title became *Tillie Wakes Up*, since the movie's action revolved around Coney Island in midday.[52] *Tillie Wakes Up* begins with J. Mortimer Pipkins (Johnny Hines) and Tillie Tinkelpaw (Marie) fed up with the ill treatment given them by their respective spouses. Pipkins takes his wife's money, while the neglected Tillie vows to live it up when her husband is away. The two run off to Coney Island for a wild time, and after a chase they make up with their mates.

Tillie's Tomato Surprise may have included more dangerous stunts, but *Tillie Wakes Up* nearly killed Marie. Frances' scenario called for Marie and Hines to drive a car to Coney Island beach and into the water. Marie recalled that the car[53] "was put on a raft and we were towed out quite a distance and turned loose. Johnny was on the front seat and I was in the back. After we had floated for some time we felt the car toppling and Hines jumped. This upset the car and I found myself being closed into the hood which frightened me extremely. I finally managed to extricate myself and dived to the bottom. Fortunately I headed for land without knowing it."

On September 1, after filming at Coney Island, Frances and Marie drove back to Frances' hotel. It had been an unusually happy day with Marie entertaining children in the park. At the hotel, the two women found a telegram announcing that Frances' older sister Maude, a beautiful and well-respected musician from Oakland, had committed suicide by gunshot.[54]

Frances was taken to the hospital in nervous and physical collapse and remained there for one week. Marie visited every day. Sometimes she just held her hand, sang songs, delivered homemade food, or softly read to her. When Frances was released from the hospital, she continued to convalesce at the farm in Vermont. Marie was growing increasingly anxious about cash flow, but she didn't share her worries. Instead, she cared for her with all the tender concern of a loving mother. Frances sums up the dark time: "I think that I would have been finished if it hadn't been for Marie."

During her stay at the farm, Frances came to realize that this maternal friend 20 years her senior needed some motherly advice herself. Frances could not figure out how Marie supported the unproductive Oasis on her irregular income. And she was none too fond of Jim.[55] "His courtly manners ... made me uneasy; they seemed studied rather than from the heart out," she wrote.

After the cow and pony sales, Marie could not bring herself to sell or slaughter her remaining animals. "I wouldn't dream of chopping off the heads of my feathered friends," she said.[56] "It makes me shudder to think of it. I even refuse to sell them for fear they'll be killed."

The Vermont Oasis that *Tillie* bought but Marie could not sustain.

"How about the pigs?" asked Frances.

"Pigs!" screamed Marie. "Is there anything cuter than a little brood of pigs?"

Frances resorted to sarcasm. "A farmer is supposed to live off his farm. Maybe you should turn vegetarian. Or can you bring yourself to bite off the heads of your dear little onions and radishes?"

Marie gave Frances the fisheye. "You're worried about me. I can hear it behind your kidding. ... Time will prove that I'm absolutely on the right track." Frances was not convinced, and she wrote that she felt "uneasy about this big hearted woman. How often we have premonitions, almost clairvoyantly seeing the path that lies ahead for those we love, long before they have even mapped out its route."[57]

By November, with *Tillie Wakes Up* finished and ready for release, Dressler was on stage in New York in a new revue called *The Century Girl*. Featuring songs by young Irving Berlin, produced by the formidable team of Florenz Ziegfeld and Charles Dillingham and enlivened by an all-star cast, the revue had Marie performing a song specialty in the last act that included a belly-flop slide headfirst down a manufactured mountain slope.

The producers were not amused. They dropped her from the lineup after three performances by announcing that "in the necessity of eliminating certain scenes from *The Century Girl* in order to shorten an overlong performance, Miss Marie Dressler has retired from the cast."[58] Marie wasn't too upset; she felt that her act was pretty rotten anyway. Dillingham and Ziegfeld also had a valid point — opening night began at 8:25 P.M. and ended at 12:58 A.M. Sime Silverman, the droll cofounder of *Variety* magazine, noted that "as there are only ninety or one hundred minutes to be taken out, [*The Century Girl*] doesn't require much of a knife, just a hydraulic dredge."[59] With machetelike pruning, the show was shortened to a manageable length and went on to be a hit in Marie's absence, prompting Silverman to declare that "it's the biggest thing of its kind New York has ever seen, and no one will side step it. No one can afford to."

Marie could have been embittered by the *Century Girl* setback, but Dillingham's good nature kept the two cordial. Soon after the firing, Marie was driving near suburban White Plains, New York, and nearly collided with him.[60]

Marie had heard that Dillingham had recently bought exclusive real estate with his *Century Girl* profits. She wished to make agreeable small talk, but she unwittingly set him up for a punchline. "I hear they're thinking of putting your name in the Social Register, now that you've got a place with a lake on it."

"Lake! Sure I have one, Marie, but some sneak came along with a sponge and stole it." Such corny humor won Marie over, and she decided that Dillingham was a gentleman after all.

She also had a grand time in New York City with Frances just as *Tillie Wakes Up* was released. They joined their mutual friend Enrico Caruso backstage at the Met when he appeared in *Carmen*. He got the idea to put them in costumes and let them sing in the chorus. Caruso "sneaked up behind Marie and gave her a pinch on her bottom while he was singing an aria."[61] Frances laughed at "the squawk she made, wanting to be heard."

In *Tillie Wakes Up*, movie audiences got their first taste of Marie's potential for drama. Crushed by her husband's thoughtlessness, Marie as the neglected wife cries over a table into a cup of tea. The inner parts of her eyebrows went up as the outer corners of her mouth went down in a broadly mimed indication of sorrow. To simulate Tillie's growing agitation, she confused the functions of toast and a handkerchief. As Pipkins, Hines made "an excellent foil to Tillie's elephantine antics,"[62] while "everyone remembers with affection the Tillie who had a nightmare and exhibitors in advertising this picture should connect the name of Marie Dressler with this uproariously successful farce of the vintage of 1910. ... The combination of Coney Island and Marie Dressler provides enough comedy to pack and overflow the prescribed five reels." Taking a cue from Keystone, the plot becomes a mere convenience on which to hang a wide variety of silly happenings. At Coney Island, the hapless couple is bombarded by bumper cars, a manufactured cyclone, and a revolving barrel. Hines was a lithe and appealing actor, but he was no Chaplin, and in *Tillie Wakes Up*, one senses a comedy style suffering creative exhaustion.

Tillie Wakes Up was Marie's last full-length movie for ten years. Unknown to her at the time, her miserable professional drought had begun. As her 50th birthday loomed, audiences changed. The youth culture was gaining strength, and Marie's brand of humor looked evermore corny. Work for older clowns was increasingly rare. Legal problems and creative shortfall only exacerbated Marie's plight. By 1917, it appeared clear that her silent film career, so strongly associated with *Tillie's Punctured Romance,* would never realize the potential of its beginnings. She may have sensed the changes in public taste. As no stage opportunities were forthcoming, and partly to save face, Marie repeatedly claimed in interviews and to friends that her priority was filmmaking. One may be tempted to attribute this to a stage career that had floundered badly since *A Mix Up* in 1914. Certainly her ample ego and pride skewed her self-knowledge. But her sincere love and longing for a film career had been revealed in the *New York Dramatic Mirror*, when she had still been flush with the success of *Tillie's Punctured Romance*:[63]

> Why, I would rather play for the five cent audience any day than any two dollar audience you can give me. It is our five cent audience who fills our libraries and our art museums. When I want a lot of personal applause, I can engage some ballroom at the Plaza or Ritz-Carlton, say, and play and sing to my friends. But these will never mean to me what it will when ten, maybe twenty years from now one who sees me now will go to look at my moving pictures. That is work worthwhile; it is registered for posterity to really see, not just hear about according to the vagary of someone else's memory.

President Wilson had hoped for an end to the killing in Europe to prevent American intervention. The United States was then a third-string military power, and yet pressure for American involvement increased from the Allies as the war dragged on. Americans, in response, were reluctant. "There will be no war," Wilson said on January 4, 1917.[64] "This country does not intend to become involved in this war. It would be a crime against civilization for us to go in."

The German submarine offensive against England and other Allies virtually assured U.S. participation. Public mood changed; the popular Al Bryan song "I Didn't Raise My Boy to Be a Soldier" gave way to George M. Cohan's rousing "Over There." When Czar Nicholas II of Russia abdicated on March 15, Wilson declared that the autocracy had been "shaken off" and the "great, generous Russian people [had been added] to the forces that are fighting for freedom in the world."[65] The United States ostensibly joined the same fight by declaring war on Germany on April 6, the same day that Austria-Hungary declared war on the United States. Wilson raised a host of moral imperatives for his provincial nation unaccustomed to transcontinental combat. "There is not a single selfish element, so far as I can see, in the cause we are fighting for. We are fighting for what we believe and wish to be the rights of mankind and for the future peace and security of the world."[66]

With her work in films and on stage uncertain, Dressler discovered latent patriotism. A conflict this enormous merited her attention and engaged her steely righteousness. She may also have seen an opportunity to coast on her celebrity as stage and movie offers evaporated. Thanks to the Keystone-Alco settlement money, she didn't need work right away and certainly didn't need the embarrassment of another *Sweet Genevieve* or *Century Girl*. Despite her confessed love of movies, Marie took an indifference to her career during the war. She may have even enjoyed watching it grow moribund as the war was so consuming. She and Jim had been vacationing in Europe after Frances' convalescence and the making of *Tillie Wakes Up*. With the April 6, 1917, declaration, they took a steamer home immediately.

Dressler was later to note that her life divides into three parts. Part one ended with the war. "I had been a hoyden," she wrote.[67] "I had had responsibility, but it had not sobered me. ... For thirty years, America had looked at me. Now I looked at America. ... And what I saw there made me burn with a passion to give, give, give! I began to live for others, and all unwittingly to find my own soul."

Chapter 7

Give Till It Hurts

Dressler was dedicated to the war before America's official involvement. By February 1916 she had already appeared at 30 benefits.[1] At an ongoing bazaar in New York, she purchased several lottery tickets every day for donated prizes on behalf of the Allies, but she never won. Hoping to get *something*, she entered a dance contest and did a mad foxtrot with a doctor named Horace Fletcher. While lottery winners took home silver, typewriters, a piano, and a Packard automobile, she and Fletcher were the proud winners of a pair of goats.[2] They were immediately named Marie and Horace.

Meanwhile, litigation for Marie and Jim seemed never to end.[3] In May 1917, after returning from Europe, they were sued by two actresses. The plaintiffs claimed that Marie and Jim had sold them worthless stock in Yulida Copper, Jim's Nevada mine. They took the besieged couple to the New York State Supreme Court and were awarded damages totaling $6,300. Marie also lost a judgment of $800 that she failed to pay.[4] By 1919 the *New York Times* noted[5] that she might go to jail if payments continued to be delinquent. Neither she nor Jim went to jail, but they did suffer a string of public embarrassments, including a failed $3,850 court battle in 1914.[6]

Two years later, Marie appeared in the suffragette charity opera *Melinda and Her Sisters,* which included a song for Marie called "Ballet Russe," written by Elsa Maxwell.[7] Society friend Alva E. Belmont, tireless campaigner for women's vote and "originator" of *Melinda and Her Sisters,* produced the event at the ballroom of the Waldorf-Astoria. She exhibited her gratitude to Marie as director by giving her a lovely parasol as a goodwill gift. Then Belmont demanded that Marie return the "Ballet Russe" music after the performance, as she had exclusive ownership. Marie countered, claiming that she had witnesses to Maxwell's agreement that the song belonged to her. The matter, replied Belmont, was "in the hands of [my] lawyer."

Marie wasn't about to be cowed by Belmont. She paid a visit to Belmont's Georgian manse at East 51st Street and Madison Avenue, the gift parasol in hand. After she rang the front doorbell, a turbaned major-domo answered.

"Do you know me?" asked Marie.

"Certainly, Miss Dressler," replied the turbaned one.

Handing him the parasol, she asked "will you return this to Mrs. Alva Economical—I never knew what that E stood for before—Belmont with my compliments?" Millionaire Belmont apparently forgot that Marie had given her the selfsame parasol last Christmas.

Belmont relented; Marie did not return the music and she sang the song again at another benefit one month later. A poor southerner by pedigree, Belmont made a name for herself by first marrying William K. Vanderbilt and then Oliver Hazard Perry Belmont, a millionaire banker and keeper of fine horses. She then steered her way through New York's society by extravagant entertaining and passionate activism. Aided by Belmont's considerable efforts, New York State at last said yes to suffragettes in November of 1917. It had been a hard battle. Many other states had approved women's right to vote; Montana had already elected Jeannette Rankin as the first woman to join the House of Representatives. Belmont was front and center for the efforts in New York; she was no one to underestimate. She and Marie never mended their friendship, and Belmont's ingratitude temporarily soured Marie to society hobnobbing. Marie felt wholly justified in fighting, but she didn't necessarily come off as the moral victor. Her career had noticeably ebbed as Belmont went on to be president of the National Women's Party.

Dressler experienced peculiar years in 1917, 1918, and 1919, as the war, romance, upside-down career moves, and oscillating finances turned her life into an absurd comedy-drama. She was never more foolish with her money and she was never more charitable. Under Jim's management, her money was mishandled and her professional decisions were inconsistent and naive. The circumstances were coming together for a miserable emotional, financial, and professional drought that would consume her in the 1920s.

During the war, Marie found some rare time with Jim on the Vermont farm. They both conducted themselves publicly as Mr. and Mrs., but the lie was wearing on Marie. She had given him large sums of money to aid his efforts to divorce his wife. When was it going to be official? How much more money was needed to avoid Marie being named a correspondent in the divorce? As Marie ran out of patience, Jim announced that the investment had paid off, the divorce would soon be final, and that they would be free to marry.

Marie was overjoyed at the news and full of schoolgirlish glee at her romance and upcoming union. She tore herself away from the farm and made a trip to New York without Jim to visit Frances, who was returning to Los Angeles to write movies for the new sensation Mary Pickford. When Marie and Frances reunited, Frances felt free to express her fears that Marie was too careless with her money and her career.

As she had in the past, Marie dismissed the concerns.[8] "I've never been so secure, Frances, as all my present and future interests are in the capable hands of a man who sincerely cares for me. ... We intend to be married just as soon as he can get away from —"

Frances interjected "—the wife who doesn't appreciate him?"

"Exactly."

The details of Marie and Jim's "marriage" will never be known.[9] He lied to the press in 1914 when he announced that he had been sued for divorce in 1905 and that he and Marie were already married. He eventually delivered the good news to Marie, announcing that his divorce from Elizabeth was final. He and Marie planned to sail off to London, where she could perform a new comedy show and get hitched. With a minister Jim had found, they were "married" in a small ceremony. "I wanted to cable my joy to [my friends, but Jim] insisted we keep it hush-hush, afraid the American press would take a whack at me for breaking up a home."[10] She and Jim would also be obliged to craft an explanation for doing business as husband and wife for several years before their English wedding. They both agreed to stay quiet. When Marie suggested they return to the States and spend a subdued honeymoon on the farm, Jim suggested they sell it and invest in producing more shows in

London. That city, he felt, was a safe long-term investment, since he was certain the English theatergoers had forgotten the 1909 performance debacle. Marie would effectively double her market by playing England and the United States on stage while continuing to pursue film work.

Though she loved the farm and loved her animals, Marie could not deny that the enterprise had become a money-eating albatross. She spent little time there and lacked the discipline for the demands of farm life. Jim convinced her to divest. She was "happy as happy can be, matrimonially speaking."[11] Only later would she correctly identify herself at this time as "a blind, happy fool." By the time of that later statement, the farm had been sold and the proceeds had been spent.

In the early days of America's involvement in the war, various New York society women coordinated relief work. "We started shops and sold whatever we could," said Anne Morgan,[12] one of the prime organizers. Marie joined the effort and was an instant success. "Every day Marie would appear," said Morgan. "As soon as she came in, it was like a dynamo charging the room. She could take the worst contributions we had and sell them." Marie seemed to be everywhere, appearing at dinners, auctions, and raffles. She sold produce at the Washington Square Neighborhood Garden Party to benefit the National League for Women's Service.[13] She reportedly entertained with a benefit dog show on Long Island hosted by flamboyant millionaire Frederick E. Lewis.[14]

During her work in a charity clothing store, Marie met Hallie Phillips, a woman of rare good humor who became her closest East Coast friend.[15] While they were both working, a "rawboned Irish woman" was perusing the racks and lit upon a showy, blue-sequined gown from Paris.

"Isn't that a lovely thing?" said Hallie. "I don't mind telling you that that dress is one which belonged to Mrs. [socially prominent] so-and-so."

The potential buyer turned the dress over, examined a few key spots and said, "Well, she sweats the same as another, it seems, and I wouldn't be wantin' it." Marie was standing nearby and overheard the comment. She guffawed so hard that she pulled an entire rack of clothes over and buried Hallie and herself underneath the load.

"We emerged friends," said Hallie. They frequently socialized, dined, and traveled together, with or without the company of Jim and Hallie's husband Robert. "Things just happen to Marie and me," said Hallie. "Without any preparation that we can remember we find ourselves on the boat for Europe. ... But wherever we are we always seem to laugh until actually we are thrown out of dignified restaurants." Marie snuck away from New York with another friend, actress May Robson, for a brief trip to England and a visit with sister and brother-in-law Bonita and Richard Ganthony. Traveling by cattle boat, they arrived in London with a local wag noting "a cargo of cows and May Robson and Marie Dressler arrived yesterday from New York."[16]

Marie's charities overshadowed her paying work.[17] She had the bright idea to buy a failed shoe factory, take home the inventory, and invite the destitute to each take a pair. Unfortunately, her benefactors were not content with shoes alone and denuded Marie and Jim's flat of "everything except the linoleum." One poor family really grabbed her emotions. She had visited them more than once and on one occasion delivered some clothes and groceries. The mother had been ill and when Marie arrived one day she found the husband and children sobbing over her lifeless body. They had no money to bury her, and so Marie gave them several hundred dollars. The family kissed her and called her a saint. On the street, she realized she had forgotten her umbrella. She tiptoed back inside, careful not to disturb the grieving family. Once there, she saw the corpse counting the loot for her funeral.

For her part in the war effort, Marie had wanted to go to France as an entertainer for the allied fighters, but she wound up singing at various domestic training camps instead.[18] Her efforts were recognized when one of the first detachments to land in France named a street and a cow after her. Marie humbly wrote that "the reason for the first compliment still eludes me."

The times were exhausting. Dressler shuttled between London, movie sets, and a cross-country Liberty Loan drive for war bonds over a two- to three-year period. She and Jim also used the floundering Marie Dressler Motion Picture Company to find and produce work for its titled owner.

A few short films emerged from the corporation in 1917 and 1918, including *The Scrublady, Fired,* and *The Agonies of Agnes*. *The Scrublady* was a two-reeler Dressler production made under a new and exclusive contract with the Samuel Goldwyn Company. She put on a long, black, curly wig, a dainty apron, and a ribbon with "Sanitary Squad" emblazoned across her bosom. She entertains a male visitor by changing into various costumes and characters and doing a silly dance for each: the Turk, Society Girl, Hula Girl, and Girl Scout. The finale includes a chase through a bomb factory for hidden money and munitions followed by the requisite explosion.

Fired was also produced by Goldwyn and released in December 1917 through World Pictures, the same company behind *Tillie Wakes Up*. Marie once again plays a Tilliesque over-aged maiden brought down by temptation. *Fired* "begins with the ejection of that celebrated character for the 'steenth' time in her rather checkered career, from the hash foundry operated by Simon Legree."[19] Marie wrote the *Fired* script and confessed to her improvisational acting method:[20] "I find that this game of nip-and-tuck with which I had the pleasure of having a hand in in the old days (of Weber and Fields) helps me beyond measure in my motion picture work. Directors have complained that I don't follow their scenarios, but they've been obliged to agree when I finished a picture that there were some funny situations they hadn't thought of." *The Agonies of Agnes,* a burlesque treatment of *The Perils of Pauline* with Pearl White, appeared in February 1918 at New York's Strand Theater. World released the film from Marie's production company, with the *New York Times*[21] stating that "Miss Dressler's size and facial expressions are capitalized to the amusement of the audience."

Marie had fun making these movies, though they weren't very good. "I love the photoplay because it is creative," she said.[22] "Every moment there is something new, every moment we create, we build, we make something out of nothing." Despite her enthusiasm, the short comedies did not advance her career, nor did they make great sums of money for backers Samuel Goldwyn, World Pictures, and Mutual. The Marie Dressler Production Corporation stopped producing and the promised stream of *Tillie* movies went dry.

Everything took a back seat to the war, which brought Marie out of the self-absorption of show business and into a world conflict. The United States government needed money fast. Tax hikes were as unpopular an option as ever, and so the idea of selling bonds as a loan to the government took hold. The loans began at a low percentage rate so as not to catastrophically alter the investment habits of Americans and throw the economy into chaos. The first loan drive, scheduled for May and June, had a $2 billion goal, paying 3.5 percent interest. "The great bond issue which will soon be offered to the public will be known as Liberty Loan of 1917. The two billion raised by this loan is for the purpose of waging war against autocracy," announced William Gibbs McAdoo, President Wilson's shrewd secretary of the treasury.[23] With the government pledging to repay its citizens over succeeding generations, the Liberty Loan bill easily passed in Congress and was signed by Wilson.

McAdoo knew what was needed. "Any great war must necessarily be a popular movement. It is a kind of crusade; and, like all crusades, it sweeps along on a powerful stream of romanticism."[24] McAdoo orchestrated a plea to all Americans for moral, physical, and financial support. "We went direct to the people; and that means to everybody — to businessmen, workmen, farmers, bankers, millionaires, school teachers, laborers. We capitalized on the profound impulse called patriotism. It is the quality of coherence that holds a nation together; it is one of the deepest and most

At the commencement of a Liberty Loan drive, a heavily bloomed Marie kneels down beside Charlie Chaplin, with Franklin D. Roosevelt, Douglas Fairbanks, and Mary Pickford behind.

powerful of human motives."[25] Dissenters were silenced. When Senator Warren G. Harding called the loan drive "hysterical and unseemly," he was verbally assaulted by his colleagues.[26]

The propaganda machine started rolling, and it was fierce and effective. One Liberty Loan poster featured a drawing of New York City engulfed in blazing orange flames and a decapitated Statue of Liberty with the reminder "That Liberty Shall Not Perish from the Earth; Buy Liberty Bonds." The most indelible marketing image was Uncle Sam (U.S.) and his pointing finger accompanied by the slogan "I Want You." With such potent new symbols, the government was wildly successful at recruiting young men as soldiers and at raising money. The second Liberty Loan drive, in October 1917, aimed at $3 billion and raised more than $4.5 billion.

No one was a more idealistic mouthpiece to the government's efforts than Marie. She believed citizens had more than an opportunity, they had an obligation to give back to their country in a crisis. She found her niche as the Liberty Loan drive's most ebullient spokesperson. She was swept along with the rampant anti–German sentiment and embarked on a punishing speaking schedule full of fiery oratory:[27] "Every person who refuses to subscribe or who takes the attitude of let the other fellow do it, is a friend of Germany and I would like nothing better than to tell it to him to his face."

Marie was a frequent visitor to the Wilson White House during her Liberty Loan work. Though he was a great fan of the cinema, Marie found the president to be cold and unapproachable.[28] She got on better with General John Joseph "Black Jack" Pershing, commander of the American Expeditionary Force in Europe.[29] When the two of them spoke at a rally, several in the throng shouted, "Pershing for president! Pershing for president!" which was countered by, "Marie Dressler for vice president!" Marie made her ambitions clear. "If you go to the White House, I will go, too," she told him. "I could see right there that his hopes were blasted. He never seemed to take any interest in the nomination after that," she wrote.

Marie and Jim had moved from their expensive Upper West Side apartment to more modest housing on East 40th Street. Marie was frequently out of town, and her costs rose to dizzying amounts, considering the "requirements" for life on the road with a major star. She was financing her trips with money from the sale of the farm and paying all of her and her entourage's expenses as well. She took over an entire train car wherever she went, and during the second Liberty Loan drive she kept the following inventory:[30]

> Item: Marie Dressler.
> Item: One Japanese butler, who stammers, but is otherwise undamaged.
> Item: One French maid who speaks French.
> Item: One secretary (feminine).
> Item: One parrot, taught to talk by the Jap and the maid.
> Item: One canary bird, which took music lessons from Marie herself.
> Item: 14 trunks.
> Item: etcetera.

Marie met Assistant Secretary to the Navy Franklin D. Roosevelt during the third Liberty Loan drive in the spring of 1918 and immediately liked him.[31] In Washington on April 18, she and Charlie Chaplin spoke with him at a large football field. Chaplin told Roosevelt that he wasn't used to public speeches and the whole affair made him quite nervous. Roosevelt said, "There's nothing to be scared about. Just give it to them from the shoulder; tell them to buy their Liberty bonds; don't try to be funny."

"Don't worry!" said Chaplin.

The speakers' platform was made of crude boards adorned with flags and bunting. When Chaplin heard his name, he bounded to the platform and let fly with a breathless speech: "The Germans are at your door! We've got to stop them! And we will stop them if *you* buy Liberty bonds! Remember, each bond you buy will save a soldier's life — a mother's son! — will bring this war to an early victory!" By this time, Chaplin's remarks were so impassioned that he toppled off the platform, grabbed Marie and took her with him as they both landed on top of Roosevelt.

The stars did not always travel together. More often Douglas Fairbanks and Mary Pickford covered the northern states and Chaplin went south. Marie, snubbed by Fairbanks as a has-been, did not have a specific geographic region but rather went all over the nation. Wherever Marie went, she was met by governors, suffragettes, and various civic dignitaries. Throngs gathered at the observation car to hear her rile them into a frenzy of giving. While local brass bands played patriotic anthems, assemblies were usually attended by no "less than five thousand. ... sometimes, I scolded, sometimes, I coaxed — my methods varied," she noted.[32] In a Fox newsreel, Marie sports an enormous multibloomed corsage as she shouts, claps, and points fingers to shame thousands of onlookers into buying bonds.[33] On another occasion she donned a seaman's uniform and posed saluting an Uncle Sam recruitment poster. At New York's Public Library on Fifth Avenue, she and young actress Hedda Hopper implored the daytime passersby to "loosen up a bit in the financial district."[34] In perfect keeping with her improvisational habits as an actress, she sometimes "asked celebrated persons to write these talks for me, but when the moment came that I went upon the platform, I always forgot everything I had to say and impromptu words came to me."[35]

In a time when the moral defense of war was unquestioned, Marie showed absolute intolerance for all nonparticipants. She even devised a handy "Slackers' Comfort Kit" to aid those stay-at-home sufferers.[36] The kit included one ounce of cotton batting and one pound of cyanide of potassium. The cotton "is to be used for ear plugs to keep the slackers from having to hear mean things people say about them and the cyanide is for the purpose of suicide when the cotton runs out."

For the servicemen she could produce a tear on cue. "If I had ever doubted the existence of a divine spark in my fellows, the sacrifices I saw during my travels at this period would have entirely reconvinced me," she wrote.[37] During one speech a young blue-eyed marine approached the platform and handed her one hundred dollars in cash. "For a bond," he said, and started to leave.[38]

"But, where shall I send it?" asked Marie.

"Who knows?" He shrugged as he was absorbed into the crowd.

In Portland, Oregon, Marie expressed her full devotion on behalf of the Allies.[39] "My family name is Koerber, my grandfather was a general in the German army, my father was born in Germany and I am touring the country ... as a protest against my ancestry. ... my special task is to get under the calloused skins of those blithering idiots who still waver because they have German blood in them. I want to wake them up and bring home to them the fact that the best means of atonement for them is to get behind Uncle Sam in this war and help wipe out the Kaiser and the bunch of brutes who are supporting him."

With an astonishing ability to rouse patriotism, Marie sold more bonds than anyone else.[40] At significant cost to her health, she spoke 149 times in 29 days during the third loan drive. A typical portion of her itinerary had her in St. Louis on April 7, Jefferson City on April 8, and Kansas City on April 9. In a single day in St. Louis, she spoke at 14 engagements.[41]

In May, Marie shot a topical two-reeler called *The Cross Red Nurse* for her none-too-active production company. The American movie industry had become deeply involved in the war. Besides bond sales by movie stars, theaters were used for fund-raising rallies and one-reelers were made to urge the purchase of Liberty bonds. Marie had volunteered for Red Cross duty already and well understood the stock characters such as the stoic infantryman, heartbroken mother, spy, saboteur, and Red Cross nurse. The national obsession was no surprise; more than one million American troops were in Europe by July, while Red Cross parties became a regular excuse for social gatherings and neighborly comfort.

After completing *The Cross Red Nurse* and logging in more than 10,000 miles, Marie was bedridden with flu and exhaustion in her rented Los Angeles home on South Rampart Boulevard.[42] She denied that her seclusion and illness had anything to do with threatening letters she had received from German sympathizers. Released in August, *The Cross Red Nurse* was a patriotic short well suited to Marie's strong feelings on the war. It was to be the last effort of the short-lived Marie Dressler Motion Picture Company. With Jim's customary ability to bungle business, the company soon faced litigation, reportedly over the authorship of *Fired*. Marie claimed to have written the scenario, but someone else challenged her on its originality. None of Marie's productions was a huge success, and when her distributor World Pictures dissolved in 1920, the production company died of financial and creative stagnation.[43]

By the fall of 1918, the German armies were receding as England, France, and Italy began to negotiate the spoils of war. The United States was not closely involved in these negotiations, but Wilson exercised international moral leadership. He offered a place for Germany among the community of nations again if it would honor self-determination, disarm, and replace the Kaiser with a democratic body. At the Versailles Peace Conference, terms for peace were harsh for Germany, which lost valuable eastern land to the newly created Poland while France reclaimed Alsace-Lorraine. Amid brass bands, ticker-tape parades, cheering, and weeping, a truce was signed and Armistice Day became a national holiday on November 11, 1918. "The Great War" signaled the beginning of a world recognized today as distinctly modern. Chemical warfare, air raids, the spread of democracy, the fall of monarchy, the slow collapse of colonialism, ongoing international suspicion, and women in the workforce are among its legacies. So, too, is a death toll of nine million.

Dressler had managed to stay in the public eye and protect her aura of stardom because of the war, not because she had any recent smash hits to her name. Armistice Day saw her great raison d'être over, her film and stage career in limbo, the farm sold, the production company ruined, and her finances ebbing. What was she to do now?

She was nearly broke and had to find work. Her agent, Alf Wilton, approached the mighty Benjamin Franklin Keith's vaudeville management organization looking for employment for his client. He returned to her embarrassed.[44] "I don't quite know how to tell you, Miss Dressler. Your last salary was $2,500."

"Yes, yes. Go on."

"Well, I can't get your old salary. They say you have been out five years and must have deteriorated."

"All right," Marie shot back. "Go back and ask him how much I have deteriorated."

Wilton was ready with an answer. "They are willing to give you $1,500 a week."

Marie put it in perspective. It's a drop in wages for sure, but how many people earn $1,500 a week? She went to work and played the Palace, far and away the greatest vaudeville house in the world, for three weeks. Advertising the engagement as a benefit for herself, Marie was greeted by a two-minute standing ovation at her first entrance. "She was in all her cut-up glory, exactly like the old days of Weber and Fields," wrote the *New York Dramatic Mirror*.[45] For her 22-minute routine at the coveted next-to-end spot on a mixed bill, she incorporated Liberty Loan travails with the standard comedy poems, coon songs, recitations, and travesties of grand opera and Russian ballet. One naysayer complained her routine was too slow, but happily reported a brisker pace when she went on tour. When she played Cleveland, Archie Bell wrote,[46] "Eternal justice will probably give her a welcome something like this: Enter, Marie Dressler, and take a front seat, for you have done more than any single human being of your generation to make the world giggle."

The success of this latest tour was minor. It did not herald a lasting comeback. After the war, Marie seemed more content with philanthropy on behalf of the new American working woman. Most often she performed for free in benefit to the American Red Cross, the Women's International Alliance, and National League for Women's Service. She volunteered for the Stage Women's War Relief and produced and starred in a well-received lampoon of auditions called "Rough Perfect." "The satire was broad and the humor broader," concluded the *New York Times*.[47]

The postwar euphoria gave way to the quiet and solemn warehousing of the wounded. Marie regularly went to hospitals to sing for young veterans now among the blind, amputated, disfigured, or shell-shocked.[48] On her first visits, she did a boisterous clowning routine, but one young man in a wheelchair took Marie's hand and asked for a favor. "Miss Dressler," he began softly, "sing something sad so we can cry." She obliged, and they all wept. She did, too, as she stood witness to the costs of war. "I know they want to cry," she told a friend.[49] "But their manhood won't let them. Yet tears are sometimes good for the soul. The right kind of tears wash away bitterness and rebellion and hatred. They ease the heart. When I sing sad songs they may weep unashamed. It is just Marie Dressler singing." She wrote in her autobiography:[50] "Men are not ashamed to cry over a sentimental old woman singing foolish songs, but they are too proud to weep over their own lost dreams and broken hopes."

Veterans' miseries were soon overshadowed and forgotten. The war had brought America out of a provincial complacency just as movies reinvented popular entertainment. Women were voting, cities were swelling in size as millions sought industrial jobs, and anti-immigration sentiments ran high in the wake of postwar hatreds. With campaigns begun decades earlier by the Women's Christian Temperance Union and Anti-Saloon League, the Eighteenth Amendment to the Constitution was signed and Demon Rum was outlawed. Speakeasies came into fast vogue and a vast underground of bootleggers was born. Liquor prices skyrocketed. In 1918 bars sold decent shots of whiskey at 15 cents or two for 25 cents and brandy at 50 cents. Now inferior booze was served for one dollar, with restaurants charging up to two dollars. Such were the standards of drinking for the rest of Marie's working life. When Prohibition was at last repealed, Dressler was near her deathbed.

Actors' Equity had its origins in nineteenth-century England, when actors banded together in an organization called the Water Rats of London, "rats" spelling "star" backwards. The Water reference came from the actors' favored sport of excursions on the Thames. Fifteen actors began the White Rats of America counterpart very early in the twentieth century. "Up to that time, an actor might rehearse six weeks without pay only to find, when his play opened, that it was a failure and he was on the street with only two weeks' salary for two months' work," wrote Marie. With no binding contracts, powerful managers such as Abe Erlanger could cancel acts when they felt like it and leave actors high and dry.[51]

Discontent was rising among the laborers. By 1910 the Rats graduated from a good old boy fraternal order to a trade union. From their efforts, greeted by indifference from the press, Actors' Equity Association (AEA) was organized in 1913. The occasion was precipitated by a disastrous performance of *The Enchantress* on stage in Los Angeles.[52] Its star, Kitty Gordon, collapsed in a heap. The engagement was canceled and the 67 cast members "were stranded, abandoned to their own resources, three thousand miles away from Broadway and the next prospective job." Given the tenuous rights of theater employees, an episode of such calamity was probably inevitable. For the next several years, a convoluted history of mergers, alliances, and betrayals marked the painful birth of theatrical labor organizing in the United States.

Once the theater workers met and shared stories, their complaints were many.[53] Out-of-town expenses were covered by the actors and pay was unpredictable. Costumes were routinely paid for by actors and shoes alone could cost as much as $60. Conditions backstage were often horrible — little or no heat, running water, or closet space. There was no standard contract and no limit to an unpaid rehearsal period, and any agreements could be broken without explanation or liability. As happened with the early tryouts of *Tillie's Nightmare*, an actor could be dismissed without redress in the middle of rehearsals. After opening, a role could be eliminated or played by someone else for less pay after the original actor had donated rehearsal time.

A breakthrough of sorts for labor occurred in 1917 when managers agreed to a contract that limited unpaid rehearsals and guaranteed pay regardless of the length of a show's run.[54] This was acceptable until the agreement came up for negotiations again in the spring of 1919. The managers hedged on two critical points: they would not pay the actors for extra matinees on legal holidays and they would not limit the number of paid performances to eight per week. The hostility was growing as producer Charles Cochran announced that he would not employ any actor or actress who was a member of the AEA.[55]

The terms were altogether unacceptable to the actors. Many among the famous supported the cause of Equity, including Eddie Foy, Lillian Russell, Ed Wynn, Ethel and Lionel Barrymore, and Eddie Cantor. With festering resentments and high-voltage endorsements, Actors' Equity voted to strike on August 6, 1919.[56] The next night, just minutes before curtain time, 12 of New York City's 43 professional theaters closed. In their condescension, managers underestimated the actors' resolve for better conditions and the strike turned very serious indeed. The timing was particularly vexing to managers, since 1919 was a banner year at the box office. Eighteen musical comedies and revues were on the boards. Demand was keen and tickets shot to an all-time high of $5 per seat.

Marie was with Jim in Atlantic City on her first vacation in years when the strike began. She could hardly believe what she was reading in the newspaper. "They can't strike," she said.[57] "We can't do anything without the press and the managers have got the press." But the strike was real and it "shoved the President of the United States off the front page and the proudest day of my life was the day we did it."

Actors' Equity was meanwhile forging relations with the already organized International Alliance of Theatrical Stage Employees and the American Federation of Musicians. "The stage hands will give you all the support the law will permit," they announced,[58] while "the musicians are absolutely in sympathy with the Actors' Equity Association." It was time to lay out the concerns for the chorus members, perhaps the most mistreated among theater employees. Sam Bernard, who had starred with Marie in *The Man in the Moon* and numerous benefit performances over the years, was outlining changes to chorus work at a crowded meeting at the New Amsterdam Opera House on West 45th Street. Marie was back from vacation and over at the Hippodrome Theater stirring up the chorus and imploring them to join the strike. "But nothing has been said to us about it," said a chorine.[59]

"I'm saying it," said Marie.

"We're not organized," said another.

"I organize you!" announced Marie.

The Opera House was soon joyously overrun by 50 chorus girls from the Hippodrome who had "walked out and are coming in." The show they abandoned was *Happy Days*, produced by Charles Dillingham, the very man who dropped Marie from *The Century Girl*. Strike headquarters took on the heat of a revival meeting as the "girls were marching in two by two into an ovation which shook the not very solid rafters of the hall."[60] Later during the strike, Marie would capitalize on such spectacles by introducing the full 300-member *Happy Days* chorus to the strains of "Hail, Hail, the Gang's All Here." During the strike, the *Happy Days* sign at the Hippodrome was painted over with *Nothing Doing* so that the entire sign read "Nothing Doing, Twice Daily."[61]

Recognizing that chorus members needed their own striking terms, a new organization was born called the Chorus Equity Association of America.[62] Initiation fee was set at $1. As an indication of the solidarity behind the labor movement, a star no less bright than Ethel Barrymore spoke at the first meeting for Chorus Equity. In the heat of the moment, and in recognition of her union efforts, Marie was unanimously elected its first president. She happily accepted the responsibility. "Audiences do not laugh because they want to, but because they can't help it," she wrote in a syndicated newspaper article.[63] "It takes years of study and thought to learn how to demand that laugh. That is why I want my own chorus people to feel the independence, the pride and self-respect which comes only to the true artisan who has begun at the bottom and learned his way step by step to the top. That self-respect is what I know their spiritual and actual affiliation with labor will give them."

By August 17 Marie announced the acceptable employment conditions for Chorus Equity Association members. Each member was to receive a minimum salary of $30 a week in New York and $35 on the road for eight performances a week with payment to be pro rata for any performances over eight. Chorus would give four weeks of free rehearsal, half pay for the next two weeks, and full pay after that. Managers would be expected to pay for Pullman berths for any overnight gigs. Through President Dressler, the association presented its terms to the managers and waited.

The Lexington Avenue Opera House became the site of an Equity benefit performance on a muggy night of August rain.[64] The curtain rose on a setless stage with 200 co-ed chorus members from various darkened shows around town assembled together. Marie came forward and addressed the standing-room-only house. She announced that, with the assistance of choreographer Kuy Kendall, she would teach the group a new set of steps in 6 to 16 minutes, though managers routinely demanded from 6 to 16 weeks of free rehearsal.

Apart from the unique circumstances, it was a standard rehearsal. Mistakes were corrected and dancers' genuine embarrassment told the audience that this was not a phony affair. The dance steps were mastered and performance-worthy with time to spare. The crowd roared its approval as everyone went dancing into the wings.

Marie became a genuine hero among the chorus girls. "She gave three years to working for the boys in soldiers' clothes and now stands ready to give as much time to the girls. She is the general of an army of tinsel and tights."[65] She saw to their well-being and treated them with a certain maternal conscientiousness, sometimes handing out ten-dollar bills to her "girls" as they exited the stage door after a good show. Though Marie didn't tell the chorus members, Mrs. John D. Rockefeller, Jr., endorsed their cause and pledged to build them a clubhouse when the dust settled.[66]

If Marie was worshipped by her union supplicants, she was reviled by managers. Some were reported to exit their office via the fire escape when she approached. Abe Erlanger, the producer who had earlier blacklisted Marie, refused to go to any of the meetings held between committees of managers and committees of actors.[67]

"Look here, Abe, we need you at these meetings," urged a fellow producer. "You ought to come. You'd have a good effect on these actors."

Abe was resolute in his refusal. "Why not, Abe?"

"Well, that Dressler'll be there. And would sorta look at me and say, 'Vell, Abe?' and — no, I guess I won't go. I would be no good to you if Marie's there."

Actors, meanwhile, used their considerable talent to entertain themselves and the public as one show after another closed. George M. Cohan's famous wartime hit "Over There" was reworded as an anthem for the cause. The travesty was all the more amusing and ironic since Cohan was aligned with the managers. He predictably hated the new treatment of his melody:[68]

> Over fair, over fair
> We have been, we have been over fair
> But now things are humming
> And the time is coming
> When with Labor we'll be chumming
> Everywhere.
> So beware, have a care,
> Just be on the fair, on the square, everywhere.
> For we are striking, yes, we are striking,
> And we won't come back till the managers are fair.

Though some actors were sympathetic to managers, most saw years of abuse and agreed that change was necessary. They were collectively blowing the whistle at last, and *Variety*, the day's leading entertainment news source, was on their side. "The strike should never have started," it proclaimed.[69] "The managers brought it on themselves, and through that left the actor, represented by Actors' Equity Association, with the best basis there can be for a strike — a just cause."

Marie was never less than dead center in the melee. She was using her Keystone court settlement money to finance the effort and avoid working at anything that would divide her energy. She took direct aim at Erlanger, the Shubert brothers and even popular Lew Fields when she said,[70] "I'm hoping to God that this struggle will be the means of bringing the managers and actors nearer together. Now the manager hates the actor and the actor hates the manager. It wasn't so in the olden times. A manager hadn't much money then and he took a chance and the actors were willing and glad to take a chance with him because if he lost he lost as well as they. But the commercialism of today has ruined art and that's why I'm hoping the strike will mend our relations."

On August 18, as the *New York Times* warned that all legitimate theaters in the country might soon close, Marie marched with thousands of actors, stagehands, and musicians from Columbus Circle down Broadway carrying a sign that read "No More Pay. Just Fair Play." On August 23 *Variety* proclaimed her to be "a great scout with the mob, loves a good story and knows how to tell one. A good woman, that's all." She exceeded that endorsement four days later at a New York State Federation of Labor meeting in Syracuse. At a time that saw the unionizing of train, postal and electrical workers in the United States and Europe, she was the first actress ever to be seated as a delegate in the history of the labor movement.[71] She, De Witt C. Jennings, and Ed Wynn were warmly welcomed and proceeded to attack producers Arthur Hammerstein and Jake Shubert. With thundering approval, an adopted resolution declared the Actors' Equity Association as the only actors' organization affiliated to and recognized by the American Federation of Labor. "The most inspired moment of my life," Marie recalled. From Syracuse, she felt "a sense of oneness, of closeness to one's own people — the workers of the world."[72] Two days after the Syracuse meeting, she was back at the Hippodrome with Frank Gillmore, secretary of Actors' Equity; Charles Shay, president of the International Alliance of Theatrical Stage Employees and Motion Picture Operators; Joe Weber; and others to draft a peace settlement.[73]

Demands had not yet been satisfied. The strike spread to Boston, Chicago, and Los Angeles and lasted through the testy dog days of summer. Actors continued to stay away from the theaters and were staging successful all-star fundraisers. Finally, on September 8, 1919, members of Actors' Equity and the Producing Managers Association (PMA) met at the Lexington Avenue Opera House and hammered out a truce.[74] Present were Equity stalwarts Frank Gillmore, Ethel Barrymore, Lillian Russell, and Marie amidst a sprinkling of lawyers and several managers. Equity insisted that striking actors be allowed to return to the positions they held at the time of the walkout. The PMA agreed. In an omnibus moment, members of the PMA, Actors' Equity, American Federation of Musicians, International Alliance of Stagehands, and the American Federation of Labor signed the agreement for various terms of employment. At three o'clock in the afternoon, Marie and others faced a wall of reporters and announced: "Gentlemen, we have reached an agreement. The strike is ended."

Eleven Broadway theaters reopened that night but the strike's reverberations were felt for years. With sweeping reform, several careers were destroyed or badly damaged by the strike. Ed Wynn went back to work, but actor-composer-manager George M. Cohan, as a sympathizer to Erlanger and defiant opponent of the actors' battle, was deeply embittered by the strike results.

Producers were appalled when calculating the strike cost at an estimated $500,000 per week. Theaters lost $250,000, actors $100,000, stage crew and musicians $40,000. More than 60 shows were stopped. Thirty-five theaters were closed, adding up to $140,000 per week in overhead. Total losses of the 28-day strike were estimated at $2 million.[75]

Equity reveled in its victory. Its members, once consigned to the class of the "bullied, belittled, despised, cheated and enslaved," were now recognized by the American Federation of Labor.[76] Its membership zoomed from 2,700 to 14,000 as minimum standards of pay and working conditions were established and enforced. All that is good from unionizing could be realized, including the cultivation of great young talent. A new order was coming. The future was uncertain, but after the strike, everyone knew that the old days were gone forever.

Chapter 8

Ghosts

By 1920 New York was exploding with new theater, but the hinterland was sick of its steady diet of mediocre leftovers. Patrons were turned off by the hyperbole that fueled highly competitive road-show campaigns, and a sharp rise in automobile ownership sent potential audiences to the great outdoors. Only 49 professional shows toured the United States, down from hundreds at the turn of the century.[1]

Dressler's Broadway had vanished and in its place was jazz and bareskin revues. Simultaneously, great excitement was generated by playwrights Zona Grey (*Miss Lulu Bett*), the young Eugene O'Neill (*Beyond the Horizon*) and Elmer Rice (*For the Defense*). Marie didn't benefit from the poststrike infusion of talent. American drama was maturing in a remarkable era of creativity, but there was no place for her. She was stuck in derivative vaudeville routines. She could not, or was not offered the opportunity to, break from her reputation as a low comedienne.

Since she had not been employed at the onset of the strike, no one owed her a job according to the union rules she helped create. But it wasn't merely her Trust-busting, strike-inciting ways that got her into trouble. She was blacklisted to be sure, but she was also a casualty of America's postwar changes in entertainment. As vaudeville declined and movies took over, she was remembered as an unstylishly rotund comedienne hopelessly tied to earlier sensibilities.

She still stayed with the cause of actors' rights. At a meeting of the Women's Trade Union League on the night of the Lexington Avenue Opera House treaty, she told of the benefits received by the chorus girls.[2] She expressed hope that managers and actors could work together agreeably in the future. On October 24, 1919, she was reelected president of the Chorus Equity Association in a general membership meeting, but she was not there.[3] She had begun rehearsals for a revival of *Tillie's Nightmare* immediately after the strike ended and was already touring.

She was neglecting union responsibilities. Dorothy Bryant, a newspaper woman of some repute, had approached Marie about handling union publicity.[4] In Marie's absence, Bryant was signing her letters as "Secretary to Miss Dressler," but she was given far more authority than was appropriate to her position. She proved so efficient in her duties that her title was unofficially raised to executive secretary and the operation ran smoothly without Marie's involvement.

On November 14, 1919, while she was performing *Tillie* under "Dalton Enterprises Company (Inc.)" in Kansas City, Marie sent a letter to Chorus Equity resigning as president.[5] She was succeeded not by Dorothy Bryant, but by actress Blanche Ring. The tour to Kansas City, Cleveland, Detroit, Philadelphia, and Boston was meanwhile losing money from an oversized payroll. Marie held out on paying over 30 Equity company members, claiming that $665.31 had already been extracted by Equity from Dalton Enterprises for sleepers and extra performances. As if to nullify her campaign during the strike, Marie had paid her non–Equity performers in full before they left Boston. When the limping production closed in Boston and returned to New York, the mightily angry union actors stormed Equity headquarters demanding their wages. Everyone was paid within a week, but not before shouting matches and near blows. For Marie, the incident was worse than humiliating; it exposed her as a hypocrite at odds with her own generous reputation.[6]

Frances Marion had divorced her second husband Robert Pike and married Fred Thomson. By any standards, he was a dreamboat. A world champion track and field athlete, Occidental College graduate, Princeton postgraduate, and Presbyterian minister, he had the studly and chiseled good looks of a matinee idol. He was a vivid contrast to Jim, who was not in attendance when Marie appeared at a farewell party for Hollywood-bound Frances and Fred. Partygoers saw that Marie had traded in her usual festive garb of feathers, sequins, and bright colors for a conservative black gown and a single long string of pearls. To prepare for an upcoming return to London, she sprinkled her conversation with "My hat, old thing," "Good show" and "Lor' love a duck" while party guests stood slack jawed.[7] "You've noticed the change in me?" she asked Frances, who nodded. "It's not only for Jim, but when I was selling government bonds in Washington I met the crème de la crème of the Four Hundred and, my dear, I've become society's pet."

Frances murmured something insincere about being sorry Jim couldn't be at the party when Hedda Hopper piped in with "Ah, Lady Throckmorton, your A is broader than your rear. Come off that high perch, Marie. You're among pals."

Marie laughed and said, "Stinker. I'm bustin' a gut to behave like a lady and nobody appreciates the effort it takes." The women then strolled into the living room, where the others were listening to a young man at the piano. There were demands for Marie to sing a comic number, but she was distracted. "I'd rather listen to this young man play," she said as she watched him.

Everyone was soon spellbound. Frances wrote that "he played on and on; no one wanted to interrupt the flow of melodic sound that aroused varied emotions in us; gaiety, momentary sadness, then the joyous warm feeling that we were alive and young at heart."

He stopped and apologized for playing at length.

"No, no," said Frances. "You inspired us."

"Was it all improvisation?" asked Marie.

"Not the last thing I played," said George Gershwin. "It's a composition I'm working over. I'm not quite sure, but I think I will call it 'Rhapsody in Blue.'"

Jim and Marie returned to London after the last *Tillie* tour hoping to mount a new musical comedy, but they were besieged with labor and casting troubles. Her latest showcase never got off the ground and money was still owed for the 1909 *Philopoena* disaster. With professional ruin looming, Marie finally began to see Jim as Frances, Hedda, and all her other friends saw him. On that last trip to London, he looked to her like "a plunger [and] a born gambler [who] couldn't be stopped until we were faced with bankruptcy."[8]

Having failed with creditors and producers in London, Jim and Marie hopped on a steamer and returned to New York, where Marie had few options but to try to rustle up any work offered. Something happened on the trip that broke Jim's ruse. He told Marie everything: he was still married to Elizabeth, who had merely laughed at the divorce offer. What about the thousands of dollars Marie gave Jim to pay for the divorce and avoid her being named a correspondent? It was spent, some went to Mrs. Dalton but most went to gambling. What about the marriage ceremony that she and Jim enjoyed? Jim hired a man to act as a minister. The lie of "Marie and Jim Dalton" they gave to the world was also a lie Jim gave to Marie.

Jim swore he had trumped up the phony marriage to keep them together, but Marie did not believe him. Before the steamer docked in New York harbor, she was screaming at him: "Liar! Blackmailer! Thief! I never want to see you or hear from you again!"[9] Back on shore, she calmed down a bit and assessed the circumstances. Her life looked too much like *Tillie's Punctured Romance* with her as the betrayed titled character, Jim as the opportunistic Charlie Chaplin, and Elizabeth as the other woman, Mabel Normand. But the ending was different in real life and she couldn't get around the fact that Jim deceived her to protect his steady flow of embezzled income.

Fate would not let Marie dump Jim and resurrect her own health and happiness. From the combustible combination of diabetes, overeating, and heavy drinking, he suffered a diabetic stroke that left him paralyzed and helpless. He was wheelchair bound, unable to walk, dress, or feed himself. In his incapacitation, Elizabeth Dalton wanted nothing to do with him and responsibility fell on Marie to maintain his medical care.[10] She could not afford nurses, and so the daily duties were hers. She gave him opium to relieve some of the misery and, weather permitting, she took him in his wheelchair on a pass through Central Park. They often stopped to chat with the aging Lillian Russell out for a carriage ride, a meeting of the Beauty, Beastie, and her Burden.

Diabetes had been identified and diagnosed for centuries but there was little to be done for a patient like Jim whose health had been compromised for years. He gasped heavily as his lungs failed to expel carbon dioxide.

Food was not metabolizing into energy. It passed through his system by ferocious urination with accompanying intense thirst, hunger, and high blood-sugar levels. He was wasting away and had hypoglycemic fits, coma, and death to contemplate in his near future. He likely suffered the classic symptoms of preinsulin diabetes: severe dry skin, weight loss, cataracts, boils, carbuncles, gangrene, impotence, and sterility. Jim's body was starving itself and no amount of food and drink would make a difference.

Marie told Frances that "I knew I could never trust him again. But it's true, the weak are mightier than the strong and when Jim had his stroke I couldn't set him adrift."[11] Decimated finances, ruined career and an invalid companion — Marie had to find work fast. She knew what people said about her. She waited outside Jake Shubert's office and knew he was inside asking his secretary to lie.[12] "I don't want to see her," he said. "I can't use her. She's through. I hate to tell her — just say I'm not here."

Marie's finances had been eroding away for some time. "The Armistice found me broke, except for a few Liberty bonds," she wrote.[13] "It is those who inherit money that part with it most reluctantly. They say, 'When this is gone, there isn't any more.' People who make money slowly and by dint of great labor have a proper respect for it also. They save. When old age comes, their nests are neatly feathered. It is the quick easy earners who are the greatest spendthrifts. They say, as I did, 'I made it once. I can make it again.' A form of egotism to which the artistic temperament is peculiarly and unhappily liable!"

Friends Helena Dayton and Louise Barrett wrote a play for Dressler, but producers gave them a standard response:[14] "The public doesn't want Dressler anymore. She's too old. They've forgotten her. Most of them never heard of her. Audiences want youth. We wouldn't have Marie at any price." An attempt by actress Nella Webb, Dayton, and Barrett to fashion a motion picture for Marie, with older actors Lionel Barrymore or George Arliss as her costar, was similarly aborted.[15] Work was spotty at best — small town vaudeville, tent shows, and a brief nightclub engagement in Florida. "I travelled from one state to another doing anything I could get," she said.[16] "I lugged [Jim] around. Poor devil, he couldn't talk; his eyes kept pleading with me to forgive him. I suppose I should be ashamed to admit this, but I never stopped caring for him."

In September 1920, one month after the first licensed radio broadcast was aired and the new Nineteenth Amendment giving women the right to vote was ratified, Marie had a prestigious job again. Though she locked horns with the Shuberts, they kept a high admiration for her skills and found her a bit part in their new spectacular. Jake added a small role for her in the lavish and already running *Cinderella on Broadway* at the Winter Garden Theater. In it she solved the problems of the League of Nations and offered imitations of Theda Bara and fellow union organizer Ethel Barrymore that were reviewed as "a veritable scream."[17] In defiance of every soothsayer who said she was over, Marie was in top form and well received, but *Cinderella on Broadway* was gone by October.

Later in 1920, after a run of *Cinderella on Broadway* in Boston and within days of Warren G. Harding's election as president, Marie was hired for *The Passing Show of 1921.*[18] The Shuberts, who found Marie substantially more agreeable to work with since Jim's stroke, borrowed the title from a nineteenth-century George Lederer revue. Attempting to rival the more ornate productions of Florenz Ziegfeld, *The Passing Show* was actually an ongoing act first staged in 1912. The productions were mostly variety patchworks of songs, sketches, and minimally clothed chorus girls within large and impressive set pieces. As a novelty, the 1921 incarnation boasted a thin storyline.

Marie was elated to be in a *Passing Show*, but there was no denying her waning marketability. Vaudevillians Willie and Eugene Howard received top billing; their names were twice as large as Marie's in the program. She appeared in just four scenes out of 26 total and sang none of the Harold Atteridge tunes. She made do with a comedy skit called "Spanish Love," in which she played a much sought-after señorita.[19]

The Passing Show suffered in comparison to the Ziegfeld Follies or Weber & Fields' Music Hall, but it lasted at the Winter Garden Theater for 200 performances. Every night, Jim waited backstage motionless in his wheelchair. Marie cried easily if anyone asked about him. "He's very, very sick," she'd say through her handkerchief.

In August Lew Fields declared bankruptcy and listed a $7,500 outstanding debt of Jim Dalton's as one of his assets.[20] Fields must have known he was not going to collect. Marie could barely pay medical bills and placate angry creditors in London, much less settle other old debts. She was grateful for the continued attention of the Shuberts. Their office released a statement announcing that their great triumph "is the signing of Marie Dressler to a twenty week contract" for their new touring vaudeville show *Moments from the Winter Garden.*[21] "Bask in the sunshine of Marie Dressler for fifteen minutes and you will feel that this sordid old world has not only been rejuvenated but that pleasure has displaced business and that joy has knocked out gloom."

Marie did her travesty of Ethel Barrymore, with costars John T. Murray and Arthur Geary providing their interpretations of John and Lionel, respectively. Francis Renault came along, too, as a female impersonator. "He brings new gowns for this occasion," announced the *Cleveland Plain Dealer.*[22] The paper's Archie Bell declared that "the billboards tell about a brand of cigarette for which anyone should be willing to walk a mile. Marie Dressler is like that cigarette ... she's about the most effervescent, bubbling and joyous thing left in American life ... she'll never fail. Give her the chance and she'll make you forget the war, the high cost of living, politics, xylophone players, singing neighbors, crowded street cars and all other annoyances of life."

Bell was a lone voice among critics and lavish press releases weren't fooling anyone. It became fashionable to write of Marie as dated, and the material she was given appealed to an

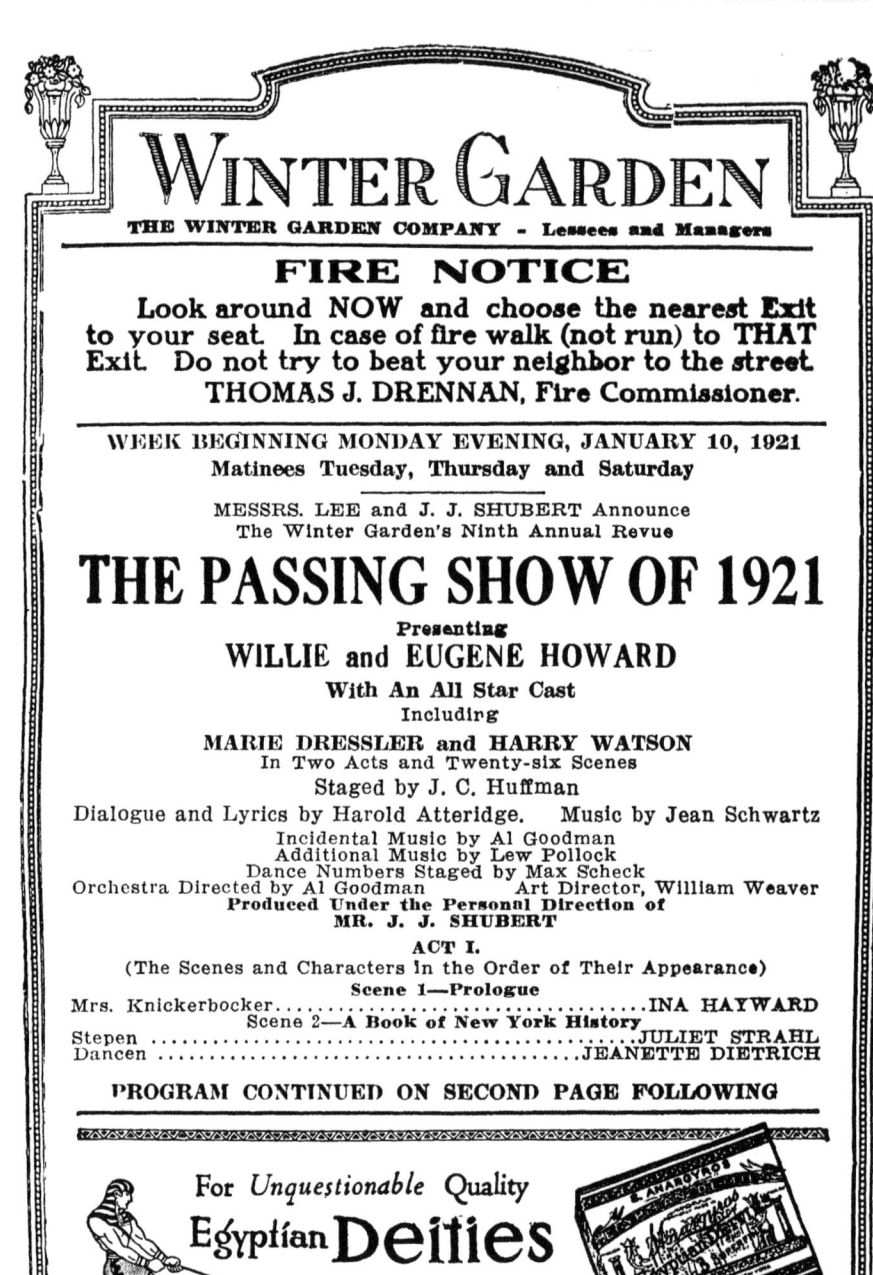

Title program for *The Passing Show of 1921*, complete with Marie's reduced billing. (Courtesy of the Shubert Archive.)

ever dwindling crowd. Depression came over her easily and she had to work like a Trojan just to keep the dull ache of her life from appearing on stage. "I wonder if by any chance you might know how happy and proud your kind generous article made me," she wrote to Bell on her 53rd birthday.[23] "In these days of commercialism when one is so held down it is a treat to meet up with fearlessness. I do hope you do not lose your job."

Marie and Jim were in Chicago when he took a bad turn. Marie was obligated to take the show to St. Louis and left Jim in the care of a Christian Scientist named Henry Davis. Jim was Irish Catholic, but there was little that any religion could do for him at this point.* Marie was out of town when he died at the Congress Hotel the night of November 29, 1921, 25 days before his fiftieth birthday.[24] The St. Louis performances were canceled and Marie was back in Chicago the next morning. Bessie McCoy Davis took over for her in Milwaukee.

Two men from the undertaker's office arrived with a policeman to remove Jim's body from the hotel. Marie had planned to bury Jim in Chicago, but Elizabeth Dalton, Jim's sometime wife, suddenly took control. She demanded that he be buried in his hometown of Corning, New York. Marie agreed and sent revised instructions to undertaker James Marshall to ready the body for a train ride to Corning. "I did not see Mrs. Dalton. I received instructions through one of her assistants. Yes, she is Marie Dressler, the actress," said Marshall.[25] "I understand that Mrs. Dalton is going east with the body tonight." When Marie was at the train station for an 11 P.M. departure, reporters were there, too. The real Mrs. Dalton had told the press of marital desertion and suddenly Marie was being followed.

"I have nothing to say. I have done my duty," she told them.[26]

"Did you meet Mr. Dalton on a railway train as this other woman says?" one asked.

"I have nothing to say. Mine is the burden and mine is the sorrow. I do not see why I should discuss it," Marie said as she boarded the train.

She arrived in Corning on December 2 and was driven immediately to the home of Timothy Murphy, Jim's cousin.[27] Also present were Jim's mother and assorted other relatives. Reporters immediately began calling the home. Who was Jim Dalton's widow? His death certificate listed "Marie Dalton" as wife, and so who is Elizabeth? Christopher Dalton, Jim's younger brother, told them, "We have nothing to say. It's none of the public's business."

From her home in Boston, Mrs. Dalton took no hesitation at revealing her status as Jim's one and only wife. Though newspaper men were initially denied access to Marie or Hannah Dalton, Marie gave up her strategy and divulged everything as well:[28] "A representative of Miss Dressler stated today that Dalton was married to Mrs. L. A. Dalton." To Marie's considerable embarrassment, the 1914 accusations made by the Gaiety Theater management of Jim's bigamy went public as the truth. The sworn affidavit made by Mrs. Dalton was rejected by the courts at that time but was wholly accurate:[29] "This is to certify that I was married to James H. Dalton in Jersey City, New Jersey, in 1900 and I have never secured a divorce from him, and that no papers have ever been served on me to indicate that he had ever applied for a divorce, and, to the best of my knowledge and belief, I am still his lawfully wedded wife." Elizabeth Dalton was not present for her husband's burial at St. Mary's cemetery on Corning's "Irish Hill," though she had told reporters she intended to be. After the small funeral, all Jim's property and savings went to her and her daughter.

Dressler went into emotional isolation after Jim's death and the handling of his estate and body. "I have known several persons who seemed to derive comfort and satisfaction from a number of mates," she once said.[30] "I think it is quite safe to say I shan't do it again." When a woman marries, said Marie, she "should make up her mind that marriage is her job and

---

*Jim was never given insulin. The first successful injection of insulin in the treatment of diabetes was given to Leonard Thompson at the Toronto General Hospital on January 23, 1922.

that it's up to her to make a success of it. I didn't and I failed."

Did she genuinely love Jim Dalton or was their "marriage" a camouflage for a convenient business arrangement and a private preference for women? Her refusal to reveal more may be from respect of a dead loved one or a means of absolving her from ever taking up with another man. In an age when homosexuality was tantamount to demonic possession, Marie may have rationalized her desire for women by stating that no man will ever replace Jim. Her drunken 1910 confession to Luisa Tetrazzini of sexual dissatisfaction could have been as much a complication from obesity and diabetes as from a relationship void of carnality.

Certainly they were more than business partners. Marie's devotion to Jim in his debilitation shows a loyalty exceeding that to her closest women friends. Marie's last words on the subject were opaque, but if her love for Jim was a masquerade, then she was a greater actress than even her most devoted fans would acknowledge. "I have always liked men," she wrote.[31] "Many of my staunchest friends have been of the male persuasion. But in all my life I have loved only one man. ... I will not tell you about him, for our love belongs to me alone." The sorrow of his illness and death was "greater than I thought I could bear," recalled Marie many years later.[32] "Except for my mother, Jim Dalton meant more than anything in life to me. I loved him. ... I still love the thoughts of those years."

Marie did not stay out of the social whirl for long. She visited the Warren Harding White House during Harding's brief tenure. She had met so many presidents there that she "could find her way to the icebox."[33] Republican Harding was the first president elected by women and Lillian Russell had worked hard for him. Marie said she "loved Warren Harding because he was so human. ... He was like me — he couldn't say 'no.'"[34] His great oil lease scandals and the conception of his illegitimate child in the Senate Office Building were only two of the shocking facts revealed after his unexpected death in 1923. In life, he knew how to pour on the charm. As his secretary began to introduce Marie, he interrupted her to dismiss the formal treatment.[35] "You don't have to tell me who Marie Dressler is. I've seen her in everything she ever did."

Lillian lived long enough to help elect Harding, but she preceded him in death.[36] She was sent to Europe as his emissary to study immigration issues and reportedly suffered a bad fall on the return voyage. Her last years were a shadow of her glorious past as she lectured on health, beauty, and hygiene. Joseph J. O'Donohue IV, a child of New York high society, witnessed one of her last public appearances. "In that era, people didn't have very many ways of entertaining themselves," he recalled.[37] "You got a card from so-and-so announcing a fancy open house on Thursday. You didn't need to r.s.v.p. It was at one of those things that I saw Lillian Russell. I was seven or eight. She seemed like an old woman with a not terribly good voice by the time I saw her. But she was a handsome woman in an era of many handsome women. She sang a little song and the grown-ups made such a fuss over her. I remember her voice cracked. It was sad." Lillian Russell, Marie's first great friend in show business, died of uremic poisoning in Pittsburgh on June 6, 1922, at the age of 61.

Jobless and despondent over the deaths of Jim and Lillian, Marie left for Europe at the invitation of Hallie Phillips, the friend she had made during the war. In Austria, they toured a castle when the guide noticed an odd expression on Marie's face. "We've been here before," she finally said.[38] Hallie assured her that this was their first visit. Marie was unconvinced. "I don't care. I've been here before." In a gallery of the castle hung a portrait of an Austrian nobleman. Marie stood before it transfixed. "Hallie," she said. "That might be a picture of my father!"

On further investigation, they learned that the castle had been owned by a von Koerber family, which was proof to Marie that she was a descendant of the castle's noble clan. Alexander had died at the onset of the war and with her family's older generation gone, Marie was urged to do a genealogy by writer Adela Rogers St. Johns. "What difference does it make?" said

Marie.[39] "Don't misunderstand. I believe that breeding is a fine possession. Good blood shows in many ways. But, thank God, in our day and age people are judged for themselves. Besides, there have been plenty of times when I didn't have any silver to put it on and there may be again. You can't get so much for silver from a pawnshop if it's got a crest." Marie could move from majestic Old World aristocrat to destitute vaudevillian in one sentence, but it didn't stop her from henceforth including a von in front of her birth name.

Marie had a special affection for Italy, in part from her friendships with Enrico Caruso and Luisa Tetrazzini. She and Hallie were in Rome as Benito Mussolini took power on October 30, 1922, and her odd affection for him was solidified on this extended trip. Rarely was her gift for naive flippancy more apparent than in her musings on Italian Fascism. Without the slightest trace of irony, she declared that "some folks regard [the Fascisti] as a body of crazy fanatics, [but] I believe with many more that they are earnest in their wish to serve their country."[40] It seemed she likened Italian Fascism to a stern parent. A little intimidation is good for the masses. "I'm not for dictators generally, but I firmly am for Mussolini," she wrote. She credited him with Italy's postwar comeback and she had "a great respect for the Fascisti movement." She may well have been ignorant of Mussolini's brutal but underreported invasion of Libya and the full brunt of Fascism was otherwise not in evidence in 1922. Marie was primarily fond of Fascism's efficiency. "The Italians were snails for speed before they got Mussolini on the job," she noted.[41]

Through an invitation negotiated by her friend Richard Washburn Child, Marie was to meet the pope, Pius XI. Lacking the proper black veil, she cut up her black lace evening gown and wore it on her head. This worked beautifully for their meeting, but she had to climb a long row of stairs to reach the audience chamber and was winded when she reached the top. Once she got there, a young reporter greeted her.

"Now, Miss Dressler, what in that noble old pile impressed you most?" he asked.

Marie sets sail for Europe, refusing to put on a long face during her era of great personal losses.

"The absence of an elevator," said Marie, still panting. "I do wish they'd get a lift for fat old women like me." The reporter saw no humor in Marie's remark, and the next day's headline read "American Actress Annoyed Because She Had to Climb Vatican Stairs!"[42]

In Venice, Dressler visited her friend Lady Alice Colebrooke. Together they attended a huge charity ball. The American wife of an Italian noble sent a message to Marie, asking her to appear during the evening, but Marie refused. "I don't like that woman," said Marie. "She's cruel, she's unkind, she hurts people. Just giving a charity ball won't make up for it and I want nothing to do with the affair."[43]

Marie did not keep her feelings secret and the woman confronted her. "I hear that you say I am cruel. How dare you make such a remark?"

"I'm sorry that you heard that," responded Marie. "But I did say it and I think that it is true."

"And for that you refuse to help for charity, to give your talent to help the poor people?"

"I will come to your ball," countered Marie. "I will buy a table and I will be there. But I will not perform — unless the ball is a flop. If I see that it is not a success — well, I'll be there."

She was there. The most anticipated appearance of the evening was by the notorious Gilda Gray, whose famous shimmy dance was the talk of more than one continent. It was very briefly the rage and everyone seemed to have an opinion on its proper execution. Rudolph Valentino said that "if you must do the shimmy, do not shake the shoulders, shake only the hips, but just gracefully, lightly, otherwise the shimmy is suggestive and vulgar."[44]

Apparently Gray's shoulders were shaking that night. In front of royalty and dignitaries of every stripe, her dance was a dud. Guests were declining champagne and leaving. Marie, in her endless desire to fix things and as promised to the hostess, decided to rescue the proceedings. The orchestra had begun playing the "Blue Danube Waltz." Marie silenced them by lifting her hand. "Play that shimmy music, boys," she instructed the orchestra. "And put twice as much wiggle in it. Remember there's two times as much of me as there is of Miss Gray." Venetian society loved Marie's interpretation; those who rose to leave sat down and the hostess approached her to voice appreciation. "You have been very kind."

"It's a nice thing to find in other folks sometimes, isn't it?" said Marie. "I bid you good night."

Marie summarized her love for Italy by noting "all that wonderful artistry that I never thought I'd get a chance to enjoy; things I have been starved for all my life" were found there.[45]

She even wrote a poem in celebration of the place:

If your World goes wrong,
Or your Heart is clogged;
If you're tired of Life,
Or your Soul seems flogged,
Go to Sunny Italy, and
Take a drop from the blue in the "Heavens"
Take a drop from the Waters that run,
Take a breath from the hearts of the people
That bask 'neath that glorious Sun.
Take as much of their simple feeling
As you can crush into the bowl
And hold it tightly enfolded
As close as you can to your Soul:
And then just before mixing,
I pray you ponder and *think*
That there's not a thing in it could hurt you
So fill up your glasses and drink
To — ITALY — Io t'amo ITALY.

Marie returned to the States via Naples with 1,667 others aboard the new steamship *Conte Rosso*. She was invigorated, but America was still obsessed with youth and flappers. With the vote came hair clipping for women and flagrant defiance of Prohibition. Bathtub gin was popular, as were public displays of smoking through long cigarette holders. The new chic, slender, and naughty image of womanhood left Marie in the dust though she continued to attempt elegance and refinement. In her reactions, she was sounding evermore like a bitter has-been. She declared, in half jest as always, that if she were a legislator she would pass a law abolishing the flapper.[46] As if in battle with new trends, she remarked that "my comedy has always been clean stuff. I know how to cater to refined people. Believe me, you have to be clever and up to date to get comedy over these days. They will not laugh at horse play anymore."

After months of inactivity, she was offered a small role in another Shubert production. Lee and Jake were Marie's sole employers in the early 1920s and she was elated to be working again. She wrote to Frances and Fred Thomson in California with a vaguely worded letter suggesting her role was a star vehicle.[47] "Think what this means to me after being in Europe so long away from my American audiences to come back a Shubert star! How I wish you were here to see this homecoming."

In January 1923 Marie opened in *The Dancing Girl* at the Winter Garden. It was found to have an "absence of any real wit" and a nearly nonexistent plot concerning a ship-to-shore romance that served as an excuse for various "passengers" to provide moments of merriment.[48] The big news surrounding the production was the redecoration of the Winter Garden, done up in gold and cream, with soft mulberry-colored damask silk panels and new velvet carpets and upholstery.[49]

Marie appeared late in the performance and offered a sendup of *Rain*, the current hit play based on a Somerset Maugham story.[50] She got some good notices for her minor involvement in *The Dancing Girl*, but fellow actor Jack Pearl observed her profound anxieties.[51] "In every performance we played together, she'd have stage fright so bad I thought she'd never go on. She'd stand there, shaking, and say, 'I can't face them, Jack! I can't remember a single word. I'm sick at my stomach. I'm no good, anyhow. I tell you, I can't go out there and face them!' Never saw anybody get in such a state. But I loved her like I love nobody but my own mother."

Frances Marion was in New York to surprise Marie at her latest Broadway opening.[52] Frances's career had only been ascending since their last meeting. She directed her husband in his film debut with Mary Pickford in *The Love Light* for United Artists in 1921 and used Fred again in *Just Around the Corner* for Paramount in 1922. She was troubled by the program at the Winter Garden. Marie was wedged between Trini, the overpublicized Spanish dancer of the title, and Kitty Doner in drag singing, "I'm a Devil with the Ladies." Through her run with *The Dancing Girl*, Marie was consigned to vaudeville hell by her middle billing on an absurdly eclectic program.

When Marie came on, Frances applauded enthusiastically, only to realize that the reception was tepid at best. In one of her trademark bizarre outfits, Marie bellowed, "Hiya, boys and gals and all my pals." The audience did not respond. Her stories were poorly timed. The audience remained cool and quiet save for a derisive remark here and there.

Marie was desperate when she proclaimed, "I'm going to play an old favorite and want my pals to sing along with me." By this time, the dead audience was so upsetting to her that she staggered back into the piano, which moved several feet from her weight. This brought welcome laughter. "Mercy!" yelled Marie. The war with the piano continued until she could make her exit. She took one bow before the applause ceased. One man near Frances commented, "Pitiful, isn't it? When will those old-timers learn to quit?"

Frances rushed to Marie's dressing room. "Please show me where I'll find Miss Dressler," she asked someone backstage.

"In the underground dressing room, number six. She sure laid an egg tonight, poor old thing."

Frances found Marie backstage looking pasty and swollen in the eyes. She was sitting alone in her dressing room, staring at the long-stemmed red roses Frances had sent. In her hand was the greeting card, "Blessings and love," that accompanied the flowers. "Hello," Marie said dully, not recognizing her friend.

"Marie! It's Frances."

"Oh, my darling," said a newly animated Marie. "Isn't this wonderful! Such a surprise! Well, bless my buttons, when did you get in?"

"Today."

"Shame on you, not letting me know. I'd've gotten you a seat for tonight's opening. Wonderful show! I'm sure I wowed 'em. Haven't heard any applause for such a long time it was like rain on the desert! Come on, let's get moving. Imagine me down here, but the show is stuffed to the gills with all these new prima donnas insisting they've got to have the best dressing rooms. I just gave in to prove that a star is a star even if they do tuck her into a dingy basement."

Frances and Marie left the theater together and headed for a nearby restaurant. Outside, a group of middle-aged people recognized her.

"Hi there, Marie. Where you been hiding? We've missed you."

Once the two women had sat down to catch up, Marie could no longer carry the burden of her deceit. "I flopped tonight. Thank God you didn't see me."

"I saw you, Marie," said Frances softly.

"Then you know. This was my last chance and I blew it. There were moments on the stage when I thought I'd gone completely off my rocker. But somehow, some way, we pick ourselves up and go on."

The waiter delivered champagne and two glasses. "From your friends over there," he reported as Frances and Marie saw the middle-aged people leaving. They paused to wave good-bye and Marie blew them a kiss. "Old fans who remember me. Know something? I still like this business of living in spite of hell and high water."

"Marie, how often I've heard you say you'd welcome the day when you could retire and take a well-earned rest."

"Hogwash! No actress really wants to retire. It's the kind of talk we bolster ourselves with when we get a whiff of that old skunk failure." Marie raised her glass of champagne. "Can't let this go flat on us like my act tonight. Let's drink and be merry. There's always tomorrow."

The Dancing Girl lasted for three months and toured without Dressler. She still had loyal followers, but they were not loud enough to keep her in audience favor. What was she going to do? Months after *The Dancing Girl* ended its undistinguished run, her options grew fewer. She "communicated delicately and indirectly to various managers that she was ready to return," but no one responded.[53] No doubt aided by the generosity of wealthy friends such as Hallie Phillips, Marie took off for Europe again in search of work. The greeting there was even colder. She played London's Alhambra Theater, where they booed her for past bad behavior.[54] Critics were indifferent to her new show, yet she managed to finally retire a $5,000 debt for the 1909 failure of *Philopoena*. Marie was desperate when Lionel Barrymore spotted her in Venice,[55] playing a dump in the "Italian Subway Circuit." Even the glories of a sunny day on the Piazza San Marco couldn't revive her. Lunching with Lady Alice Colebrooke, Marie was "not wisecracking, but being bravely witty, really witty. She didn't look happy however. She looked to be an aging woman who'd been about a bit and knew it wouldn't get her anywhere to let down."[56] On the trip home, she booked passage third cabin,[57] knowing that most steamship hosts, when eyeing her name on the register, moved her gratis to first class. She often entertained aboard ship in grateful exchange. Once ashore, she told the *New York Times*[58] that if she could not find work here, she would either return to Italy, where living was cheap in *pensiones*, or enter an old ladies' home.

She did neither, but instead took the advice of friends and published an autobiography titled *The Life Story of an Ugly Duckling*, which she wrote in longhand while in Europe. Printed in a dignified burgundy-colored jacket by Robert M. McBride and Company with a cameo-sized profile of Marie embossed on the cover, it sold well and was serialized. There was still an audience for her, or at least for her life's story, but producers were not impressed. Even written praise for the Shuberts made no difference. "The publication of the book did not bring her engagements," noted a reporter.[59] "It was as if she had written of a career that had ended." She didn't have the fire to write as she did to act. Despite authorship of *Ugly Duckling* and several magazine articles, Marie was ambivalent about the written word. She read newspapers devoutly but didn't bother with contracts and scripts. She didn't know how to type and her surviving letters are terse, unpoetic and written in a hurried scrawling hand. With her lack of formal education and the striking difference between her letters and all other writing attributed to her, it is likely she had more than one ghost writer echoing on the page her great extemporaneous witticisms. Friends Helena Dayton and Louise Barrett, it would seem, put together the pieces of *Ugly Duckling*.

In 1924 Marie moved into the Ritz-Carlton Hotel at 46th Street and Madison

Avenue. Her furniture, furs, and jewels were sold to pay various debts and she was left with a small savings account and a few bonds. Friend Albert Keller was manager at the Ritz and he saw to it that she paid next to nothing for the smallest room in the hotel usually occupied by a servant of a guest. Her accommodations were barely enough to fit a bed and dresser. Keller let her stay in exchange for hostessing at the hotel restaurant. "If I had wanted to feel sorry for myself, I never had a better chance," she said.[60] "I just wasn't wanted anywhere — except at parties — and you can't live on banana cake!" She had long since failed to support maid Mamie Steele, who had married affable, cigar smoking Bahamian Jeremiah (Jerry) Cox since working for Marie. Both refused to abandon her. Securing work elsewhere, they paid some of her bills as they were able and brought her food. The Coxes even sneaked into the Ritz to give Marie a massage or press her gowns.[61]

She was astonishingly stoic through the miserable circumstances of her reduced life. "Your public front and your self-confidence are your most important assets," she maintained.[62] She fought hard to be sociable. At a meeting of the Newspaper Women's Club of New York at her new home, she got a note from Will Rogers, a bright new Ziegfeld star. Please come to his table immediately, it said.[63]

"Look here, Muree, I'm in a peck of trouble and you got to help me out," he pleaded through his overworked chewing gum.

"Anything I can do, Will," said Marie as she noticed a gold laurel wreath on the table.

"Well, it ain't much, Muree. Nothin' I wouldn't do for you, if you was caught in a pinch like me."

"Out with it."

"It's like this," said Rogers. "I'm chairman of the committee to award this durn thing (the wreath) to the most beautiful woman in the room. There's so many good-looking dames here I'm scared to pick one for fear the other'll jump on me and tear my hair out by the roots. So I thought — that is, I kinder thought, Muree, if you'd stand there and let me put this durn thing on your head, the crowd would kinder laugh it off and nobody'd get mad!" Nobody got mad that night, including Marie. She had encouraged people to laugh at her looks for years and wrote that "it is some comfort to know that mine is a face which once seen is rarely forgotten."

She amused contributors of the Central Park Association as toastmistress at their gala and served tea in complete barmaid regalia for the Dug-Out Club House war charity, but she was more deeply involved with the American Women's Association, which she cofounded in 1925.[64] The AWA was created to help women with the postwar changes in economics and business. This was to be a full-service association with a meeting place for lectures, concerts, bridge, study groups, dances, and dates. With society doyennes Anne Morgan (daughter of J. Pierpont), Alva E. Belmont, and Anna Steese Richardson involved, they set a $2 million fundraising goal.

Marie kept busy by organizing benefits. She wrote and appeared in plays. She handled radio programs, made speeches, and remained popular with the social bluebloods. She was dropping press releases here and there hoping for a bit of exposure, but in 1925 she had a hard time staying in view. "I knew that when my time came to return to the stage, the public must not realize I had been away from it," she said. The Shuberts sent her on a brief, lackluster vaudeville tour. Actress friend Nella Webb later rustled up some work for her doing one- or two-reel movies in Europe called *Travelaffs*.[65] She was a sort of Mrs. Malaprop with wanderlust at such landmarks as Fontainebleau and Versailles, where she fell into the lake. Funded by press agent Harry Reichenbach, only two were made and the results were worse than bad. With no story or director, they amounted to photographs of beautiful and historic places with Marie coming on to hog the camera and belabor a few laughs. She was so unhappy that she refused to have *Travelaffs* shown and did not even pay for their duty when returning to the United States. They were never recovered from the customs office.

Marie was in Paris when the AWA approached the Rockefellers for a donation.

They originally blinked, believing perhaps that this charity was a bit too bohemian for them. Anne Morgan planned a luncheon for the Rockefellers and she was careful to invite the most conservative contributors and committee members. Marie returned from her *Travelaffs* debacle on the morning of the luncheon, having won some badly needed cash in a shipboard poker game.⁶⁶ As soon as she disembarked, Marie called Anne Morgan's house and was told about the luncheon. "I'll be right over."

Marie was quickly bored by the proceedings; they struck her as unusually stuffy. There was no fun, no life to the gathering. She decided to take action. How about a joke? On her Paris trip, a taxi driver was trying to explain to Marie that her friend lived behind the Hotel Continental. "C'est derrière l'Hotel Continental, c'est derrière l'Hotel Continental," he said, but still she did not understand.

"Que signifie derrière?" asked Marie.

The driver had enough. Using flawless English, he replied, "If madame does not know the meaning of derrière, nobody does!"

The audience was convulsed with laughter; Anna Steese Richardson was in such hysterics she had to be slapped on the back to keep from choking. Still, the Rockefellers were not amused and declined to contribute to the AWA. Only later did Marie learn of the conservative nature of the lunch. "Somebody should have told me! Never mind. I'll sell more bonds in a week than they'd have bought anyhow." She did.

For all her charities, Marie was increasingly despondent. She took comfort in Mark Twain's words, "I have had many troubles, most of which never happened," but her troubles *were* happening. On October 13, 1925, at a dinner for the AWA, she announced her retirement. ⁶⁷ Later she elaborated: "The other night during a speech which I made at a dinner, I said 'I've left the stage!' The sound of those words in my own voice gave me a strange sickening feeling. But it is done and I'm glad to be through with the terrible nerve strain of theatrical work." Her newly announced career was in Florida real estate, where property values were going sky high in the robust postwar economy. She bought what she could but was taken in by con men. A hurricane disrupted the bull market as well, but Marie's woes were brought on primarily by bad judgment. "I allowed myself to be urged into something I knew nothing about. ... Almost beside myself with distress, I did what I could to straighten things out. This experience was one of the most humiliating of my life."⁶⁸ She did not settle the Florida real-estate debt until 1932.

Edward Darling, the compassionate chief booking agent for the Palace, was in the market for veteran troupers. He had luck with nostalgia shows at his vaudeville temple, with Weber and Fields and May Irwin recently cutting up like they did so long ago at the Music Hall. He signed Weber and Fields, Marie Cahill, Cecilia "Cissie" Loftus, and Irwin for an *Old Timers' Week*. When Darling offered a spot to Marie, she told him, "Oh, dear, no; they don't want me anymore."⁶⁹ The same sentiment had already been spoken by Irwin, but a guaranteed $2,000 stopped everyone's coy talk.

Irwin, at 63, was the oldest of the old timers. She was used to dressing at home then reporting to the theater, but she was looking tired and needed to conserve her energy. Marie respectfully said, "I want to give my room to dear May; there's a couch in it, too."⁷⁰ Proud Irwin said no and added "these legs are as good as ever. I'll stand in the wings and watch the acts. Maybe I can steal a few gags."

As the opening night approached, Weber and Fields were incensed at being billed below Marie on the lobby placard. They were quick to point out that Marie had been their employee, not vice versa, and that vaudeville protocol had been breached. They claimed "illness" and didn't appear, but many knew it was a simple case of wounded pride.⁷¹ Marie and her cohorts, including the fine old pros Cahill and Loftus, did well enough without the men and were held over a second week. Marie and Loftus did a sister act and recited some racy dialogue:⁷²

"She never married, did she?"
"No, her children wouldn't let her."

Marie managed a brief solo show during her "retirement," in which she regaled her audience with tales of Europe. "The incidents do not arrive as per schedule," noted one reviewer.[73] "Each anecdote being side-tracked by another, suddenly remembered."

These minor engagements were not enough to restore Marie's optimism in ever again earning a living in the theater or movies. In her memoirs, she was pragmatic and shrewd at hiding her deep pain:[74]

> A time comes when people cannot or may not make the same money as previously and the fact should be accepted as gracefully as possible. When such a situation arises, people off the stage as well as on should be ready to resort to some other means of livelihood. If an artist or a poet starves because the world does not appreciate his talent in dollars, why should some other occupation be scorned? In watching theatrical people, penniless, and with no prospect of a job on the stage, I have never been able to understand why those who were clever enough to play in a show could not be clever enough to try something else — sell goods over a counter or in some way be self-supporting when out of jobs. At any rate, when stage doors are barred to me, I shall be found either buying or selling winter flannels at Baltman's or balancing fish balls at Wild's.

To prove her sincerity, Marie began telling her friends that she would move to Paris and open a hotel for American travelers, even though she spoke no language but English. The theater is too grueling at this point in her life, she added. She was in her late fifties and well past menopause. In her day, such chronology was considered old age, particularly for women. No question, Marie was aging rapidly; her silky skin became corrugated with fine lines, her reddish brown hair grew coarser and flecked with gray, and her impressive singing voice lost much of its range.

There was the damaged psyche to consider as well. She was constantly reminded that there was no place for her in New York or the theater. In 1926 Lew Fields produced *Peggy Ann*, a Freudian reworking of *Tillie's Nightmare*. He bounced back with another hit, but Marie was not even allowed to keep her greatest stage success as hers alone.

Old buddies had their own sagging fortunes to sustain. "A whole volume could be written about the meteoric careers that sink into oblivion, but it is all part of the passing show," she sighed.[75] Two comedy stars of Marie's approximate vintage, Fay Templeton and May Irwin, were retired. Templeton happily set up housekeeping with a Pittsburgh businessman and Irwin saved enough to chill in New York luxury after her *Old Timers'* engagement at the Palace. Maurice Levi, music director for many of Marie's shows, was now selling jewelry in Baltimore.[76] Fondly remembered buildings were going, too. Philadelphia's venerable Chestnut Street Opera House, site for stints of *The Lady Slavey* and *Miss Prinnt*, was demolished in 1913 and Koster and Bial's Music Hall, where Marie performed when she first got to New York, was demolished in 1924.

Most depressing were the many deaths of friends and professional colleagues. George Edwardes, the London impresario, and Mrs. Fish, the society leader, both died in 1915. Brother-in-law Richard Ganthony died in 1924, leaving Bonita as Marie's only close living relative. Marie's allies among producers and managers were gone: *Stag Party* producer Albert Palmer died in 1905, Oscar Hammerstein in 1919, Percy Williams in 1923, and *1492* producer Edward E. Rice in 1924. The great tenor and good friend Enrico Caruso died in 1921. *Tillie's Nightmare* composer A. Baldwin Sloane and actor-friend Sam Bernard both died in 1926. To Marie, the entire business was now run by a flock of young strangers.

"I'm through," she told humorist Irwin Cobb at a dinner party.[77]

"Marie, you're never through until you admit it."

"I don't admit it, I'll never admit it. But I'm a minority of one. Most of these new managers around New York never heard of Marie Dressler. A few of 'em remember that I could clown once. But they think I'm too old now. So I'm going to Europe to live. I can open a hotel in Paris or sell dresses — pick up a living like a sparrow. Yes, it looks as though Dressler is through — and I don't like it."

The opportunities in Paris seemed particularly meaningless one night. So, too, was the charity work or any other pitifully modest ambition. How many more Elizabeth Daltons and Florida real-estate salesmen were waiting? How many more professional ventures would end in ruin and debt? How many more jokes were left about a fat body and a hound-dog face? Dressler saw only more poverty and humiliation waiting in her future. Her career was nonexistent. Even the Shuberts stopped offering her bit parts.

She ate dinner alone at the Ritz, quietly and unrecognized. Show business legend has it that she carried less than $1 in her pocket. She intended to finish dinner, leave the money on the table, walk upstairs to her room, and throw herself out the window.

Chapter 9

The Undying Affection of Friends

Dressler didn't get to her room to commit suicide.[1] Instead, a Ritz Hotel staff person gave her a handwritten note from respected film director Allan Dwan. The note mentioned that he had seen her on stage and admired her, and wondered if she might like to appear in a new film he was directing.[2] Dwan was in the restaurant and watched Marie stagger on the stairs and grab the railing as she exited while the headwaiter rushed over to assist her.

Soon after, a bellboy came to Dwan's table and gave him an invitation to Marie's room. When they met upstairs, Marie asked Dwan if he was serious. When he repeated his offer, she told him she had intended to kill herself that very night. In giving her the role of society matron Mrs. Heath in his new movie *The Joy Girl*, Dwan might be credited not only with giving Marie her first break in years but with saving her life. Dwan went further: he wrote letters of introduction for Marie and paid her way to the Florida movie location.

The circumstances of this meeting and new opportunity with *The Joy Girl* are veiled in mythology. The version found in *My Own Story*[3] and as told by Marie for *Liberty*[4] magazine in 1933 is different from the chance-meeting-in-a-restaurant story. In Marie's recounting, it was Nella Webb who came to the rescue. Marie and Nella's friendship dated back to the Lillian Russell–George Lederer days of 1893, when Marie was just establishing herself in New York.[5] By 1903 Nella was appearing in the Broadway smash *Babes in Toyland*. Seven years Marie's junior, Nella was "a small, dark, animated person with the grace of a humming bird and the persistence of a bull pup." She had abandoned her stage career to devote herself to astrology. In 1926, unmarried and unattached, Nella invited Marie to share a spacious apartment on upper Broadway. No doubt the bill paying burdens were not shared equally between them, as Nella had a thriving astrology business while Marie had a dwindling savings account and a few bonds. Friendship saved Marie yet again and it did her morale substantial good to escape that dreary little bedroom at the Ritz.

With an old friend as roommate, discontent lingered. There was still the professional inactivity, the financial burdens, and the lingering feeling of uselessness. The misguided dream of running a Paris hotel persisted. Marie concluded that her meager savings were just enough to book passage and establish herself abroad. She had purchased her ticket and was ready to leave.

It was Nella, according to Marie's possibly imaginative hindsight, who insisted she stay in the States. "You can't go, Marie," Nella said. "The stars show great things for you — greater things than you have ever had yet. In January — on January 17, 1927 — you're going to get a message offering you new work. You must listen to me!"

"I'll give you until the 17th," said Marie.

Nella held onto that date and insisted that Marie return from a trip to Atlantic City to be home for the "message." On January 17, in the afternoon, Marie and Nella were in their living room entertaining two friends. At five o'clock, the phone rang.

The call was from Allan Dwan. Would Marie be interested in taking a small role in his new film shooting in Florida? Marie was again disappointed. Her original thought was "no thank you," this job was not worth sacrificing a trip to Paris, the chance to begin a new life and leave behind the many ghosts of New York.

By Nella's repeated consultations with charts and graphs, the horoscope boasted that Marie's greatest years were ahead, not behind. The stars foretold amazing success, worldwide influence, activity, and happiness. Nella had to persuade Marie to accept *The Joy Girl* part. Marie sniffed at the tiny role of Mrs. Heath, but Nella was adamant. "It's all here, Marie," she insisted.[6] "Motion pictures must be the thing for you. You've got to take whatever offers, for that way opportunity lies."

"Humph!" said Marie. "You've been singing that tune a long time. We made motion pictures last year, didn't we, and where did it get us? Yes, sir, we made motion pictures. I've made a lot of motion pictures. Once before I got my own company and I'm still paying back money to folks who invested in that. I don't want anything more to do with them!"

"We were premature," Nella continued as she consulted the charts and books spread out before her. "Didn't I tell you you'd get a telephone call this very day about motion pictures? I tell you, this is too plain to be wrong!"

"Nope," she told Nella. "I'm not going to do it! I'm going to Paris and start my hotel over there. I'm going to devote myself to that."

Nella called on their mutual friend, playwright James Forbes, to intervene. He came over that night, as did friends Helena Dayton and Louise Barrett. Nella read off Marie's chart, predicting greatness around the corner. The others did not have faith in astrology, but they felt obligated to prevent Marie from making a foolish decision. With everyone fully assembled, Marie spoke of her hotel plans.[7] "An ideal conclusion for a female entertainer, because I'll never have to diet again," said Marie as she sipped one of her favorite drinks, ginger ale and lemon rind. "Nothing but American cooking. Think of all the Americans who'd love some real ham and eggs! And plenty of baths. And I'll kinda make things lively around there, so it'll seem like home. You can come and stay, Jimmy, and Nella."

Marie recited her long list of friends, then one of the women interjected, no longer able to contain herself. "Hotel keeper, my eye! She'll never collect a bill!" Then came Jimmy's turn. "Who's going to stay at your hotel besides your friends, Marie?" He drove his point home. "You know what'll happen, don't you? You'll be running the finest free boarding house in Europe. Oh, you'll be a fine hotel keeper, Marie! Every American girl, ever down-and-out actor, every poor hungry art student, anybody you ever knew or heard of that's broke in Europe will be eating off you. You'll never turn anybody away, and you'll never collect any bills, and you'll give most of them money to get back to America. It won't last six months — unless you've got the United States Mint back of you."

Marie conceded. "Oh, all right. But you'll make yourself awfully unpopular some day, Jimmy, being always right!"

"You're going [to Florida]," said Nella, "if I have to ship you by freight."

Dressler reported to the Palm Beach set of *The Joy Girl,* not so secretly thrilled to be in front of the cameras again. *The Joy Girl* was a light comedy about the exploits of pretty showoff Olive Borden snaring handsome and wealthy playboy Neil Hamilton. Marie's role was indeed tiny. She appeared on the set Tuesday morning, and by Wednesday night she was on the return train to New York. The minor assignment in *The Joy Girl* was less important as a role than as a promise of more employment in movies. Talk of house cleaning, hotel hostessing, and breadlines ended, at least temporarily. The experience made her a convert to astrology.[8] "I have checked up on my horoscope many times and have never once failed to find them accurate. They don't fail. All of the scientists in the world don't know the meaning of life. The stars and influencing bodies of the heavens do."

Marie played her role with enough vitality to earn some notice, if not employment. Returning to New York, and not daring to dream of the future Nella promised, Marie found that the offers did not come tumbling in. It was very difficult to shun the taint of decline that marked so much of her public life after World War I. Friends noted a "sad searching look in her eyes."

Frances Marion's star was still rising. After defining Mary Pickford in more than a dozen films, she wrote profitable movies at Fox, United Artists, and First National before being nabbed by young Metro-Goldwyn-Mayer. Her creative output was staggering, and she now enjoyed an enviable position as a powerful player within the secure walls of a thriving new studio. MGM executives, most notably the "boy wonder" head of production Irving Thalberg and the paternalistic studio kingpin Louis B. Mayer, regularly deferred to Frances for production decisions.

Frances had not forgotten Marie or her wretched condition at the Winter Garden Theater two years earlier. She was foremost a loyal friend. Fellow Hollywood writer Adela Rogers St. Johns noted that "behind a Madonna-like face and a shy-and-lady-like manner, Frances Marion had the rugged determination of a boa constrictor where a friend was concerned."[9] She was more modest about her loyalty, noting that "Marie's kindness is something you could never forget."

While she was thinking of Marie, a letter arrived for Frances from Elisabeth Marbury, a former theater producer now a high-powered literary agent. Marbury was aware of Marie's desperation — she, Anne Morgan, and Marie had lunch together only days before. She wrote to Frances:[10]

> I know that our mutual friend, Marie Dressler, has been writing you about her bonanza year in Florida, that she is still being sought after by theatrical producers and has done another successful movie. Not a word of this is true, but that's our Marie; she wants to spare anyone she loves. The Florida deal was a fiasco. She hasn't had a single offer from any theatrical source, even second-rate roadshow companies. The movie "success" was a very small part Allan Dwan gave her out of the kindness of his heart. ... Today, I found out that she is planning to accept a job as a housekeeper in a Long Island home. Isn't it possible for you to write a part for her in one of your movies?

With timing perfect enough to melt any skepticism about Nella's astrology, Frances perused a list of projects in development at MGM and lit upon *The Callahans and the Murphys*. Based on a novel by Kathleen Norris, the story revolved around two raucous Irish matrons. Why not match Marie with that Irish comedienne Polly Moran, currently under contract at the studio? Here were two plum parts for character actresses and Marie, she believed, would be perfect. Frances got to work writing a screen adaptation. She was willing to make a professional sacrifice on behalf of Marie, and so she approached Thalberg. She dropped the working script off at his office and made a return visit a few days later. Thalberg, with whom Frances was chummy, told her he had read it and liked it. The casting question was broached. "Who do you see in it?" he asked.

"Polly Moran," Frances answered casually.

"Yes, she'd be good as Mrs. Murphy," Thalberg said. "But whoever plays Mrs.

Callahan must be a dramatic actress as well as a comedienne."

"Do you remember Marie Dressler?" Thalberg nodded.

"She's the only actress who could do it justice," she said.

"But I haven't heard of her in years," answered Thalberg.

"You haven't! Why she's one of the greatest comediennes on Broadway. That's just it. If we want to get her back in pictures, we'll have to give her a big salary — say, $2,000 a week."

"Irving," Frances said, "Marie's a friend of mine. She needs a job." On that, Frances took Elisabeth Marbury's letter out of her purse and handed it to him.

"I thought so," he answered. "I'll talk it over with L. B."

By the time of their next meeting, Thalberg was convinced: "My theory is that anybody who hits the bull's-eye — it doesn't matter in what profession — has the brains and the stamina to do it again. So I figure a woman who scored as often as Miss Dressler did should be able to repeat. She's probably been the victim of bad writing — and bad advice. Send for her. We'll start the picture as soon as she gets here. And her salary will be — $1,500 a week."

"Glory be!" shrieked Frances. "The marines to the rescue!"

Marie had been hesitant to get too excited about *The Joy Girl*. Not so when *The Callahans and the Murphys* was confirmed. Frances was given the pleasure of telling Marie the good news. Marie and Nella were both home the night Frances called. Marie was making a dress in her usual way.[11] She put the material on the floor and cut it without pattern or markings. Then she lay down over it on her stomach and sewed it up.

Marie received the unexpected phone call in New York late in the evening. "Pack up your pie box," said Frances, "and come to Hollywood. I need you!" She outlined the highlights and Marie was instructed to catch the next train to California. Nella danced a jig in her nightgown. Racing with excitement, they stayed up all night drinking black coffee. Mamie packed Marie's shabby belongings and early the next morning she and Marie were at the train station with their tickets to Los Angeles. Jerry, Mamie's husband, had to stay in New York indefinitely for his work. Whatever possessed Mamie to such heights of devotion? "Miss Dressler is a darned good woman and can't be beat," she declared.[12] "Look for a long time — you'll never find another. That's from the heart."

Their anticipation must have made the trip aboard the Chief very long. The women spent most of the trip in their compartment, not taking full advantage of the impeccable service and esprit de corps that was the fashion of transcontinental trains of the 1920s. Instead, they played endless rounds of honeymoon bridge, a game that soothed Marie's jangled nerves.

The train arrived in Los Angeles on March 7 with Frances waiting at the station. She was initially shocked at how haggard Marie looked, changed even since their last meeting. "She looked old and shabby," remembered Frances.[13] "Gone was the spring in her walk, the upward thrust of her chin, the way she used to pull her shoulders back. ... Her flesh seemed flabby, her eyes dull. What hell she must have gone through."

"Frances! Am I glad to see you again," Marie roared as she stepped off the train. "It's been donkey's ears. I almost fainted when I got your wire! Came at a time when I was juggling a big deal! Almost settled for it instead of your movie, but decided on the latter because I didn't want to miss the chance of a visit with you." Frances saw through the lie immediately and found the display a bit pitiful. Marie was openly enthusiastic. "Gee, I'm glad you asked me to stay with you, we'll have lots of time for chin wags."

Marie and Frances proceeded to talk excitedly. It was only then that the sequence of events were fully revealed to Marie, how the letter from Elisabeth Marbury arrived on her desk, how the novel of *The Callahans and the Murphys* struck Frances as a perfect vehicle for Marie, and how she beefed up the role of Ma Callahan. Marie and Mamie's brief stay with Frances and Fred Thomson was agreeable with everyone, particularly infant son Fred Junior. Frances credits Marie with eliciting his first smile.

Marie had her first taste of new Hollywood splendor. The Thomsons were at the top of their games, Fred was a major movie star, and they lived in a spectacular estate nicknamed the Enchanted Hill.[14] Perched on more than 20 acres in Beverly Hills, the rambling Spanish-style house featured a stone fireplace, beamed ceilings in the living room, a library, photo lab, aviary, tiled barbecue, film editing room, huge windows, swimming pool, and tennis court. The Thomsons loved to entertain and their parties were populated by educators, athletes, artists, scientists, archaeologists, and explorers such as Robert Flaherty, maker of the landmark Eskimo documentary *Nanook of the North*.

Shooting began immediately on *The Callahans and the Murphys* and Marie's broad brand of comedy was an instant hit at MGM. During those first days on the set, with a candor reserved for real friends, Marie finally told Frances the whole story of her life with Jim Dalton. She told of her deep betrayal, how her love for him had turned ugly, how it came to be that their marriage was a fraud, how he had paid a man to pose as a minister, how he insisted she sell the Vermont farm to produce musicals in London, and how her fortune was lost on his bad management and gambling. She told of his stroke and diabetic debilitation and how his wife supplanted her in Jim's burial—the final indignity. Frances found Marie's professional inactivity painful, but her personal life made the whole scenario grotesque.

"That belongs to the past, Marie," Frances said quietly.

Breaking free of the horrible memories, Marie returned to the present. "Now tell me if you think I'm putting on a good show in *The Callahans and the Murphys*."

"You and Polly will make the greatest team in the business."

During the early days of her Los Angeles return, Marie made many new friends and became reacquainted with old ones. She saw more of actress Hedda Hopper, who was

Watching out for Marie: Frances Marion, circa 1928. (Courtesy of Cari Beauchamp.)

devoted to Frances. Though she and Marie were friends as well, more than once they vied for Frances's affection. Marie found Polly Moran agreeably daffy and together they grew chummy with puckish young comic William Haines. His homosexuality was the worst kept secret in Hollywood and he and Polly were forever joking about their imminent marriage. The older women loved his wit and style. If Fred was busy, Billy escorted Frances to a premiere or some other industry event.

Marie was filled with love and gratitude for friends old and new. She was fierce in her demands, and some associates—Frances most notably—met her requirements. In *My Own Story*, she demonstrates the generous spirit that won her so much love:[15] "If I have a gift in this world, it is for picking friends. Those I've made have stuck to me through thick and thin. Maybe because I've tried to be a friend. Friendship is worth any hardship, any sacrifice. It is the one bloom that remains fresh and fragrant when the years have stripped our lives of frailer blossoms. Fame, money, health—these come and go. But real friendship persists."

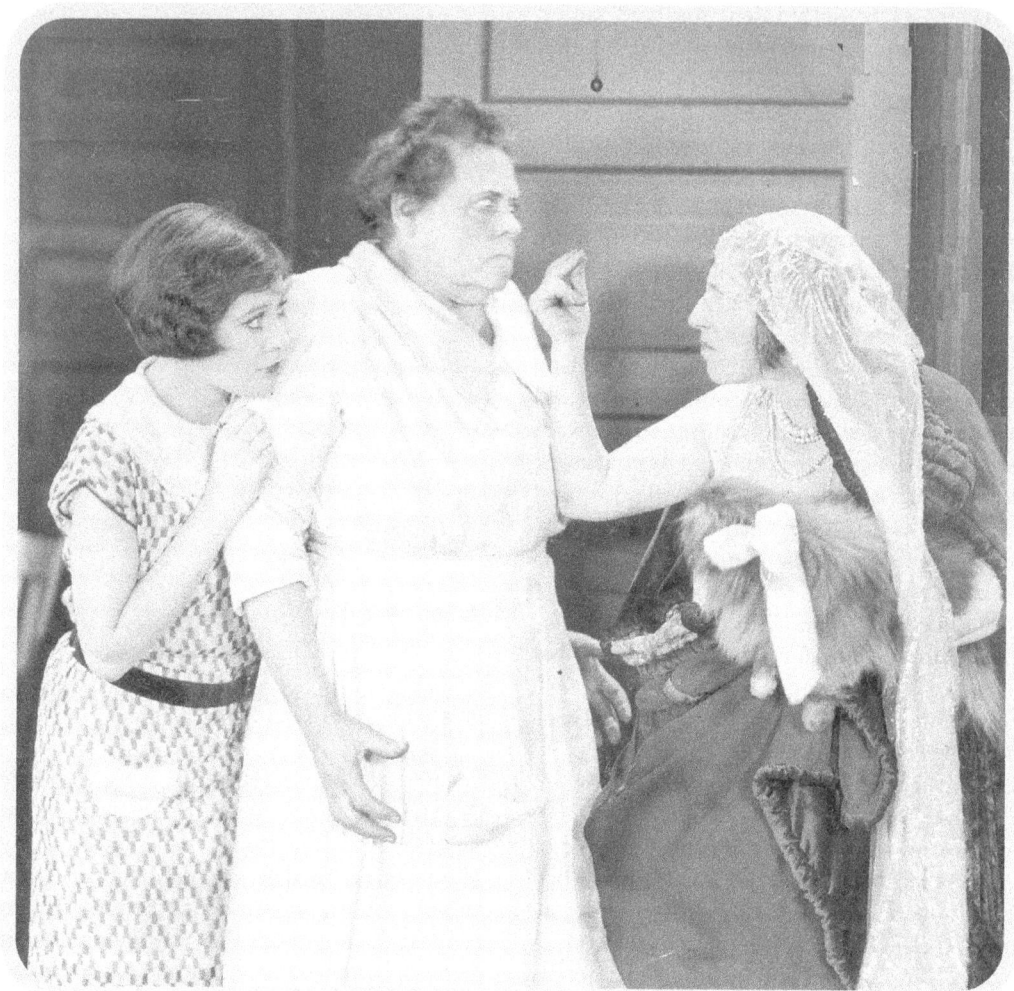

Sally O'Neil demurs, Marie seethes, and Polly Moran threatens in the infamous *The Callahans and the Murphys* (1927).

Marie enjoyed making *The Callahans and the Murphys*. She found the cast and crew good fun and, not surprisingly, she adored having a starring film role again. *The Callahans and the Murphys* was a silent movie, and the set was filled with the familiar assortment of human and mechanical noises. Still, technological advances had occurred. The camera was more fluid and acting was less broad. Gone was the improvised style of the Keystone days — character development was more important than hurling physical tricks.

Hollywood, too, had changed. The HOLLYWOOD sign went up in 1923 as a real-estate gimmick. The tiny hamlet that fostered Keystone had become a chic and wealthy enclave. The chaos of moviemaking had given way to a more formal hierarchy of status based on professional duty and rank. Studios had learned how to make and sell stars, and enormous fortunes came to successful producers, directors, and actors. In this new environment, Marie thrived. Southern California agreed with her as always. She delighted in the open space and the fragrance of orange blossoms that reached into downtown Hollywood from the surrounding orchards.

Preview night arrived for *The Callahans*

and the Murphys, and sitting with the nervous Marie and Frances was visiting New Yorker Nella Webb.[16] James Forbes, who had moved to Hollywood as Mayer's handpicked studio dialogue director, was there too. Frances detested Jimmy. He was a vicious editor of her scripts, but she was tolerant because he was Marie's friend. George Hill, a longtime family friend of the Thomsons, directed the simple story of two slum families. The Callahan daughter (Sally O'Neil) has a baby by the Murphy son (Lawrence Gray), but the movie centers on the two mothers, who take to beer, gossip, picnics, and laughter with unbridled zeal.

The preview audience howled on first viewing. Marie, Frances, Nella, and Jimmy wept at the audience's response. Apparently, the studio had struck pay dirt with the pairing of these two rowdy gals. The crowd nearly mobbed Marie at the movie's conclusion. She was a new discovery to these young filmgoers who had no memory of her years on stage. Intoxicated with happiness, Marie and her friends headed for the Enchanted Hill to celebrate. They were up all night.

"The stars were right," Nella reminded the group.

"I knew you'd do it, you old hotel keeper!" needled Jimmy.

"Your future is all set," said Frances. "You'll be such a hit in this picture you'll never have another day off."

Marie could no longer contain herself. She sobbed, "I'm a fool, but I'm so happy."

When *The Callahans and the Murphys* opened in June 1927, the studio had an unprecedented challenge in selling the comic appeal of two middle-aged frumps. The marketing was substantial, with MGM using a litany of now-forgotten silent comedy teams for comparison. "There was [Wallace] Beery and [Raymond] Hatton in *Behind the Front*; there was [Charlie] Murray and [Chester] Conklin in *McFadden's Flats*; There was [George K.] Arthur and [Karl] Dane in *Rookies* and now — the first comedy woman team surely the greatest of all!"[17] For a brief time, everyone had reason to believe the hyperbole. The *New York Times*[18] reviewed it as "a rough and tumble comedy that plays for loud laughs and occasional sentiment. ... a flower pot, a keg of beer and a baby [are put] to proverbial uses and, with those who have always liked such, hilarity results." Marie and Polly drew laughs as they tippled gin before the intertitle that read, "This stuff makes me see double and feel single."

"The cast speaks for itself," continued the *Times*. "Those who have followed stage and screen at all know Marie Dressler and Polly Moran. To them falls most of the work — and they work industriously at their mugging for comic effect and fighting for the fun of the thing." *Variety*[19] announced that "the playing of the two featured women is never out of key. ... it is a fine faithful transcript from life, and therein it is a bit of art, a credit to its producer, its director and its excellent cast." Even Charlie Chaplin and Harold Lloyd proclaimed it as one of the funniest movies ever.

The early enthusiasm to *The Callahans and the Murphys* was short-lived. A storm of protest rose from Irish Americans just before the movie went into national release. Headed by the Hibernian Society, the Roman Catholic Church, and various Irish American organizations, the movie was blasted for its many episodes of insulting and defamatory drinking and fighting. "One thing you learned when you wrote for the movies, all nationalities were sensitive except Americans," noted Frances,[20] who had larded Kathleen Norris's story with much slapstick on behalf of Marie and Polly. "You can make [Americans] the most sinister villains and never hear a word of protest from Washington, Chicago, Kalamazoo or all points west. But should you describe a villain belonging to any other country but America, you found yourself spread-eagled between the Board of Censors and the Diplomatic Service of some foreign power. That is why we exploited gangsters, cattle rustlers, robber barons, pickpockets and con men and gave them good old American names like Steve Carter, so we would not be embarrassing Mexicans, Chinese, Egyptians or what have you."

Frances deviated from her rule and was stung for it. *The Callahans and the Murphys* was seen as a giant ethnic joke, a laugh at the expense of the Irish.[21] One scene had a band playing while the musicians pass out one by one until only the drummer is left hitting a snare drum unrhythmically. In another, Mrs. Callahan picks fleas off her nightgown and young Terrance enjoys putting the chamber pot on his head. Outrage moved to destruction as a chemical bomb, rocks, rotten fruit and vegetables, acid, and ink damaged theaters and wounded patrons wherever the movie was showing. Theaters were picketed, and a scroll with more than a thousand signatures was sent to the studio decrying this crime against the Irish.

Through 1927, as the movie was screened regionally for representatives of the powerful Motion Picture Producers and Distributors of America (MPPDA),[22] numerous objections were raised. The chief recurring complaint was the women's drinking, though certain lines were ordered to be struck before it could be screened in Ohio, Texas, Wisconsin, and Virginia. To one MPPDA group, the title card "Goat Alley is a section where a courteous gentlemen [sic] always takes off his hat before striking a lady" had to be deleted. Still other groups winced at Mrs. Callahan's remark after changing the diapers of a newly adopted baby boy. She discovered her charge "ain't a Jew baby."

Black Americans were as maligned as anyone in *The Callahans and the Murphys*. Not commented on by the MPPDA or the Catholic Church are the script's references to "nigger toes" and the butting of heads between a goat and a "negro down on hands and knees." The goat, not the man, goes flying in the head-on collision. Ignoring these scenes, the censoring brigade got hot only when the script implied that the Irish were of a lower status than African Americans: "Several colored waiters arrive at the picnic, put on an apron and get ready for work. When told it is an Irish picnic they yank aprons off in a hurry and run for their lives." The scene was cut and the Irish regained a modicum of dignity.

Not everyone was outraged by the Irish smears. Jason S. Joy, director of studio relations at MPPDA and chief abolitionist of blasphemy, profanity, and vulgarity from original scripts, reported that he spoke with a hundred priests and nuns and found "no one who had any objections against the industry on the grounds that it offended the church. I had many conversations with them regarding *The Callahans and the Murphys* and similar pictures and found no evidence that the church was offended."

Plenty of others were mightily offended. Carl E. Milliken, secretary of the MPPDA, reported 125 complaints from various Irish American organizations by August 26. Some written responses were particularly ugly. *Irish World* delivered these remarks:[23] "Marie Dressler, who appears as Mrs. Callahan, has successfully impersonated a gorilla. Miss Dressler, as she appears in this film, might take the beauty prize as an ape in the jungle. That Miss Dressler chooses to look like this is her own business — or misfortune. That she should pretend to be an Irish woman is an insult to every woman of the race." The passionate reactions were dumbfounding to the Irish who worked at the studio, including producer Eddie Mannix and Irish-descended director George Hill. The Irish Polly and the quarter–Irish Marie were similarly shocked. So were the young leads Lawrence Gray and Sally O'Neil, both of Irish descent.

Frances suggested renaming it *The Browns and the Joneses*, but it was too late. MGM attempted to quell the protests with select editing, but they realized the movie would be incoherent if all complaints were answered. The studio then searched for endorsements from Irish Americans who liked the movie, but none came forward. Even the original author, Kathleen Norris, joined in the protests. Loew's theaters received so much nasty mail that owner Marcus Loew declined further distribution. In November MGM withdrew *The Callahans and the Murphys* from release still $44,000 in the red.*

**Loew died unexpectedly during* The Callahans and the Murphys *brouhaha on September 6, 1927, at the age of 57. Mayer, Thalberg, and others mourned him as a giant in the motion-picture business.*

One piece of correspondence from the MPPDA office expressed "serious regret" at the retirement of the movie, but the National Catholic Welfare Conference noted that the withdrawal "so tardily and reluctantly taken by producers, is an admission on their part that the criticisms of the production on the ground of offense to race, religion and public morality were well founded."

Dressler was devastated by the disappearance of *The Callahans and the Murphys*, but she was typically stoic with Frances and others.[24] "Don't worry about me, dear. My friend, Nella Webb, studying my astrological chart, says that I'm passing through a sabbatical year. With Jupiter going backwards, and with my progressed Moon in opposition to my progressed Mercury, I must expect these little setbacks." Frances was disappointed and hurt as well, but she understood that the movie meant much more to Marie than it did to her. For the prolific writer, it was only another potential hit in a string of successes. Knowing Marie had to persevere as an actress to save her sanity and possibly her life, Frances and others persuaded her to stay in town. They all assured the despairing 58-year-old that other projects would come along, though Marie wasn't easily convinced.

Marie may have stayed in Los Angeles not because of tenacity and willpower, but because she neither could afford nor had compelling reasons to live on the East Coast. She announced,[25] "I was homesick for New York, went back, passed Christmas in freezing weather — and now I'm in California for good." Back in Los Angeles, with film roles nowhere to be found, she was again reduced to working party gigs. One such event, a "frolic and ball," featured her with Hedda Hopper and Sam Chipman, Marie's longtime piano accompanist.

Even such minor engagements were rare. After leaving Frances and Fred's Enchanted Hill, Marie checked into the Ambassador Hotel on Wilshire Boulevard. More than a few industry types were in residence, and the Cocoanut Grove nightclub in the hotel was a favorite haunt for early Hollywood. True luminaries lived in the mansions of Beverly Hills or Whitley Heights above Hollywood, while the lesser lights resided at the hotel. Marie lasted there for two months. "It grew embarrassing to live at the Ambassador," she confessed.[26] "When I arrived there, everybody assumed that I was up some company's sleeve. I naturally let this assumption ride. Then they would say, 'Let us in on the secret. What picture are you scheduled for?' In reply to these questions, I had to smile and look mysterious and it's mighty hard to say nothing and look mysterious for two months with my open nature."

Marie next rented a bungalow on Hillside Avenue above Hollywood Boulevard, placed an ad in the Standard Casting Directory, and waited. Many days were spent playing solitaire, playing the piano, singing, and attending to her mutt Friday. Her *Callahans and Murphys* salary had been generous, and occasionally she saw a check for some revival of *Tillie's Punctured Romance*, but finances again dwindled to almost nothing. She was rescued once more by wealthy friends. Marie, ever full of Victorian discretion, did not name her benefactors, but they gave her a check large enough to carry her an entire year.

When the familiar deprivation returned, Marie turned to prayer and friends for comfort.[27] Without the benefit of a church she could pray almost anywhere, on a set, in a park, or at home. She once said that "if you pray this and mean it, it's all you'll ever need." She often recited her favorite prayer, by Louise Wheatley:

Teach me to love not those who first love me,
But all the world, with that rare purity,
With that true ecstasy of broad outreaching thought
Which bears no earthly taint
But holds in its embrace — humanity.
Teach me to love.

She continued to work at benefits and parties at a depressed fee hovering around $150. Some months after *The Callahans and the Murphys* was yanked from distribution and *The Joy Girl* came and went from theaters, Marie was given a small role in *Breakfast at Sunrise,* a seven-reeler directed by Malcolm St. Clair at the First National Studio. Its leading lady was Constance Talmadge, a major silent-screen star who was not coincidentally a good friend of Frances.

This adaptation of a French farce of romantic jealousies was not particularly well received. The *New York Times* review dwelt on the sets and costumes, not finding anything else worth much comment. Marie made a few customary funny faces as Her Royal Highness Queen Sophia of Hernia, in consort with General Vibration and Prince Cyril Nitwitz. Silly names notwithstanding, the film did little to advance her stalled position among Hollywood character types. *Breakfast at Sunrise* made such a minor impression on Marie that she obliviously called it *Breakfast in Bed* to a reporter. Work dried up again until a stage offer presented itself.

The character actor Edward Everett Horton was mounting a stock production of Ferenc Molnár's *The Swan* to play in Los Angeles.[28] Knowing Marie was in town, he offered her the role of dowager princess Beatrice, mother to Lois Wilson's princess. She was to receive $125 a week, 5 percent of her top vaudeville fee, for an eight-week run. She accepted with gratitude.

The Swan was playing in Los Angeles when film work was again available. Hungry for more opportunities in movies, Marie unceremoniously left Horton and his company. Horton, known for his generosity and good nature, was disappointed, but Marie's ambition for a comeback was acute. He recalled the episode: "She ... was most efficient in the role [as Beatrice]. The cast loved her and waited on her constantly. She received an offer to sign with MGM and I was pleased to release her from her contract." Horton bore no grudge; they remained friends and he worked to secure Marie another film offer in 1929. Actors' departures from stage productions for more lucrative and higher-profile movie gigs has been the bane of theater producers in Los Angeles for decades. For Marie, however, this episode was different, for *The Swan* was to be her last stage appearance. Her preference for making movies, and more money, was clear. She would not, after all, have persevered for so many years if film work had not been her first priority. As she puts it in *My Own Story,*[29] "I had given up knocking at stage doors to wait for an opening wedge in a movie studio."

Marie left Horton and *The Swan* for *Bringing Up Father*. Penned by Frances, the movie was an adaptation of the popular comic strip by George McManus that ran in William Randolph Hearst publications. It seemed only fitting, therefore, that *Bringing Up Father* be supervised by MGM's Hearst-owned unit company Cosmopolitan Productions. The cast included J. Farrell MacDonald as the henpecked milquetoast Jiggs and *The Callahans and the Murphys* survivor Polly Moran as Maggie. *Bringing Up Father* was another comedy of rough hewn Irish slapstick, which made everyone tense.[30] Eddie Mannix defended the project to Jason Joy, who wrote a cautious memo to Will Hays at the MPPDA office during *The Callahans and the Murphys* mess: "Metro-Goldwyn-Mayer are now contemplating the making of a picture based on the comic strip *Bringing Up Father* ... because of the agitation among the Irish folk created by *The Callahans and the Murphys*, extra care ought to be taken with any picture dealing with this subject."

A collective sigh was heard when *Bringing Up Father* opened in March 1928. This time, the Marie-Polly team had benign comic appeal. There were no picket lines, perhaps because Maggie and Jiggs were already well recognized cartoon characters. In the supporting role of Annie Moore, Marie was praised, but *Variety*[31] announced that "it does not flatter the Irish. It represents an Irish wife and mother as a vile-tempered nagger." The public was none too impressed with the abundant "rolling-pin humor," and *Bringing Up Father* did only middling business. Marie's morale was boosted by a trip to Europe studded with her usual preferred company of nobility and aristocrats.

Marie's next movie, *The Patsy*, was more successful. *Bringing Up Father* had brought

J. Farrell MacDonald checks his likeness to Jiggs as Marie holds original George McManus cartoon drawings of Maggie and Jiggs during the production of *Bringing Up Father* (1928). Marie is made up as Annie Moore and looking on is director Jack Conway. Even with William Randolph Hearst's marketing machine behind the movie, it met with a tepid public reception. (Courtesy of Eric D. Bernhoft.)

her to the renewed attention of publisher/art collector/politician/film producer Hearst[32] and his longterm girlfriend, the actress Marion Davies. Made in a glitch-free 30 days, the film was financed by MGM, where the eccentric newspaper giant had enormous influence. He in fact conducted much of his newspaper and film business from a two-story Spanish-style house built on the studio lot. In the cozy arrangement, Hearst produced MGM films at Cosmopolitan Productions while MGM movies were guaranteed abundant free coverage in the nation's many Hearst-owned newspapers.

Davies is often painted as a woman of limited abilities who rode on the coattails of powerful men. The dismissal is inaccurate. Though she is remembered primarily as Hearst's inamorata, the former Ziegfeld girl was in fact a talented comedienne. Her biggest film hits, *The Patsy* and *Show People*, even got good reviews beyond the Hearst press. Her association with Hearst gave her opportunities other actresses of equal talent were denied, but Hearst was also an unwitting enemy of her career. His overbearing attention stifled Davies's comedic abilities and his constant media blitzes were more than any performer could endure. With her $10,000-a-week salary and 14-room bungalow on the MGM lot, audiences expected a star the magnitude of Greta Garbo, but they got a charming light comedienne instead.

Davies adored Marie's performance as her monstrous mother in *The Patsy*. In a demonstration of her considerable clout, Davies insisted that none of Marie's scenes be edited from the final print.[33] The studio agreed to her demand, and Marie dominated the shenanigans in a rare unsympathetic turn. In the family scenes, she is consistently amusing as the dictatorial matriarch. The film's comic highlight took place at a stuffy yacht club where a party is disrupted by a flying celery stalk that lands in Marie's cleavage.

The Patsy did well, logging in a $155,000 profit.[34] Marie scored, as did Davies as a revenge-hungry Cinderella. Davies offered astute impersonations of Mae Murray, Pola Negri, and Lillian Gish, but *The Patsy* is most noted for the revelatory direction of King Vidor. He directed silent dramas so masterfully, including *The Big Parade* and *The Crowd*, that it was assumed he was capable of handling heavy material only. Upon the opening of *The Patsy*, famed critic Mordaunt Hall of the *New York Times*[35] wrote that "the audience was frequently thrown into gales of laughter by the performances of the players and the frequently clever captions." About Marie he wrote that "the mother is that substantial and clever actress, Marie Dressler. ... under Mr. Vidor's guidance, [she] gives her best contribution to the screen." But Marie is not conventionally funny in *The Patsy*. Her character's obsession with upward mobility approaches desperation and suggests that Vidor had not abandoned *The Crowd*'s harsh critique of capitalism.

Hearst was so impressed by Marie's talents to amuse that she became a frequent visitor to San Simeon,[36] Hearst's fabulously excessive estate and vacation retreat. Marie was intimidated by the man with the icy stare, but she would not refuse an invitation to "the Castle." There was no land access to San Simeon, and the trip required two days by boat up the California coast to Hearst's private dock. At the Castle, she could socialize with motion-picture luminaries Pola Negri, John Gilbert, Norma Shearer, Alla Nazimova, Buster Keaton, and Irving Thalberg while staying in one of the ornate art-packed guest rooms. The parties are legendary. At a masquerade ball Hearst gave in 1928, Charlie Chaplin arrived as Hamlet, while Marie finally realized her ambition to play Lady Macbeth.

Dinners at San Simeon were informal and served in the huge refectory on a long dining table that seated 40. Days were spent swimming, playing tennis, reading, and relaxing or strolling the grounds admiring the abundant animal life. Marie's lifelong love of animals was put to the supreme test at the Castle, known worldwide as a great menagerie. Jerry the chimpanzee was unruly and disrespectful. He seemed particularly offended by humans who were colorful and distracting, including writer Elinor Glyn, the Countess Dorothy di Frasso (nee Dorothy Taylor), and Marie. He honored all three by throwing his feces at them. This was Jerry's downfall. Davies, the exacting hostess, and Hearst, never known for his sense of humor, were appalled at Jerry's befouling of select guests. He lived out his life at a midwestern zoo.

With or without the scatological primate, Marie loved socializing at the Castle and wanted to return the favor. Hedda Hopper recalled a disastrous dinner party Marie hosted at her humble home on Hillside Avenue for her, Frances, Hearst, and Davies.[37] Wishing to honor Hearst's love of simple food and drink, Marie gave Mamie the night off and served her "special cocktail" of bathtub gin and vanilla ice cream. Stomachs churned and appetites were lost. The corned beef and cabbage were similarly received and "guests left the house green around the gills." So much for Marie's reputation as a great chef.

By early 1928, work was becoming more frequent for Marie, though she was floating from movie to movie without benefit of a long-term studio contract. Next up was a role in a First National release, *The Divine Lady*,[38] a sweeping eighteenth-century costume spectacle on the affair of Lord Nelson and Lady Hamilton. Frank Lloyd directed; Marie played Lady Hamilton's mother, the modest cook Mrs.

Marion Davies and Dell Henderson respond differently to the arrival of the celery in King Vidor's *The Patsy*. (Cleveland Public Library Photograph Collection.)

Hart. Lloyd gave Marie some odd business. Wide Mrs. Hart can't fit through a carriage door and tumbles out to the ground in a comic moment at odds with the pageantry of the drama.

Mrs. Hart was so small a role it was barely noticed, and *The Divine Lady* was inconsequential to Marie's reemerging career. Mordaunt Hall[39] only mentioned that she "chooses to make the most of her avoirdupois during certain junctures." The production was plagued with setbacks. More than $1 million in expenses and a fire on the set led to excessive memo writing, cost itemizing, and hand-wringing by First National executives. Marie was a minor player in the on- and off-camera drama, though her $2,000-per-week pay was more than double the remuneration of the movie's other supporting players. Despite spectacular scenery and epic scale, reviews were cool. Lloyd won the Best Director award of 1928–29 from the Academy of Motion Picture Arts and Sciences, though it no doubt helped his chances that he was a charter member of the two-year-old organization.[40]

The Divine Lady, Marie's last silent movie, came at a peculiar moment in film history. *The Jazz Singer* had been released in October 1927 and *The Divine Lady* in March 1929. *The Divine Lady* included special sound effects and Corinne Griffith as Lady Hamilton lip-synching in a dubbed singing sequence delivered via Vitaphone. Applause, rolling drums, firecrackers, and cannon blasts were also simulated. *The*

Divine Lady awkwardly straddled two film worlds, appearing when silent movies began their precipitous decline and talkies were a frightening and unknown commodity. "I did not care for talking pictures at first," confessed Marie.[41] "I used to go to the picture houses and rest there. The symphony orchestras were so soothing. ... The first talking picture I saw, I thought, 'All my peace and quiet is gone,' but now I love them."

So Marie at last was synchronized with technology and public taste. The industry was changing at an alarming pace; the replacement of silence with sound was nothing if not swift by 1929. Marie was ready.

Chapter 10

The Raspberry Season

Sound was used in movies before *The Jazz Singer*, the commercial release that heralded the rapid but not immediate decline of silents. Thomas Edison first envisioned moving pictures as an extension of his phonograph. The pioneering Lumière Brothers of Paris registered a patent on a proposal to synchronize their cinématographe with a phonograph as far back as 1896. Experiments on synchronization and aural fidelity were conducted in France, Germany, Sweden, Japan, England, and the United States throughout the early twentieth century with mixed results. Sound was even introduced in the early twenties, but it did not catch on. Financially cautious studio executives were in no hurry to promote sound and render their silent technology obsolete. As long as the public was satisfied, it made no sense to encourage a revolution in entertainment.

A revolution came just the same. Many producers were entrenched, but audiences grew hungry for the gimmick. Sensing a shift in public taste, Warner Bros. Pictures broke from the herd and took the first chance on this novelty. On August 6, 1926, when Marie's fortunes could not have been lower, the Refrigerated Warner Theater on Broadway and 52nd Street presented *Don Juan*, a movie starring John Barrymore and Mary Astor. It included a Vitaphone sound-on-disk synchronized musical score and sound effects. Among the shorts shown was a filmed speech dryly delivered by Will Hays, head of MPPDA, announcing Warner's Vitaphone. The invention, he promised, would turn the movie world upside down.

William Fox inaugurated the Fox Movietone News with a sound-on-film system in December. By May 1927 news films included spoken words from Benito Mussolini and Charles Lindbergh. Warner's convinced stage star Al Jolson to record his voice for their new feature *The Jazz Singer*. With synchronized musical numbers and Jolson's prophetic words, "You ain't heard nothin' yet," sound was finally and irrevocably an integral part of motion pictures.

The advent of sound was one of Dressler's good fortunes. Since she was hardly an object of fantasy, she had no fear that sound would shatter a carefully constructed aura. For her, it meant another means of making people laugh.

Sound, timing, talent, and Frances Marion alone did not save Marie, however. The tastes of studio executives, directors, and the public were diversifying. She observed[2] that "movie moguls belatedly realized ... there is more to living and loving than a handsome young man engaged in amorous acrobatics on the parlor sofa with a doll-faced young woman ... dramatic things can happen to men and women after they are thirty — or even forty."

It was quickly becoming essential for producers and directors to cast films with actors who had strong vocal training. Many silent-film careers fell when incongruous lisps and tinny voices were revealed to an unforgiving microphone. A few fortunate performers, Marie among them, saw their stock rise through the strength of their speaking voices. Marie's voice was well suited to sound; she could boom or whisper persuasively and modulate her delivery for an emotional effect. With sound, her prospects looked richer. Professionally, her long night was over.

Just as social life and career were both looking rosy, Marie received word that Frances's husband Fred Thomson was ailing. Suffering from a high fever, he had checked into the Queen of Angels Hospital in mid–December with Frances keeping vigil in a room across the hall. The world-class athlete turned western movie idol was mortally sick with tetanus. "As I got off the elevator on the floor where Fred was, I heard a horrible sound: hard, labored breathing. I was told it came from Fred's room," remembered Hedda Hopper.[3]

Frances was at his hospital bed on Christmas morning and asked Marie to entertain 2-year-old Fred Junior and his baby brother Richard. They loved her and she was delighted to be useful. "Don't worry, you poor darling," assured Marie.[4] "I'll trick myself out like Grandma Santa Claus and give them a whooping good time." She was in her car and on her way to the Enchanted Hill.

That afternoon, Marie and the boys were at the hospital alongside a small army of friends waiting just outside Fred's room. Hedda recalled Marie's benevolent if overbearing take-charge attitude, as she "barged in like a schooner under full sail" onto the scene.[5] When a doctor saw so many people lingering, he asked Hedda to help him escort them outside.

"I can do it all, except for one person," she said. "Marie Dressler. We won't be able to budge her."

"Leave that to me!" he assured her.

As Hedda was saying good night to the Thomsons and putting on her coat and hat, Marie approached her and said, "I'm staying. The doctor asked me to."

"Oh, fine," said Hedda and headed for the elevator. Just before she left, Marie called out, "Wait for me, Hedda. I'll go with you."

Hedda dropped Marie off and was driving home when she was seized with the compulsion to return to the hospital. A sister spoke to her as soon as she came through the front door. "Oh, I'm so glad you've come!" she said. "Mr. Thomson just died."

Frances was in shock, holding onto Fred's body until Hedda and the doctors pulled her away. Sleeping pills brought her rest, but for days she was near sobbing or collapse. It fell on Marie and other close friends and family to make arrangements. In the days that followed, after the funeral at Forest Lawn in Glendale, the reading of the will and the vague semblance of a routine reappearing, Frances decided to sell the Enchanted Hill.

Frances was happy to get her asking price of $450,000 and touched that Hedda suggested one last party at the house. Marie got involved, of course, and announced, "I must be one of the hostesses."[6] The "gala" was attended by more than 250 friends. Somehow the local press interpreted the event as Marie's, noting that "the great motion picture star gave a farewell luncheon party for her dearest friend, Miss Frances Marion, who is leaving her hilltop home to take up residence at a smaller place." Hedda was none too pleased with the newspaper's spin on the fête, but Frances found some momentary happiness in seeing her friends assembled to laugh and remember.

Ten years after the actors' strike paralyzed New York theater in the summer of 1919, union rumblings were heard in Los Angeles.[7] With sound storming the industry, labor issues resurfaced that echoed, but did not duplicate, those from the early days of Actors' Equity.

The union had already opened a Los Angeles branch office when the film industry began its systematic raid of New York theater talent. By 1923, under direction from the New York headquarters, Equity was encouraging Los Angeles film producers to accept standard Equity contracts. As the *Los Angeles Times* noted, "Equity officials submitted a proposal for Equity control of film players and virtually set themselves up as a Moses come to lead the film folk to plenty." Appealing to the MPPDA did not get Equity very far. Will Hays gave unionizers the runaround for years.[8]

When the Academy of Motion Picture Arts and Sciences was founded later in the decade, the original officers temporarily quashed Equity's efforts. The Academy, composed of directors, producers, and other executives, pledged its assistance at writing contracts, arbitrating disputes, reducing costs, and eliminating any taint of employee exploitation. Equity would have none of the Academy's promises; it looked like the fox guarding the henhouse. Equity continued to establish itself in the film industry. Nonunion forces, including the Academy founders, were challenged in 1929 when Equity announced that no member of its union could enter into a contract with a motion-picture producer except under Equity conditions.

Since theater had been unionized for nearly ten years, and Hollywood was recruiting actors, writers, and other talent from New York with hungry zeal, the Actors' Equity hold on the film industry was probably inevitable. Even so, unionizing was not a widely supported notion in Hollywood. Sentiment at keeping Los Angeles "the country's outstanding open-shop city" ran high, and many film players denounced Equity "intrusion." The conditions that brought unions to the theater, they maintained, did not exist in the West Coast movie industry.

Marie became one of those early naysayers to Equity in the movies. She even found herself a spokeswoman against the cause she had so passionately supported during the theater strike:[9]

> When Actors' Equity Association was formed I was one of the first to join. In the difficulty of 1919 I organized Chorus Equity and was its first president. ... Conditions similar to those of 1919 do not prevail in motion pictures. And a point I would like to make is this: Let the people who find so much to complain of in motion pictures go back to the stage. ... [W]ith the coming of the talkies, we faced new conditions. And it seems to me that Equity is taking an advantage, perhaps an unfair advantage, of a situation ... But it's a privilege to live in the glorious Southern California and doubly a privilege to have one's work here. ... [Organizing film actors] can only result in trouble and unhappiness where everyone has been prosperous and contented. It is unwise and I don't think they can succeed.

Dressler was wrong, of course. Actors' Equity did succeed and gathered support with the arrival of sound. Unions for writers, designers, crew, and directors followed closely behind. She was shortsighted to predict Equity's failure or to deny the presence of exploitation in the early talkies. One disgruntled film actor wrote to Equity[10] noting that layoffs without salary were common and cast members were expected to pay for their transportation and lodging on location. But the whole issue was downplayed in the press. This time Marie was not responding to decades of abuse leveled at nameless theater aspirants. The latest controversy centered on how best to conduct business in a new industry. This was no cause célèbre as was the strike of 1919, and her anti–Equity efforts of 1929 made only tiny ripples. Marie's outspokenness did not imperil her professional position; studio executives continued to seek her services.

Years earlier, Marie had been convinced that the strong arm of union activism and Fascism had cured the ills of the New York stage and Italy, respectively. Both worked more smoothly as a result of such intervention, or so she believed. Years later, the relative luxury of the film business in balmy southern California blinded her to any potential for abuse of labor. But she came around to another way of thinking and eventually saw the worth of unionizing and became an advocate for Actors' Equity in Hollywood. The turnabout may have come when Marie fell victim to Louis B. Mayer's vacillating salary scales. Still, as a woman ruled by her own voice of experience and little else, no one ever accused Marie of being consistent.

Metro-Goldwyn-Mayer,[11] Marie's chief and ultimately exclusive employer, made movies on a 53-acre lot in Culver City on the outskirts of Los Angeles. Founded in 1924, it had grown to include 22 sound stages and projection rooms, a park, and a greenhouse. A commissary thrived "where $6,000-a-week actors can lunch on Long Island oysters for fifty cents." Pampering was in order, right down to the lunch menu. Mayer loved food and instructed the commissary staff to "try not to lose more than $20,000 a year."[12] Private lives were shielded from public scrutiny, medical treatments were discreetly paid, and, as long as healthy profits continued, lucrative employment was guaranteed. Studio employees practiced 117 professions on the lot, but "the colored shoeshine boy outside the commissary considers himself an actor because he frequently earns a day's pay in an African mob scene."

The $250,000 weekly payroll supported the hefty salaries of Marion Davies, Norma Shearer, Greta Garbo, Joan Crawford, Buster Keaton, Ramon Novarro, Wallace Beery, and John Gilbert. At the top were Mayer and Irving Thalberg. They were an unlikely pair.[13] Mayer was gregarious and authoritarian and would pal around with the studio barber before hosting a senator or prime minister on a visit to California. Thalberg was quiet and private and avoided talking to anyone outside his office. He was sensitive, softspoken, and empathetic to the creative talent on the lot. Mayer was bombastic and old-fashioned in his tastes and he could outact any star at the studio to get what he wanted. Contractees typically warmed to Thalberg faster than to Mayer.

Under their guidance, the studio didn't so much set trends as it set standards. For surefire, high-gloss productions, MGM had no peer. But it was a stodgy institution that acquiesced to censorship efforts as it simultaneously became the undisputed champion of lavish musicals and family entertainment. When tastes grew ever more conservative in the 1930s, the studio responded by preserving and perpetuating the day's ideology of racial separatism, family unity, and national patriotism. "I worship good women, honorable men and saintly mothers," Mayer once summarized.[14]

MGM, like the other studios, was scrambling to devise ways to present new and returning stars in the untried sound format. Everyone seemed to get the same idea at the same time: with talk came song. As a genre, musicals were born alongside sound and for a short time they were everywhere. Studios were cranking out revue-style entertainment that "introduced" talking and singing stars to audiences without the benefit or burden of plot. There were *Fox Movietone Follies*, *Paramount on Parade*, and *Show of Shows* at Warner Bros. MGM mounted the most ornate effort with their *Hollywood Revue of 1929*.

It was a most complex and unwieldy production. Under orders that would never be acceptable to Actors' Equity, Marie and nearly all other stars at MGM were called to perform on a sound stage for their part of the *Hollywood Revue* during the graveyard shift. After all sequences were shot, the studio had 90 songs on 3 million feet of exposed film.[15] This was edited to 20 songs on 11 thousand feet running more than two hours.

As film history, it is a fascinating spectacle. The assembled smorgasbord is astounding. It opens with a minstrel show and dance routine, as masters of ceremony Jack Benny and Conrad Nagel are introduced. From there, the showcases alternate from delightful to regrettable. Stars who had no business singing or dancing were put through humiliating paces. Newcomer Joan Crawford warbles and hoofs her way through "Gotta Feelin' for You" with galumphing sincerity. Norma Shearer and John Gilbert attempt an age-inappropriate *Romeo and Juliet* balcony scene. They then update the scene, with Lionel Barrymore's guidance, using flapper language. Shearer cloys badly and, more disastrous, Gilbert's thin voice accelerated his career decline. Motion Picture Academy founder Conrad Nagel sings "You Were Meant for Me" to Anita Page, and Bessie Love emerges from Jack Benny's pocket in miniature to sing "I Could Never Do a Thing Like That" with a male chorus. Also featured were Laurel and Hardy, Marion Davies, the Brox Sisters, Ernest Belcher's Dancing Tots, and Buster Keaton doing an underwater drag ballet.

No one came off better in *Hollywood Revue of 1929* than Marie. This was her first exposure to sound, and she was not surprisingly more comfortable with her mouth open than closed. She was better in talkies than in silents, "while she looked you over, she told you off, and there was simply no one else around who did it as well."[16] Her voice was just right, "deep, powerful, almost masculine at times, with a resonance that bespeaks capacious lungs and much practice."[17]

She was teamed with Polly Moran and Bessie Love for the songs "Marie, Polly and Bess" and "Strolling Through the Park" and with everyone for the movie's hit "Singin' in the Rain." But the comic number "For I'm the Queen" established her great potential in the talkies. Behind a bank of chorus girls, Marie enters with Polly as Eucalyptus, her lady-in-waiting. When the queen's flourishing-bugle-call entrance ends with a rude blat, she turns to Polly and speaks her first words on film. Her regal ears offended, her expressive eyes shooting daggers, she asks, "Eucalyptus, is this the raspberry season?"

She then recites rather than sings "For I'm the Queen" and has a rollicking good time at self-mockery. During her serious proclamations, a shoulder lost control and rolled to faux Egyptian rhythms. When a jazzy tempo invaded the orchestra, she momentarily cut loose and forgot all queenly dignity, though decked out in glittering jewels, a crown, and a long train. The Martin Broones and Andy Rice lyrics included many silly lines.

Audiences had never seen or heard anything like *Hollywood Revue of 1929*. Released in June, it was a big hit, played an extensive run at Hollywood's famed Grauman's Chinese Theater, and was later nominated for the Best Picture Academy Award. Crushing crowds were reported from Singapore to Brazil. "Brimming over with good fun and catchy music," noted the *New York Times*.[18] "Metro-Goldwyn-Mayer's audible picture ... won frequent outbursts of genuine applause. ... two beautiful color sequences that are something for the eye to feast upon. ... Marie Dressler delivers a hilarious bit when she warbles, 'For I'm the Queen.'" *Photoplay*[19] deemed it "a great show for the money. ... [T]o date, the best of its kind and great entertainment." The *Brooklyn Times*[20] critic noted that "we still show our preference for a star whose art defies time and rivals. When Marie sings 'For I'm the Queen' we listened to a bit of recording and saw snatches of pictures that will be lifted out of this revue one of these days and laid aside as part of the 'history' of talkies."

Hollywood Revue of 1929 was released three months after *The Divine Lady,* another oddity of late silents and early sound. Both became obsolete almost immediately; the revue era was short-lived. *Hollywood Revue of 1929* remains entertaining because of, not in spite of, its antiquatedness. Through many creaky passages, it holds an ironic appeal as a precious historic document. It lies sandwiched between the cobbled efforts of late vaudeville, radio, the narrative musical film, and, still later, early television variety shows. Its awkward technology is on constant display. The production's sound log[21] includes notes such as "N. G. did not have switch on," "wrong setting on 8C," "cameras not ready when motors started," and "belt came off process wax machine."

Hollywood Revue of 1929 offers an unmatched roster of entertainers. The full cast reprising "Singin' in the Rain" for the finale aboard Noah's ark is a loving scrapbook of ancient movie personalities. And then there's Marie. She found a way to stand out in the heavyweight star lineup. She stood next to her pal, Jack Benny, and is the only singer juggling a small umbrella as "rain" comes pouring down onto MGM Sound Stage 15.

Marie still wasn't easy to cast. A few workless months went by and she proclaimed it "another low tide. It was so low there wasn't enough water to float a pollywog, much less a whale."[22] Eventually she won a modest assignment at Paramount Pictures called *Dangerous Females*. Written for Marie by Florence Ryerson and Colin Clements, the two-reeler reunited her with Polly Moran. Its producer was Al Christie, who one year earlier had made a remake of *Tillie's Punctured Romance* at Paramount.

Dangerous Females was well received. In it Marie attempts to use her sex appeal to capture an escaped convict. Her shenanigans included taking her dress off one mountainous shoulder, sending her voice into falsetto, batting her eyelids, getting drunk as her lips move inadequately, and capturing the bandit by sitting on him. As Sarah Bascom to Polly's Tilly Cram, Marie was buoyed with the results and so wrote to the authors:[23] "You are just too nice and I do want you to know how much I appreciate it — Polly and self are just delighted re *Dangerous Females* and wish you had another like it."

When filming was complete on *Dangerous Females*, Marie stopped in at MGM to see Frances, who had returned to work after months of grieving. Marie was effusive about the movie she had just made and the chemistry generated between her and Polly. She was additionally grateful to Edward Everett Horton, who negotiated the role at Paramount even though she had abandoned his stage production of *The Swan* one year earlier. "Bless his heart," she said as she dabbed away a tear with one of her man-sized handkerchiefs.[24] "Yes, siree, if it weren't for Eddie, Polly and I wouldn't have been able to do that comedy for Paramount. And maybe we'll be ending up here again. With you still prospecting for me, and my astrologist friend, Nella Webb, telling me that all my planets are doing handsprings, who knows what lies ahead?"

By the summer of 1929, she managed to secure another assignment at MGM. *Chasing Rainbows* was a backstage musical comedy directed by *Hollywood Revue*'s Charles Reisner. Originally titled *The Road Show, Chasing Rainbows* starred Charles King, a pert and pretty Bessie Love, Jack Benny and Polly Moran as the wardrobe mistress of a traveling theatrical company. Marie played Bonnie, a veteran character actress. Even in these supporting roles, Marie and Polly sparred in their scenes together, only to reconcile with Benny's intervention. The on screen warring friendship between the two was being developed and would bloom in starring roles the following year.

Chasing Rainbows included early Technicolor scenes, but they are lost. Among the missing footage is a number with Marie called "My Dynamic Personality." Remaining footage includes a strange talk-singing number with Marie and Polly and a rare example of Marie throwing away a line. ("Oh, pardon I," she mutters away from the camera.)

Chasing Rainbows is not of substantial quality. Love and King hoped to repeat their *Broadway Melody* triumph of one year earlier, but it didn't happen. The *New York Times*[25] concluded that "except for a few interludes of passable comedy and two clever recitations by Marie Dressler, *Chasing Rainbows* ... is a hapless piece of work." *Chasing Rainbows* was also caught in the crossfire of wildly capricious public tastes. Plotless entertainment such as *Hollywood Revue of 1929* had upset the delicate balance of supply and demand, and when *Chasing Rainbows* was being readied for distribution in early 1930, MGM was compelled to include a cautionary tagline that it was "Not a Revue."[26] It was, however, a backstage musical, and audiences were weary of that formula as well. Though *Chasing Rainbows* made money, it made no lasting impression. Its chief distinctions are Technicolor scenes and the movie debut of the hit song "Happy Days Are Here Again."

Mayer and Thalberg had not yet made a blood pact with Marie and she was therefore available for freelancing. After making the lackluster *Chasing Rainbows*, she moseyed over to the nascent Radio-Keith-Orpheum (RKO)

Tilly (Polly Moran) warns Sarah (Marie) of the evils of homemade brandy during an apparent pursed lips contest in *Dangerous Females* (1929). (Wisconsin Center for Film and Theater Research.)

studio for a special project. "The Vagabond Lover" was an enormously popular song from young bandleader, saxophonist, and vocalist Rudy Vallee and a movie of the same name would be his debut as movie star. Vallee was the heartthrob of the day and was adored as Bing Crosby, Frank Sinatra, Elvis Presley, and the Beatles would be later. The affection is hard to comprehend from the results of *The Vagabond Lover*; a more wooden and uninspired debut is hard to imagine.

Much ado was made of Vallee's entrance into film. He arrived in Los Angeles on Labor Day weekend accompanied by his parents on the Santa Fe Chief and was greeted at the train station by the mayor and six chorus girls from RKO.[27] A band played "The Vagabond Lover" as Vallee and his parents emerged from their chauffeured Rolls-Royce at the Roosevelt Hotel.

Makeup and lighting tests proceeded apace. Marie was signed for the role of haughty society matron Mrs. Ethel Whitehall. Sally Blane, Loretta Young's little sister, was hired to play Jean, Mrs. Whitehall's niece and Rudy's love interest. Marshall "Mickey" Neilan, the highly regarded director of such silent films as *Rebecca of Sunnybrook Farm*, *Daddy Long Legs*, and *Tess of the D'Urbervilles*, was also brought on.

Complications ensued shortly. One night while the cast and crew partied in a Roosevelt Hotel suite, Marie introduced Vallee to Frances. She was still numb from losing Fred, but Marie insisted that she begin to socialize again. Upon meeting Frances, Vallee was pragmatic:[28] she "was anything but my ideal, but I knew [she] was a very gifted writer and occasionally a producer and director for motion pictures." According to him, while taking a drive in the Hollywood Hills that night, she smothered him with kisses. He pulled away and they both returned to the Roosevelt. Frances did not speak or write of the experience and the forwardness was uncharacteristic of her.[29] She was 40, Vallee 28. She was diplomatic and businesslike with film people, as evidenced by her negotiating skill that won Marie *The Callahans and the Murphys*. If she threw herself at Vallee, it was likely from grief rather than passion.*

Whatever the awkward circumstances, Vallee was more interested in an MGM starlet. Back at the Roosevelt Hotel, he approached Marie and asked, "Will you get me Fay Webb's phone number?"[30]

"Certainly not!" she responded. Vallee assumed that her refusal came from a desire to unite him with her grieving friend Frances. Eventually, Marie gave in, saying, "You'll regret calling her." Vallee and Webb wound up married, then divorced.

There were plenty of problems on the set.[31] Neilan was earning a reputation as a heavy drinker and when his mother died during production, he disappeared for days on a bender. Sally Blane recalled that the problems in production came from Vallee, not Neilan. When cast and crew had to work into the wee hours to accommodate Marie's next quickly scheduled picture, Vallee threw a tantrum. "He was selfish," Blane said.[32] "He wanted to leave early and have his close-ups shot before he got tired and everybody else was expected to stay late." By next Monday, perhaps feeling contrite, Vallee invited everyone as his guests to the Cocoanut Grove for a party. Afterward, one of the film editors stopped him on the RKO lot and said, "Mr. Vallee, no one but no one has ever given a dinner and invited all of us in the crew and the cutting department. But I must tell you that we have been instructed in the cutting of this picture to give you the works!"

"Every small town has its small town band with its big town ideas," begins the story of *The Vagabond Lover*. Members of the Connecticut Yankees, a college orchestra led by Rudy Bronson (Vallee), set out to find Ted Grant, a famous impresario. In an effort to make good, they take over his swanky Long Island home for a jazz session, but Grant is away. When the nosy neighbor Mrs. Whitehall notifies the police of the intrusion, Rudy tells the police that he is Grant. Not knowing what Grant looks like, Mrs. Whitehall believes him and hires the orchestra for a children's charity performance. Rudy's lie is revealed, but the band is a big hit and Grant arrives to prevent further damage. A happy ending results for all.

Vallee's reputation as a ladies' man was propelled by *The Vagabond Lover*'s trailer announcement: "Men hate him — women love him!" Apparently so, for enough of Vallee's radio fans turned out for *The Vagabond Lover* to guarantee a profit for RKO. Once the Valleephiles had had their fill, however, the movie quickly died. Vallee may have been egotistical, but he was self-aware enough to suffer regret over his film debut. Decades hence, he still forbade its mention at family gatherings.

The Vagabond Lover was not all his fault. Not even talented veterans, much less callow Vallee and Blane, could dignify the execrable dialogue:

> VALLEE: (after seeing a saccharine performance by young girls of the nearby orphanage) Cute, don't you think?
> BLANE: I just love children, don't you?
> VALLEE: I guess our likes are pretty much the same.

Marie's Mrs. Whitehall is pure shtick, and she runs away with an otherwise comatose movie. Her funniest scene involves a police call to report a burglary in the Grant residence. She talks to the police with a mixture of doomsday anxiety and nouveau-riche pride. She nearly squeals in her wide-eyed concern

---

*There is reason to believe Frances loved sex. "I guess you could have called me [a swinger] when I was young," she told Hedda Hopper for the record in the 1960s. "I liked to dance and sing and I liked the boys. ... We did a little [bed hopping], too."

for neighborhood safety. Tugging at her pearls, rolling her eyes, and dabbing her brow, she is possessed by incessant bits of business and offers blessed relief to the dull proceedings. Mrs. Whitehall is far from Marie's best work, but Blane said "she was a big plus on the set."[33]

The Vagabond Lover is "certainly no great shakes as a picture," reported *Variety*.[34] Neilan "could have phoned this one in from the golf course. Marie Dressler isn't any more to this picture than its heart. Veteran and fully capable comedienne is all over the screen as a flighty social climber who has her ups and downs. ... One thing in the film's favor is that it runs only sixty-nine minutes."

The 1929 advice of John J. Raskob in the *Ladies' Home Journal* could not have been more bitterly inaccurate:[35] "If a man saves fifteen dollars a week and invests in good common stock, and allows the dividends and rights to accumulate, at the end of twenty years he will have at least $80,000 and an income from investments of around $400 a month. He will be rich. And because income can do that, I am firm in my belief that anyone not only can be rich, but ought to be rich."

Economic historians are not in agreement on the chain of events that caused the stock-market crash. The bull market of the 1920s was fragile and doomed; stock prices had been climbing at a rate that far exceeded worker productivity, available technology, and earnings. America's postwar prosperity and speculative investment spree ended on Tuesday, October 29, 1929, when stock values on the New York exchange plummeted $14 billion in one crazy day of runaway selling. There had been warnings earlier, as industrial production lagged over the summer and $3 billion in market value of stocks was lost on October 24. Like some sickening and predictable play of tragic destiny, investors panicked, factories shut down, and workers were laid off. The economic crisis only intensified, and by 1933, $74 billion in paper wealth had disappeared.

Marie began showing the signs of success just as the disaster struck. She moved into a rented home on Milner Road in Whitley Heights in the hills above Hollywood.[36] The neighborhood was undeniably chic. Heavily treed with pine and eucalyptus, homes were harmoniously designed with Spanish-tiled white stucco that dotted the hillsides and canyons, evoking the Mediterranean coasts of Italy and Spain. The narrow, steep, and winding streets sported addresses of Charlie Chaplin, Wallace Reid, and W. C. Fields.

Marie's secluded home had an arched entryway, iron detailing on the doors and windows, hardwood floors, and a view of downtown Los Angeles. Her bedroom opened onto a sunny terrace. At the end of the terrace lay a deep, narrow pool, one of Los Angeles's first, but she didn't use it. When asked whether she swam, Marie answered, "No, I've given the world enough laughs."[37] A large kitchen, a pantry, three bedrooms, and three bathrooms provided ample space for guests. Marie's growing paycheck meant that Jerry Cox could at last quit contracting work in New York and join his wife in California.[38] Chauffeuring was among his duties; Whitley Heights was a lengthy distance from the MGM studio.

Marie met Idaho-born, convent-educated Claire DuBrey, whose real name was Clara Violet Dubreyvich, in 1928.[39] Born in 1892, Claire was proud to have arrived in California by covered wagon. For a time she was respectable, becoming a nurse and marrying a surgeon. But she longed to act, and in 1915 she began appearing in Thomas Ince films at New York Motion Pictures, based in Los Angeles. The thick-auburn-haired, brown-eyed Claire was particularly well suited to westerns, which she made for the protean Ince and then for Universal. She made two- and three-reel titles such as *Six Shooter Justice*, *Prisoners of the Pines*, *The Ghost Girl*, and *The Devil's Trail* and was briefly elevated to leading-lady status. When her career grew viable, she tired of the surgeon and they were divorced.

When Claire got Marie's attention, they were found to have much in common despite a 25-year age difference. Claire was autocratic, strong-willed and ambitious; an excellent golfer and tennis player; and a believer in getting to the point. After sound arrived and her career nosedived, she took out page-sized ads

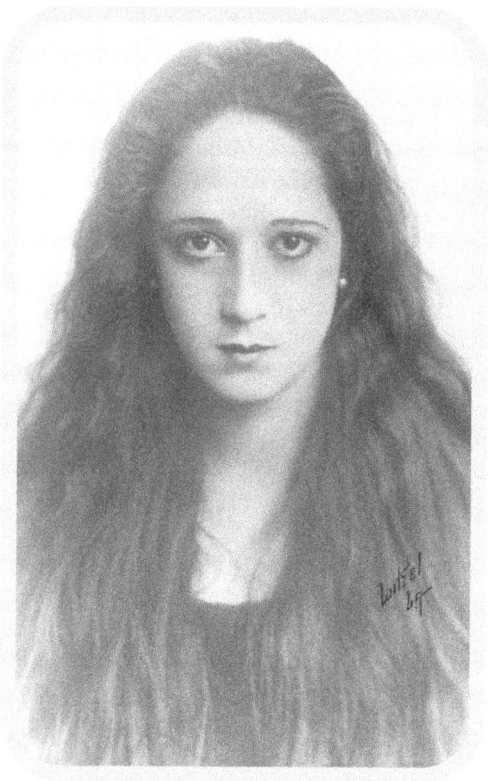

A striking Claire DuBrey in 1915, soon after she began making movies for Thomas Ince. (Courtesy of John Phillip Law and Sierra Pecheur.)

in the Standard Casting Directory looking for work as leading lady, extra, or anything in between. The ploy won her a few bit parts, but the talkies did not offer much for her.

Claire made more than a dozen movies in 1919 but was making only one or two per year by the late twenties. When Marie offered her work, she said yes and agreed to suspend her career. "I helped her check her bank stubs," Claire said.[40] "I was with her in the high society she loved. We spent countless hours alone. I shared her bedroom when we traveled." Claire became Marie's nurse, secretary, confidant, and travel companion. In time, they drifted into a romantic friendship as unlikely as it was private.

Marie was quite thoroughly in love with Claire, though she would adamantly deny lesbianism. Claire, in contrast, was a sensualist, attracted and attractive to men and women.[41]

She was more comfortable with their iconoclastic relationship than was Marie, and only their closest friends and employees, including Jerry, Mamie, and Frances, knew of their romance. The rest of the world could graciously note their constant company without threat to the heterosexual assumption. Both Marie and Claire had been married before, though Marie kept quiet on details concerning George Hoppert and Jim Dalton. Claire seemed older than her years; her face and carriage had a maturity that suited her to character roles. Both women could cultivate images of a sexless middle-aged friendship. There was no public expectation for them to be with men. They were "between husbands," and Claire was Marie's nurse, after all. When Marie suffered from gallstones, Claire was there to put her in the hospital. Finally, Marie's matronly looks and aura served to shield her personal life and private happiness.[42]

Under a code of absolute silence and denial, Marie was free to love Claire, but boss Mayer could not abide homosexuality. He retained the likes of Billy Haines because his movies made money, but he was loath to cover for gay actors, and he dreaded blackmail and scandal. With Marie, the quintessential mother icon, he could afford to look the other way, and there is every reason to believe that he was clueless. Marie and that friend of hers in an unnatural relationship? Blasphemy!

Marie was happiest when holding court among the smart set. As she enjoyed increased prosperity at work and contentment at home, and as if to insulate herself from harsh reality, she cultivated an impressive list of Depression-resistant friends in and outside the film industry. There was former RKO president John J. Murdock, *New York Times* publisher Alfred Ochs, rich feminist Anne Morgan, and Morgan's constant companion Anne Vanderbilt. In addition to the William Randolph Hearst–Marion Davies crowd, there were Allen Breed Walker and his wife Katherine, a Santa Barbara couple who ran the swank and secluded La Quinta resort three hours away in California's Mojave desert. Tucked away at the foot of the Santa Rosa Mountains in the Coachella Valley, La Quinta was nothing if not remote. Opened in 1926 and featuring quiet courtyards and 20 blue-shuttered adobe-bricked casitas; anyone traveling east from Los Angeles had to be chauffeured from Palm Springs in cars without air-conditioning by the hotel staff. The mountains and dirt roads caused frequent blowouts, but privacy-starved movie stars made La Quinta a Hollywood playground second only to Hearst Castle. "It was the kind of place everyone was looking for," said director Frank Capra.[43] Once there under Claire's orders, Marie could recover from neuritis or counteract the stresses of working into her advanced years. In the guest lounge, far from Prohibition's censure, guests spiked fresh orange juice with whatever filled their flasks. Marie had a deep fondness for the place, for the California desert solitude was like nothing she had ever experienced. She also adored the Walkers, particularly Allen, with his unfailing business skills that well suited his concomitant hospitality.

Old-timers used to tell of Marie's more memorable visits to La Quinta. As legend has it, one morning she stepped from her walled casita to get the newspaper and the gate shut and locked behind her.[44] Wearing nothing but a revealing negligee, she deftly covered herself with the newspaper much as a bullfighter uses his cape. Eventually a staff person came to her rescue.

Dressler was just as happy to sneak up the coast with Claire to Santa Barbara. In late 1929 she joined the exclusive Valley Club in Montecito, a stylish community adjacent to Santa Barbara. There she could socialize with the elite while sipping lemonade or playing croquet on manicured lawns.[45] A more influential friend than the Walkers was Cornelius K. Billings, a

Marie looks surprisingly youthful and rested at La Quinta.

millionaire Republican industrialist, horse breeder, and sportsman from Chicago. His 158-acre estate at Santa Barbara was subdivided into guest "cottages" of multiple bedrooms and spectacular views. As she had done so adroitly in New York in the 1890s, Marie the social climber assumed her place among an affluent and staid crowd. She was, by all estimates, an absolute expert at charming everyone in the vicinity of a swanky party or worthwhile benefit. She also increased her own hostessing, sometimes at a moment's notice. When Mamie suspected that Marie was lonely, she would call a few friends over for lunch, dinner, bridge, poker, or backgammon. One of Claire's later employees[46] remembered her saying that "Marie loved to play poker with her friends ... and her house keeper." Mamie had an uncanny knack for selecting the perfect guests to cure the melancholia gnawing at Marie.

As the Depression gained momentum, Marie kept a safe distance from the disaster. By invitation, she joined the actors' branch of the Academy of Motion Picture Arts and Sciences. She was ever more secure financially as demand for her services rose. This woman, Hollywood was learning, could turn the most wretched material into something funny. And audiences loved her. Imperceptibly at first, she was assuming a profoundly important place as an icon for the newly destitute. It would take shrewd casting to complete Marie's makeover. In the month of the crash, October 1929, Irving Thalberg, Louis B. Mayer, and director Clarence Brown met to choose the costars of *Anna Christie*, their great Greta Garbo sound vehicle. Marie was given an important role in that picture and, by March 1930, she would see her fortunes zoom even higher. The role of Marthy would require real humanity, not just buffoonery — the character was a raging alcoholic in a heavy drama. Her public makeover as screen star was even more startling than the extraordinary changes in her private life.

Marie's life is steeped in irony. She blazed a place in high society but admitted to economic reversals. And while the gilded rich welcomed her into their homes, clubs, and vacation retreats, she became evermore a screen symbol for the lower classes — the country yokel, the charwoman, the tenement lush, the maid. And now the greatest irony of all was imminent. As the United States enjoyed unchecked abundance and new urban sophistication in the 1920s, Dressler languished as a forgotten, broken-down vaudevillian. In 1930, as much of the world sunk into an economic morass, she found success on film that no one, least of all herself, could ever have imagined.

Chapter 11

Anna Christie

MGM had a dilemma. Greta Garbo was a huge star, but she had not yet appeared in a talkie. Mayer was understandably nervous about her thick Swedish accent; he had seen too many foreign-born stars ruined by sound films. Stalling for time, he and Thalberg paraded Garbo in late silent films in 1928 and 1929 such as *The Single Standard* and *The Kiss*. Time was running out—*The Kiss* would be MGM's last silent film.

The studio had wanted her for *Hollywood Revue of 1929* showcase, but contract fine print prevented her appearance. A studio memo[1] explained the problem: "Garbo's present contract is still a 'silent' one as she has never signed an agreement to talk. ... She is the one exception in our stock company. The question of her signing was discussed with the advent of sound pictures, but she declined to sign, giving as her reason ... lack of confidence in the English tongue."

Thalberg spent two years searching for Garbo's first talking picture property. He finally lit on the fallen heroine of the play *Anna Christie* as an atypically sooty role for the star. The drama had prestige. Written by Eugene O'Neill, it had won the Pulitzer Prize in 1922. Fortunately Anna was Swedish; at least Garbo's accent would be consistent with her character. O'Neill detested the play and even by 1930 it had aged badly. Nonetheless, Thalberg charged ahead with the necessary arrangements. He went to First National for the screen rights, since they had produced a silent version in 1923. It was Marie's good luck that Thalberg assigned Frances Marion to pen movie dialogue from the play.

True to her disposition, Garbo flinched at *Anna Christie* early on. With prostitution, drunkenness, child abuse, neglect, and impoverishment in the original play and in Frances's treatment, she felt it was insulting to Swedes. She didn't want the role but finally said yes. Why did she accept? A few explanations circulated. One includes professional jealousy; rumors flew that Blanche Sweet, the first screen Anna and D. W. Griffith favorite, would replace the great indecisive one. Another story maintains that the stock-market plunge forced Garbo to be less choosy. Thalberg told Frances that Garbo needed the money.[2] "The Beverly Hills bank where she kept her savings went under in the crash," he said to her privately. To gain Garbo's eventual cooperation, Mayer promised her a subsequent German-language version of *Anna Christie*. She was more comfortable with German than with English, and would be given Jacques Feyder, the French director she had worked comfortably with before. The deal was sweet enough. She relented and would endure the first version to be rewarded with the second.

Certainly she had other concerns beyond money, Swedish-American relations, and linguistic proficiency. The business of talking movies caused Garbo substantial anxiety, and she had avidly avoided the microphones.[3] In 1928 Garbo visited Thalberg's office with the suggestion that she leave MGM. "Silent, I'm a star all over the world. How will it be with dialogue? Can I handle it?" Thalberg was concerned about her future, too. He had seen Pola Negri, Vilma Banky, and Emil Jannings disappear from the screen and he knew that foreign accents were particularly unattractive to American audiences. Even so, everyone seemed to realize that Garbo's rite of passage into sound had arrived.

More problems plagued the creation of *Anna Christie*. The MPPDA, the organization so watchful over *The Callahans and the Murphys*, was again on alert for *Anna Christie*. Formed in 1922, the MPPDA had grown to be enormously powerful and exercised great influence over studio production decisions.

Chief among its self-appointed responsibilities was censorship of content found objectionable by political, religious and ethnic groups. The MPPDA leader Will Hays had been a lawyer, the U.S. postmaster general, and the chairman of the Republican National Committee. For a salary of $100,000 a year, he was expected to clean up the movies and keep busybodies off producers' backs. Though the infamous "Hays Code" was not instituted until 1934, the MPPDA had chilled Hollywood since its inception. Jason Joy, the MPPDA's director of studio relations, anticipated trouble with *Anna Christie*. Just prior to completion of the first script, he wrote to MGM production supervisor Albert Levin[4] that "if Anna's past life is indicated and not actually picturized, there will be no objection raised to the picture by the various censor bodies." In August Frances, director Clarence Brown, and Thalberg had a conference with Joy at his office on Hollywood Boulevard to review possible concerns and objections.

As Frances refined her screenplay, she noted the role of Marthy Owens, the waterfront hag and mistress to Anna's father. As originated on stage by Eugenie Blair and first written by O'Neill, she's an odd character. She appears early to give Anna support and friendship, only to disappear from the action. Frances, ever faithful, began enlarging the role of Marthy, intuiting that Marie would be perfect.

Frances voiced her casting idea to Brown, who was initially unsupportive. "Marie Dressler!" he exclaimed.[5]

"Yes, she's the one actress who can play the part."

"Look, I know you're friends with her, Frances, but she's a Mack Sennett comic!" insisted Brown.

Though Marie had two years of solid character performances to her recent film credits, Marthy was an altogether greater risk. The role was small but prominent and she had to convey faded dignity saturated in beer. Marie's trademark burlesque antics were not enough. More significant, whoever played Marthy would share the screen with Garbo as she enters and speaks her first words ever heard on film. To settle the casting question, Frances suggested and won a screen test for Marie. Everyone agreed that she was spectacular. Casting was completed and production began on October 7, just days before the stock-market crash.

"I have learned my lines, Mr. Brown. I am ready to rehearse," Garbo announced as she reported to the *Anna Christie* set.[6] The speculation on this, Garbo's first talkie, was monumental. Security was intense — special passes were required for everyone.[7] Even Thalberg was rejected from the shooting one day, having left his pass in his office. Several key participants were uneasy for different reasons. Brown had directed only one talkie before *Anna Christie*, Marie still lacked job security, and Charles Bickford, the fiery actor who played Anna's boyfriend Matt Burke, was forever agitating the front office with his union activism. Garbo had met Marie before, in Hollywood and at San Simeon, but they had not spent significant time together. She was initially terrified of that big bear of a woman.[8] Her fears evaporated quickly as they became better acquainted and grew to admire each other.

The close relationship formed on the *Anna Christie* set prompted rumors that Marie and Garbo became lovers, but a sexual union is unlikely. Garbo's attraction to women is documented, while Marie's sex life remains a less scrutinized mystery she took to her grave. Marie's public statements about Garbo were laudatory but professional, while Garbo, like so many others in Hollywood, treasured Marie for her warmth, generosity, and good humor. Garbo the beauty and Marie the comic were both conditioned to avoid public speculation and they were additionally separated in age by nearly 40 years. A romance seems doubtful; Greta Garbo was not Claire DuBrey.

Still, rumors persist. Antoni Gronowicz[9] quotes Garbo as writing that "I will never forget her [Marie's] warm body, simple love, wisdom and perceptive, friendly attitude toward me. ... She gave me the opportunity to meet other women and displayed great love for all her friends. She taught me not to be ashamed of this kind of love." Barry Paris, in his Garbo biography, painstakingly dismantles much of the "facts" found in Gronowicz's *Garbo: Her Story*, including the alleged Marie Dressler– Greta Garbo love affair. Robert Payne, another Garbo biographer, respected Marie's insights into Garbo but did not see the older actress as either in love with Garbo or "blinded by her beauty."[10] Whatever their exact relationship, the two women maintained a friendship and mutual respect to Marie's death. Never one to contain her emotions, Marie cried when a rumor circulated that Garbo was returning to Sweden.[11] Marie even reportedly agreed to appear in *Grand Hotel* as Garbo's maid for no salary, but Mayer refused the idea.[12] Marie is also credited as giving Garbo an early suggestion to make a movie of the life of Queen Christina of Sweden.[13] The result was 1932's *Queen Christina*, one of Garbo's greatest successes.

Relations between Clarence Brown and Garbo were more ambiguous, even though he would direct her in several subsequent films. In a filmed interview on the making of *Anna Christie*, Brown noted that Garbo "was very backward and I think she had a bit of an inferiority complex. There was lots of rehearsing because she had some old pros along with her, George Marion* as the waterfront captain and that gal named Marie Dressler in alongside her, so she was in some pretty high class talent."[14] In contrast, decades earlier he announced that "her judgment on matters affecting screen technique is excellent. So highly do I regard it that often, as in *Anna Christie*, I adopt Garbo's ideas rather than my own."[15]

Damnation or praise, Brown's flip-flop reflects so many views of Garbo. She could always draw strong responses. John Barrymore, when working with her on *Grand Hotel*, was intimidated. "Not because she is difficult," he said.[16] "Far from it. But because she is so perfect as an artist and as a woman." From an opposing camp, film critic Pare Lorentz[17] wrote "if you insist on calling her an actress, we then have something to bicker over."

Marie's assessment, leaning in Barrymore's direction, is most remarkable for its insight into Garbo's allure both on and off screen:[18] "She is lonely. She always has been and she always will be. She lives in the core of a vast aching aloneness. She is a great artist, but it is both her supreme glory and her supreme tragedy that art is to her the only reality. The figures of living men and women, the events of everyday existence, move about her, shadowy, unsubstantial. It is only when she breathes the breath of life into a part, clothes with her own flesh and blood the concept of a playwright, that she herself is fully awake, fully alive."

Incorporating sound into early films was

George Marion had directed Dressler on stage in Higgledy-Piggledy *in 1904.*

a laborious process and conversion of studio equipment was expensive and cumbersome. While in New York, Mayer's aide Eddie Mannix received a cable[19] commanding him to "make sure our sound truck is not shipped back [to California] before we can take exterior scenes for *Anna Christie.*" In these early years, MGM was using newsreel visual and audio equipment for exterior shots. Interior shots required the camera to be encased behind a soundproof booth to prevent its mechanical noises from being received by the overhead microphone. The results were long conversations and an earthbound camera. For its time and available technology, *Anna Christie* is typical, even down to the use of dissolves to indicate the changing "acts" of the filmed play.

Dressler was keenly aware of the stature of this project, its closely watched production, and its potential to her career. She reported to work promptly and was the epitome of professionalism. With time-tested methods, she worked this assignment with a motto that served her well:[20] "Play every part as if it were your first and last. Temper the enthusiasm of the novice with the fine restraint of a mature artist." Perhaps more revealing, and more confessional of a notorious scene stealer, was her comment when featured on a *Time* magazine cover in 1933:[21] "All I want is a small part to come in and upset the plot." With *Anna Christie*, made on a strict 30-day shooting schedule, she got her wish.

By December 1929, as the first rough print of *Anna Christie* was screened for insiders, MPPDA representatives were crawling over the script, characters, and plot. Plenty of fuss was made over Marthy calling Chris a "punk," noting the word could be interpreted to mean a male whore. Early screenings were cautious. Jason Joy suggested "toning down of the drunken character of Martha [sic]."[22] Another early commentator, W. F. Willis, had a different impression, right down to capital and lower-case lettering for emphasis:[23]

I think [Marie's] is the most convincing acting in the whole film, it is just too bad that the censors will fail to appreciate it as I do.... The censors always look askance at the degradation of a woman. ... I think the public, if it ever sees the picture, will rate the four principals in this order:

DRESLER [sic]
MARION
BICKFORD
Garbo

and much as I regret it, I will agree with them.

Anna Christie was on the brink of distribution when Hollywood was jolted by Mabel Normand's death. The young enchantress of Keystone comedies, most notably *Tillie's Punctured Romance*, died of tuberculosis and pneumonia at the age of 35 on February 23, 1930.[24] After a scandal-ridden career involving heavy drug use and accusations of murder, she fell out of public favor in the 1920s and many theaters refused to show her movies.

Her funeral service was attended by her husband Lew Cody, Irving Thalberg, directors King Vidor, Marshall Neilan, her former intimate Mack Sennett, and most of the great movie clowns: Ben Turpin, Buster Keaton, Harry Langdon, and *Tillie's Punctured Romance* stars Marie, Charlie Chaplin, Mack Swain, and Chester Conklin. It was a remarkable collection of comic talent, "tears flow[ing] plentifully over tragic countenances," as Vidor noted. Marie's grief may have been as much in remembrance of her lost years after the war and *Tillie's Punctured Romance* as it was for her former costar. Whatever the reasons, in neither grief nor comedy was she subtle. No one wept more copiously at Mabel Normand's service than Marie.

Less noticed by the filmgoing public, but equally noteworthy for Hollywood, was the sudden wedding of Frances Marion and director George Hill.[25] Seventeen years prior, Frances had been introduced to Hill, then a cameraman, by novelist and family friend Jack London. She didn't love him as she had loved Fred Thomson, but he was a close friend and wonderful with Frances's two young sons. They held a small, private ceremony in Phoenix. Once back in Hollywood, the union became known. More than a few friends expressed surprise at the impetuousness of the newlyweds.

With its references to prostitution obscured but unmistakable, *Anna Christie* previewed in San Bernardino east of Los Angeles with no fanfare. It was a decidedly unglamorous and disrespectful affair.

Garbo is absent in the beginning; she does not appear before 15 minutes into a 74 minute film. The suspense was overwhelming for the first-time audience. Before Garbo uttered that immortal first line, someone yelled, "I tank I go home," and the audience broke up. With a crew member shouting, "Shut up!" the crowd settled down and watched attentively. When she finally enters, she carries with her the despair of an embittered and abused young woman. Shuffling across the barroom toting heavy literal and metaphorical baggage, she sits down wearily and speaks: "Gimme a whiskey, ginger ale on the side — and don't be stingy, baby."

It is an electric moment; a star had just reinvented herself. As caught by the crude sound system, the voice was husky, not overly accented, and mellifluous. Mayer was delighted with the results. "Why, her voice is almost perfect for this role," he remarked.[26] "She has just the right Swedish accent." When the audience applauded at an important scene between Garbo and Charles Bickford, Mayer was gleeful. "It's in the bag! Garbo's a winner!" Frances was not surprised. Resisting the urge to say "I told you so," she reflected, "I have no idea what they thought would come out when Greta opened her mouth. They were addled by the smell of fear wafting through the industry."

Mayer paid little attention to the autograph hounds surrounding Marie at the preview. He was preoccupied with his final makeover of Garbo as talking-picture star. On the morning after the preview, he directed studio publicists Frank Whitbeck and Howard Strickling to spread the news of Garbo's triumph.[27] Downplaying the movie's somber plot, MGM flooded newspapers, billboards, and placards with the exclamation of the era: "Garbo Talks!"*

By the fifth preview, the studio realized it had a blockbuster in *Anna Christie*. The San Bernardino screening had had such éclat that the *Los Angeles Times* reported it as a news story rather than as a movie review. *Anna Christie* was released on March 14, 1930, and Garbo's talking was greeted with pandemonium. Like Marie before her, she actually seemed more comfortable with sound than with silence. The money rolled in.

Eleven days after *Anna Christie* opened, Jason Joy wrote a memo to Thalberg.[28] Certain lines of dialogue ought to be cut to sanitize the movie for wide release. Objections were raised over "there's plenty of guys and plenty of boats waiting for Marthy" and "them Swedes — woman-hungry." "You Irish swine" needed to be shortened to "you swine" to avert "any possible trouble from that quarter." Other minor changes were necessary as censorship boards from British Columbia to Ohio reviewed the film between March and June.

At her first appearance in *Anna Christie*, Garbo's beauty was very much present beneath a drab dress and hat. She made a startling contrast to Marie, who was already sitting at another table in the bar. If life's cruelties had not yet made their mark on beautiful Anna, they had on wasted Marthy. Tattered in spirit and costume, here sat a formidable human shipwreck of drunkenness and inertia.

Marthy exists outside the central plot, her relationships with Chris and Anna begin to be developed just as she leaves the screen never to return. It is, even under Frances's careful writing, a part to dismiss and forget in the hands of a careless or uncreative actress. Marie, of course, was neither. Her Marthy Owens is certainly one of the most accomplished characterizations she committed to film and stands as a monument to her art. More than a few observers say *Anna Christie* belongs to Marie and would be virtually unwatchable without her. At the very least both she and Garbo found

---

*When Whitbeck was introduced to Garbo as the man who coined "Garbo Talks!" she gave him a withering stare and murmured, "Aren't you ashamed?"

incalculable career advancement in making this movie.

For Dressler, notices were almost uniformly rapturous. She brought "an incomparable combination of the proud, the self-pitying and the vulgar" to the film.[29] Welford Beaton effused in the *Film Spectator*[30] that "Marie Dressler contributes one of the grandest performances I ever saw on the screen. ... She dominates every scene she is in, even those which Miss Garbo shares with her. Every flutter of her eyelids, the twist of her lip, her faintest gesture, everything she does, is an exquisite example of screen acting." The notice in *Life* magazine[31] was similarly effusive: "Marie Dressler is so convincing as [George Marion's] hard-boiled, whiskey-sodden wife [sic] that there are times when it takes the combined efforts of director Clarence Brown and the entire cast to prevent her walking off with the piece bodily." Perhaps she did just that; early audiences applauded as she completed each scene.[32] She had proven her comic appeal in sound with *Hollywood Revue of 1929*, but her dramatic potential was not revealed until *Anna Christie*. This wasn't simply her first serious turn in talking movies, this was the first sustained dramatic role of her career.

Film writer Ethan Mordden[33] observed that "you just can't bother with anyone else when she's in view. Unlike most movie actors, [Marie] always played to an imaginary audience, gauging the house, timing for laughs, mugging for the balcony, yet observing character. She was *theatrical*, and it shouldn't have worked in film, but it did." To Garbo biographer Robert Payne,[34] in Marthy "no richer, riper character ever graced the screen." He made several shrewd observations on Marie and the film:[35]

> Marthy Owens is a real character, and as played by Marie Dressler, she is as memorable as Garbo. It is not really fair to put Garbo in a film with Marie Dressler: perfect beauty encountering perfect humanity. ... In the past Garbo in her American films was pitted against actors and actresses who had not a fraction of her talent. Confronted by Marie Dressler, for whom she possessed a genuine affection, Garbo was at a disadvantage. There was never a moment when Garbo was a convincing prostitute who had worked in a house in St. Paul and there was never a moment when Marie Dressler did not resemble to perfection a fat and hilarious wharf rat.

Marie built Marthy Owens from a series of small acting details. This time her scene stealing was slier than in *The Vagabond Lover* or *The Patsy* but no less effective. It helped her enormously in developing character to note that Marthy spends every second on screen hopelessly drunk. She grabs attention from the opening scene, dozing restlessly in a rocking chair on a coal barge. Her face is partially obscured. She sings a song with drunken sloppiness. She rises from her chair and begins talking to herself as the full expressive range of her face is witnessed. First-run audiences applauded. This is potent testimony to Marie's power, since crowds were, after all, eagerly waiting for Garbo to utter her first words.

Throughout Marie's moments on screen, there are similar flawless bits of character development. Her futile efforts to appear unruffled at the "ladies' entrance" sign for the bar give Marthy a dignity that elevates her way beyond stock drunkard. "Lar-ry," she intones to the bartender when ordering a beer, her voice and body struggling to stay controlled. One hand reaches back to adjust her hat in a failed attempt to appear fully-assembled.

Marthy's love for alcohol is brilliantly realized in a bit of business by Marie. Anna and Marthy sit down to share a beer but propriety keeps Marthy from attacking the drink. As small talk is exchanged with Anna, Marthy keeps her eyes on the glass, hand twitching, retreating, followed by the other hand twitching. One hand pulls on the cuff of her sweater and exposes a hole in the mesh. At last, the time arrives to imbibe and Marthy nearly finishes her ale in one open-throated gulp. Marthy's obliviousness to her behavior makes it all the more amusing and real.

Marie also runs away with the Coney Island scene between Garbo and Bickford. Marthy wobbles over to their table and recognizes Anna, her acquaintance from the waterfront bar. Bickford as boyfriend Matt is annoyed by Marthy's presence. She gets the hint and leaves, careful not to reveal Anna's secrets. The playing of Marie and Bickford throws the movie off center, since Matt's bad treatment of the sympathetic Marthy makes Anna's affection for him appear ill placed. Marthy was made lovable prior to this scene by her kindness to Anna and her insistence to Chris (George Marion) that he treat his daughter well. When Matt calls Marthy a "sea cow," he seems in need of etiquette training.

For her last scene, Marie was given the line "well, kid, it's a hell of a life at best." "Hell" would have to go, but Marie devised an inspired alternative that was mentioned in only one censorship report. Her delivered line: "You've only got one life to live and it's a *hiccup!* of a life at that."

In *Anna Christie*, Garbo elicits the mixed, uncertain response typical of so much of her work. The star's intriguing mystery may be interpreted as allure, fatigue, boredom, or selfishness. She is what you read into her; Simone de Beauvoir once said that "Garbo's visage has a kind of emptiness into which anything could be projected." She remains the most striking example of the subjectivity in watching film actors work.

As with the woman herself, there was no consensus on her performance. The *New York Herald Tribune*[37] printed that "Miss Garbo proves entirely triumphant in her defiance of the microphone. ... there is never an instant in *Anna Christie* when you doubt that Greta

Marie shows off the Anna and Marthy puppets. Garbo presumably made herself unavailable for such marketing.

Garbo is the outstanding actress of the motion picture world." To Alexander Bakshy of *Nation*,[38] Garbo was "rather uneven, failing pitifully in the big scene at the end, while the picture as a whole, largely through poor direction, fails to maintain dramatic unity and suspense."

The two male stars did not register well. George Marion played Chris, Anna's father, in the stage play and the 1923 silent film, but by 1930 his repeating line "that old debil sea" in thick accent verges on the ludicrous. Charles Bickford is all bombast and bravado. He plays

Matt as a tough-talking brutish sailor, sounding more like one of Anna's johns than her lover. Clark Gable, Ramon Novarro, or John Gilbert might have brought some sexual and romantic charm to the role.

Anna Christie, like *Tillie's Punctured Romance* 16 years before, succeeded in part from brilliant timing. Film historian Lewis Archibald[39] assessed *Anna Christie*'s acclaim as deriving from the public's thrill at hearing Garbo's deep, throaty voice for the first time: "Like *The Jazz Singer* (the first talkie, 1927), *Bwana Devil* (the first 3-D film, 1952) and *The Robe* (the first CinemaScope film, 1953), it was the wrong movie at the right time." Garbo was none too impressed with the results. "Isn't it terrible?" she asked her friends.[40] "Who ever saw Swedes act like that?" She was happier with the German version, produced later when MGM kept faith in 1930. Salka Viertel, Garbo's close friend and screenwriter for several of her talkies, played Marthy. If Garbo disliked the English *Anna Christie* overall, she adored Marie's performance. After seeing the completed movie, she arrived at Marie's house on Milner Road with a bouquet of chrysanthemums. Garbo may have known then what time has since made clear, that *Anna Christie*'s chief asset is Marie.

However mixed its critical reception, *Anna Christie* was a giant box-office winner. It broke all records at the Fox Criterion Theater in Los Angeles. Combined accounting with the German and English versions calculated a domestic and foreign profit of $576,000.[41] Patrons were seeing the movie multiple times. Even marionettes were made of the Anna and Marthy characters and proudly displayed in photos alongside Marie. At year's end, the critics bearing praise overwhelmed the naysayers. Garbo was nominated for the best actress Academy Award and competed with herself in Clarence Brown's *Romance*. Brown was nominated as best director for both films as well, but he lost to Lewis Milestone for Universal Studio's *All Quiet on the Western Front*. Garbo lost best actress to fellow MGM star Norma Shearer in *The Divorcée*. Marie was not nominated for the simple reason that the supporting actress category was not inaugurated until 1936.

The production code's stranglehold on Hollywood in the years following *Anna Christie* grew stronger. In 1940 Joseph Breen, movie censor extraordinaire, wrote to Mayer on the occasion of a suggested revival of *Anna Christie*:[42] "We had the pleasure this afternoon of reviewing your old Garbo–Marie Dressler production of Eugene O'Neill's *Anna Christie*, and I regret to be compelled to advise you that the story, in our judgment, is quite definitely a violation of our Production Code, and because of this, could not be approved."

Similar obstructions were raised with an attempted remake in 1946.[43] Breen wrote to Al Block at MGM that "you will note that our basic objection to this story is suggested by the fact that your leading character is definitely established as a prostitute. ... if you were to remove entirely from the story any suggestion of prostitution, it might be safe to proceed with development of a new treatment." Removing "any suggestion of prostitution" in *Anna Christie* is like taking the Civil War out of *Gone with the Wind* and the studio never again bothered to suggest a remake.

Awards and controversy aside, Dressler got what she wanted. Based on executives' impressions and an enormous amount of fan mail, she was signed to a seven-year contract at MGM.* Mayer no longer harrumphed about *The Callahans and the Murphys* and was urging Frances to write stories for Marie. To Mayer, the veteran actress was now in company with his sainted late mother.

Marie had profound affection for the character of Marthy. In a January 1934 interview,[44] she revealed that it had been her favorite role and asked, "Remember that dissolute old drunken Marthy, who told too much when she was in her cups? I loved doing that part. Because deep down beneath the sordidness of

---

*In her memoirs, Marie writes that the studio contract was verbal. Closely guarded files prevent confirmation of the contractual agreements.

the character I wanted her fine soul to show through."

Marie reveled in her new success.[45] "Fortunately for me, Metro-Goldwyn-Mayer were delighted with the success of *Anna Christie*. And I? Well, after ten years on the shelf, how do you think I felt? Letters poured in. People liked me. They wanted to see me again. It didn't matter to the public that I was no longer young. The hurt in my heart was healed."

Nothing Marie had done on stage or film quite prepared audiences for the sublime merging of comedy and drama she exhibited in *Anna Christie*. Certainly her acting could be overblown and hammy even under sensitive direction, but Marie's glorifying of character brushed aside most objections. Despite Marie's penchant for drawing her own personality into every role, her Marthy is actually close to O'Neill's original creation. Forever lost in her "suds," Marthy was "that rare happening in films when a performer makes a magical transference of humanity from screen to audience."[46]

Marie was gracious with all the fuss surrounding her performance. She wrote of the experience in courtesy to the star while managing to bring attention to herself[47]: "At once [*Anna Christie*] established Garbo on a throne which in my mind has never been threatened. She was magnificent. And some of the critics said an ugly old woman had stolen the show from the beautiful young star!"

Marthy's heartrending twin qualities of failure and pride are echoed in Marie and her humor. The unmistakable overlap, the traces of Marthy's life in Marie's, are reflected in a recollection from *My Own Story*:[48] "After *Anna Christie* was released, several persons wrote in to ask where on earth the studio found that 'broken-down hat Miss Dressler wore as Marthy.' One woman said: 'It was perfect. That hat alone was sufficient to establish Marthy as a besotted old hag.' Besotted old hag, indeed! That was one of my own hats. I still have it and there's a lot of good wear left in it, too!" Hard to know where character ends and woman begins; so much of Marie's experience informs her Marthy.

Back in New York on the eve of another European sojourn, Marie was basking in adoration even greater than that of her stage heyday. She loved to tell stories of recognition such as one between her and a New York policeman.[49] "Hello, Marie," he called after stopping traffic to let her cross. "You've made a big hit in movies, haven't you?"

"Hello, yourself. I'm still on the job anyhow." Later she would elaborate.[50] "I've been on the stage forty years, and I played on Broadway thirteen years and the old-time policemen are all my pals. ... a good many of them call me Marie. And do you know it gives me a thrill when they stop me on the street and tell me they like me in *Anna Christie*."

In *Anna Christie*, Dressler won acceptance as she had never before known. "Heavens, I'm walking around in a daze!" she exclaimed with honest disbelief.[51] "Everyone has been so good to me and the screen and I have become the best friends in the world." Marthy was arguably the most consequential performance of her career. Now 61 and suddenly in great demand, she would reign as *the* grand old lady of movies for the rest of her life.

Chapter 12

Working

Dressler's late career trajectory didn't just reflect a public that had rediscovered her. Marie had changed, too. Those grim and fallow years in the 1920s brought a humility and humanity to Marie the person and Marie the actress. Why shouldn't they have? The combative star who alienated Lew Fields, Abe Erlanger, Mack Sennett, and the Shuberts with lawsuits and contractual breeches, and who waged war on the entire New York theater establishment, had failed. She may have felt justified in her prima donna antics and righteous causes in the past, but they had left her broke and unemployed. And she most certainly fell victim to a sexual double standard: her qualities were admired in men but considered pushy and unladylike in women.

Age and hard-learned lessons had mellowed Marie into an immensely lovable older woman, and Claire's love only boosted her already upbeat disposition. Her peculiar politics and past comments about Fascism and labor unions did not damage her public standing in the slightest. She may have been dismissed by intellectuals as a misguided mainstream comic, but it is nearly impossible to find negative press about Marie from *Anna Christie* onward. An aura of grandeur accompanied her through 1933.

The public loved her story: the down and up fortunes, the triumph over physical pain, bankruptcy, and her frank joy at late-life success. Her eagerly awaited homilies sounded like Will Rogers crossed with Franklin Roosevelt. Meanwhile, she luxuriated in Hollywood comfort, never failing to acknowledge her friends and employers. Energy and drive were waning, though, just as millions caught sight of her in *Anna Christie*. Even before that breakthrough, Marie declined a well-paying stage offer with an unusually pithy explanation: "I am content."[1]

Not that she converted to sainthood overnight. "Marie can be cold; she can have a temper; she can indulge in ladylike profanity under her breath; she can stamp her foot; she can glare with a concentrated balefulness and belligerence — and she frequently does all five," wrote Elizabeth Bordon in the *Boston Herald*.[2] "She by no means goes around mothering people. ... Ramon Novarro may rush up, saying 'Hello, Marie darling,' and be seized and kissed heartily, or thrust aside, with the words, 'Now go get me a sandwich, will you, and don't stand around fussing over me, I'm hungry and I'm mad.'"

Her diminishing vanity was perfect for the friendly but corporate atmosphere of MGM. Both parties, studio and star, responded to this union with a veritable lovefest. Experience molded her into an ideal studio player — tough, gracious, grateful, accommodating, funny, and hardworking. Mayer in turn wrapped Marie in a gold-lined embrace that was nurturing but unyielding. She saved her complaints for private conversations.

Thalberg and Mayer were not prepared for the outpouring of affection for Marie in *Anna Christie*. She needed more projects, and they both instructed Frances to pen features for her. Still, they were uncertain what to do with her and how best to exploit her unusual talents. One thing was certain: Mayer loved no one on the studio lot more than Marie. He defined himself as the studio's ambassador and figurehead, and he often asked her to cohost studio luncheons for visiting royalty and politicians. Marie complied, and Mayer made sure she was seated at his right side. She relished the attention and saw it as some postponed but well-deserved affection since her aborted comeback in *The Callahans and the Murphys*.

Though she desired relaxation, 1930 was the most productive year of Marie's life. Except for a few weeks in May and June for a European respite, she worked continuously. Under the system of such massive factories as MGM, actors would shuttle from one set to another making movies in punishing succession.[3] If MGM developed roles that were not always worthy of her talent, she did not complain, at least not openly. She was cooperative to the extreme, accepting assignments without first reading the scripts.

In one performance after another, Marie proved that *Anna Christie* was no fluke. Mediocre productions were being delivered to the public with furious speed, and Marie often found herself the most praised actor in otherwise lackluster efforts such as *The Girl Said No*. William (Billy) Haines starred as a rogue who comes to realize that there is more to life than car racing, girl chasing, and irresponsibility. Marie's role was minor; she had just one scene that was rehearsed and shot in three days, yet she received fourth billing. She got drunk — again — this time playing a crabby millionairess. The high point of the movie had her dropping a fountain pen down the front of her dress and Billy retrieving it with a pair of tongs. Though she could play this scene in her sleep, and though it looked cheap on the heels of *Anna Christie*, it was greeted with howls of approval. "She could play a drunk better than anyone," noted Frank "Junior" Coghlan, who played the kid brother.[4] Billy acknowledged that Marie stole the movie "right out from under my nose" as he was savaged by the critics.[5] "They thought it was too lightweight and he was making a damn fool of himself," said Coghlan.[6] Short on plausibility and frequently stilted, *The Girl Said No* managed to bring in nearly $1 million in gross revenue and $245,000 in net profits.[7] With the celery-in-the-cleavage routine from *The Patsy* and now this, Marie was agreeing to gags much more risqué and earthier than ever before. No more was she congratulating herself on being a "clean" entertainer. If she could roll them in the aisles by drawing attention to her gigantic breasts, so be it. She was having a blast and her pleasure in front of the camera was evident to her audiences.

Revues were dying, but MGM had already sunk a considerable amount of money in *The Hollywood Revue of 1930*.[8] Another star-heavy production, it was hobbled from the beginning by wrongheaded nostalgia from silver-haired producer Harry Rapf and graceless direction from Charles Reisner. This "concept" revue was to feature various entertainers from yesterday, today, and tomorrow. The elders were culled from the Weber and Fields Music Hall survivors and included Marie's old theater cohorts Joe Weber and Lew Fields, Fay Templeton, Louis Mann, and De Wolf Hopper. The hot young stars included Bing Crosby and Ramon Novarro while Gus Edwards' kid acts constituted the future. Polly Moran, the Duncan Sisters, Charles King, and a dog routine were later added.

The production schedule was modified for Marie, who suffered an unidentified illness and stayed home for one week.[9] When she returned, she worked ten-hour days. She was done up in some Grand Guignol version of an ingénue for a burlesque of the horse racetrack. She played "the girl" while Weber and Fields played "rescuing jockeys" who "save" Marie from the villainous Mann. Andy Rice, who penned the "For I'm the Queen" showstopper in *Hollywood Revue of 1929*, wrote "Ballet for Marie Dressler" that was mostly sound effects and reaction shots. "That's How It's Done on Stage" had her and William Collier, Sr., demonstrate how melodrama, tragedy, and comedy are performed on stage as opposed to real life. Yet another number was added in which she played Susie Glububberson and sang "But Father Mustn't Know I'm Going on the Stage — He Thinks I'm a Shop Lifter."

Dressler was back in her element making a revue movie and enjoyed the set thoroughly. Through the shooting, Marie and Weber were expressing mutual affection and seemed to have forgotten the Palace *Old Timers'* billing snafu six years earlier. "Well, Marie," said Weber during an off-camera moment.[10] "You aren't quite so thin, but you're four times as funny." She surveyed the wreckage of her body and speculated, "Maybe I've lost my sex appeal." Actress Marion Shilling was a young newcomer working on a stage adjoining the revue. When she was asked to pose with Marie for a photograph, "the famous actress put the little beginner immediately at ease, keenly attentive to my answers when she asked me about myself," recalls Shilling.[11] "We hear the expressions, charisma, charm, graciousness, magnetism, warmth, presence, good vibes, lovely aura. ... She personified them all!"

Big stars, expensive color processing, chorus lines of 500, and extended shooting drove the budget through the roof. Rapf was bombarded with ideas from no fewer than 15 writers. As if *The Callahans and the Murphys* didn't teach them anything, there was a scene making fun of German Americans that had to be excised. On and on the project limped. Reisner's anxiety on the set was palpable as he kept getting new production schedules daily. With the pompous new title *The March of Time*, Reisner attempted to make sense of the mess and reorder the scenes into one of the first narrative musicals. His efforts were futile. The results may have been worth releasing, but the public was downright hostile to revues by the summer of 1930. After months of fruitless tinkering, the decision was made to shelve the movie and take the estimated loss of $750,000. Segments of the catastrophe showed up in later films, most apparently in *Broadway to Hollywood* in 1933, but *The March of Time* was never released to the public.

It is sad that Marie's last appearance with Weber and Fields should be so ignominious, but the disgrace of *The March of Time* does not belong to them. The two men were used to control on stage, but here they were manipulated into a vision of the past that rendered their old comedy routines pointless. As for Marie, compared to former setbacks, this was nothing more than a minor inconvenience in an otherwise brilliantly ascending late career.

United Artists, the company founded in 1919 by Mary Pickford, Douglas Fairbanks, Charlie Chaplin, and D. W. Griffith, purchased the rights to film Ferenc Molnár's *The Swan*. Marie had played its dowager Princess Beatrice of an unnamed empire on stage in Los Angeles to some success in 1928 and the studio was eager to have her services. When the movie was being cast, *Anna Christie* had not yet been released and MGM did not yet know what a phenomenon it had in Marie.

After *Anna Christie*, *The Girl Said No*, and so many others, fans wanted to know: why all the drunk roles? Who is "the real Marie"? Alma Whitaker of the *Los Angeles Times*[12] took a slightly chiding tone in an interview: "Now, Marie, don't you dare tell us you are a total abstainer in real life, as the ladies who play wicked vamps always want to assure us they are simple innocent maidens behind the scenes who always share a bedroom with their mammas."

"Certainly not," bellowed Marie. "But all the same, well, anyway, you just see me in *The Swan* when it opens, for I am a high born queen in that, every inch of me, even if I have sort of made a specialty of lowdown, sodden women in so many productions. I'm dignity personified."

The film was renamed *One Romantic Night*. Its lead was Lillian Gish, the star of D. W. Griffith silent dramas now making her sound debut as the young blue blood Alexandra. The movie's heroine is wooed by the fun-loving Prince Albert (Rod La Rocque). She has no interest in him, which troubles her mother, the very sober Beatrice. To pique jealousies, Beatrice invites a brilliant astronomer (Conrad Nagel) to a ball in Albert's honor. Her plan backfires as Alexandra and the astronomer become too amorous. Believing that Alexandra is in love with the astronomer, Albert declares his love for her. Nobility wins, the plebeian scientist is banished, and the royal couple skip off to a marriage in South America.

Directorial responsibilities for *One Romantic Night* were shared.[13] Paul Stein, nominally the film's director, was reported to take a backseat to the more talented George Fitzmaurice. Harry D'Abbadie D'Arrast, Charlie Chaplin's assistant on *The Gold Rush*, was also mentioned as another participant. *Variety* reported that whatever merit *One Romantic Night* possessed was due to Fitzmaurice, who had directed the 1926 Rudolph Valentino sensation *The Son of the Sheik*. He declined credit for *One Romantic Night*.

Fitzmaurice was wise to keep his name off *One Romantic Night*. The movie was routinely panned. Gish, camped out in Mary Pickford's United Artists bungalow during the shooting, disliked the film and complained that Marie was asked to play Beatrice as she had played Tillie. Gish's skill at movie dialogue accompanied the scuttlebutt of *One Romantic Night*, though there was no avalanche on the order of Garbo and *Anna Christie*. Gish appeared prissy, backward, and oh so dull; the movie failed to ignite her talking film career. By the time *One Romantic Night* opened, she was doing *Uncle Vanya* on Broadway and devoting herself to the stage.

Once again, Marie escaped a bad movie nearly unharmed. There was plenty of giggling reported during her scenes at the opening of the film at New York's Rivoli Theater in May 1930. But with no consistent director to keep her clowning instincts in check, some saw her performance as coarse. Still, her reviews were shining compared to the conclusion that *One Romantic Night* was "one of the very worst motion pictures that we have had to sit through in months."[14] Thalberg, Mayer, and Frances, meanwhile, had not abandoned Marie to bit parts and rival studios. *The Girl Said No* and *One Romantic Night* were mere diversions as they fashioned more showcases. *One Romantic Night*, in fact, was her last movie made outside MGM. From that time on, her freelance days were over. Marie was now the exclusive property of MGM.

There was scarcely breathing time between movie assignments. Marie's social life was curtailed, too, as most evenings after shooting she could do little more than eat dinner prepared by Mamie, relax with Claire, take a hot bath, and collapse. Production for Marie's new starring movie, *Caught Short*, began on January 28, 1930. Yet another teaming with Polly Moran, *Caught Short* tells the story of two rival boardinghouse keepers. Marie speculates on a stock, the Brazilian Banana, and it goes belly up in the crash. Later, "the shekels [come] pouring in when she buys American Cheese."[15] By the finish, the two quarreling women, Marie and Polly, put aside differences, pool their resources, and run the boardinghouse as partners.

Caught Short excited no rumors of smash hit in the making, although Louella Parsons prognosticated that "if this picture isn't funny, I am going to say all hope is lost."[16] When Frank Whitbeck, MGM's ace publicist, previewed *Caught Short* and reported to Thalberg, he could not contain his ire. "This is a criminal waste of talent of a grand old lady, Marie Dressler," he said.[17] "What should have been no more than two reels is stretched to five reels. It is an insult to the intelligence of an audience."

After reading Whitbeck's report, Thalberg asked, "Is this the way you feel about this picture?"

"Yes."

"You realize this is a very bad report?" Whitbeck nodded. "It's the way I feel."

Apart from its topical humor aimed at the stock-market disaster, *Caught Short* is noteworthy in being one of William Randolph Hearst's Cosmopolitan Productions made through MGM. Suggested from a gag book by actor-singer Eddie Cantor, early audiences "enjoyed Miss Dressler's and Miss Moran's vociferous and unrestrained conduct."[18] Polly's character is prone to malaprops, and the two enjoy a memorable sequence trying to negotiate an unruly Murphy bed run by "electrocution." The daring maneuver was filmed in 17 takes and left Marie depleted.

Not everyone was ready to laugh at the stock-market toboggan; some found the comedy of *Caught Short* too timely. The story is not funny, suggested *Life*, and might have made an effective drama played without exaggeration.[19] Though "it is practically impossible to prevent Marie Dressler being funny. ... Most Americans are so resilient or something that they can find humor in the most discouraging situations." Many critics were similarly dour, but audiences ignored them. Made for just $171,000, *Caught Short* grossed $1,027,000. When it was confirmed as a stunning financial success, Thalberg called Frank Whitbeck.[20]

"What is playing at the Loew's State, Frank?"

"*Caught Short.*"

"How did it do, Frank?"

"Broke records."

"Do you remember your report?" persisted Thalberg.

"Yes," replied Whitbeck and quickly added, "I still feel the same way. How do you feel about it, Mr. Thalberg?"

Thalberg laughed. "The same way."

Dressler was similarly ambivalent about *Caught Short*. She was delighted with its success, but none too proud of the product. She wrote that it was not "a part after my own heart"[21] and believed that "there's a place ... for the *Caught Short*s of the industry; but there's a bigger need for the real stories that people live."[22]

After *The Callahans and the Murphys*, *Bringing Up Father*, *Chasing Rainbows*, and now *Caught Short*, it was obvious that Mayer and Thalberg were grooming Marie and Polly Moran as an ongoing team. It worked for a time, but Polly was not of Marie's comic stature. She was a wonderful physical comedienne and expert at playing selfish, vain, and bossy women, but her comedy didn't carry the poignancy that Marie's did and she had little facility with melodrama. That burden fell on Marie, who consistently won higher praise in their mutual screen efforts. As a veteran of vaudeville and Mack Sennett silent comedies, the buck-toothed sleepy-eyed Pauline Therese Moran was liked and admired by her fellow film workers. "Oh, Polly was a fun gal. She and Marie had a certain magic together," said Anita Page,[23] who costarred with them on three occasions. "They worked together like a dream."

Polly had a reputation for kindness; she fed stray dogs and never ventured a callous remark about anyone. She took part in offcamera high jinks that costars and studio personnel talked about for years. One morning she amused everyone by driving her car to work while her chauffeur sat by her side reading a newspaper. She loved drawing attention to her ample breasts, which were nearly as distinguished as Marie's. If someone bumped into her frontside she would scold with "watch out for the avocados."[24] On another occasion, Polly showed up with two black eyes and explained she "got 'em skipping rope without a bra."[25]

Caught Short was Polly's sort of routine; she excelled at one-liners and sight gags. MGM retained Robert (Hoppie) Hopkins as "gag man" for just such stars as Polly. With Hopkins's input, her comedy was low and superficial but endearing. Marie was all personality, the comedy of familiar characters — the drunk, the dowager — in unlikely or undesired predicaments. Marie's comedy was rooted in exaggerated humanity, Polly's in pratfalls and easy jokes. "You won't find any flappers who are willing to be so undignified as Polly and me," said Marie.[26] No one challenged Marie on that statement.

For all her comic resourcefulness, Polly

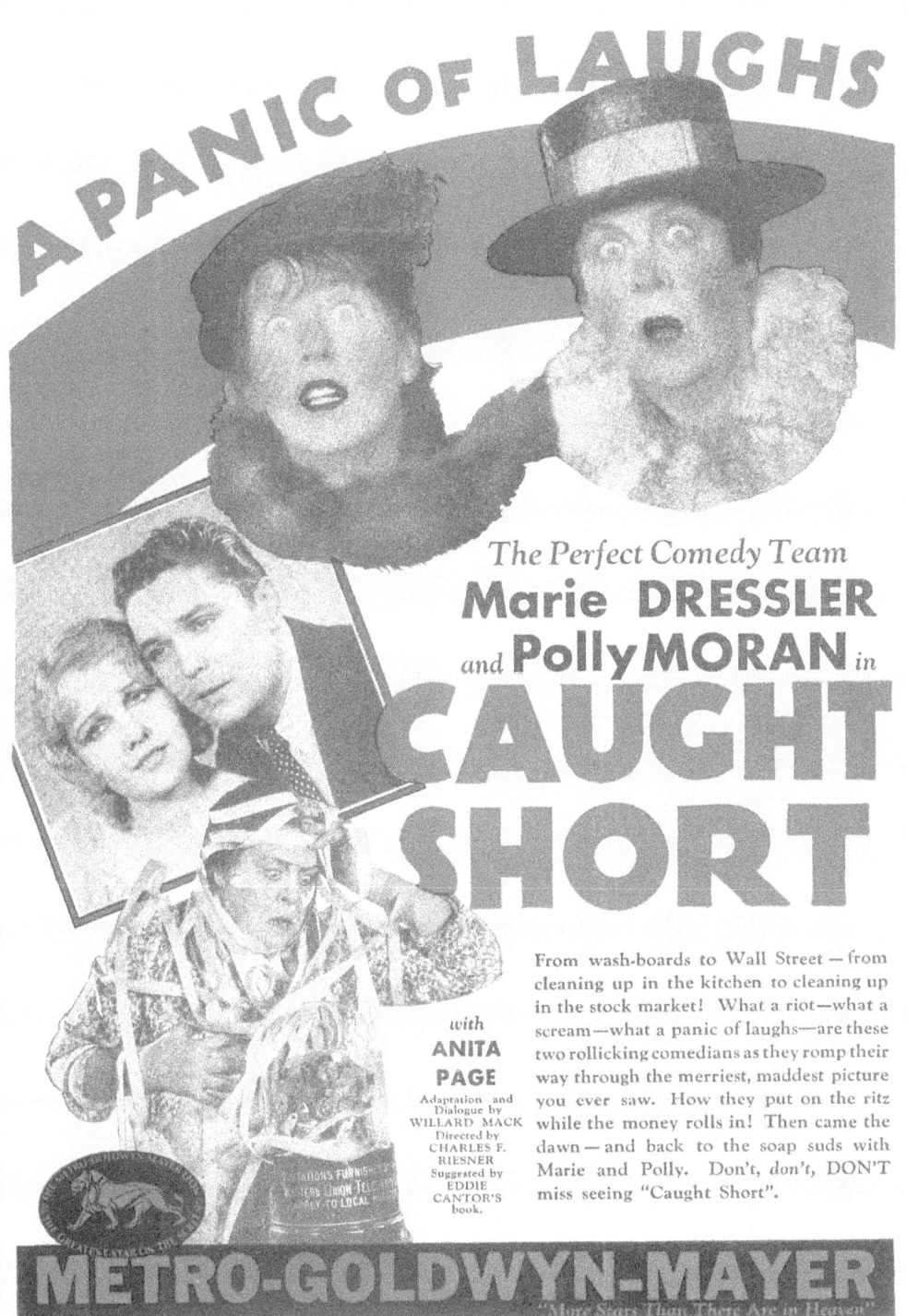

Caught Short caught on to become Marie and Polly's first runaway hit.

was often eclipsed by Marie. She explained her dilemma:[27] "That rubber face of hers makes me look like Dead-Pan Keaton when I'm in a close-up with her. All she has to do is make the slightest grimace and everyone else in the scene fades right out of the picture." Resigned to eternal second-fiddlehood, she proclaimed Marie "a genius and I am honest enough with myself to know that I could never approach her greatness. I consider myself lucky to drag along with her — no matter how far behind she leaves me."[28]

Marie and Polly were a profitable pair. Their movies were light, predictable, and entertaining, and, for a time, audiences were convinced that the two made a great comedy team. Marie was diplomatic in summarizing their protracted association, although a thinly disguised desire to break free comes through:[29] "I have a lively respect for Polly's ability as a comedienne, and, personally, I think her one of the most likable persons alive. None of which prevents me from believing that each of us plays better without the other. I'm pretty sure Polly feels the same way about it." Marie and Polly would be teamed together for three more features.

Taking a break from Polly, Marie next found a role of rare and satisfying substance. She was a natural as Mrs. Bouccicault, the crusty society matron of the recent stage success *Let Us Be Gay*. The play was a frothy tale of romantic complications, startling makeovers, and philanderers redeemed by poetry read on sweeping moonlit verandas. Frances handled the screen treatment, but she had already developed a preference for writing characters for Marie that were on the skids. "I was not overly anxious to see Marie in the role of a Newport grande dame," wrote Frances.[30] "Frankly, I was afraid that she might drift into those broad A's again."

Let Us Be Gay starred Norma Shearer, the princess of MGM who had enormous clout throughout the studio as a box-office champion and wife of Irving Thalberg. Production was set at a very tight six weeks, since Shearer was pregnant and showing by the spring of 1930. Fortunately, the many interior shots allowed her to hide behind tables, chairs, and drapes. "It took a miracle to keep her svelte," noted famed designer Adrian.[31] "But we performed that miracle and Irving later said it floored him."

"That Norma is the most ambitious woman I ever met in my life," Marie told Frances.[32] "I can't accuse her of stealing scenes; she's gracious enough about giving her players their head, but does she pay close attention to herself — mirrors, lighting, fittings, makeup, cosmetics, the whole kaboodle! I don't know where she finds the time to get in there and act, but she manages that, too. And pregnant, too!"

More interesting dynamics occurred on the set with Marie and Hedda Hopper, who was cast in a supporting role. The longterm friends had never appeared in a movie together and once again Frances found herself in the middle of their ceaseless sniping. "Where does Marie come off with that English accent?" asked Hedda.[33] "She's better at Weber and Fields stuff. I shall advise her to cut it out." Marie approached Frances later and said, "How come Hedda is suddenly so veddy, veddy British? She was born in some one-horse town in Pennsylvania. I must advise her that she'd better cut it out."

On its inaugural release, *Let Us Be Gay* proved a success, raking in a sizable profit and glowing reviews for Marie, Norma Shearer, director Robert Z. Leonard, and company. The movie's origins, a 1929 play by Rachel Crothers, made for a pleasing comedy relying on the skills of its players to deliver witty repartee at fast speed. The proceedings were aided immeasurably by Frances's screen adaptation filled with suggestive asides that barely avoided the censors' surgery. Hedda dismissed her performance as "just another of those thankless roles" but was gracious enough to give Marie her due.[34] "Stars today yell 'Foul!' when they're made to work with babies or dogs," she remarked. "Making a picture with Marie Dressler in camera range was more rugged than working with quintuplets of all of Lassie's clan."

Though she was frankly exhausted by the unrelenting work schedule, Marie delivers a vigorous performance in *Let Us Be Gay*. Delighted audiences burst into applause at her first appearance.[35] With her thick brown hair in an unusually elegant do, an imperious Marie bosses her quietly exasperated butlers, directs the seating plan at a card game, and is all hot air and churlish authority. Her unexpected appearance late at night, wearing an enormous nightgown and cap adorned with dozens of little bows, was an assured laugh-getter. Cigar smoking, a character eccentricity written into the play, was denied the screen Mrs. Bouccicault because of censors' disapproval. Marie managed to convey the woman's neurotic energy by vigorous knitting instead. As with Marthy before her and Min after, the audience knows that the barnacled Mrs. Bouccicault is hiding a sweet nature. The wise old busybody wants only for the young people to be coupled appropriately. "I loved playing this woman who has nothing but money," she told the *Los Angeles Times*.[36] "I know so many of them over in Europe, with their peculiar little characteristics and transparencies. They are trying to find life through the eyes of the young whom they must constantly have around."

By late 1930 Marie's standing as a great comic actress made criticisms nearly felonious. *Theatre* magazine[37] wrote, "After witnessing a preview of the Rachel Crothers comedy, *Let Us Be Gay*, Norma Shearer went forth and sent a wire. 'Marie, you're a great actress.' ... Laughter, but thoughtful laughter, is the keynote of her art. All of her effects, subtle or simple, are produced in an attempt to evoke intelligent and sympathetic responses. Through all those years when she was unrecognized she steadfastly maintained a high opinion of the critical judgment of the man-in-the-street."

"There are three worthwhile things in life, laughter, music and religion," Marie explained. "I always combine the first and the last. So that, really, laughter is my religion." Playing the ever-cooperative star, her pontifications must have left Mayer smiling. "As an educational and cultural organ," she stated in the same interview, "the movies stand supreme as the greatest civilizing influence ever perfected."

Marie and Claire left for a sojourn to England, France, and Germany on May 9 aboard the White Star liner *Olympic*.[38] Marie was approached by a *New York Times* reporter as the boat was set to depart and assured the inquirer that she would continue to work in Hollywood, not New York, upon her return. "My next film is going to be *Dark Star*. Frances Marion is writing the continuity, and her husband, George Hill, is going to do the directing. I'm looking ahead to that when I get back. ... I haven't any ambition to go [to Europe], but I know that I need the rest and that is the place to get it."[39] The trip did allow her a rare reunion with her only living natal family member, sister Bonita, who was a longterm resident of Richmond, Surrey. Catching up with her friend, 72-year-old actress May Robson, Marie was deprived of that needed rest in London. She had to be rescued by bobbies when she was mobbed by fans. At a press luncheon for Marie, 45 were invited and 45 attended.[40] Marie had been insulated by work since *Anna Christie* opened in March, shuttling from home on Milner Road to endless social and acting assignments at the studio. It wasn't until the spring retreat in Europe that she felt the full impact of newly regained popularity.

Though her life had changed, she hung onto her traveling habits of the past. In Paris restaurants, she collected drums, hats, and dolls given as favors. When motoring in remote villages, she would leave the effects near a group of children and then hastily drive off. As much as she loved fine jewelry and clothing, and her weekly paycheck hovering around $1,500, she kept a carefully maintained public humility. "I get on a train. I look out of the window and I see a little house going up, I bless it and the people who are building it. Maybe if I ever met them I'd want to kick them in the afterpiece."[41]

Marie and Claire returned from Europe on the White Star liner *Majestic* on June 24, having missed the American premiere of *Caught Short*. Marie was loaded down with souvenir gifts such as costume jewelry, cigarette boxes, and cigarette holders for various employees at the studio.[42] She stormed a story conference and dumped a ready-to-assemble cocktail service shaped like a zeppelin onto the table for Harry Rapf. From the doting of reporters at the New York docks, to the mob scene in London and the dual hits of *Anna Christie* and *Caught Short*, she was beginning to understand the impression her recent screen portrayals were making. She was distracted more easily than ever and flatly misspoke herself when saying that "they tried to produce [*Anna Christie*] in Germany but gave up the attempt because they were unable to find any one to play Marthy as it was played in the American original."[43] Salka Viertel, the actress who played Marthy in the 1930 German version of *Anna Christie*, knew eight languages. No one bothered to correct Marie in print.

Irving Thalberg, Jr., was born on August 25, 1930, less than seven weeks after his mother's film, *Let Us Be Gay*, opened to turn-away business at the Capitol Theater in New York. Marie was one of the few to receive a photo of the child. A message was written on the back: "To Marie from Junior. My mama says you steal pictures from her, but we love you just the same."[44]

The idea for *Min and Bill* came to Frances while she observed Marie on the *Anna Christie* set. Marthy Owens was most alive on the waterfront, and Marie's weatherbeaten appeal was in perfect harmony with seedy, fog-shrouded docks and ships. The possibilities for repeating Marie in similar surroundings inspired Frances. By the time of *Anna Christie*'s release, she had nearly finished her treatment of *Min and Bill*, another tale of dockside lowlifes. Frances grew accustomed to personal triumph in production meetings after her successful lobbying for Marie in *The Callahans and the Murphys* and *Anna Christie*. She remained Marie's closest friend and ally at the studio and her job got much easier. After *Anna Christie*, *Caught Short*, and *Let Us Be Gay*, Mayer and Thalberg hardly needed convincing of Marie's versatility, skill, or marketability.

Frances was astute at casting as well as screenwriting. She envisioned the studio's two character stars, Marie and "the lovable old rascal" Wallace Beery, as a team for her new script. Beery was a potbellied bellicose actor from Kansas City with a colorful background.[45] Son of a policeman, brother to actor Noah Beery, and uncle to actor Noah Beery, Jr., Wallace's early career included a stint as an elephant trainer in the Ringling Brothers circus. As a young man, he was vaguely handsome and possessed a fine singing voice. He began making movies at the age of 28 for Essanay in 1913, just one year before Marie made *Tillie's Punctured Romance*.

His early years in film did not set the world on fire. If he wasn't playing a stock bad guy he was wearing a dress and wig. He repeated his drag character Sweedie, an idiot Swedish maid, in one- and two-reelers and was married to teenager Gloria Swanson for two years while they made Mack Sennett comedies together. For much of the 1920s, Beery worked as the villain in a parade of movies for Universal and Keystone.

As with Marie, sound served him well. He reached his greatest popularity in middle age after his face had contorted into hound-dog expressions and his voice had turned to gravel. At the time of casting *Min and Bill*, he had just made a hit in *The Big House*, a gritty prison drama that won him a best actor Academy Award nomination and Frances her first Best Original Story Award. There was no dissonance, only enthusiasm, at the proposed teaming of Marie Dressler and Wallace Beery.

Whatever qualities audiences saw in Beery, he was as atypical a movie star as Marie. Publicly, he could be gracious, funny, and charming, but just as often he was loud, oafish, and insensitive. He gave his employers plenty to worry about off screen. He was a devout amateur pilot and his reckless flying left studio bosses fearing for his life. He repeatedly tried to coax Marie up into the sky, but no one ever talked her into leaving the earth. Privately, Beery physically and emotionally abused women. He raped Swanson on their wedding night in 1916, leaving her shocked and bloodied. Swanson did not report Beery's attack, joining "the great conspiracy of silence" in "a man's world."[46] The extent of his brutality was kept from the public gaze and Marie did not know of his penchant for such violence.

Min and Bill was not the exclusive creation of Frances. Lorna Moon, a tubercular young Scottish woman, had written it as a book first, and it was selling briskly. Moon was on the writing staff at MGM, and she and Frances formed a formidable sorority with Kate Corbaley, head of the reading department. Frances loved Moon's story and once again took charge. She had her secretary type the manuscript when Moon became too ill. She then instructed Corbaley to help her advocate the property at a story meeting.[47]

"Has anyone here read *Dark Star*?" asked Corbaley.[48] No one had. Frances, listening at the door, entered at that moment. "Frances thinks it will make an excellent movie, so I'll let her tell you the plot."

Before Frances spoke, Harry Rapf commented that "anything dark in the title sounds gloomy."

"It's anything but gloomy," began Frances, who then outlined the plot of her new screenplay. "This is a rip-roaring comedy, laid right here in San Pedro, where the tuna fleet is anchored. Besides, we can change the title to one that fits the rowdy main characters named 'Min' and 'Bill,' who live in Cannery Row."

"Give us more details," said Hunt Stromberg, an unconvinced producer.

Frances outlined the plot. "Be great for Dressler," Rapf said. "Who do you see for Bill?"

"Wallace Beery," answered Frances.

"A great combo," said Rapf, not bothered that Beery was 15 years younger than Marie. At the same meeting, Frances negotiated a $7,500 sale of *Dark Star* for Lorna Moon, who would use the money for tuberculosis treatment at an Albuquerque sanitarium. Final credit for the scenario went to Frances and Marion Jackson, with *Min and Bill* "suggested from the book *Dark Star* by Lorna Moon." The production was approved, and as the meeting was breaking up, Frances gave Kate Corbaley a wink.

As she had demonstrated with *Rebecca of Sunnybrook Farm* and *Pollyanna* for Mary Pickford, and *The Callahans and the Murphys* for Marie, Frances could be both a slashing editor and clever dialoguist when adapting literary properties to suit screen personalities. *Dark Star*'s central character was young Nancy, while "Divot Meg," named after the grassy sod of earth that protects potatoes from cold weather, was secondary. Frances's script moved the story from Scotland to southern California, turned Divot Meg into Min Divot, made her the primary character, and enlarged Bill for Beery. Nancy was hardly eliminated, but actress Dorothy Jordan had tough competition for audience attention with the expanded parts of Min and Bill paving the way for a Dressler-Beery mug-o-rama.

"Frances made Marie as far as Hollywood was concerned," said Elaine St. Johns,[49] daughter of Hollywood writer Adela Rogers St. Johns. "Frances could be tart, she could cut you to pieces like Dorothy Parker. She didn't get along with everybody. She and my mother used to poke fun at people, Mayer included. Never at Marie, however. Frances and Marie were a pair of popular and beloved people. And when they teamed up together, they made a great deal of money."

Lorna Moon wept at receiving a check that far exceeded her expectations. She quickly gathered her belongings and checked into St. Joseph's Sanitarium in Albuquerque, where she died a few days later.[50]

Production began on July 29 under the working title *Dark Star*. Marie tore into the role of Min like a starving carnivore. She openly gushed upon her acquaintance with the character, a gruff but loving hostess of a rundown maritime boardinghouse who loves young Nancy enough to sacrifice herself before Nancy's strumpet mother Bella (Marjorie Rambeau). "I knew that here was the role I had been waiting for all my life," she wrote.[51] "The characters were so rich, so meaty."

Min "was a very tough physical role for Marie," stated second assistant Joseph Newman.[52] "We shot most of the picture on location at Wilmington which is part of Los Angeles Harbor. We built the set at Fish Harbor which at that time was home to almost as many fish canneries as Monterey. We stayed at a small hotel called the Don. It was no easy task for Marie." Hill strove for seedy realism, and

Relaxing on the set of *Min and Bill* with costar Majorie Rambeau (center) and screenwriter Frances Marion. (Courtesy of the Academy of Motion Picture Arts and Sciences.)

everyone agreed the movie wouldn't work unless the atmosphere was believably tawdry. Fish Harbor consisted of decaying saloons and the dilapidated boardinghouse, "where the odor of barracuda, halibut and sea bass filled the air."[53] Both Marie and Beery were ill during the production, he with laryngitis and she with another "throat affliction," and a layoff was called from August 26 to September 5.[54] While ill or during production, Marie preferred to spend her nights at home rather than at the Don.

Renamed *Min and Bill* before its release and billed as a comedy, the movie was not initially a critical favorite. The *New York Times*[55] believed it "regrettable that Miss Dressler and Mr. Beery should have been cast for the first time together in this far from pleasant film." Chinking in slapstick bits and labeling *Min and Bill* a comedy was a stretch, what with murder, disfigurement, maternal sacrifice, abuse, and alcoholism propelling the story. *Min and Bill* is ultimately downbeat and pulls most vigorously at drama.

Marie's Min reflects the uneasy mix found at all levels of the movie. There are moments when her facial reactions are extreme even by her standards. But she dominates the film and skillfully navigates dozens of emotions. When George Hill controlled her rubberized face, she could be deeply effective, as when she anxiously waits among the trunks for a glimpse of her returning daughter Nancy. When Marie kicks a can in dejected solitude, it becomes a textbook study of lumbering heartbreak. The final scene, as Min is taken away on suspicion of murder, is a haunting moment somewhere between fear, poignancy, and satisfaction. Marie aims an expression toward the camera as sublime as any of her career.

She never looked more perfect for a role. That great shelf of a bosom became the resting place for so many comforting nights with her beloved adoptee Nancy. The eyes perpetually darkened in their sockets, flashing anger and fear if Nancy or Bill were threatened. The tangled hair and those surprisingly feminine hands were punctuated by a wide-brimmed black hat, a floor-length skirt, and a small purse hanging from her belt. As for the teaming of Marie and Wallace Beery, here was the apex of early Depression sentimentality. In *Min and Bill*, they were two old boozers who enjoyed a clandestine nip now and again. As the innkeeper and her boat captain boyfriend, their harsh affection for each other made an indelible impression on audiences. This aging couple, antiglamour personified, offered a refreshing alternative to so much standard screen romancing and beauty. Audiences went wild. With America crippled by a profound uncertainty for the future, the sight of two old veterans playing humble folk, scraping by on love and hard work, was a rare comfort.

Beery and especially Dressler do wonders with the material. More buddies than sweethearts, Min and Bill's years together become stunningly real as she gives him a shave or the two share a private joke on a quiet evening. The relationship between Min and Nancy is equally moving. The playing of Marie and Dorothy Jordan is tangibly beautiful, but their scenes were forgotten when so much to-do was made of the Dressler-Beery "love team."

George Hill was intimidated when given the assignment of directing two notorious hams in one picture:[56] "I had visions of having to tear them apart when they were before the camera. I thought I'd need all of my tact and all of my authority to keep one from scene stealing from the other. It worked just the other way around. I had to fight them separately, to keep their faces in front of the camera. Each

Min and Bill print ad.

wanted the other to have all the business. It must be love!"

Puff pieces in movie magazines had the two adoring each other, but Marie reportedly told her sister Bonita that she hated Beery and that they weren't getting along at all well, that they "just weren't the same type."[57] Joseph Newman said that Marie was "successful for the most part in keeping Wallie Beery in a good mood."[58] "Major" Carl Roup, a child actor and script supervisor at MGM in the late 1920s and early 1930s, also recalls that Marie kept Beery on his best behavior. "He could be a mean man," said Roup.[59] "When I was working with him as script supervisor, then called script clerk, I had to go through the director for any changes Beery needed to make. He could explode very easily." Marie was wise to keep her feelings about him closely held while many dubbed this one of the all-time great film teams. As *Variety* summarized: "They fit so snugly."[60] To demonstrate their affection, the

Marie dressed down for a photo session as Min. Notice her rarely unpancaked freckles.

studio released a tender and "candid" photo of the two stars "napping" in each other's arms. It seemed irrelevant that Beery married actress Rita Gillman the same year *Min and Bill* was made.

When Frank Whitbeck, the publicity and advertising man who confronted Thalberg on the low quality of *Caught Short*, saw a preview of *Min and Bill*, he turned to Thalberg and said: "That's one of the greatest I've seen."[61]

Thalberg felt Whitbeck overreacted. "It's not that. It's just a little comedy that we hope will go." Still, Whitbeck's comment stayed with Thalberg, who mentioned it to Mayer. The next day, Whitbeck was called into Mayer's expansive red-carpeted office, with Thalberg and third-in-command Eddie Mannix also present.

"Now, repeat what you told Irving about *Min and Bill*," ordered Mayer.

"It's one of the greatest you've ever made."

Mayer was in agreement with Thalberg and shook his head. "Why, it's nothing, Frank. It has no production value."

Whitbeck was adamant, even in confrontation with the boss. "It has one thing, Mr. Mayer. It has *entertainment*. I want to put it into the Carthay Circle."

Carthay Circle was Los Angeles's showcase theater for important movies, and Mayer had no confidence that *Min and Bill* could survive such marketing. "I think you're crazy," he told Whitbeck. Turning to Thalberg, he said, "But go ahead and give the goddamn fool the picture and let him play it where he wants to!"

It helped the marketing campaign of *Min and Bill* to have Whitbeck's enthusiasm. He billed the film as "a comedy drama with heart interest" and ran a teaser campaign for several weeks trumpeting the new rough-and-tumble love duo. On opening night, hundreds of fans collected outside the Carthay Circle clutching autograph books and pencils. Whitbeck installed a big book on a dais in front of the theater, called it *Min and Bill's Album*, and invited celebrities to write messages to the "new" stars. Printed in the book was, "In tribute to Marie Dressler and Wallace Beery in recognition of their glorious contribution to the screen — in appreciation of their immortal characterizations of *Min and Bill*." When Marie's car arrived, Beery met her at the curb and opened her door "with all the grace of a courtier," and then bowed as she got out.[62] He then led her on his arm to the radio microphone and they kissed. Marie was charmed, and she was completely dazzled by the cheering crowd — while the studio staff was stunned at such cordial behavior from Beery.

Whitbeck's instincts were on target. *Min and Bill* became a runaway audience favorite, playing 14 weeks at Carthay Circle, where it appeared with Fox Movietone News, a Walt Disney cartoon, and a short about the tuna industry called *Fisherman's Paradise*.[63] In New York, *Min and Bill* was held over at the Capitol Theater where *Let Us Be Gay* had recently done booming business. In San Francisco it played to a record 31,460 people in the three days following the premiere. At the final tally, *Min and Bill* outran all other MGM features released that year. The dissenting critics were silenced when it was selected among the

Directors Charles Reisner, left, and George Hill snuggle up to their adored star. (Courtesy of the Academy of Motion Picture Arts and Sciences.)

year's top five films in *Film Daily*'s nationwide poll.[64]

It was all too much for Marie. One critic[65] called her "a magnificent mountain of energetic sorrows and impulses," but she was never as robust as her screen image. She managed to get out of the house on November 25 to attend the premiere of *Morocco* starring Marlene Dietrich and Gary Cooper,[66] but by the 28th was in exile at La Quinta with an attack of neuritis.[67] "My dear, I guess I can't stand success," she concluded.[68]

Marie was getting royal treatment, and no wonder. In ten months, seven movies in which she appeared were released, all of them financial successes: *Chasing Rainbows, Anna Christie, The Girl Said No, One Romantic Night, Caught Short, Let Us Be Gay*, and *Min and Bill*.

A vaudeville circuit offered her $10,000 a week for appearances,[69] but she couldn't consider the even more grueling schedule of the theater. On the studio lot, a portable dressing room on wheels with small windows and art deco details was given to her as a Christmas present from Marion Davies. Soon, in true regal fashion, she and her dressing room were transported Cleopatra-like from one location to another by human labor.

A permanent retinue was growing around her. Cook Irene Allen was hired to ease Mamie's work in the kitchen. Claire had stopped pursuing acting jobs to work for Marie as nurse, companion, and confidant. Secretarial duties were assumed by young Mildred Kelly and later by Ida May Roycroft. Lawrence Weingarten, a studio production supervisor, would become

Marie's assistant. Weingarten benefited from old-fashioned nepotism by marrying screenwriter Sylvia Thalberg, Irving's sister, but he was genuinely apt. Mamie became well known at the studio, frequently visiting to assist with wardrobe and various attending duties. She sat offstage and watched Marie work. "I certainly am proud of her," announced Mamie.[70] "And getting prouder and prouder!" Husband Jerry, happy to be reunited with his "family" of Mamie and Marie, became Marie's butler and meticulously maintained her 1931 Ford.[71] He shared driving duties with Jean Meadows, one of the first women chauffeurs.

Other studios teetered close to bankruptcy during the early days of the Depression, but not MGM. Even after *The March of Time* sting, the studio was doing better than any other, consistently showing budgets in the black. It was well known that Marie Dressler, startling new screen darling, was a major cause of MGM's solvency. She wanted the world to know it, too, even if deceit was necessary. She bought a $5,000 diamond ring and flashed it around announcing it as a Christmas gift from the studio.[72] It was more likely a purchase she made from jeweler Sol Laykin during one of his regular sales visits to La Quinta.

The adoration of Dressler was in full flight. "She was an old shoe," remembered Elaine St. Johns.[73] "She loved people, believed in them, it didn't even matter that they had betrayed her. And her screen portrayals are closer to who she was than most others." As an industry reporter[74] noted: "Mayer, Thalberg or whoever else got Marie to put her signature on the dotted line took out insurance for the whole MGM product in doing so ... [her] great heart, like a sun, should warm all the minor planets, such as producers, directors and other players. ... people with chill, constricted natures thaw under the hard, sweet humanness of a Dressler."

Chapter 13

Queen Marie of Hollywood

Min and Bill continued to do heady business into the early months of 1931. MGM kept grinding out the publicity, making as much as possible from the runaway hit. On January 31, Dressler and Beery appeared at Grauman's Chinese Theater to cement their celluloid union with hand and foot prints as "America's new sweethearts." The studio even used them in a two-and-a-half-minute public service denunciation of the daylight savings time proposition on the ballot. Marie as Min described it as "a new idea they got to push the clock ahead so's to squeeze in another hour of daylight." With her trademark angry eyes flashing, she added, "They *pay* men to think up things like that."

After Marie and Frances took a brief holiday together in Hawaii, George Hill checked into the Beverly Wilshire Hotel in a trial separation from Frances.[1] The *Min and Bill* director and screenwriter had been married for one year, but Hill suffered severe bouts of depression and had a secret addiction to bourbon. The long-term friendship between him and Frances had been strained by marriage and both expressed hope that the separation would be temporary.

Movie magazines meanwhile continued the hoax of a Dressler-Beery romance. In language that smacks of canned public relations, *Motion Picture* magazine ran twin columns in April with Beery "writing" an article called "Her" and Marie "writing" another called "Him."[2] From Marie: "He's brought a lot of laughter to the world, but things haven't always been so funny in his own life. ... The recent financial depression cost him his entire fortune. ... But I better quit this gasping about it, it would never do to have this big ape find out how wonderful I really think he is!" From Beery: "I don't know anybody who deserves [success] more, or who enjoys it more. ... She's just about the most generous giver that ever lived, I guess. She gives that big salary of hers away so fast that it would make your head swim."

Directors joined in the hosannas. Charles Reisner, who worked with Marie five times and was her most frequent director, teamed with George Hill for a *Los Angeles Times* article on her glories.[3] "She is a great comedienne because she has built her laugh-making on the ashes of a personal tragedy. She was born an ugly duckling, overgrown, awkward. People laughed at every move she made and it was cruel laughter. But this young Canadian girl merely gritted her teeth and said, 'all right, apparently people want to laugh at me. Why shouldn't they?' ... she knows how close laughs are to tears." Hill remarked that Marie "has the most delicate sense of the dramatic that I have ever seen. She can take a line or a situation and so augment it that it becomes a mighty thing. ... [She] has brought to us a new conception of the art of acting." Marie was effective to her audiences no matter which "kid" was directing behind the camera.

Other studios tried to duplicate the magic of the Dressler-Beery coupling. Two other old characters, Edna May Oliver and Hugh Herbert, starred in RKO's *Laugh and Get Rich* with nowhere near the effect. W. C. Fields and Alison Skipworth were delightful in Paramount's *Tillie and Gus*, *If I Had a Million*, and *Six of a Kind*, but no one could match the team of *Min and Bill*. By late 1930, Marie was not only the chief purveyor of folksy comedy, she was commonly referred to as the most popular actress in Hollywood. The loving epithets started surfacing with more regularity and revealed Marie as an icon to moviegoers. She was alternately dubbed "the first lady of American comedy," "that grand old fire horse," "the most beloved crook" (in reference to her scene stealing), "mother spirit of the world," and the often used "Queen Marie of Hollywood."

As accommodating studio star, Dressler practiced her goodwill wherever she went. In April 1931 she tried radio. Louella Parsons began a "chitty-chatty gossip" radio show on CBS featuring top film stars.[4] Marie was her usual charming, homily-infused, unspecific self over the airwaves. "We're all perched upon mad horses, rushing madly through the world working for the big thing," she said on the air. "In our mad rush we're passing by the little things. It's from helping the other fellow that all the big things will come to us." As payment for her observations, Parsons gave Marie crates of oranges and lemons donated by California Citrus Growers, the show's sponsor.

These live appearances were never easy.

Even past the age of 60, and with the love of the world all hers, Marie still fell victim to stage fright. In 1932 she appeared on Rudy Vallee's radio program, gave a beautiful speech, and then collapsed. Jack Pearl, one of Marie's former stage costars and later a popular radio comedian, was nearby to help her. She fell into his arms, shaking. Audiences never had a clue to these attacks and clamored for more programs with Marie. The demand was ferocious—Hedda Hopper said that Marie was offered a radio contract of $5,000 per week, but the studio brass talked her out of accepting it.[5]

Most often, Marie was a good sport. In addition to accepting fruit for her services on radio, she posed in swimwear to promote Olympic gold-medal swimmer Johnny Weissmuller before he began his reign as the movie Tarzan. To riotous effect, she donned a wig to "test" for the coveted role of a tenement trollop who sleeps her way to the top in *Red-Headed Woman*. The role became the 1932 star-making performance for Jean Harlow.

Marie was now sought by and posed for top-notch star portrait photographers Ruth Harriet Louise, Clarence Sinclair Bull, and George Hurrell. She came closest to real glamour with Hurrell. For their session, she entered his studio and announced, "I've got the whole day. Let's do something interesting."[6] Hurrell remembered that "her face was the most expressive I had shot up to that time. She reacted instantly to my moods. I didn't have to worry about making her look slim. She slapped her well-corseted derrière. 'That's all me!' she laughed." The results of their collaboration are carefully composed portraits radiating wily but good-natured intelligence and a surprising trace of sensuality.

Beginning in October 1930, Marie was given two standard Polly Moran comedies in quick succession, which she accepted graciously just as she suffered constantly declining energy. The move motivated the *New York Times*[7] to chide that the studio was "determined to bury Miss Dressler's talents under tons of grotesque slapstick."

Reducing was directed by Charles Reisner and starred Marie as Marie Truffle, the dowdy country sister of Polly Rochay, a beauty salon expert from the city. With country bumpkin Marie arriving with her husband and three rambunctious kids at swank sister Polly's home, the comedy setups were inescapable. Marie is predictably inept at the ways of modern beauty salons and proceeds to make chaos from a treadmill, mud bath, skin plaster, and fat-reducing electric belt. *Reducing* reveled in the ceaseless quest for the slender form as Marie Truffle proclaims such truths as "always have someone around to keep you from eating things you shouldn't."

Choice moments included Marie's efforts to get her elephantine self onto a train's upper berth and an opening scene that received much comment. She appeared at the station with her money hidden in her corset. She forgets the location of her cash, believes she has been robbed, and then realizes that the stash has fallen to her waist. Desperate and running out of time, she jumps up and down madly until the money falls out her skirt. "When you analyze it this is a really tragic situation," summarized Reisner in an overstatement.[8] "We laugh at the plight of Marie Truffle because we are all saying in our subconscious minds, with a subconscious sigh of relief, 'my—I'm glad that isn't happening to me.'" More genuine drama came in *Reducing* when Polly's unmarried daughter becomes pregnant. In a fine example of the discretions in 1930s American filmmaking, the shocking fact is never spoken

George Hurrell captured a sophistication rarely seen in photos of Marie. (Courtesy of the Academy of Motion Picture Arts and Sciences.)

but is left to easy interpretation in several instances.

Reducing wasn't made for the approval of academic circles or *New York Times* film critics. The Marie-Polly comedies were strictly lowbrow, made for fast returns and aimed for the great rural masses. "The banana peel sense of humor, with a flavoring of sentiment almost as hokey, and all saved by the genius of Marie Dressler for getting the human quality into everything she does," read a review for *Reducing*.[9] The newspaper ads[10] screamed "The Funniest Women Alive ... ARE HERE!" as Marie and "her sharp-nosed playmate Polly Moran" invaded theaters across America. *Reducing* packed huge belly laughs that left early audiences limp and was yet another demonstration of Marie's potency at the box office. Made for $222,000, it grossed more than $1.5 million. *Photoplay*[11] ran a Questions and Answers column with one inquirer wondering if Marie was reducing in real life. Answer: "Marie Dressler is 5 foot, 7; has brown hair, blue-gray eyes, and weighs around 200 pounds. Yes, the title of one of her latest pictures is *Reducing*, but she isn't! Her face and her figure are her fortune, and Marie is wise enough to let well enough alone." Louella Parsons was happy with the status quo as evidenced in *Reducing* and rhetorically asked, "When a recipe is good, why not stick to it?"[12]

Near the release of *Reducing*, Marie is credited with one of the enduring truisms of Hollywood and moviemaking: "You're only as good as your last picture."[13] She did not need to worry at this point; she was cranking out hit after hit. Mayer explained to cash cow Marie that the studio needed another one of her movies in a hurry. Would she consider postponing her annual spring European vacation? She agreed, and Mayer handed her another Polly Moran movie with a $10,000 cash bonus. He also began earmarking a weekly sum with annuity rights to Marie should she ever retire from acting. Most spectacularly, he approved her weekly salary raised from $1,500 to a reported $5,000.[14] If her salary actually reached such heights, she matched W. C. Fields's and was among the highest anywhere. After paying her many expenses and her staff, and sending sister Bonita a $150 allowance each month, she still had huge amounts left over for charity and savings.

The golden handcuffs secured, Marie had few options but to work on *Politics*. The formula returned with director Reisner and the well-worn comedy duo. Together they created a precursor to the cozy familiarity of a long-running situation comedy. Polly is the stubborn one who makes Marie look bad, she gets her comeuppance, providing laughs along the way while Marie provides the heart. In *Politics*, crooked politicians incite gentle widow Hattie Burns (Marie) to run for mayor and clean up her town of Lake City. Polly played Ivy Higgins, Marie's campaign manager, and Rosco Ates had a well-received turn as Peter, Polly's stuttering husband. Claire appeared unbilled as a rally leader.

Early talking screenplays were often penned by several credited and uncredited writers. One anonymous collaborator[15] on *Politics* jotted on a draft copy that "this story is written with a positive disregard for those 'Astringents' placed upon us by Censorship." Indeed, *Politics* turns dramatic and racy and includes a plot of women's emancipation nominally by Wells Root, Malcolm Stuart Boylan, and Zelda Sears.* Hattie's daughter Myrtle (Karen Morley) is involved with a young hoodlum who has been framed for the murder at the speakeasy of Ivy's daughter Daisy (Joan Marsh). Using tactics from Aristophanes's *Lysistrata*, Hattie implores the townswomen to go on strike and cease their wifely duties in "parlor, bedroom and bath" until the murderous political machine is broken. The men of Lake City put up much resistance as represented by Ivy and Peter's constant sniping:

> PETER: You should stay in the kitchen where you belong.
> IVY: Men like you make me tired.
> PETER: Women like you make me th-th-th-thin.

There are role reversals as "obstinate males are much impressed by the variety of work the position of housewife entails."[16] The women's strategy is successful, and Hattie succeeds the sleazy Tom Collins as Lake City's mayor. Her first duties in office include marrying her daughter to a reformed gangster and appointing Ivy/Polly commissioner of garbage.

At *Politics*' summer opening at the Loew's State Theater in Los Angeles, the house was packed to standing room, with women a clear majority of the audience.[17] "There is nothing halfway in the appeal of [Marie]," noted the *Los Angeles Times*.[18] "Either one likes her a lot

---

*The doe-eyed Sears was also an actress who participated with Dressler in the 1919 Broadway Actors' Strike.

on the screen or not at all. Filled houses at Loew's indicate which class predominates." The hasty production of *Politics* could not be camouflaged. The *New York Times* expressed the wish "that some day the producers will see fit to cast Miss Dressler in a pictorial narrative which will give full scope for her exceptional ability."[19] Once again, a Marie Dressler movie was critic-proof, and *Politics* brought in a $564,000 profit.[20] The press had begun to deify Marie just as Mayer sent riches her way. It was common to extol her invincibility: "She has the wisdom which comes with three score years of living and she speaks the language and thinks the thoughts of youth. She spares neither her energy nor her time and she never tires or grows weary. She is ageless, mentally, physically and spiritually."[21]

Marie's "commodious" Beverly Hills rental belonging to Adela Rogers St. Johns.

The reporting could not have been more inaccurate. Marie and Claire skipped off to Santa Barbara for a round of Fourth of July parties.[22] They stayed at the Biltmore "but we lunched, tea-ed and dined all over the place," recalled Claire. By day three, Marie was wearying and complained of headaches, but she still accepted lunch and bridge with Doris Nixon at her cabana on the beach. Claire begged off and rested. "Softie!" shot Marie, who paid little attention to a masseuse who spoke of an unusual lump in her abdomen.

Marie's headaches grew worse and she went immediately to bed when she returned home. The next morning saw no improvement, so Claire sent for Marie's "little doctor." Marie had a strange relationship to medicine. She didn't "believe" in it, yet her bathroom cabinet overflowed with remedies for a wide range of ailments. "Let some masseuse or manicurist tell her about a magic herb, picked at midnight in the dark of the moon, in the middle of the Black Forest, and she'd set Mamie to brewing and drink quarts of the stuff," wrote Claire.[23]

The headaches were soon accompanied by a fever. With the press alluding to her immortality, fans were shocked to learn that Dressler was sent to the Osteopathic Hospital in Los Angeles for a reported hip operation.[24] She did not receive visitors or answer phone calls for a week and didn't work for three months. Only after her death was it revealed that doctors had operated and attempted to remove what was likely to have been a malignant uterine tumor "in the lower abdomen."[25] Whether or not Marie was told that her operation revealed cancer, she and her doctors were optimistic and considered a few weeks' rest the only inconvenience and precaution necessary.

She stopped by the studio periodically but otherwise stayed home, put her name on magazine memoirs called "The Girl Stood on the Burning Deck," and rested.[26] Flowers from well-wishers were everywhere in the house and her doctors were wondering how to limit the hordes of guests who came to visit. The Coxes took care of Marie as always, but she was also attended by Claire, who stayed at the house part-time. Her training as a nurse was most welcome; she accompanied Marie during the operation and afterward dressed her wound twice a day. The crisis got Hallie Phillips out to California from New York. "I want Hallie," Marie announced,[27] and Frances sent a dispatch immediately. "I just have to make Hallie laugh." Hallie came, she laughed, and Marie briefly recovered. "We were all concerned about Marie. All of us, except Marie, were afraid," observed Adela Rogers St. Johns.[28] Marie dismissed suggestions she should ease up on the physical demands of movie making and travel, saying, "I just had some poison in my system that had to come out. Hard work never hurt anyone."[29]

Mayer was alarmed by Marie's sinking health and insisted she leave her multistaired perch in Whitley Heights for a home on flat land closer to the studio. With a seemingly inexhaustible ability to relocate, she rented a large four-bedroom house on Bedford Drive in Beverly Hills from her friend Adela Rogers St. Johns. The two-story, steep-roofed brick house had servants' quarters downstairs for Mamie and Jerry and a rose garden in the back, but Adela's daughter Elaine remembered it as "unimaginative. The house didn't have much personality. I don't think Marie was very turned on by it either. It was commodious, convenient and first-class, but that doesn't make a house a home."[30] Still, on Bedford Drive the public Marie could give way to a private, exhausted, and ill woman. If not working at the studio, she would read or make dresses and drapes while Claire answered fan letters. If guests came by, she'd challenge them to bridge and usually win.[31] And in late September, just as soon as she was able, she took a hastily planned trip to New York.

Though *Reducing* and *Politics* were released to packed theaters, many had not forgotten the mysterious smile and awesome sacrifice of Min. When the fourth annual motion picture Academy Award nominations were announced on October 5, 1931, Marie was up for Best Actress for *Min and Bill*. Hers was the film's only nomination. Competing with Marie for the prize were four young glamour stars: 30-year-old Marlene Dietrich in *Morocco*, 28-year-old Ann Harding in *Holiday*, 32-year-old Irene Dunne in *Cimarron*, and 31-year-old *Let Us Be Gay* star Norma Shearer in *A Free Soul*. While still in New York, Marie proclaimed the nomination was the "silliest thing I ever heard! Imagine this old mud hen running competition with a star like Norma Shearer. Probably some pal tossed in my name to give me a plug and the crowd a good laugh."[32]

The awards were moved from the Ambassador Hotel, Marie's former residence, to the more spacious Sala D'Oro Room of the Biltmore Hotel in downtown Los Angeles. Marie was well enough to attend the ceremony on Tuesday, November 10, one night after her 63rd birthday. Broadcast on live radio for the first time, it was a mismanaged affair with dinner scheduled for 8 P.M. but postponed to 9 P.M. because of confusion over place settings. Marie's table was populated by her nearest and dearest Hollywood friends, including Claire, Hedda, and Howard Strickling. Frances, freshly divorced from George Hill, was at the table with escort Billy Haines.[33]

Finally the ceremony began at 10:30. It was a glittering affair that paid only callous attention to the destitution of millions across the country. With 2,000 in attendance, American Newspaper Publishers Association president J. N. Heiskell made a flippant comment on the unemployment problem. It would go away, he claimed, if the government would employ the unemployed to collect statistics on unemployment. The evening slid downhill from there as many swilled from their flasks in defiance of Prohibition. Between awards for art direction, cinematography, sound recording, writing, and direction were long-winded oratories by Mayer, Will Hays, California governor James "Sunny Jim" Rolph, Jr., and Herbert Hoover's vice-president, Charles Curtis. Also in attendance was Dolly Gann, Curtis's sister and the centerpiece of Washington society. She and Curtis were guests of the Mayers while visiting the West Coast.

Marie accepts the Best Actress Academy Award from Norma Shearer in the company of Best Actor winners George Arliss (*Disraeli*, 1929/30) and Lionel Barrymore (*A Free Soul*, 1930/1931). (Copyright Academy of Motion Picture Arts and Sciences.)

By the time the Best Actor award was announced, the seating plan had gone helter-skelter and 10-year-old *Skippy* nominee Jackie Cooper was asleep on Marie's lap. He slept through the announcement of Lionel Barrymore as winner for *A Free Soul*. "I fell asleep on Marie Dressler's lap," Cooper recalled many years later, "so when Mr. Barrymore won the award he's limping a little (arthritis). He came by our table after all the applause and I'm in her lap and she wakes me up and says 'It's Mr. Barrymore, it's Mr. Barrymore.' He said 'This really belongs to you but they gave it to me because they think I'm going to die.'"[34]

A radiant Norma Shearer was the Best Actress presenter. Suspense was artificial for the winners had already been announced to the press. Still, considerable emotion electrified the room. As Shearer read a prepared statement, Billy leaned over to Frances and whispered, "This is the feline moment of truth":[35]

> I will be in my dressing room, some mornings, making up, and I will hear the heavy tread of Marie Dressler's feet carrying her to her room. I'll know that she is tired, that she has not been feeling well, that she has been working the previous night. I'll hear her dressing-room door slam. Then, in a few moments, a boy will shout, "Calling Miss Dressler! On the set Miss Dressler!" The door will open and down the long corridor of the dressing-room building will come the thump, thump, thumping footsteps of that Grand Old Fire Horse Marie

Dressler! Made up, ready for work. Ready to carry on! Ready to give everything for the profession that she loves."[36]

Shearer continued, her voice breaking toward the end: "I want to thank the Academy for allowing me to present this award for the most distinguished actress this past year. To someone who is not only a great artist but someone we all dearly love. A grand old trouper who has carved her niche of fame for two generations, Miss Marie Dressler."

Dressler sat in stunned silence for a moment. "Like an old Model T Ford, I had to be cranked up," she later said.[37] "I sat there and winked back the tears that smarted behind my eyelids; choked back the lump in my throat that threatened to leave me speechless. I was so happy that it hurt." She eased Jackie Cooper into his mother's arms and headed for the podium. Marie remembered luminaries coming into view as she walked forward. Will Rogers and Wallace Beery were grinning, Lionel Barrymore was blowing his nose, and Billie Burke was crying. Looking back at her table, she saw Frances "smiling a triumphant I-told-you-so smile."

Surrounded by applause, she arrived at the podium and planted a vigorous kiss on Shearer's lips. By then Marie was grand, composed, and eloquent in her brevity. Dressed in a simple black lace evening dress, she warmly acknowledged Frances and the late Lorna Moon: "You can be the best actress in the world and have the best producer, director and cameraman, but it won't matter a bit if you don't have the story. ... I have always believed that our lives should be governed by simplicity. But tonight, I feel very important. In fact, I think Dolly Gann should get up and give me her seat."[38] The crowd laughed and Mrs. Gann stood up and offered her chair to Marie. They clapped and cheered as Marie returned to her own table. When she was seated again, Vice President Charles Curtis approached. "I admire you so greatly, Miss Dressler. Do you mind if I call you Marie?" The Academy Award winner leaned over to him and replied, "Charlie, you can call me anything you like."[39]

Cimarron, a sprawling western from RKO, was announced as the best-produced picture and the ceremony at last was over.* The next day's reviews for the awards were dismal. In *Daily Variety:* "A long winded, verbose, political and dull evening of a nature which will repel many a Hollywoodian next year (unless memories dim and time makes 'em forget)."[40] The guest of honor, Vice President Curtis, got the worst reviews. "That dull Republican oratory started dishes to rattling, silver to clinking and conversation to humming," noted the *Hollywood Herald.*[41]

There was no carping over the selection of Marie as Best Actress, however. In no uncertain terms, she claimed the award as "the crown for all the years of suffering and hardship that have gone before."[42] Her joy, however, was tinged with sorrow. While enjoying a late breakfast the day after the awards, she read a small obituary for a forgotten actress who committed suicide. She had been one of Marie's friends when she was just starting. "I looked back along the highway of the years," Marie wrote.[43] "Dark, pretty little Jane and big, homely Marie Dressler, dancing together in the pony ballet for a third-rate musical comedy in Kansas City, forty-odd years ago. Jane on Broadway, while Marie was still stalking the provinces. ... And now Jane was dead at sixty, a self-confessed failure. And I, Marie Dressler, was alive, with the Academy Award of last night standing within reach of my hand. I slip the golden figure into a bureau drawer. I cannot bear to look at it right now."

Dressler continued to exercise her patriotic fervor. In November, she spoke about President Hoover's unemployment program on NBC radio.[44] She also went back to her first film production since the summer medical scare and surgery. Once again, the script was penned by Frances to showcase her dear friend. This time, however, the physical demands were

---

*By coincidence, the first four Best Actress Academy Award winners—Janet Gaynor, Mary Pickford, Norma Shearer, and Marie—were Canadian born.

scaled down by Frances and Thalberg, who both voiced concern for Marie's health. The project was called *Emma*, and in it she had the titular lead as a longstanding housekeeper to inventor Frederick Smith, played with understatement by Jean Hersholt.*[45] Wishing to avoid the ache of old age loneliness, he proposes marriage to Emma and she accepts. He dies shortly after, setting into motion a chain of events evocative of Shakespeare's *King Lear* and E. M. Forster's *Howards End*. The story is essentially somber, exploring children's ingratitude, late-life romancing, inheritance, and the sting of betrayal after years of service. It includes death, an improbable courtroom showdown, emotional turnarounds, and several effective comedy routines.

Marie with Myrna Loy, who hated her role but loved her leading lady, in *Emma*.

Emma appeared destined for success. The stylish designer Adrian was assigned the costuming. Frances knew Marie's acting style better than anyone and had been fine-tuning script drafts for five months. Marie was given able support from Hersholt and Richard Cromwell as the favored child. The director was Clarence Brown, who had worked so well with Marie on *Anna Christie*. The studio budgeted a respectable $350,000 to give *Emma* the proper trappings.[46]

Emma contained the expected mix of melodrama, sentiment, and slapstick more in service to the star than to plausibility. "Gruff but lovable" hangs on Emma Thatcher as it does on so many of Marie's other characterizations. She drops an armful of towels, misfolds a diaper, and is all flustered when the kids get unruly. One minute she's telling them off, the next she is as sweet as the sweetest grandmother. Marie was so joyously alone in her *Emma* tour de force that the studio's decision to continue her in "team pictures" is downright baffling. The movie is foremost a monument to her skill, with additional kudos rightfully aimed at Brown. *Emma* is sentimental but not maudlin, funny but not vulgar, dramatic but not turgid.

Marie made the set warm and friendly. *Emma* was the first film for Myrna Loy under an extended MGM contract after Thalberg spotted her in Fox Studio's *Skyline*. A beguiling 26-year-old from Montana, Loy had been languishing in a succession of thankless exotic vamp roles. She recalled the *Emma* experience:[47]

> Metro started me out with a string of relatively normal, definitely minor ingénues. After six years and sixty pictures, it didn't

---

Though he had a long career as a character actor, Hersholt had a bigger impact elsewhere. He was president of the Academy of Motion Picture Arts and Sciences for four years and a generous philanthropist. During the production of Emma, *he persuaded cast and crew to make small weekly donations toward the building of a home and hospital for motion picture veterans. He won two Academy Awards for his service and inspired the naming of the Jean Hersholt Humanitarian Award given by the Academy.*

At about the time she made *Emma*, Marie and her floral print dress appear to take root amidst the vines of the Bedford Drive backyard stairway. (Courtesy of the Academy of Motion Picture Arts and Sciences.)

seem like progress to be playing a spoiled snot who ill-treats Marie Dressler. My disappointment must have showed. "Get your chin up, kid," Marie advised. "You've got the whole world ahead of you." *Emma* was fun because of her. She was a delight, a lovely woman, high-spirited and caring. I was crazy about her. She inspired awe, too, with her robust presence and extraordinary achievements. In her sixties she'd returned from near oblivion to become the movies' biggest box-office draw, beloved as few stars ever have been. It seemed that she'd go on forever.

The critical response to *Emma* was predictable: okay movie, spectacular star. "There is only one Marie Dressler, a character woman of unique distinction, a trouper with a genius for characters of comic surface but profound pathos. The hoke sympathy here is the jolt and it has been laid on very thick," wrote *Variety*.[48] The *New York Times*[49] called Marie's Emma "one of the finest character studies that has come to the screen. This Emma is a good-natured, utterly unselfish woman whose only thought is for Frederick Smith and his family." *Liberty*[50] went all out, proclaiming that "The National Academy of Motion Picture Arts and Sciences gave Marie Dressler the 1931 acting award — a neat little statuette — for her playing in *Min and Bill*. A statue about the size of New York Harbor's ex–Liberty is in order for Miss Dressler's work in *Emma*."

Emma opened in January 1932 and was an immediate hit. Critical judgment was overly harsh, though the film stands guilty of tear jerking. The central relationship between Emma and Smith is poorly developed, in part because the overpowering Marie wipes the mild Hersholt right off the screen. But *Emma* has a lasting poignancy and several scenes of tenderness: when Smith helps Emma put on her jacket for a vacation, she greets the gesture with a combination of surprise, embarrassment, and uncertainty. Emma has, after all, been caring for everyone but herself for more than twenty years. When Smith lies ill on his bed, Emma sings him a sweet song at the piano. Smith quietly dies, Emma chides the maid for entering loudly, and she continues her song.

Treacle is just around the corner, but *Emma* avoids it. While boasting excellent production values, the action and intent remain appropriately modest. It isn't burdened with the portentousness of *Anna Christie* or the forced folksiness of *Min and Bill*. It is rather filled with shrewdly observed visual jokes, as when the camera lights on dull magazines called *World's Work* and *Review of Reviews*. Emma grabs movie gossip magazines for her entertainment and in a pre-code moment, she opens a copy of *French Model* to find photos of bare-breasted women. At 73 minutes, the whole affair moves with great dispatch. The requisite comedy, especially Emma chasing a wayward knitting ball through a train station* while a shoe and a corset fall from her full arms, is delightful. It is vintage Marie, and it serves to create the character as a bumbling, well-intended lady. The finale was highly anticipated in production meetings. One executive was teary imagining that Marie "turns around with that marvelous face of hers and says [to her charges] 'be happy ... be happy,' and walks out. That kills you."[52]

Emma grossed nearly $2 million, with profits to rival *Min and Bill*. As with the Polly Moran comedies, it played particularly well in rural theaters, where patrons saw the movie repeatedly. One fan letter reveals the power and wisdom Marie was perceived to have at a time when movie sound was young and personal sacrifice was heroic. The writer was a 20-year-old woman from rural Michigan:[53]

> Dear Marie Dressler — Last year my only sister, who was eleven years older than I, died, leaving three small children. Their father was a good man, hard-working, loyal but totally incapable of providing three growing girls with more than food and clothing and shelter for their bodies ... nothing for their souls. No imagination, no ambition. They have nobody but me to look to. I had just finished working my way through college when my sister died. I wanted to be a doctor. Four years of study ahead of me. I couldn't earn my way and look after the children, too. I gave up my dream, but I did it grudgingly, in meanness of spirit. There was no glory in my giving. Day by day, my sacrifice was harder, more hateful to me. I had got to the point where I thought I couldn't go on. Then I saw you in *Emma*. Things aren't so hard now. I know I can manage.

Emma includes one of the sweetest scenes Dressler ever played. She and Hersholt are

---

*Someone at a rival studio gloated to Brown that his railroad station set was superior to the one used in *Emma*. Brown replied, "Well, anyway, we've got Marie Dressler."[51]

drifting on a small rowboat, aglow with happiness at their new marriage. With uncanny knack, Marie lets both serenity and haunted sorrow pass across her face. The collapse of actress and character into one public image is unmistakable: "I was never so happy in my life, I never had anything like this," she says pensively. "When people like we, well, grow old, we've had all the bad things in life and then when the good things come they seem so much better." Early audiences reportedly wept.

As *Emma* made its first run, Marie and Claire went off for a weekend at Aguascalientes, the flashy Mexican gambling and vacation resort.[54] Also attending were Margaret and Louis B. Mayer, director Raoul Walsh and his wife, and Major John Zanft and his wife, fashion designer Hattie Carnegie. Marie once again held court with the smart crowd, at one point ogling the mink coat worn by Carnegie. Then Mayer noticed a rash on Marie's arms and hands.

"Marie, do you want to do something to please me?" he asked like a father second-guessing his child.

"Of course, I'd give you my right arm. You know that."

He gave her a friendly pat. "Keep your arms, my dear, but let my doctor look at them, that's all I ask. I'll make an appointment for you when we get back."

She reluctantly submitted to an exam while Mayer gave his doctor, Edward B. Jones, instructions to reveal the results to him, not her. The rash proved to be systemic. When Mayer received the diagnosis of cancer, he sent for Claire. Together they devised a plan to promote Marie's recovery. Claire told Marie she was diagnosed with anemia and low blood pressure. She also spent extra time at Marie's home to better attend to nursing duties. She would try to keep Marie quiet and, with Mamie's collaboration, encourage her to rest. Claire was also to report periodically to Mayer. The secret was kept by five people: Mayer, Jones, Mamie, Claire, and Ida Koverman, Mayer's matronly and well-liked executive secretary. Her credentials were impeccable. As executive secretary to the presidential campaigns of Calvin Coolidge in 1924 and Herbert Hoover in 1928, she knew how to keep secrets.

Marie was a most disagreeable patient. "Keeping [her] in bed when she didn't want to stay in bed was a job a lion tamer would decline," noted Claire.[55] On and on Marie would rail: "I'm not sick! Fire the doctor!"

In the spring of 1932, unaware of or denying death's proximity, Dressler bought her first house. The homes she had rented in Whitley Heights and Beverly Hills had served her well for nearly five years, but with her new wealth, home buying seemed an obvious investment. One more time she was willing to move, this time with the hope it would be permanent. With young friend Newell Van Derhoef as her agent and insurance broker, she chose a handsome five-bedroom mansion at 801 North Alpine Drive in Beverly Hills formerly owned by the late razor titan King Camp Gillette. "I don't know what it was that attracted me to the house. Perhaps it was the garden. ... Perhaps it was the red brick Georgian simplicity of the house itself. It looked so strongly rooted in the soil, so perfectly at home in the midst of the trees and the shrubberies. I liked its simple straight walls, its green shutters against the white window frames, its green-shingled roof. It was solid and substantial and I knew that it belonged to me as soon as I looked at it."[56] She knew what she wanted. "I've sat in too many uncomfortable chairs in too many white drawing-rooms in Hollywood," she noted. "This is going to be a place where people can be comfortable and sit around in their carpet slippers if they want to." She christened her new home Loafhaven.

Almost immediately, Marie started having guests. On June 4, she hosted an old friend, minor British actor Quentin Tod. He brought with him Meher Baba, the avatar from Ahmednagar, India, who had taken a vow of silence.[57] The stocky, long-haired holy man with limpid brown eyes and large nose was a celebrity among celebrities in Hollywood. Using letters on an alphabet board as his voice, he enchanted press and film stars at parties in his honor at Mary Pickford and Douglas Fairbanks's Pickfair

Jerry and Mamie Cox pose with Marie's car in the Loafhaven driveway. (Courtesy of the Academy of Motion Picture Arts and Sciences.)

estate, Grauman's Chinese Theater and the Knickerbocker Hotel.

Marie received visitors with her customary hospitality, warmth, and humor. In the middle of lunch, she said "Baba, if you permit me, I would like to take you out to the woods and dance with you. And even if you want to speak a few words to me, I promise not to tell anyone!"[58] She was so impressed with Baba's serenity and warm gaze that she promised to stand beside him on the day he broke his silence. Marie and Meher Baba never met again.

Loafhaven residents included Mamie and Jerry, a menagerie of caged birds, a mutt named Friday, and a "canine aristocrat" named Peter.[59] "My friends ding-donged me into acquiring Peter. They think Friday is a disgrace. Peter is all right, but I just can't warm to him as I warm to Friday. Friday and I have been through a lot together. We see eye to eye. Friday used to lie at my feet and doze during those two long years that I sat on the veranda of my hillside house and waited for something to turn up."

Billy Haines was earning a reputation as a fine interior decorator and was drifting out of acting altogether. Marie hired him and announced that she was ready to spend a lot of money. She filled her new place with an eclectic assortment of things: Persian rugs, antique English prints, early American and Spanish chairs. Much of it set eyes on edge, including a large hand-painted lamp with a bright pink shade, which was made by an old friend and had to stay. In the living room, she combined strié wallpaper, chintz draperies, a sofa of silk moiré, and cabinets filled with tshioke collected at auctions and junk stores. In the dining room, her glass, silver, and pewter collections were displayed over English wallpaper of pastel-colored hollyhocks. There was an abundance of cut flowers and plants. She had walls full of photographs and sheets of music at her piano. Above all else, she made the home a warm and casual magnet for friends. She boasted that "there isn't a stick of furniture in my house that a man couldn't prop his feet on. ... I like a living room to look a little mauled."[60]

Mamie always loomed nearby. She usually pampered Marie and treated her like a child; the two appeared amused by their well-rehearsed relationship. In the evenings, Mamie would serve guests coffee on a Chinese tray in Dresden china cups atop an Italian carved table. Marie would pine for a cup, but Mamie would scold, "Miss Mary, you know you can't have no coffee at night."

Mamie and Jerry's bedroom featured cream-colored enameled furniture covered with glazed chintz of deep yellow background, matching window draperies, and a creamy tan rug. Marie was the boss, but Mamie was the adviser. Mamie did most everything — bought food and planned the meals, prepared Marie's bath, laid out her clothes, and worked with her at the studio. By any standard, the devotion Mamie and Jerry showed to Marie over 20 years was extraordinary and perhaps smothering. Each was paid $20 per week plus room and board. Marie was more than aware of their exceptional service. Mamie "is the priestess of my kitchen and my chink-filler," wrote Marie for a newspaper article.[61] Her "devotion makes me very humble. ... The bond between Mamie and me is simple. Her problems and interests are mine and mine are hers. What could be easier? I value Mamie's love and loyalty because nobody knows as I do how important backgrounds are in our lives."

At this stage in her life, with money and dotage to spare, Marie's daily routine was set.[62] She was awake by 7 A.M. and was usually given tea and muffins by Mamie. Breakfast was often delivered in bed and, honoring mother's advice to know the world, she read the newspaper every morning. A cigarette was usually burning between her slender fingers all day. Her dressing closet had an abundance of hats, with green her favorite clothes color. Accessories included rings on both pinkies and a string of beads. Jerry chauffeured her to the studio and they usually arrived by 9 A.M. If she was not expected at the studio, she would see visitors, shop, or hold an interview. She did not snack, but ate three hearty meals a day.

At the studio, the door to her portable dressing room was always open, except when she was changing. Friends dropped by regularly between scenes while she sewed or knitted. She ate lunch in the commissary, but "her entrance and exit are real processions. It consumes at least ten minutes for Marie to walk from the front door the few feet to her favorite table. Everyone stops her to talk a moment or merely to say 'hello.'"[63] There were always tangled lives to manage and egos to pacify. "Everyone should have a Marie in their lives," said Elaine St. Johns.[64] "The younger stars hung onto her like crazy. She was a very open person and a friend to everyone. She didn't have any feuds. Nobody was out to get her."

She usually left the studio at about 5:30 P.M. and was driven home by Jerry. A working day might have her on all fours in some undignified predicament with Polly Moran, while at night she was in an original Adrian black velvet gown with pearls to preside over a benefit dinner or awards presentation. If she went out, to a tea, premiere, or weekend in Santa Barbara, it was in the newspapers. Less often noticed was the constant presence of Claire.

Marie made no secret of preferring the luxurious and staid socializing of Santa Barbara and La Quinta to Hollywood. When in town, however, she was often escorted by urbane young gay men such as Billy Haines, Ramon Novarro, director George Cukor, and Jack Winslow, who joined her staff in 1932. She half-jokingly insisted that men over 26 didn't interest her. A typical blurb from a Los Angeles newspaper:[65] "Marie Dressler Brown Derbying with a nice looking young fellow."

Most often she went home in the late

afternoon. "I don't think she had much of a private life," said Elaine St. Johns.[66] "She didn't socialize in Hollywood much," observed Joan Marsh Morrill,[67] who played Polly's daughter in *Politics*. "She kept to herself." She rarely went out to the movies. "If [the] performances are better than mine, I feel uneasy — if they aren't, I'm bored," Marie rationalized.[68] With enough daylight, she preferred to putter in her rose garden.

Dinner was usually at 6:30 P.M. She especially liked Mamie's delicately spiced broiled chicken. In the evening she had the radio playing music softly in the background. Sometimes she would send Mamie or Irene Allen from the kitchen, don an apron, and be creative. One photo session posed "candid" shots of Marie at home cooking her "tail steak" concoction.[69] With the usually discarded end of a steak, she would finely mix the meat with vegetables, crack an egg on top, and bake it. Her culinary skills inspired Jack Pearl to compose a Teutonic-inflected poem:[70]

Act Got! How dot woman can cook:
I can't explain it to you:
She makes ham unt noodles a vunder of art
Undt a symphony out of a stew —
Her sauerkraut simply vould melt in your mouth
Undt der ribs is a t'ing for der book
Undt her noodles mit flares (???) is simply malicious —
Act Got! How dot woman can cook!

If friends were not coming over for dinner, bridge, or singing around the piano, she often had dinner in bed. If good friend May Robson stopped by, they'd play double solitaire or rummy. "Muzzie May" didn't have the aptitude for cards that Marie did, but she revealed that "I do believe Marie makes up her own rules."[71]

A masseuse visited her in the evenings two or three times a week. Just as often she visited her favorite beautician for a facial and neck massage. "If I am working I always have the masseuse in the evenings, so that I can tumble into bed and go to sleep."[72] To relax, she preferred baths to showers. Her bedroom featured a velvet carpet, silk draperies, and a bed covered with crepe de chine, lace, and plenty of pillows for comfortable reading. By about 9 or 9:30 P.M., she was reading or falling asleep. She giggled as she told a reporter "I'm wearing pajamas now around the house. You should see me. But they're so comfortable and easy to get around in."[73]

Rarely was she alone in the house. Mamie and Jerry had a rule of taking their days off separately, so that someone would be nearby should their boss need help. Marie remembered when they were invited to a wedding and "I insisted that they both go together. I promised I would go to bed early and assured them I would be all right. And, besides, I was to dine out that evening. Before they left they wrote a note and propped it against the lamp in the entrance hall, where I would see it when I came home. It read: 'Please lock the front door and leave the light burning in the upstairs hall. Then be sure to lock your door until we get home.' I did as I was told. But they didn't stay till the end of the party, anyway. They got worried about my being in the house alone and came home shortly after I had arrived."[74]

In 1932 Quigley Publications and the *Motion Picture Herald* polled 12,000 film exhibitors nationwide and asked them to name movie stars with superior earning power. The top ten included Janet Gaynor, Joan Crawford, Greta Garbo, Norma Shearer, Wallace Beery, Clark Gable, and Will Rogers. Dressler topped them all as number one.* To honor the occasion, she posed for photographs in the backyard clutching a press announcement of her top status while secretary Mildred Kelly looked on.[75] Marie's movies were grossing three times their cost on average; no other star came close to her value. As if to speak for most moviegoing Americans, one observer[76] wrote that "anytime Marie Dressler will stand in front of the camera and make faces I'll go see her. And if she does more than that — well, a team

---

**Dressler was ranked fifth in 1931.*

of army mules couldn't keep me out of the theater."

Loafhaven stayed open and in easy view from its palm-treed boulevard in Beverly Hills. Marie had her home address printed on her stationery. Security and fears of personal danger were minimal. It was all part of studio efforts to cultivate a homey image for Marie. Not that it was difficult. So many accounts of generosity, delicious cooking, and convincing mother roles fueled the reputation. But Mayer and the studio were also in the business of shielding the public from sex scandals, medical problems, and assorted peccadilloes. Marie's health was her great vulnerability, and her fans were unaware of the cancer that was growing. She remained the jovial, lovable, and supremely inspirational elder star of the movies. For as long as possible, the studio made sure she continued in such a capacity, free from the taint of sickness and mortality.

Chapter 14

"Careless Rapture"

Dressler was her own worst enemy where health was concerned. Although her stamina waned as the cancer cells proliferated, she loved her new life too much to slow down. She was "relishing every moment of her success," according to Frances,[1] and it was killing her. She may have avoided Hollywood parties in favor of her Loafhaven, but she didn't give up her travels. The doctors told her to stay put and "stop racing back and forth across the continent, and wearing yourself out, and you will live for years."[2] But at the studio's insistence, she had to leave Hollywood between movies to rest.

Her response to the conflicting orders was to do as she pleased, which further compromised her health and left her perpetually fatigued. She rarely admitted any decline and was forever evoking the grueling years of road shows as demonstration of her hearty constitution. Just to prove that she could, she and Claire often got in the car after a day's shooting and went north to Santa Barbara for a dinner date with the Walkers and other friends.[3] Her refusal to slow down was a source of increasing anxiety for Claire, Mamie, and others in her inner circle, but what could they do short of locking her in her room? Claire counted 17 trips in one year, usually to San Francisco, Santa Barbara, or La Quinta.[4]

Through the months of secrecy, Mayer played God, occasionally calling Claire into his office for a progress report on Marie's condition. He had insisted that Marie see his doctor, leave her home in Whitley Heights, and meet with him frequently at the studio, but he still wanted more intervention. Seeing that she was too active for her own good, he decided to give her Edward B. Jones's medical report. Claire and Mamie agreed to the decision, hoping it would motivate her to a more sensible schedule. They waited outside as Mayer delivered the news in his office, both terrified by the uncertainty of Marie's reaction. She wasn't hysterical and she didn't rail at anyone for withholding valuable medical information. Instead, when the three women were alone, Marie said, "Poor Claire. Poor Mamie. What you must have gone through! Why didn't you tell me? We'll lick this thing yet. I love a good fight."[5] She remembered show business tycoon John J. Murdock's 1926 cancer battle that was "won" by potions of honey and the blood serum of horses. Marie agreed to a regimen of horse serum injections administered by Murdock's controversial doctor, Thomas J. Glover. The experimental and hush-hush treatment had Mayer's full approval.[6]

Mayer wanted Marie to keep working. Late in 1932, she showed up in another early talking oddity starring Jackie Cooper, the tyke who fell asleep on her lap at the late-night Academy Awards ceremony. *The Christmas Party* was a mere 12-minute short with hundreds of kids enjoying a huge party hosted and catered by Lionel Barrymore, Clark Gable, Ramon Novarro, and Marion Davies, who got advice on dealing with boyfriends from one of Cooper's pals. Behind the warming trays were Marie, Wallace Beery, and Polly Moran serving a turkey dinner while gently humming "Happy Days Are Here Again." At the conclusion, Cooper speaks directly into the camera to wish a "Merry Christmas and a Happy New Year" from everyone at Metro-Goldwyn-Mayer.

Marie was simultaneously involved in a much larger project. In a profound lack of creativity, the studio assigned her to another comedy with Polly Moran called *Prosperity*.[7] Marie was to play Maggie Warren, a widowed mother and retired bank president in a small town hit hard by the Depression. Leo McCarey was originally hired as director; he had joined Lawrence Weingarten and Wanda Tuchock for their first story conference meeting on November 17, 1931, just one week after Marie won the Academy Award.

Prosperity had one of the longest gestations the talkies had yet seen. The collaborators were grappling with the plot, particularly the finale involving an attempted suicide, but the script was not coming together. "[W]e don't quite have it," wrote Tuchock. Drafts and redrafts continued into 1932, but the *Prosperity* script eluded everyone's satisfaction. At least five writers contributed to the story, and production began before a completed script had been approved.

As befitting the Queen of Hollywood and the most popular actress in the country, Marie received the world's largest postcard while she was making *Prosperity*.[8] Postage was $3 paid in 100 three-cent stamps. "Congratulations, Marie!" it read. "We the undersigned residents of Fort Wayne extend you our sincere best wishes for having won the 1931 Academy of Motion Picture Arts award for the year's best performance by an actress. We are looking forward to seeing you in your first real starring picture, *Emma* when it comes to the Rialto Theatre the week starting Friday, April 1st. Signed — [850 residents of Fort Wayne, Indiana]." The occasion was honored with a photo session as a cheerful Marie embraces the postcard, which was as long as the full reach of both her arms.

Anita Page, the young actress who had played Marie's daughter in *Caught Short* and *Reducing*, played Polly's daughter in *Prosperity*. During production, Marie confessed to Page that she was beginning to be ill from the cancer (or perhaps from the treatment of horse serum) and would have to limit her hours at the studio. "She was so brave, such a trouper," recalled Page.[9] "We loved her so much. We wanted her to feel fine, but she worried when she had forgotten things. She couldn't bear the idea that she was slipping." Discretion prevented details, but there was plenty of gossip buzzing around the studio. "We didn't know what kind of cancer she had," said Page.[10] "She didn't talk about it. It wasn't discussed in those days."

Marie's declining health was but one problem in the making of *Prosperity*. The first version of the movie had a gloomy preview. Had the Marie-Polly magic finally evaporated? The consensus was that there was too little slapstick and too few reactions between the two. A certain inertia was hampering the good time and several scenes would have to be reshot.[11] Production expenses rose to $628,000, a sum far beyond the cost of the women's previous efforts.[12]

On May 13, 1932, Thalberg, Weingarten, McCarey, and newly added writer Zelda Sears held a story conference to salvage the project. Thalberg felt the movie needed a more human touch and so threw another writer, Willard Mack, at it. McCarey felt the movie lacked romance and a strong conflict between Marie and Polly. He presented his interpretation:[13] "This version starts with the presumption that we now have between 5,000 and 5,500 feet of footage where the audience will laugh almost continuously. ... [It is] my opinion that unless the central character [Marie] stands out, we will never have a great picture no matter how many laughs we get." By June 18, Sylvia Thalberg and Frank Butler had written a reconstructed *Prosperity*. In July, Sam Wood replaced Leo McCarey as director. In August a shooting script was at last issued from Wood's office and production began again.

Mayer and Thalberg, in a panic and wishing to avoid any bitter irony in the film's title, mounted an unprecedented marketing campaign. The studio appealed to theater owners and film distributors nationwide with screaming announcements in multipaged ads industry magazines:[14]

> PROSPERITY IS *POSITIVELY NOT* AROUND THE CORNER! Face the Facts! Don't be FOOLED! Metro-Goldwyn-Mayer dares to tell the TRUTH! IT'S HERE RIGHT NOW! Introduced by those beloved ladies — DRESSLER AND MORAN in "PROSPERITY." The Greatest Comedy Ever Made — Bar None — Will be ushered into Box-Office History with NATIONAL PROSPERITY WEEK Nov. 18th. Simultaneous Day-and-Date Engagements Everywhere! ... [MGM's Leo the Lion is captioned:] "I ROLLED UP MY SLEEVES and went to work on the BIGGEST PROMOTION campaign I ever produced on any picture before! ... ASK ME for the SPECIAL CAMPAIGN BOOK. ... It's a showman's paradise, crammed full of sensible promotion ideas. ... Planned by practical field exploitation minds, not swivel-chair exploiteers." ... from your pals MARIE, POLLY and LEO!

The studio didn't stop there. Marie and Polly posed for a chummy photo with President-elect Franklin Roosevelt.

> GIVE AMERICA "PROSPERITY" Mr. ROOSEVELT! Hooray for our new President! Sincerely Yours, Marie Dressler, Polly Moran, THE MGM "PROSPERITY" GIRLS!

Prosperity's appearance on the eve of Roosevelt's first term and his New Deal for American prosperity gave the movie an urgent topicality. Playing the role of no-nonsense bank president Mrs. Warren, Marie offered a solution to the ongoing economic crisis. All the unemployed and idle can help themselves by working the materials that also lie idle. If people have no money, they can make barter arrangements — plumbing for laundry, cooking for rent, etc. Mrs. Warren's pleas for independence, pride in the family name, and passion for hard work were so obviously meant to transcend the movie and speak to the audience that *Prosperity* sometimes sounds like benign propaganda from Roosevelt's transition team.

Once again, Marie and Polly were warring mothers-in-law in what the *Hollywood Reporter*[15] termed "the friendly enemy style of belligerency." Polly was particularly shrewish this time, while Marie poured on her fidgety sweetness and high stoicism. For once, it aided a movie to have multiple authors. With comedy and drama more seamlessly intertwined, *Prosperity* was better received than *Caught Short*, *Reducing*, or *Politics*. The comedy starts early when Marie and Polly hire two different clergymen to marry their children and the women stage a brawl that audiences loved. With surprising restraint, Polly ran afoul of only one pie. Marie lets loose with her customary girning, at once puffing her cheeks, bulging her eyes, and furrowing her brow. The spat ends when Marie shoves a pickle in Polly's mouth.

Pies and pickles notwithstanding, Dressler was actually called upon to develop a relatively subtle character. The drama involves her son becoming prey to swindlers. Marie also plumbed her emotions during a speech about her late husband. She had fed him radishes and buttermilk on his deathbed when he asked for strawberries and cream, but he didn't know the difference. The comedy counterbalanced the drama, but Marie dissolved into tears at the end of the scene. Production notes by writer-actor Ralph Graves[16] came true as he predicted that *Prosperity* held "a great opportunity for pathos in spots where a woman has to knuckle and grub for existence the way Dressler does. Here is an optimist faced with real poverty. She's probably got the greatest chance in her whole life to get pathos if that is borne in mind as well as the laugh qualities."

The finale of *Prosperity* is a high expression of Depression-era merging of comedy and drama. Mrs. Warren decides to kill herself so her son can collect insurance money and avoid jail. She begins the scene by writing a suicide note, utterly determined in her actions. She believes she has ingested poison, though the audience knows better. Polly reveals the "deadly liquid" as Prune-O-Lax. The happy ending, with son John catching the criminals and the townspeople cheering the bank's reopening, is tempered by Mrs. Warren's hasty retreat to the nearest lavatory.

Prosperity had "a litany of gags," including ice down the dress and some messy cake business, mixed with near tragedy. Some critics did not take kindly to this potpourri. "Now that Marie Dressler has proven herself one of the greatest emotional actresses of the time, why should they wish to push her back into the rough and tumble comedy of custard?" huffed one observer.[17] "From *Emma* to this! Marie Dressler is entitled to kinder treatment."

Critics pooh-poohed the Marie-Polly movies, claiming they were undignified. They forgot Marie had a long history of low comedy on stage and that wild reactions, exaggerated gestures, and proven shtick were rote for her. Naysayers blamed writers, directors, and producers for saddling her with such business, but she was too habituated to resist her comedic impulses. If she hadn't been so good at it, perhaps the incongruous slapstick in her prestige movies *Min and Bill* and *Emma* would have been eliminated. "Certainly no director told her how to be funny," observed David O. Selznick's assistant Marcella Rabwin.[18] "She had far more experience than they did." Whatever the movies' shortcomings, they were undeniably entertaining, sometimes even trenchant, and they never approached the all-out screaming silliness of Marie's stage work.

Gloomy preview, protracted rewrites, and huge costs made no difference to Marie's army of followers. *Prosperity* did turn-away business at Loew's Metropolitan Theater in New York, where doors opened at 9:30 A.M. to accommodate thousands of patrons waiting in the November 1932 chill.[19] It came to log in a hearty $378,000 profit.[20] *Time* magazine's reviewer[21] liked the opus in spite of the shortcomings: "If you took any comic strip joke about a mother-in-law, multiplied it by two, added a bank failure, four platitudes about the silver lining and a vaudeville fox terrier you would have all the ingredients of *Prosperity* except the one which makes it human and amusing. This ingredient is Marie Dressler, who always impersonates grunting, sympathetic, noisy, witty, violent, immensely courageous old ladies but somehow manages to do it with enough vitality to make them seem alive."

Prosperity is an overlooked gem — modest, evocative, and full of Zeitgeist. Marie is forever buoying those with wounded pride and flagging spirits. Her status as "mother spirit" and personification of hope was never more obvious. Lovably crotchety, crabby, and impatient, but never scary or threatening, she need only be taken seriously when imparting sage wisdom. She can't resist telling someone what's what if they steal, forge, or abandon a romance for the wrong reasons.

Prosperity also smashes the stereotype of Depression entertainment as all fluff. The economic crisis had seeped into every corner of American life, and *Prosperity* was just one of many movies designed to boost morale without retreating into escapism. At MGM alone, there was Clarence Brown's *Looking Forward*, Gregory La Cava's Roosevelt rouser *Gabriel Over the White House,* and King Vidor's *Stranger's Return*. With more panache than *Caught Short, Prosperity* abounds in foreclosures, cramped living arrangements, investment scams, and mob hysteria over lost fortunes. Leading the way toward a happier future is Marie, nearly addressing the camera when she says, "We've been through a rough time, this town and this grand country of ours. ... We've learned that the stock market may go down, but the sun will always come up."*

Once *Prosperity* had succeeded in spite of its setbacks, Mayer and Thalberg decided not to repeat the Marie-Polly formula. *Prosperity*, arguably the women's best effort together, was their final joint appearance. One writer saw the pain creeping into Marie's face and noted that her "features seem to have undergone some mysterious change, giving her a haggard countenance and a smile bleaker than it should be."[23] When Marie mentioned to Anita Page during the production of *Prosperity* that she was beginning to feel sick, she wasn't kidding. In September 1932, she had surgery to remove a malignant tumor on her vulva.[24] The news was not made public and her problem was not widely known. Doctors feared that the cancer had spread to vital organs, and their prognosis was grim. Still Marie kept active. "I don't feel old or decrepit. I refuse to sit in a corner and watch the world go by," she had told a reporter in August.[25]

Fans had no clue to the seriousness of her condition. "Her general health is much better these days," reported columnist Harrison Carroll.[26] Tidbits were dropped in the press about her dining at a restaurant in Chinatown, shopping for garden furniture, or attending the summer games at the Olympic Stadium in Los Angeles. She added handsome young Jack Winslow to her staff.[27] "He's my secretary, businessman, adviser. ... Joan Crawford just gave him a title. She says just call him 'My Everything.'" With public appearances, press whitewashing, and increased personnel, Marie appeared to the public as the epitome of late-life vigor.

She did everything to maintain that image. After a mere two months of recovery from the September operation, she and Claire took the train to New York and were there for the opening of *Prosperity* and the 1932 Academy Award ceremonies. During their stay, Marie stepped out to see the acclaimed Abbey Theater Players of Ireland. Adoration can be fatiguing, and Marie had hoped not to be detected. After the final curtain call, she stood up to leave and found a large fireman waiting at the door of her box.[28] "Will you come backstage for a minute, Marie?" he asked. "The company knows you're here and they're crazy to have a word with you. They're too shy for asking themselves, so I said I'd bring you." Backstage the players were drawn in a line. Upon her arrival, there was a palpable pause, followed by a gushing sound from the leading player: "We can't believe it. We can't believe we are really *seeing* you. This is the happiest moment our company has ever had!"

Still more love was lavished on Dressler during that New York sojourn. She was eager to see *Music in the Air*, a new production by her 1903 accompanist Jerome Kern. When she walked down the aisle of the Alvin Theater arm in arm with Jimmy Forbes, the entire audience rose *en masse* to greet her. Jimmy whispered, "Bow. Do something, Marie! They're saying, 'Hello, Marie, we love you!'" More fuss was made over her than over Kern's show. Between acts, she was approached by Jane Cowl, Anne Morgan, Irving Berlin, Edna Ferber, Jack Pearl, and Anne Vanderbilt. She was absolute royalty that night.

Outside at a red light, her car stopped and was almost immediately surrounded by a mob, "their tired faces alight with love."[30] The car drew throngs from Central Park to Washington Square. At that moment Marie was "more beloved than any other woman in the world. ... She is the woman for whom, above all others, this old world has borrowed its mirth during the darkest days any of us remember."

The annual Academy Award banquet was held while Marie was in New York. She found herself nominated for another Best Actress Award, this time for *Emma*. She was in the running with only two other actresses, Lynn Fontanne for *The Guardsman* and Helen Hayes for *The Sin of Madelon Claudet*. The Academy banquet had a new treat this year: The Walt Disney Company color short *Parade of the*

---

*The plot of *Prosperity* hit too close to home when the bank to the stars, First National of Beverly Hills,[22] closed its doors in June 1932. Marie was among its depositors suffering undisclosed losses.

Award Nominees was screened with animated versions of each actor and actress marching to heralding bugles and tossed flower petals. Marie's cartoon as Emma came with her sight gag from the movie involving a corset and an alarm clock.

This time there was a faint breeze of protest for Marie's possible second triumph. This was the fifth year of the Academy Awards and Hollywood was not used to multiple awards for individuals. Some felt that former winners such as director Frank Borzage, writer Frances Marion, and Marie should be prohibited from repeating their victories. Back on November 18, the Academy had already voted down a petition for exclusion at the Ambassador Hotel in Hollywood.

Frances won her second Academy Award that night, and Wallace Beery won his one and only, both for the boxing tearjerker *The Champ*. Best Actress went to Helen Hayes in *The Sin of Madelon Claudet*, a movie Irving Thalberg called "crap." The finale of the evening was a radio broadcast from New York. Producer David O. Selznick spoke on the wireless, followed by Marie, who said, "It is honor enough for me to be mentioned for an award in company with Helen Hayes and Lynn Fontanne. Dear Helen, you will know that my hand clasps yours under the hand that hands you the gold prize which you have won so brilliantly."[31]

The crowd applauded Marie, but then gasped when she continued.[32] "I am under strict doctor's orders to remain in New York for several weeks." News of Marie's illness was now far beyond the trust of close friends or the guarded walls of the studio. Her trip to New York wasn't all business and adoration — she was being examined and treated by the nation's top cancer specialists. She was given a new diet, and more horse serum, but little else could be done for her. Mayer was disturbed by her public revelation, but Marie's illness could not remain a secret forever.[33] She had been vague about her condition, and loath to talk about it, while her public persona was so energetic that it was easy to forget she was mortally ill.

On their return trip to California in December, Marie and Claire shared a train with Dore Schary, Mayer's eventual successor at MGM. He recalled that "the trip came alive when word spread through the train that [she] was a passenger. At each stop, we got off and gawked at the car in which she was riding in drawing-room splendor. But it wasn't until Albuquerque that Marie appeared on the steps, posed for pictures, waved a royal hand at her fellow passengers and then retreated into her curtained room."[34] Marie was inaccessible on that trip across the country not from vanity but from increasing frailty.

With a cursory nod to doctor's orders, Dressler arrived in California on December 17 and began planning her next round of social calls. Claire and Mamie's incessant efforts to get her to rest failed. Marie kept encouraging her friends to visit, even when she was weak. In a thank-you note for a tribute by Cleveland critic Archie Bell,[35] she confessed that "When one is on a picture — that ends everything — I go so early to the studio and get home too tired to do anything but flop — but flop is the word." In almost the same breath she asked, "Why not take a run out here? I promise you a really good time and I should love to see you."

Claire had been a nearly constant companion since late 1930. She was Marie's most intimate friend, but Marie was also paying her as a nurse. By the time the two returned from the latest New York trip, a wedge had appeared in their relationship.[36] There was a new frostiness attributed to jealousy and Marie's increased desperation about her health. The two were arguing ever more frequently.

Claire was never convinced of the sincerity of Mayer's affection for Marie and told her so. She believed he saw Marie foremost as a commodity. He wanted her back at the studio not for her own morale but for the guaranteed lucre of her movies. Marie hated to imagine Mayer so callously, but Claire gave her reasons to suspect him. On one occasion, when he called Claire in, ostensibly for an update on Marie's condition, he veered from the topic and began to ramble about how he kept his stars under control. For some he cried, for others he used reason. Claire sat rapt as he told her that most of them were convinced that he truly cared about their lives and well-being. To Claire, it was a nauseating spectacle. To Marie, it was a fact best ignored.

Claire did not specify the exact reasons for her departure, but she later wrote that "I tried to hold her back when she began to descend." Both were stubborn, dominating women, but Marie had the additional burden of possessiveness. One report has Claire's mother being ill with heart problems in late 1932. She was resting at Claire's Santa Monica home and needed her daughter's attention. Marie was ready for a trip to La Quinta, but Claire declined. Marie summoned all her grandiloquence and pettiness, drew a line in the sand, and gave Claire an ultimatum. Claire left and they never saw each other again.

Dressler was not one to stay at home and pout. She charged through anxiety by keeping an exhausting schedule. After Claire departed, Marie packed and was off again for a New Year's Eve party with the Walkers at La Quinta.[37] She tried heroically to hide the blues of losing Claire and gregarious Elisabeth "Bessie" Marbury, a major architect of Marie's comeback, who would die in January 1933. By March, she was back in New York for more meetings with more doctors. She endured yet another operation and told reporters she regretted missing George Bernard Shaw on his swing through Los Angeles.[38] She also agreed to a salary cut, since her productivity had declined and other stars were taking cuts to keep the studio solvent.[39] Marie's weekly income was now just $2,500, far below the sums of less bankable stars. But without bullish Jim Dalton to storm the front office, Marie was more likely to suffer and complain privately.

Reporters and fans expressed concern at her health, but "she didn't mention the fact — she never mentions it — that she has been desperately ill," wrote Adela Rogers St. Johns.[40] "Why, you've got to be a fighter, honey," reasoned Marie.[41] "Don't folks know that? Everybody gets socked." By the spring of 1933, Marie was perpetually sick and denying rumors of her retirement. Though she barely managed a few productive hours a day, usually 10:30 A.M. to 1 P.M., she longed to keep working. Missing plum roles was more painful than getting out of bed, which by this point was a challenge.

She was keen on the role of Annie Brennan, the proud skipper of a rundown Seattle tugboat called the *Narcissus*. MGM had bought the property and Zelda Sears and Eve Greene adapted it from a serial in the *Saturday Evening Post*. Marie's name was on it from the beginning, as Tugboat Annie was described as "large-framed, solidly built, with rugged, almost masculine features and shrewd, quick blue eyes and her movements had an elephantine energy that galvanized everyone with whom she came in contact. When she passed through a room, dust and odd bits of paper danced in her wake. And when she stood, she looked not unlike a blowzy but exceedingly combative bulldog."[42] Marie explained her attraction:[43] "I love any role which shows that if you aren't afraid of life, life can't hurt you. That is what Tugboat Annie does. She licks fate because she can look it in the eye and not be afraid.... I think that's the kind of stimulant that we need in American life right now."

Harry Rapf, the kindly man who rode *Min and Bill* to success, was the producer. Mervyn LeRoy was the director, still hot from the Warner Bros.' hits *Little Caesar* and *I Am a Fugitive from a Chain Gang*.[44] Mayer convinced LeRoy to defect to MGM to direct. LeRoy knew the *Tugboat Annie* stories and felt "they had tremendous possibilities for the screen." Baby-faced Robert Young played Annie's son Alec and Maureen O'Sullivan came aboard as his love interest. To complete the principal cast, who better to play Terry, Annie's bibulous husband, than Wallace Beery.

Mayer spared nothing for his favorite actress, even buying her a cottage[45] she and Howard Strickling had admired on the way to Washington. Mayer had it moved, tied a blue bow around its front door, and attached a card that read, "Welcome Home, Marie!" It became her residence while in the Northwest. "Oh, yes, they spoil me handsomely ... and I just sit back and lap it up like a cat with her nose in a saucer of cream," wrote Marie.[46]

The prolonged stay in the Northwest

would be taxing enough, but Dressler had the additional burden of a physically demanding lead role. She confessed that the storm sequence at the end of the movie was the most difficult shooting of her career. Another difficult scene was shot on the Puget Sound waterfront with 10,000 extras and a huge crowd of onlookers. The hired extras, crew, and all-star cast were issued badges to get through the police lines. Beery and Marie were on board the boat, but shooting was postponed when LeRoy forgot his badge and couldn't get through the police barricade he had orchestrated for crowd control.

It would appear careless of MGM to subject its most profitable and fragile asset to the elements and suicidal for Marie to accept. But Annie was a part she desperately wanted to play, as though the onslaught of death motivated her to work even harder at assembling a legacy. Instructions from Mayer and Thalberg to LeRoy and crew were strict:[47] Marie was to appear only when well and she was never to be kept waiting. LeRoy, in his self-congratulating autobiography *Mervyn LeRoy: Take One*, steps in line with Myrna Loy, Wallace Beery, Greta Garbo, Louis B. Mayer, and so many others in his praise and awe for Marie's commitment:[48] "Poor Marie ... was dying of cancer and she knew it. ... She could only work three hours a day because of her physical condition. Marie was always a lady, always kind and considerate and she worked like a Trojan, to the limit of her health. That limit was very limited. ... When [she] went home at night, I couldn't help wondering whether she would be able to make it to the studio again in the morning. She was in constant pain and the pain mirrored itself on her face, on her bearing but never on her professionalism when the camera was rolling. She never lost her skill."

In sharp contrast, Beery could be monstrous. LeRoy called him "a bull of a man, crude, impatient, unable to understand weakness of any kind."[49] Beery lost his temper over Marie, who was frequently tardy. On one occasion, he was ready and she had not yet appeared on the set. "Where's Dressler? Get the old bag in here. I'll be in my dressing room. Let me know when she gets here."[50]

Cast and crew were offended and shocked. LeRoy interjected with "Wallie, that's not worthy of you—and you know it." He blushed, apologized, and behaved cordially afterward. "I've seen her work and smile when she was in actual pain," said a repentant Beery.[51] "They don't come any better than Marie."

Unlike the notorious *Anna Christie*, *Tugboat Annie* received few objections from the MPPDA.[52] "We found it to be a delightful picture, clean and wholesome in theme and cleanly and wholesomely picturized," concluded James Wingate. Objections were limited to a few "hells," "Gods," "Lords," and a "reference to 'male companion' should be deleted as an inference to sex perversion." Mayer complied, and a print was ready for preview by July. The world premiere took place at Seattle's Fifth Avenue Theater on July 28.* "Seattle Scoops the World!" roared the local *Tugboat Annie* ad. No stars were there, but Marie sent a telegram. She ventured out infrequently that July, spotted only once with the Walkers for a late night dinner at the Miramar Hotel.[53] Three weeks later, LeRoy escorted a noticeably frail Marie to the Hollywood premiere at Grauman's Chinese Theater, where she and Beery had made their foot and hand impressions in the cement as *Min and Bill*. Predictably, *Tugboat Annie* was a tremendous hit. MGM gloated that the movie bested *Prosperity*'s business in Boston, New Haven, Providence, and Denver. At Loew's State Theater in Los Angeles, it broke the record set by *Caught Short*. Produced at a pricey $614,000, it grossed more than $2,500,000.[54]

Unlike *Min and Bill*, *Tugboat Annie* focused directly on the Marie-Wallie relationship. This time they were married and both had a dose of parental instincts. The story, built

---

The Northwest did not soon forget the making of Tugboat Annie *at Puget Sound. A plaque honoring the film's debut at Tacoma House was fitted to the Roxy Theatre on its refurbishing in 1974 and the "Marie Dressler Tugboat Race" was inaugurated in Tacoma after cast and crew had left.

around Annie's frequent coverups of Terry's inebriation and a parent-child estrangement and reconciliation, was weak. The narrative doesn't so much move forward as it goes around in circles, but its flaws were neatly camouflaged by some sharp dialogue and one-liners. For the sake of character, Marie once again looked like hell, dressed in a dark shirt, old sweater, and tattered hat.

Annie is a softer and less coarse creation than Min. When Maureen O'Sullivan as Pat asks whether she's invited on board the *Narcissus*, Annie blurts out that she is more welcome "than a grasshopper in a crate full of turkeys." Annie becomes a lovable salt immediately as the audience learns she is nearly illiterate. While reading from her son's book, she mispronounces such fancy words as *enthusiasm*, *Worcestershire*, and *philistine*.

Made during the last gasps of Prohibition, *Tugboat Annie* offers a unique look at attitudes toward drinking. Marie's tippling in *Dangerous Females*, *The Girl Said No*, and *Anna Christie* is either funny or pitiable. She does no one any harm. Beery in *Tugboat Annie* is quite another matter. Terry is either selling pieces of the hawser to buy his brew or running the *Narcissus* into a gleaming cargo ship. For too long in *Tugboat Annie*, Beery's character is downright despicable, full of "alcoholic stupidities."[55] Beery's performance ages badly; it's hard to laugh at drunks putting others in danger. Marie, in contrast, remains timelessly funny, tender, and patient. She is once again the heart, soul, and muscle of a movie. Fortunately for all concerned, Terry overcomes the bottle and acts heroically in the last reel, and Annie is found to have well-placed loyalties after all.

Noted *Variety*:[56] "In the hands of the co-starring couple, its deficiencies are barely noticeable. Those who will be irritated or annoyed by the story's hokey, sobby, stale baloney nature are likely to be a very small minority. The average Dressler-Beery fans, of whom there are many, will eat it up as is without asking for Worcestershire sauce."

"It all seems so maddingly simple," wrote *Newsweek*.[57] "All Marie Dressler has to do is to call her drunken mate 'you old lummox' and

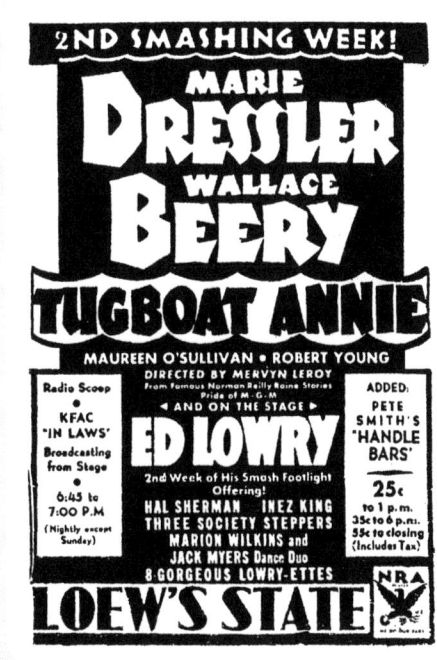

Breaking more records. As suggested by the ad design, the stars were more important than whatever movie they appeared in. (Courtesy of the Marie Dressler Foundation.)

strong men and stronger women burst into tears. At any rate that's what happened to first night New York audiences last week at *Tugboat Annie*. ... [She is] God's gift to the movies." From the discriminating pages of *Rob Wagner's Script*,[58] one wag found it quite vulgar: "After all, money *is* what counts. Art? Pfftt!"

Tugboat Annie succeeded not just on the strength of its stars, but because of its clear message of love and forgiveness. This is a movie filled with tender relations: husband and wife, son Robert Young and daughter-in-law Maureen O'Sullivan, an old couple and the sea, a woman and her boat, a mother and son, and a father and son. Even Terry's love for the sauce is treated gently in a postscript as Annie finds him imbibing yet again.

Tugboat Annie may falter in storytelling, but it looks perfect on screen. Sets, props, and costumes created such a cozy and worn-out *Narcissus* that one can almost smell sea salt. It

The incomparable guest list for *Dinner at Eight*: Marie, Edmund Lowe, John Barrymore, Wallace Beery, Jean Harlow, Lee Tracy, Billie Burke, and Lionel Barrymore. (Courtesy of the Academy of Motion Picture Arts and Sciences.)

was masterfully shot, with striking scenes of shafts of light, burning boilers, and restless waterways. Credit goes to Gregg Toland, perhaps the greatest cinematographer of black-and-white film. His career is studded with ravishing and eclectic work such as *Wuthering Heights*, *The Grapes of Wrath*, *Citizen Kane*, and *The Best Years of Our Lives*.

Annie lived on after Dressler. In 1940, Warner Bros. produced a sequel with Marjorie Rambeau, *Tugboat Annie Sails Again*, and in 1941 Beery was *Barnacle Bill* with Marjorie Main at MGM. Jane Darwell took the helm in Republic's 1945 *Captain Tugboat Annie*. In 1957 Minerva Urecal became Annie for a television series. It is commonly agreed that no subsequent efforts equaled the charm of the original.

The making of *Tugboat Annie* was protracted because of Marie's limited workday, but the studio also wanted her for another altogether different project. Shot during the lengthy production of *Tugboat Annie*, *Dinner at Eight* was a witty comedy of New York high society by George S. Kaufman and Edna Ferber and had been a Broadway hit in 1932. Also in 1932, MGM mounted the box-office bonanza *Grand Hotel* as a star showcase. The studio bought the film rights to *Dinner at Eight* for $110,000 with the intention of making another star-powered movie of the highest

order.[59] Irving Thalberg, just 33 years old, had suffered a heart attack late in 1932 and was sidelined. Mayer brought his son-in-law David O. Selznick to the studio as vice president and producer, where his first production assignment was *Dinner at Eight*. Selznick was followed to MGM by friend and neophyte director George Cukor. A former dialogue coach, the 33-year-old Cukor had directed Tallulah Bankhead in *Tarnished Lady* and John Barrymore, Billie Burke, and Katharine Hepburn in *A Bill of Divorcement* before winning the *Dinner at Eight* assignment.

Cukor had demonstrated a facility with actors, but *Dinner at Eight* would test his young skill to the extreme. Selznick was nervous with this first MGM assignment, but he aimed high and used the best talent available.[60] Adrian would design the costumes and Cedric Gibbons the sets. The biggest stars on the lot were cast in key roles. Enlisted into service was Lionel Barrymore as shipping scion Oliver Jordan. Billie Burke, the recently widowed Mrs. Florenz Ziegfeld, was cast as Barrymore's flighty wife Millicent. Wallace Beery was on hand as the nouveau-riche swindler Dan Packard. His tartish wife, trying desperately to overcome a humble past as hat-check girl at the Hottentot Club, was Jean Harlow. John Barrymore played Larry Renault, a washed-up ham actor carrying on an affair with the Jordans' daughter (Madge Evans). To further adorn the cast with names, well-known contractees such as Jean Hersholt, Lee Tracy, Karen Morley, Edmund Lowe, Louise Closser Hale, Phillips Holmes, and May Robson were given lesser roles in the comedy-drama. As MGM now billed her "the World's Greatest Actress,"[61] Marie's place was at the top of the heap. As evidence of her towering commercial power, she received top billing for her role as Carlotta Vance, overripe stage actress and courtesan of the gay '90s now an expatriate in Paris. The ensemble action revolves around Millicent's impending dinner party, with numerous intrigues, stock buyouts, and clandestine meetings taking place before everyone assembles. Each star was used anywhere from two to twelve days during a tight shooting schedule that began on March 13 and ended on April 17.[62]

The stage play was adapted lickety-split in four weeks by Herman Mankiewicz and the ubiquitous Frances Marion. Frances had a dislike for chatty screenplays and was lukewarm on this assignment. "A picture with so many characters and each individual role equally good could not fail," she wrote.[63] "But it bore the blight of artificiality to me." Despite Frances's reservations, the condensed time for creativity, and so many star egos, shooting went smoothly. "When I was assigned the direction of Dinner at Eight, my friends began dealing out condolences on the difficulties that were to confront me in handling so many stars," observed Cukor.[64] "I didn't have much trouble, stars are usually easier to cope with than less important people." The movie's success was due entirely "to those marvelous performers. With them behind me, everything seemed possible."[65]

The brilliance of Dinner at Eight arises from flawless casting according to type. Mankiewicz slyly noted that Cukor's job was ingenuously simple.[66] "It must be awful tough for you to show Marie Dressler how to perform an old actress who's very ill and I can see the difficulty in making Lionel Barrymore understand the emotions of a man who has an extravagant wife* or Jack Barrymore comprehending the feeling of a fading matinee idol." Mankiewicz also "sympathized" with Cukor for trying to make a sexy tart out of Jean Harlow and an uncouth creature out of Wallace Beery.

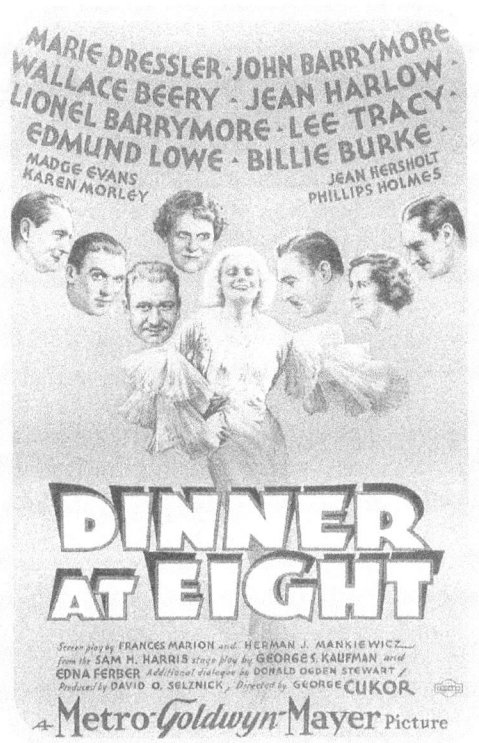

William Galbraith Crawford's illustrated poster of the *Dinner at Eight* ensemble. Marie received top billing, but Harlow revealed why she "need never worry" about machinery replacing her profession. (Library of Congress collection.)

Selznick proved to be a competent and self-possessed producer. Unlike Thalberg, he was very visible on the sets and in production. Not all was rosy during the hurried completion of *Dinner at Eight*, however. The stars avoided tantrums, but Mayer felt Harlow, so young and inexperienced, would be obliterated by the veteran pros. Cukor found Marie unconvincing as a former beauty with wealthy lovers in every port, though he adored her as a person. Harlow and Beery detested each other;

---

*Barrymore's two wives were actresses Doris Rankin and Irene Fenwick.

she wasted no time in calling him "a mean old son-of-a-bitch."

Script changes kept coming during the shooting. In one scene, Carlotta's Pekingese deposits an atrocity on a hotel carpet.[67] The episode was condemned by censoring pre-viewers but somehow managed to make it into the final print. More problematic was the dog's name. He was alternately named Gandhi and Mussolini, but the fear of international offense was too great. In a postproduction dubbed voiceover, Marie calls him Tarzan.

The final scene of *Dinner at Eight* includes the most famous moment in the careers of Dressler and Jean Harlow, but it nearly didn't happen. An acceptable ending to the movie kept eluding the writers.[68] An early draft was nearly verbatim from the play, but Cukor and Selznick considered it too downbeat. Multi-talented writer Donald Ogden Stewart, who had worked with Cukor on *Tarnished Lady* and with Harlow on *Red Dust*, was recruited for dialogue doctoring. The shooting scripts dated March 7 and March 23 include his contributions:

> CARLOTTA: *(to Kitty)* Charming gown. *(Just then Kitty turns away from Carlotta and toward the dining room, revealing a plunging back.) (To Dan)* I adore these modern gowns — they leave so little to the imagination. *(She turns with Dan to follow Kitty.)* I'm afraid they wouldn't be so becoming on me — but as I've always said, modesty is a poor figure!"
> THE END.

Stewart was dissatisfied. Shooting of the final scene took place on the last day of production and he had written a more direct exchange between Carlotta and Kitty. The scene attracted much attention and there was a large crowd watching off camera.

> *(Marie as Carlotta makes her entrance escorting Harlow as Kitty to the dining room. She is flagrantly staring at Harlow's front side as though to analyze how someone could have so many moving parts.)*
> KITTY: I was reading a book the other day.
> *(Carlotta stumbles at the notion of Kitty as literate.)*
> CARLOTTA: *(quietly and incredulously)* Reading a book?
> KITTY: Yes, it's all about civilization or something, a *nutty* kind of a book. Did you know that the guy said machinery is going to take the place of every profession?
> CARLOTTA: Oh, my dear *(once again scans Kitty like an efficient searchlight)* that's something *you* need never worry about.

The two then walk into the dining room as the film ends. Cukor yelled "Cut!" and the cast and crew broke into laughter and cheers. Twenty-two-year-old Harlow went to her dressing room and cried with joy. "The Baby (Harlow's nickname) and Dressler had a great time doing it," said assistant editor Chester Schaeffer.[69] Harlow and Dressler later exchanged compliments. "Being in the same cast with Marie was a break for me," Harlow explained.[70] "She's one trouper I'd never try to steal a scene from. It'd be like trying to carry Italy against Mussolini. She knows all the tricks." In Marie's estimation, Harlow "all but ran off with the show."[71]

"Of course that last scene was the most wonderful of all," recalled Selznick assistant Marcella Rabwin.[72] "People left the theater laughing and they loved Marie." The scene, which must be seen to be fully appreciated, is justifiably famous and remains one of the great moments in American screen comedy. Delivery and timing from both actresses are flawless. Marie's weary, sagging, all-knowing Carlotta is in perfect contrast to Harlow's alluring, crude, and guileless Kitty. Marie offers a wink and a nudge to the audience and a good time is had by all. As for "the Baby," she was an adored young actress of few pretensions. Hers was a rare comedy of seeming obliviousness, but she knew she was funny.

Several reports have Dressler and Harlow becoming friends despite the huge gulf in age and experience. They had briefly shared powerful Arthur Landau as their agent and Marie offered her shoulder when Harlow's husband, producer Paul Bern, committed a highly publicized suicide in 1932. At the very least they knew how to pal around in public. One midwestern fan saw them together on a break while shooting *Dinner at Eight*:[73] "Visited the MGM Studios. So excited we saw Jean Harlow with whom we thought must be her mother. On closer look it was Marie Dressler with Miss Harlow. Both were so kind, signed autographs. ... Jean Harlow looked so tiny up to Miss Dressler. After they signed several autographs they talked to a man at the gate, waved and walked hand in hand inside the studio. SO EXCITING!"

Dinner at Eight is Dressler's best movie. The reasons are simple — it had the best director, the best writers, and the best cast. Never mind that it's overly stagy and set-bound, or that the dramatic action from the Barrymore brothers temporarily bogs down the sparkling repartee. Marie was in professional heaven. She said it was "just like moving from your own home where you've lived for years into a new swell neighborhood" while she "eagerly watched the doings of her aristocratic neighbors."[74]

Dinner at Eight brilliantly unearths the hypocrisy, deceit, and pettiness of the upper class but still leaves room for sympathy. It's all about death of life or a way of life, yet it is consistently funny. At no time was American popular culture more adept at illuminating class conflicts than during the Depression; here is social satire chased with arsenic and laughing gas. *Dinner at Eight* is an example; it has the further distinction of being shot entirely during the special session of Congress that resulted in Roosevelt's New Deal of social and economic reform.

Marie's Carlotta Vance is a glorious invention, a pillar of decaying pride. Prone to romantic distractions and excessively bejeweled, she carries each bauble and pelt as tribute to one or another romance from the youthful past. If Marie's love life was modest, Carlotta's was spectacular, and she plays into the stereotype of actresses of a certain age as loosely moraled. Astute filmgoers caught the irony of Marie having smashed that stereotype in the 1890s. The character was originated on stage by Constance Collier and her élan is modeled after one of Marie's contemporaries, British stage actress Mrs. Patrick Campbell. She was a florid beauty and George Bernard Shaw's devoted pen pal. She and her Pekingese named Moonbeam were inseparable. With eccentricities too exotic even for Hollywood, she tried to establish herself there in the 1930s. Alas, her most enduring fame in that town came as the prototype for Marie Dressler's Carlotta Vance.

Marie's final scene with Harlow is inscribed in immortality, but she shows equal verve elsewhere. Lionel Barrymore gives her their first scene together without a fight. He feeds her lines that allow Carlotta to grow before our eyes as the little girl from Quincy, Illinois, who had dined with Noel Coward and Winston Churchill. When Jordan's secretary (Elizabeth Patterson) makes a faux pas about Carlotta's age, she receives in response a withering stare that would reduce an army to contrition.

Assistant director Joseph Newman noted[75] that "Marie was so seriously ill" but that "her respect for her art and her great determination kept her performing brilliantly." She showed unusual control throughout *Dinner at Eight*, as though all her life she had been waiting for this moment alongside George Cukor and that great cast. She and Burke played off each other superbly, as society obligations force both to enact a thin veneer of cordiality. In a scene with Madge Evans filled with references to death and hard-learned lessons, Marie brings such knowing skill that it appears as a valedictory to her entire career.

Cukor had a way with actresses that is well documented. Though there was a 30-year age difference, he made a friendship with Marie as one of her fleet of admiring young gay men. "Although she spent most of her life playing low comedy roles on the stage, cooks and charwomen on film, she was very civilized," he wrote.[76] "Marie was able to give the impression that she was a somebody. She had that quality in spite of her looks; in the way she carried herself, the way she wore clothes." Marie was affectionate to Cukor quite likely for his flattering observations of her. After the *Dinner at Eight* shooting, illness drove her to announce

Dinner at Eight ad after its "triumphant" premiere at the Astor Theater.

her retirement in *Variety*, which only made her feel more isolated, unhappy, confused, and frightened. With Claire incommunicado, she sought solace and sympathy elsewhere. In a typically brief scribbling, she reveals her friendship with Cukor[77] and her emotional vulnerability: "Dear George ... I'm lonely to see you — the flowers you so sweetly sent — are too wonderful and I did appreciate them and you but there is an empty feeling somewhere and I just got to see you soon. Love, Marie."

Retakes of *Tugboat Annie* lasted through late June 1933, two months after *Dinner at Eight* finished production. The two were released within a month of each other. There was heavy rain in New York when *Dinner at Eight* premiered at the Astor Theater on August 23.[78] Even so, police had to keep back the crowds who gathered in front of the theater to see the stars arrive. With a live radio broadcast from the theater, there was an unmistakable electricity in the evening. Celebrities present included Hoot Gibson, Max Baer, Jack Benny, Una Merkel, Polly Moran, Walter Huston, Richard Barthelmess, Jean Hersholt, Jimmy Durante, Madge Evans, and Jack Pearl. In the next morning's *New York Times*,[79] Mordaunt Hall effused that *Dinner at Eight* is "a fast-moving narrative with its humor and tragedy, one that offers a greater variety of characterizations than have been witnessed in any other picture. ... Veteran players of the stage, who have since been won over to talking pictures, are the principal assets in this film. It is a great pleasure to behold Marie Dressler away from her usual roles, dressed in the height of fashion and given lines that aroused gales of mirth from the first-night audience." *Dinner at Eight* made everyone smile. With a budget of $420,000, it actually came in at $387,000. Its box office exceeded $3 million, a huge sum for the Depression.[80] Selznick remained enormously proud of the film, noting that the chic art deco sets had a considerable effect on interior decorating all over the world.[81]

As for Dressler, her star kept rising. A radio network pleaded with her to name her price for 15 minutes on the air each week for 15 weeks.[82] Marie declined, saying she needed several months of rest. She appeared on the August 7 cover of *Time* magazine dressed as Tugboat Annie with a caption that read "they make you a star and then you starve."[83] The magazine noted that "captious cinema critics have suggested that Marie Dressler's most

14. "Careless Rapture"

On the top of the heap and on the cover of *Time*, August 7, 1933. Less than one year later, Marie would be dead. (©1933 Time Inc. Reprinted by permission.)

Socializing during La Fiesta in Santa Barbara, 1933. From left to right, New York friend Hallie Phillips, John Roche, Martha Gray, La Quinta manager Allen Walker, Marie, Milton Greene, Katherine Walker, staff member Jack Winslow, and real estate agent Newell Van Derhoef. (Courtesy of the Academy of Motion Picture Arts and Sciences.)

dependable talent is flexibility of her facial muscles. Her critics are only partially correct. What makes Marie Dressler's performances invariably exciting is the fact that even when they are careless impersonations they are brilliant records of her own robust and friendly personality."

More distinctions and accolades major and minor poured in. She and Beery were prominently featured in the cartoon *Mickey's Gala Premiere*, with animated stars rolling in the aisles over a movie within a movie of a Mickey Mouse chase. A new hothouse dahlia creation of crimson bloom called the "Marie Dressler" was engineered and shown worldwide.[84] Gimbels department store marketed a line of "Marie Dressler dresses" made of printed spun cotton and rayon and sold them for $1.99 to $5.99 in sizes 40 to 54.[85] "When warm weather comes, large ladies bless us for our beautiful selection of cotton Marie Dresslers," announced their ads. There was a jigsaw puzzle circulating with Marie's portrait on it and from the Philippines she received woven grass mats and crocheted tributes. Priests and ministers wrote to say that her movies preach better sermons on humanity than they do.[86] She was given the Gold Medal as the most popular film actress in England, the *Hollywood Reporter* named her the year's top star, and for the second year in a row she ranked first in Quigley Publications' box-office poll.

She was now, for one brilliant moment, a fully made creature of the cinema and the most popular actress in the world. "I love to act," she wrote in her memoirs.[87] "More particularly, I love to act before the camera. With its eagle eye on you, you can't skimp or fake. Less than your best isn't good enough. ... [P]erhaps one day you are inspired and do a specially good bit of work in a difficult scene, only to find when the rushes are run off that some actor who was working with you was feeling low. ... Of course the shot will have to be retaken. And, this time, you may find it impossible to recapture the fine careless rapture of your original interpretation."

In August 1933, while *Tugboat Annie* and *Dinner at Eight* both played to phenomenal business, Dressler was working again. By sheer willpower, she completed *Christopher Bean*, alternately called *Her Sweetheart* or *The Late Christopher Bean*. It was a tender movie about a posthumously famous painter and efforts by various greedy folks to cheat his widow Abby (Marie) of her rightful fortune. Beulah Bondi played the matriarch of the house and, devoid of any heart or humor, proved to be Marie's movie antithesis. Marie was especially excited about working opposite Lionel Barrymore again, whom she loved as a gentleman and as an actor. The film was directed by Sam Wood, the man who had replaced Leo McCarey on *Prosperity*.

Christopher Bean is a quiet movie; dialogue moves it along rather than action. It also had a full history, based on Sidney Howard's play *The Late Christopher Bean*, which was based on René Fauchois's *Prenez Garde à la Peinture*. It was a big hit on the English stage with Edith Evans and Cedric Hardwicke and did similarly well on the New York stage with Pauline Lord as Abby. But it was now a Marie Dressler movie and so gratuitous slapstick courtesy of Sylvia Thalberg was inserted into early scenes involving a runaway car. One is left to wonder how Mayer, Thalberg, and all the others let their star gallop after a runaway car under the hot sun when she was in such pain and so close to death. She went along with the demands, making reference to her own condition when saying, "It is human to welcome a ray of humor in the midst of life's most tragic moods."[88]

Marie's Abby is another suffering, bumbling kitchen-slavey saint on the order of *Emma*. This time the head of the house isn't kindly Jean Hersholt, but "simple country doctor" Barrymore with patients who can't afford to pay him. He turns into an avaricious demon at the prospect of selling the valuable Bean paintings. His abrupt personality change is the chief credibility gap of *Christopher Bean*, but it allows Marie's Abby to take another one of her moral high roads. At a late dramatic crest in the movie, she honks, "You should be ashamed!" to Barrymore. That's all it takes for his conversion back to decency. The old lady has made the world right again. Similarities to *Emma* did not end there. Yet again her employer's family turns against her when money is involved. Yet again there is one respectable child who is disgusted by the betrayal and deceit. As is *Emma*, *Christopher Bean* is steeped in nostalgia summoned by Abby's warm recollections, curled down lower lip, softened voice, and misty eyes.

Intentionally or not, *Christopher Bean* makes reference to Marie's life. The coincidences are eerie and leave the impression that Marie wanted some lasting tribute to Jim Dalton. Abby must prove her marriage to Bean is real just as Marie had to prove the same with Jim. Marie/Abby lives with Jim's/Christopher's memory with no venture toward another heterosexual autumnal romance. Young love triumphs in a subplot of the movie, but Marie literally has Bean's paintings as her bedmates. Marie would not admit that she was through, but her last words in her last movie have the quality of a coda. Marie as Abby is on a train to Chicago, which is where Jim had died 13 years prior. As she bunks down in her berth, she says, "Good night."

Dressler never revealed her illness before the camera. She simply refused to be defeated, and her stoicism had its benefits. "So, some mornings I don't feel so good. But that's never stopped me before and it's not going to stop me now."[89] By the time of *Christopher Bean*, though, she could not hide the visual ravages of cancer. She showed a noticeable weight loss and had acquired permanent brown-gray circles under her eyes that makeup and lighting could not hide. There was also all that the audiences didn't see—the nausea, the dramatically reduced working hours, the horrendous pain, and the easy exhaustion.

Marie still wouldn't stay put. During the production of *Christopher Bean*, she drove to Santa Barbara with Mamie and visiting New York friend Hallie Phillips to entertain at a luncheon during the city's annual La Fiesta celebrations. Ever defiant, her insistence on a full work and travel schedule destroyed her health, no doubt, but also left her with a fleeting sense of control that may have helped her forget that death was descending. "I want to sleep so much," she confessed to a reporter.[90]

Dressler was back on the East Coast in September with Mamie for a six-week sojourn after completing *Christopher Bean*. The trip was filled with quirky events. She visited President Roosevelt's National Recovery Administration (NRA) headquarters in Washington to offer her help and feel a bit of the old patriotism that so enlivened the war years and the Liberty Bond drives. Instead, she "paralyzed traffic on the fourth floor and caused a suspension of business among the girl workers."[91] Police were summoned to break up the throngs, which did not dissipate until a clerk appeared to make threats and jot down names of the workers absent from their stations.

She made a radio address on behalf of the Mobilization for Human Needs and was present at the Exposition of Women's Arts and Industries.[92] The honored guest was Eleanor Roosevelt, but Marie was the evening's final speaker. From the dais, she was nearly incoherent, saying, "I think that people really should be made happy whether they like it or not." After that remark she nearly collapsed. Mrs. Roosevelt offered support with her arm, but Marie declined. "Don't wait for me; don't worry about me," she told the First Lady.

Marie was feeling better when she and Mamie were overnight guests at the White House on October 6. She was a hit with the Roosevelt family and staff at dinner, telling them stories and delivering one joke after another.[93] With an ability to jump party affiliations that is unthinkable today, Marie had an almost evangelical enthusiasm for the president. "Franklin and Eleanor Roosevelt welcomed me with that simple friendliness which is their nature," she wrote.[94] "The President is human. He has made some mistakes. No doubt he will make others. But there is one thing of which I am certain as I am certain that God is Love. It is this: Franklin Roosevelt is ruled by one thought and one prayer—to lead the country wisely and safely out of what has been a hideous mess. He has made a heroic beginning. I believe he will take us all the way—if we have the courage and faith to go where he leads."

Back in New York by October 11, Marie was the guest of honor at the Hotel Roosevelt.[95]

Five hundred guests arrived for a benefit to the Actors' Dinner Club and to pay tribute to Marie. The MGM studio had delivered a huge birthday cake, while Marie added that her 64th birthday was still a month away. Those lies about chronology caught up with her: she had publicly announced her 60th birthday in 1932. That seemed irrelevant at the moment. New York's finest cancer specialists had examined Marie on this trip and informed her and Mayer in plain language that there was nothing more to be done.

After receiving the virtual death sentence, Marie faced a room of stage actors and writers gathered to pay her tribute. "There is nothing left for me to say," she said. "I have heard very many beautiful things said here tonight and I really don't know who it was all about. I am sure it wasn't me." She invoked her customary magical sentiment that would sound cloying and ungenuine from anyone else. "I think we are a wonderful crowd. We are always ready to help and always willing to help whether we are hungry or whether we are poor, no matter what our condition in life may be. ... If I am clever, if I am one of the kind that all these people say I am, I hope to God I'll never know it. I thank you all and I am deeply grateful." Marie was still mystified by her rampant celebrity, thriving in it to be sure, but unsure of its origins. Only three days earlier, a *New York Times* reporter[96] observed that "Miss Dressler still is skeptical and a bit confused, like Alice when she found herself a giantess." On that same trip, Dressler said that she would make another picture soon.[97] The only thing to prevent her "would be for some millionaire to come along and marry me."

There would be no millionaire, no marriage, and no more pictures.

Chapter 15

Pacific

Everywhere people expressed their love to Dressler with the urgency of realizing that she would soon be gone. When she disembarked the train in California, a large delegation from the studio was there to welcome her.[1] And the early New York birthday party was but a minor prelude of the festivities to come. Mayer had told her that an enormous birthday party and dinner dance was planned for November 9 at the studio and that she should rest.[2] Utterly exhausted from the last trip, Marie restored herself at home. Days were spent in quiet pursuits such as light gardening and writing down memories for a new autobiography.

For the big night, the studio issued a formal invitation with an embossed cameo and Marie's signature surrounded by gold. Most newspapers reported that she was turning 62 as thousands of congratulatory letters and telegrams came in from Denmark, Egypt, England, France, Italy, Germany, Australia, and Scotland. Special fan mail boxes were available throughout the United States to receive the many thousands of domestic messages.

The celebration wasn't exclusive to Hollywood. Writer Gladys Hall announced[3] that the birthday of "our first citizen ... [has] become a National Event. It was spoken of as 'Marie Dressler Day.'" Various "Marie Dressler Birthday Clubs" in the United States and Canada organized local celebrations. In Cobourg, a bronze plaque was placed at her birth home on King Street and Mayor J. P. Delanty spoke to a group at the Capitol Theater before a screening of *Emma*.[4] Though the occasion was special, the regular admission prices prevailed — 35 cents for adults and 15 cents for children. "Old-timers in town have a dim recollection of a vivacious little girl of between eight and ten, who used to like to play the piano and dance," reported the *Cobourg Sentinel-Star*.[5]

Spearheaded by the Actors' Club in New York and as a promotional tie-in for the upcoming wide release of *Christopher Bean*, the "Marie Dressler International Birthday Celebration Campaign Book" had tips galore on pulling off local fundraising birthday parties for "the great trouper."[6] They sponsored a poetry contest with a $250 prize and recommended tribute dinners be coordinated through the cooperation of various women's clubs. Custom-made "Come to Marie Dressler

Birthday Party" banners and pennants were available through mail order, as were buttons, programs, birthday cards, door hangers, theater displays, and stills. Radio scripts, cutout Marie heads and stickers were also recommended for party promotions. There were even suggestions for theater owners on how to install an electric Marie Dressler birthday cake and candles atop their marquees.

Four special wires were set up at the studio to receive telegrams for "the first national salute ever accorded an actress or actor."[7] "Happy Birthday, Marie" was spelled in red roses against velvet drapes behind the speakers' table.[8] All the governors of all the states sent telegrams of congratulations and appreciation. A proclamation was signed by all of them and then forwarded to President Roosevelt. He and Eleanor sent their own proclamation as well.

Guests at the studio bash included Lionel Barrymore, Norma Shearer, Madge Evans, Clark Gable, Polly Moran, May Robson, David O. Selznick, George Hill, Sam Wood, Cecil B. DeMille, Sid Grauman, Mary Pickford, Frances Marion, and U.S. Senator Henry F. Ashurst of Arizona.[9] William Gibbs McAdoo, the designer of Woodrow Wilson's Liberty Bond drives during the war and now a U.S. senator from California, was also there. Marie was a jumble of nerves and anxiety. As the nearly 1,000 well-wishers arrived, she was asked to wait near a makeshift restroom next to the stage until she was escorted to her place by California governor James "Sunny Jim" Rolph, Jr. Time stood still. "Why don't they come and get me?" Marie quivered.[10] "I'm so nervous. I can't stand this waiting much longer. I'll break down and cry like a fool in front of all those people if they don't take me in there before I lose my courage." When at last she was seated, the crowd cheered. Will Rogers was there to announce the party over the radio and present Marie with a huge white orchid corsage.

Dinner proceeded without a glitch. As dessert time approached, all lights were extinguished on cue and several moments passed in darkness.[11] Then spotlights flooded the center of the dance floor. There stood a 500-pound chocolate cake, eight feet tall and six feet across, hauled in on a decorated electric truck driven by chefs dressed in white. The dessert was so unwieldy it required blueprints and a construction superintendent to oversee the bakers.

The party was broadcast over national hookup with an estimated 20 million listeners. Mayer appointed himself toastmaster, nearly choking on his remarks. Testimonials from various guests were delivered. Rogers "had to hurry the end of his talk because tears were getting into his voice."[12] Marie was crying most of the evening, but writer Edgar Allan Woolf noticed that her tears weren't necessarily joyous.[13] He won a few moments with her and asked, "What's the matter? Aren't you the happiest woman in the world tonight?" She said, "I was just thinking about a lot of my dead pals I wish could be here to enjoy this with me tonight."

Dressler at last spoke to the crowd and recalled her first public appearance as Cupid on that toppled pedestal in church when she was five.[14] In a moment captured on a Hearst newsreel, she implored everyone to join her in donating the cake to a nearby orphanage. "My feeling of gratitude cannot be expressed," she said with newly found serenity.[15] "There aren't words enough. It is not Marie Dressler whom [you] are honoring, it is the profession which I represent. At last, after all these years in which they have been treated as mountebanks, or disregarded — except when they are needed — the men and women of the stage are coming into the respect which they deserve. If I have done any little thing to help us reach that place of dignity, I am proud and happy." She closed with "Good-by, au revoir, auf wiedersehen and to all, good night." Songs were performed by Nelson Eddy, Irene Franklin, Jimmy Durante, and Jeanette MacDonald, with everyone joining in for "Auld Lang Syne" to conclude the evening.[16] Cleanup seemed to take ages. Weeks later, crews were still finding stray chicken bones on sound stage five.

Since Mayer was foremost a showman, even his parties got reviewed. In no uncertain terms, it was deemed the best-attended party

While the monstrous birthday cake blazes, California governor James Rolph, Jr., Marie, and Louis B. Mayer pose with the first slice. (Courtesy of the Academy of Motion Picture Arts and Sciences.)

Hollywood had ever thrown.[17] "The Dressler party went off with both ease and dash," concluded columnist Lee Shippey.[18] "The publicity men, of course, were again the real hosts. They were the people who met and greeted, answered questions, found seats, did and said a hundred tactful things. ... [T]he best studio party of any kind we have seen. ... We felt especially sorry for the cigarette girls, because they were the only people present who were not made comfortable." Shippey deemed Marie the "Wide World's Best-Beloved Woman."[19] Alluding to the fact that Marie overcame poverty, lack of education, disappointment, bereavement, and despair, Max Baer called her "a better fighter than I am. She's licked everything and kept right on making people laugh."[20]

Marie insisted on seeing her "birthday picture," *Christopher Bean*, immediately after it opened in November. She was mobbed in the lobby and stood with the crowd for more than an hour. When she was at last pulled away by attending friends, she climbed into her car and collapsed, pale from exertion.

"It makes me mad to think that I can't stand up under a little thing like that. I wouldn't have disappointed those people for anything in the world. They had waited to see me. I would have been an ungrateful old fool if I had slipped out a side door, as the folks from the studio wanted me to do. Those people are my friends. I owe everything I am to them."[21] Later that month, *Christopher Bean* opened. Though the movie had its admirers, it was a modest success and a distinct anticlimax to Marie's string of triumphs. The similarities to *Emma* were discovered, and reviews were cool: "*Christopher Bean* is one of those standby shows that in the face of any competition has the name and entertainment values," wrote the *Motion Picture Herald*.[22] "Though neither Marie Dressler nor Lionel Barrymore have roles that equal their more recent hits, this adaptation of the Broadway play is a fairly satisfying affair," concluded the *Film Daily*.[23]

After *Christopher Bean* was released, Marie's 50-year career was complete. Versatility is a mere superficial description of the range she navigated from dowager to drunk. Whatever gifts, or tricks, she brought to her characters, they were eclipsed by her abundant pleasure at being on screen. Like many great stars, Marie's characters and personality continuously merged. She inhabited her roles, but there was never any doubt that Marie, not Annie or Emma, could skipper a tugboat and dote over a baby. Her career, while filled with ringers and duds, reveals the consistency of a hardworking, hard living, and generous woman.

As the guardian of righteousness, she was given a responsibility on film never expected of her on stage. With Lillian Russell, with Weber and Fields, or solo, all she need do was be hilarious. After her great drought in the 1920s, Mayer saw a charismatic preacher in her alongside the funny woman. With Irving Thalberg, Frances, and directors George Hill, George Cukor, and Clarence Brown, Marie's movies became something more than Mayer's preferred wholesome family entertainment. Carlotta Vance of *Dinner at Eight* was one of the most desired and expensive actress-escorts of the Mauve Decade. And what sort of excess brought her heroines of *Anna Christie* and *Min and Bill* to their wretched conditions?

With or without vice, her later roles all had in common a nobility that defied age, income, or circumstance. Their wisdom was Marie's wisdom — born from years on the road, broke or loaded, alone and destitute, or standing before a cheering crowd. None of this was lost on her vast audience. In *Min and Bill*, *Reducing*, *Politics*, *Emma*, *Prosperity*, *Tugboat Annie*, and *Christopher Bean*, she provided the moral guidance for other characters adrift in the anxieties of hard times. Without fail, she won her battles; a tragic end to a Marie Dressler character was unthinkable. So many years later, a question lingers: Why didn't MGM take more chances with her? Were Mayer and Thalberg fearful that her earning power would plummet if she played a monster or a heroine of classic drama? She never realized a lifelong ambition to try tragedy, but her potential for sustained seriousness can be seen in *Min and Bill*, *Emma*, and *Tugboat Annie*. Under the familial comforts of studio life, Marie's options remained limited and we are left to contemplate what she might have done with a role on the order of Ma Joad, Lady Macbeth, or Clytemnestra. Her career is satisfying and impressive, and there is no indication that she would have been better treated at another studio, but her talent and the terms of her employment beg speculation.

After the epic birthday party, which could also be interpreted as a living wake, she continued to decline. Cancer was complicated by nephritis, an acute and chronic inflammation of the kidneys. As her kidneys worked ever less efficiently, Dressler's bloodstream reabsorbed toxins and she suffered a steady loss of weight, endurance, and immunity. She made noble efforts to carry on, as did her friends and the studio staff, but she was too weak to go back to work. "I'm too tired to think of plans," she said.[24] Actress Joan Marsh Morrill, a cast member of *Politics*, recalled visiting Marie at home.[25] "Every time I was with her, while her cancer was spreading, there was never a word of complaint. I saw her just before she died and brought her flowers from my garden. She was in bed and I could see that she was so tired, but she was always thoughtful and sweet."

Dressler was able to continue some of her philanthropy and public speaking. On November 12, 1933, she spoke to the nation on NBC radio urging donations by women to local welfare programs.[26] "Somewhere you have tucked away some trinket, some little thingamabob which you have probably forgotten. It can be turned into money, which in turn can be turned into milk for a starving baby or medical attention for some prospective mother who doesn't know which way to turn in the hour of need." In January 1934 she attended the Screen

Actors' Guild's midwinter ball at the Biltmore Hotel.[27] She also accepted chairmanship of two lavish Franklin D. Roosevelt birthday celebrations in a campaign for the president's Georgia Warm Springs Foundation in its battle against infantile paralysis (poliomyelitis, or polio).[28]

As part of his ambitious National Recovery Administration, President Roosevelt looked to reform labor relations in a number of industries, including motion pictures. He appointed Dressler, as his favorite actress, to the Film Code committee, which was charged with curbing "unreasonably excessive" salaries and endowed the committee to levy fines on studios for such excesses.[29] Considering Marie's past union affiliations, and her weekly salary that topped the six month income of the average family of four, the appointment from Roosevelt was embarrassing. Her appointment took NRA personnel by surprise and was greeted in Hollywood with apprehension, but Roosevelt knew her involvement would silence any dissenters. How can a reasonable conversation about compensation, labor, and economic crisis take place when the president appoints to his committee an ailing and sacred actress that no one would dare criticize?

The president's committee did not take much of Dressler's time. Neither did her help with the Actors' Guild Ball or Roosevelt's birthday on January 30. She limited her travel, accepted only local appearances, and tried to stay at home. She appeared in the Paramount short *Hollywood on Parade, Number Thirteen*, blowing kisses to her admirers at her birthday party, but of course she wanted to do something more satisfying. In early 1934, she and Frances were enjoying a casual conversation near the MGM studio commissary. It pleased Frances that Marie was finally forthcoming about her health problems. When a doctor suggested more surgery, Marie told him "to put his carving knives away; my intention was to die in peace, not pieces."[30] Frances chuckled at the gallows humor that dominated Marie's wit lately. "Did it ever occur to you how much old age is like a deserted house on the fringes of a town?" she continued. "First the dust accumulates, then the kids break all the windows, somebody steals the doors and finally a blast of wind comes along and carries off the roof. Yep, that's old age." Her voice was trailing off to a whisper when she added, "Who's afraid of the big bad wolf?"

Wallace Beery came along at that moment to give Dressler a rib-cracking hug. "I've missed my old pal," he bellowed.

"I've missed you like all get-out," replied Marie, "but they tell me we're being lined up for a sequel to *Tugboat Annie*. When do you finish the one you're on?"

"Soon, or my real end will be flatter'n a Mexican tortilla," said Beery, who was in costume for *Viva Villa*. "I wasn't cut out to be no Pancho Villa riding a fire-eating nag from here to hereafter. I'll be glad when we get back to the tugboat."

"So will I," said Marie.

Dressler was feeling absolutely wretched. Efforts at a cure from the Potter Metabolic Clinic failed, and few options remained. She had been offered rest and comfort at a cottage on the Santa Barbara estate of Cornelius K. Billings,[31] a friend since the high-society days in New York. Her health care had been inconsistent at best and unethical at worst, but that changed in Santa Barbara. The days of herbs, liquid diets and horse serum were over, but so, too, was hope for a cure. A county hospital was nearby, as was the home of Franklin Nuzum, Marie's new doctor. With stables, dirt roads, and open space, the neighborhood seemed built for pleasure and comfort. Marie enjoyed visits there immensely and considered the place a sanctuary for her final illness.

In March, Dressler and the Coxes left Loafhaven after less than two years in residence and checked into the Santa Barbara Biltmore.[32] Only caretaker Emile Hangen was left behind to keep up on maintenance and yard work. Marie suffered a fever and headache at the Biltmore on April 3 when the Walkers arrived and were escorted in by Mamie. Marie wanted to discuss an offer they had made and asked Allen if he might want to take time off managing La Quinta and attend to her affairs. He was initially too distraught at Marie's illness to consider the necessary negotiations, but he composed himself on her behalf.

"How much have you been getting at La Quinta?" asked Marie from her bed.

"$500 a month," he replied.

For once, Marie sounded like a wise businesswoman. "Will half of that be satisfactory to take care of me this summer and I pay all expenses of you and your wife and the car?"

"Yes."

"I don't want my car and chauffeur used. Would you use your car for my affairs?" she asked.

"Yes."

From then on, Allen Walker took charge of business. After six weeks at the Biltmore, Marie and the Coxes moved into the duplex cottage called Casa Lo Bella, just adjacent to the main home of the Billingses' hilltop estate. For $500 a month rent, Marie had a simple pale blue and copper-colored bedroom with a bedside table and two chairs. French windows from ceiling to floor gave her a view of the Pacific Ocean that reached to the Channel Islands on a clear day. Everyone assumed brave faces, but they knew that Marie was going there to spare Hollywood friends and colleagues her quick deterioration. This didn't matter to Frances, who limited her work at the studio and rented an apartment in Santa Barbara. Frances, Mamie, and Jerry were highly protective of Marie and screened all visitors. "Her final illness was horrifying to her friends," said Elaine St. Johns.[33] "My mother thought it was selfish of Marie to withdraw, but she's not the only famous person to do that. Marie knew it would be hard on them. She was thinking more of them than herself."

Before leaving for a trip to Europe, Mayer visited her in Santa Barbara to present her a $10,000 bonus and assure her of work waiting at the studio.[34] It was a well-intended gesture, but to Marie it sounded like torture. Columbia Pictures wanted her for the choice role of Apple Annie[35] in Frank Capra's *Lady for a Day*, but Mayer refused to loan her to a rival studio.* He had previously angered Marie by insisting she stay home to await a new production rather than take a trip.[36] Now he was making promises that she knew would go unfulfilled. From her bed, she turned her face to the wall and called him a money-grubbing bastard trying to control her life. It did not occur to him that Marie, as a dying person, did not need roles. She needed a miracle or acceptance of her mortality.

Dressler was more charitable to studio publicist Howard Strickling.[37] A 36-year-old soft-spoken southerner with a stutter, Howard kept dropping tidbits in the news about upcoming projects for Marie. He was with her in the Pacific Northwest during the difficult filming of *Tugboat Annie* and had joined the surrogate family alongside Frances, Mamie, and Jerry. After long associations with overbearing men, she was attracted to his reserve, his courtly manner, and his respect for confidentiality. He demanded everything in writing and regularly issued terse memos on pink paper. "His mind was keen, his hand was firm, his heart was soft," summarized a colleague.[38] "Marie looked to Howard for everything," said Marilyn Strickling Read, Howard's niece.[39] "He in turn cherished her friendship." When he came to Santa Barbara, Marie made it clear that she was not offended by his false premonitions of recovery. "I've been so blessed by friendship," she told Frances and him.[40] "It sounded so elegant when I read in the paper that I was visiting my society friends in Santa Barbara and would soon be returning to my home in Beverly Hills where I planned to entertain some of the Vanderbilt clan. What a scoop for this old gal! I nearly died laughing and—"

"You must rest, Miss Dressler," interrupted a nurse.

"Shucks! I'll have all the rest I need after Gabriel toots his horn."

On May 29 Dressler signed her will.[41] "She sat up in bed, took the pen in her fingers and scratched her scrawling signature," declared Allen Walker,[42] who was named both witness and executor. "Then she twisted up her face, like she did on the screen, and said 'well, that's

---

*The role went to May Robson, who earned an Academy Award nomination.

that.'" She had been semicomatose on bad days, but Allen reported that she was cheerful and full of energy. She even autographed photographs for the other witnesses—Earl G. Johnstone and Marion B. Sanders of Santa Barbara—correctly observing that "I won't be signing any more of these."[43]

Dressler kept settling her accounts with remarkable poise. She gave her Academy Award to Howard Strickling as a close friend and as a great but modest film man who never stepped into the limelight. He was deeply moved at her gesture and displayed the award prominently on his mantel. She had never reconciled with Claire after their breakup in late 1932. Marie called her and forged some sort of cordial truce, but they never saw each other again. "Marie's whole life and attitude was wrapped up in how she died," explained Elaine St. Johns.[44] "Everyone had an opinion on how she handled herself at the end. I was very impressed. I thought it was wonderful, very heroic and must have been very lonely."

With nothing but death as the prognosis, plans continued for Dressler's career. There were rumors and proposals in the studio pipeline, as if more movies would save her.[45] In addition to *Lady for a Day* at Columbia, Paramount wanted her for *A Son Comes Home*, a tearjerker that went to Mary Boland. Mayer had wanted to devise a vehicle for Marie and Jackie Cooper, but it never materialized. Neither did *Mrs. Van Kleek*, a South Seas yarn being adapted for the screen in which Marie was to have the titular lead. Talk of her and Marion Davies reteaming for *Paid to Laugh* flew for a time. When Marie proved unable to work, her role was excised and the script was adapted into *Going Hollywood* for Davies and Bing Crosby. Marie and Jean Harlow had appeared together only in those magical final seconds from *Dinner at Eight*, and Mayer was hungry to reunite them. He was readying a movie for them called *Living in a Big Way*, to be written by novelist Louis Bromfield and directed by George Cukor. Harlow had already been fitted for costumes to play Marie's adopted daughter, but the movie was never made. Irving Thalberg, back at work after his heart attack, had bought the rights to Mary Roberts Rinehart's "Tish" stories for Marie. Neither he nor Marie saw that project to completion. Marie was also slated for the 1934 musical *Hollywood Party*, but declining health prevented her from appearing in what would become a major flop. MGM courted W. C. Fields to costar with Marie in the comedy *Fercke*.[46] Fields was yoked to Paramount, where negotiations for a loan of Fields collapsed from high salary demands and Marie's unstable condition. Marie and Will Rogers had always wanted to make a movie together and the press reported them possibly teaming up in a film of Eugene O'Neill's new play *Ah, Wilderness!* None of the proposed movies was made with Marie, but even with the professional inactivity, it was almost possible for fans to believe that everything was fine. Without any current film in release, but on the continued running of last year's *Dinner at Eight*, *Tugboat Annie*, and *Christopher Bean*, Marie ranked ninth among movie star favorites in the annual Quigley Publications poll in 1934.

As Dressler lay dying, Hollywood was changing. In June the Production Code Administration, or Hays code, was institutionalized by the major studios. In agreeing to the standards and morals of the PCA, and in pursuit of its seal of approval, MGM tamed Harlow's pert nipples and double-entendres. With a slight change of timing, her great scene with Marie in *Dinner at Eight* might not have happened and certainly *Anna Christie* would have been even more severely sanitized. PCA was headed by the notorious smutbuster Joseph Breen, who was described as bitter, petty, and anti–Semitic. Under the guise of protecting common decency, the PCA controlled film content for two decades.

Dressler reportedly spent much of those final months at work on a second autobiography, with a working title of *You Make Me What I Am Today*. The 1924 tome, *The Life Story of an Ugly Duckling*, was now obsolete. In her new memoirs, published by Little, Brown and Company and renamed *My Own Story*, she takes up where she left off in *Ugly Duckling*. It is a similarly anecdotal account of her life—

warm, funny, highly conversational, and bereft of a single reference to Claire.

Given Dressler's condition, her contributions to the book are unclear. She met with writer Mildred Harrington, who "acted throughout in compliance with the wishes of the author," but Marie was too ill to read or give approval to the final proofs. If they are Harrington's words, then she captured Marie's spirit impeccably:[47]

> I hope that I have succeeded in some degree in the task which is my own — of sending you out of the theater washed of bitterness, forgetful of sorrow and trouble. This much I hope I have done for you who have done so much for me. You are my friends, you people on the other side of the footlights. ... Without your quick appreciation, your unfailing loyalty and your generosity in taking a homely old woman into your hearts, I should never have found the strength to fight on to whatever good fortune has come my way.
>
> What a horde of rich memories enrich me as I glance backward down the corridor of the years! The thousands upon thousands of lines I have memorized — comedy, tragedy, vaudeville skits, the classics, opera scores, all were grist to my mill. The countless pieces of business I have worked out! The costumes I have loved; the costumes I have hated! The men and women who have walked with me from time to time! Ah, a lot of water has run under the bridge since 14 year old Leila von Koerber defied her father and went away to act on the stage!
>
> Perhaps tomorrow the curtain will go up on a new show — a show with a fresh part and fresh lines for an old trouper. Meanwhile, a full life to look back on and true friends with whom to pass the time of day.
>
> What more could any man or woman ask?

At Casa Lo Bella, Dressler was attended daily by Grace Annable.[48] She was an uncommonly beautiful 27-year-old nurse with a curvaceous figure, sharply defined face, blue eyes, brown hair, and eyelashes nearly reaching her eyebrows. She had a special way with her only patient. Grace selected Marie's diet, which was prepared by Mamie. Creamed chicken was a favorite. Because of her failing kidneys and a bad reaction to the medication, Marie suffered a toxic buildup of urine. With proper massage, Grace could get her "to urinate buckets." Grace's adeptness kept Marie from excessive doses of opium, and further massage put Marie to sleep.

Dressler responded with rudeness. Bitter from her physical deterioration and helplessness, she demanded, did not ask, for service. "She spoke sharply and shortly," recalled Grace, who earned every penny of her $49-a-week salary. "This went on day after day." Grace also saw Frances every day, who she recalls as passionate, caring, and warm. "Frances was one of the reasons I stayed," said Grace. "She, Mamie and Jerry were a big help, they kept apologizing for Marie and telling me she wasn't normally like this." Grace grew stubborn and told her husband that she would rather force Marie to fire her than quit, but she would never give her any reason to do so.

Everything changed when Annable accompanied Dressler to Cottage Hospital in Santa Barbara for three days of x-rays and tests. On their first evening there, "as I leaned over her she put her arms around me and pulled me down and kissed me," said Grace. "I thought she was going to attack me, but then she burst into tears and told a doctor how badly she behaved. Later she confessed that she believed anyone that was beautiful went on looks alone and was not worth anything." From that moment, Marie was unerringly thoughtful and complimentary to Grace. If she wasn't begging for forgiveness she was telling everyone that Grace was a perfectly wonderful nurse. "It was a relief in one way and an embarrassment in another," wrote Grace.

Annable noted that Dressler became easier to lift as she became emaciated and bedridden. Care was constant and demanding — Marie was given two 12-hour nurses and three 8-hour nurses in constant rotation. Franklin Nuzum, a brilliant and compassionate 45-year-old heart specialist, was in daily attendance by mid–June, and Harold Schalenburg was later summoned as his associate physician. "No one was ever better cared for," said Grace. Marie, in turn, gave up all the pugnaciousness of her first days in Santa Barbara. "She was most considerate of others," recalled another nurse.[49] "She was a wonderful patient and so very grateful for any little thing that was done for her."

Dressler may not have been conscious when Will Rogers spoke in a prayer broadcast across the country:[50]

> We don't know Hitler, we don't know Dillinger and we don't know the Astors. ... But, by golly, we all do know Marie Dressler. We all do—we all do know Marie Dressler. And you feel like you know her, and you do know her. You could go up and talk to her. There's not a five-year-old kid or a 90-year-old person in the world that doesn't know her. ... She was a star with a theater full of people when your fathers and mothers had to get a marriage license to see Niagara Falls. She could sing. She had a beautiful voice.

Rogers was having a hard time forming his words, but he haltingly continued:

> One of the regrets of my—when I signed my last little contract—I had it put in there that ... we'd often talked about doing a picture together. Every time I'd meet her, she'd say, "When are we going to make that picture together?" Golly, I'd open the door, or anything else. There's been nothing—nothing like her career has developed in our whole moving-picture industry; or the stage either, for that matter. That would be the proudest moment of my life—my whole amusement career—to say that I'd worked with Marie!

Beginning in late June, when her condition was known worldwide to be serious, the *New York Times* and the *Los Angeles Times* began printing something akin to a "Marie Watch." In an extraordinary testament to her popularity and esteem, the *New York Times* ran a daily report on her status. Sometimes it was no more than a one-inch paragraph tucked away in the entertainment section, but her condition became anticipated news. Nuzum supplied the world with most of the information. Headlines are from the *New York Times*, unless otherwise noted:

June 24—**Marie Dressler Slightly Better**
"Miss Dressler is much better than she was a week ago," declared Nuzum. "There is no danger at this time."

June 25—**Marie Dressler "Holds Her Own"**

June 28—**Marie Dressler Very Ill** (*Los Angeles Examiner*)
It was announced little hope for recovery was held. "Miss Dressler is critically ill and the outcome is dubious," proclaimed Nuzum.

June 29—**Dressler's End Near** (*Los Angeles Times* front page)
Nuzum announced to the press that he did not expect Marie to live through the night. Thousands of telegrams arrived in Santa Barbara, but she was unaware of the latest avalanche of affection. Marie was comatose and her face had turned a pale blue, but Nuzum marveled that "her fighting spirit is remarkable." Eleanor Roosevelt expressed hope for Marie's recovery in a press conference, and she and the president sent a get-well telegram. By midnight, in a shocking turnaround, she had normal heart respiration and no fever.

June 30—**Dressler Has Gain** (*Los Angeles Times* front page)

June 30—**Marie Dressler Passes into Coma, Physician Fears End Is Near—Message of Hope Comes from the White House.**
By the end of June, Marie had drifted into lethargy and was sometimes unable to recognize people nearby or to use her voice. Mayer is in constant contact with the Billings estate.

July 1—**Dressler in New Rally** (*Los Angeles Times*)
Today Marie used her voice for the first time in ten days. Friends and staff hovered around her bed. Due in part to Grace's

expert massages, she was not in great pain and was not taking opiates, but her temperature was unchanged at 104.4 degrees. "Everyone's so kind," she said.

July 2 — Marie Dressler Easier

Marie remains feverish and in critical condition. Mayer visited and announced to the press that "Miss Dressler is putting up a courageous fight against overwhelming odds." Howard Strickling began spending increased time at Casa Lo Bella.

July 3 — Marie Dressler Rallies

Marie is mentally clear and taking solid nourishment, her first in two weeks, but doctors do not expect a recovery from cancer and the accompanying complications of uremic poisoning. Mamie is the "dominant figure among the star's attendants." She sits by her side continuously, often just holding Marie's hand.

July 4 — Marie Dressler Has Solid Food

She recognizes the people in her sick room.

July 5 — Marie Dressler Rests Easily

July 6 — Marie Dressler Holds Her Own

July 7 — Marie Dressler's Condition

Even when conscious, she shows no interest in the radio.

July 8 — Cheery Mail Read to Marie Dressler

An "unchanged" bulletin was issued today from the bedroom. ... Returns to consciousness are growing shorter. Katherine Walker read letters aloud to Marie from Mary Pickford, President and Mrs. Roosevelt, Amos and Andy and Irving Thalberg, among others. The Walkers' secretary from La Quinta has been recruited to administer to the volumes of mail received daily. Mamie Cox has taken over the kitchen to prepare her favorite meals.

July 9 — Marie Dressler Unchanged

July 10 — Marie Dressler Holds Gain

July 11 — Marie Dressler No Better

July 12 — Marie Dressler's Condition

Those who are privileged to see her everyday believe she has lost ground in the last week. During consciousness, Marie ordered a sound projector be installed at the children's wing of the Los Angeles General Hospital and be supplied with comedy films. To Mamie she said, "never let me see you without a smile."

July 13 — Marie Dressler Easier

"She is unable to appreciate her surroundings and no longer recognizes any of those who care for her," announced Nuzum.

July 14 — Marie Dressler Unchanged

July 15 — Marie Dressler No Better

July 16 — Marie Dressler No Better

July 18 — Marie Dressler Has Good Day

July 19 — Marie Dressler Semi-Conscious

July 20 — Marie Dressler No Better

Min and Bill is reissued and opens at the Capitol Theater in New York where it first played in 1930. "Thousands, moved by sentiment, have asked that *Min and Bill* be returned as a token to the brave Miss Dressler," read the ads.

July 21 — Marie Dressler Unchanged

July 22 — Marie Dressler Failing

July 23 — Marie Dressler No Worse

Several Hollywood friends arrive and leave flowers. Marie's last weekly MGM salary check of $2,500 is deposited by Allen Walker.

July 24 — Marie Dressler "Unchanged"

July 25 — Hope for Miss Dressler Gone

July 26 — Marie Dressler No Worse

"The kidney function is very inadequate," reported Nuzum.

July 27 — Marie Dressler Unchanged

July 28 — Marie Dressler No Better

Frances sat quietly with Marie, who was comatose and had ceased recognizing anyone. "Her mouth once so flexible with laughter [was] drawn into a taut line that ended in deep pockets" and her once warm and soft hands were skeletal.[51] "Words of farewell can be spoken in silence," wrote Frances.[52] "And in this silence that lay upon us, I spoke of the many tender moments that pass between friends and are recorded in our hearts."

As Frances silently reminisced near Marie's deathbed, Marie's eyes began to open and close. Frances did not notice at first. She was jolted when the nurse shouted, "Miss Dressler is coming out of the coma! I'll get the doctor right away!"[53]

Frances leaned over to be closer. "Marie."

"Frances?"

"Yes, Marie — dear Marie."

"So ... long ... ago." Her voice was barely heard above a struggling whisper. "Remember?"

"Of course I remember."

"I said ... I'd see you ... again." Her hand rose to touch Frances's cheek. "I'll see you ... again." Her hand settled back on the bed and the light left her eyes.

In *My Own Story*, Dressler recalled that "once, a few years ago, I came close to death's door. So close that I could hear the dark wings of death beating above my head. And suddenly, to my great joy, I discovered that I no longer hated and feared death. It was as unterrifying, as natural, as life itself. *It was right.* I knew that my time hadn't come, but I knew that when it did come, it would be as simple as taking the hand of a friend and passing from one room into another."[54]

Marie died in Santa Barbara on Saturday, July 28, 1934, at 3:35 P.M.[55]

Epilogue

Frances had left Marie's bedside before the moment of death. Present were Grace Annable, Mamie and Jerry Cox, Allen and Katherine Walker, Franklin Nuzum, and Harold Schalenburg. Marie died so peacefully that Nuzum needed his stethoscope to confirm the fact.[1] He soon presented a formal statement: "Miss Dressler passed away at 3:35 P.M. The immediate cause of death was uremia (failure of the kidneys to function). This was complicated by congestive heart failure and by cancer. Cancer was found in the lower abdomen in July, 1931. During the latter part of her illness it spread to vital organs."[2]

Just before noon on July 29, Dressler's body was taken by hearse from Santa Barbara to Los Angeles.[3] She was dressed in a plum-colored afternoon dress and placed in a plain casket of cast copper with a statuary bronze finish. It had a double top of heavy plate glass and hammered bronze. Etched in plain Gothic letters was "Marie Dressler."

The Walkers took charge of the funeral details. "Although we have foreseen the end, the shock of her actual passing is none the less acute," said Allen.[4] "To avoid crowds, it is likely that the friendly cortege will visit an unannounced undertaking parlor that the body may rest there until final arrangements are made." The Walkers and the Coxes accompanied Marie's body to Los Angeles and then went straightaway to Loafhaven. The location of the body was a secret and no flowers were on or near the casket as it lay in the Pierce Brothers' chapel in Los Angeles. The body remained at the chapel until services were held at Forest Lawn on Tuesday, July 31.

Louis B. Mayer was in London when he learned of Dressler's death. He immediately issued a statement:[5] "Surely there never breathed a woman more beloved than our own Queen Marie. Her great life was one full to the brim with human kindness. Her magnificent artistry made this world a happier place for countless millions of her film admirers. To have been closely associated with her in her wonderful career for more than five years was a privilege I shall never forget. The screen has lost one of its greatest characters. Personally, I have lost a very dear friend." He telephoned from London and ordered a blanket of orchids and gardenias, Marie's favorite flowers, to cover her casket.[6] The Walkers ordered a large basket of "America's Sweetheart — Marie Dressler," the rose variety that was named for her just two years earlier. Thousands of other bouquets from all over the world flooded MGM and Forest Lawn. The whereabouts of Dressler's remains became known, and soon Pierce Brothers was receiving hundreds of bouquets as well.

Others followed Mayer with public remembrances. Irving Thalberg:[7] "Marie Dressler leaves behind a monument of success that will ever stand as an inspiration to those whose lives seem paved with obstacles. Her passing is a bereavement to the whole world."

Wallace Beery:[8] "Marie was my friend, probably the best friend I ever had in show business.... I have the consolation of knowing that the personality that was Marie Dressler is still alive and vibrant."

Polly Moran:[9] "Marie Dressler will never be dead. She will live forever in the hearts of the theater-going public and her friends throughout the world."

Mae West:[10] "Miss Dressler's courageous fight to live has been a stirring, inspirational lesson in a world where most of us give up too easily. Those of us who have been privileged to walk even near the path of Miss Dressler have learned something we shall not soon forget. We have learned to be more tolerant, to share with others and to show humility. Miss Dressler is gone but she has left a lot for us to remember."

Harold Lloyd:[11] "The screen has suffered an irreparable loss ... A consummate artist, she made age a beautiful thing on the screen. She was without doubt the greatest comedienne of this generation."

Edward G. Robinson:[12] "It seems hard that Marie Dressler should pass away at the height of her career, yet her great comeback into public favor at her age should prove an inspiration to all who today may be faced with the same despair that once assailed her."

While dozens of Hollywood's elite spoke of Dressler to journalists, the Walkers arranged her burial at Glendale's sprawling Forest Lawn Memorial Park, "the Valhalla of Hollywood." A funeral service was scheduled for 9 A.M., July 31, at Wee Kirk o' the Heather at Forest Lawn. July 31 was a typical southern California summer morning, the sun beaming through the trees and warming everything below. Approximately 100 friends and associates were given invitations, including fellow stars Norma Shearer, Polly Moran, Jean Hersholt, Lionel Barrymore, and May Robson. Also present were the many "carpenters, technicians and messenger boys who knew and loved Miss Dressler."[13] One of the more emotional mourners was Martha Watson, the studio commissary's waitress who served Dressler every day. She contributed a huge shelf of flowers to the service.

The cemetery's huge iron gates were kept closed during the service, and only those with invitations were admitted.[14] The studio agreeably collaborated with the Walkers and thousands were kept outside. In stated reference to Rudolph Valentino fans, privacy was necessary "to avoid a repetition of the undignified performances of the curious at other motion picture stars' funerals."[15] Elsewhere, flags flew at half mast. In Cobourg, many paid a visit to the cottage on King Street where Dressler was born. Even before the service, the Stage Relief Fund in New York announced a Marie Dressler Memorial Fund to help unemployed theater workers.

Limousines filled with studio personnel sped through Los Angeles streets to the cemetery and the church where services were to be held. The walnut pews were filled with early arrivals and the later guests had to stand near the entrance. Marie's body was to be sealed in a marble crypt in the Sanctuary of Benediction, a sunlit hall of marble and bronze and stained-glass windows. A replica of a Scottish church with brownstone walls and a bell tower surrounded by lawns, trees, shrubs, and flowers, the sanctuary was an idyllic resting place for the dead. Other celebrities who preceded her there were Florenz Ziegfeld and Lon Chaney.

Dressler's funeral remained simple and dignified. Wee Kirk o' the Heather was strewn with flowers.[16] The chapel housed three giant white crosses of gardenias and lilies of the valley. The largest came from Frances. Sid Grauman sent lilies, roses, and white dahlias. The Academy of Motion Picture Arts and Sciences sent a huge bouquet of pink and yellow dahlias and roses. Irving Thalberg and Norma Shearer sent orchids, gardenias, and roses. "Last greetings from Greta Garbo," read the card on a great wreath of roses. Other floral tributes were sent by Charlie Chaplin, Wallace Beery, Jack Conway, Harold Lloyd, Polly Moran, Nicholas Schenck, May Robson, Jean Hersholt, Alice Brady, Eddie Mannix, Constance Bennett, Marion Davies, Mr. and Mrs. Harry Rapf, William Randolph Hearst, the Screen Actors Guild, George Cukor, Mr. and Mrs. Cornelius K. Billings, Jack Warner, and Adolph Ochs, publisher of the *New York Times.*

Only a few of her closest friends were permitted to see Dressler's bronzed copper casket sealed and mortared behind a huge slab of marble. "Her life was so simple, and we know it was her wish that the last ceremonies be unostentatious," said Allen.[17] The most disconsolate mourner was Mamie, who wept copiously through the rites and the interment. Jerry tried to calm her, but he was unable. She approached Claire DuBrey at the service and said, "Miss Clara, if my darling could smile, I could, even though my heart was breaking."[18] When Mamie and Jerry spotted Grace Annable, they greeted each other with tearful hugs and kisses. Another one of Dressler's last nurses later approached Grace and said, "I would never let a black touch me."

"Aren't they lucky?" she retorted.[19]

Whispering subsided as the hearse arrived with the casket. The pallbearers, all wearing carnations against their dark suits, were directors who had worked with or had hoped to work with Dressler: Clarence Brown (*Anna Christie, Emma*), Jack Conway (*Bringing Up Father*), Mervyn LeRoy (*Tugboat Annie*), Charles Reisner (*Caught Short, Reducing,* and *Politics*), William K. Howard, and W. S. Van Dyke.[20] George Hill escorted his ex-wife Frances, who held onto him tightly for support.[21]

Dressler's casket was overwhelmed with the orchids and gardenias ordered by Louis B. Mayer. Back at the MGM studio, all was silent as work ceased during the service and flags flew at half mast. The Reverend Neal Dodd, pastor of the Little Church Around the Corner in Hollywood, officiated. At Dressler's request, he read her favorite poem.[22] It had been sent by an anonymous fan who scrawled a brief note: "Here is a verse written by a man named [Joel Keith]. I clipped it from a newspaper because it exactly expresses how I feel about you." The poem drew tears from the crowd:

> Her face is like a god's come back to life —
>   A face that shows the pain of mortal
>   man;
> And happiness that centuries have
>   known —
>   A god who speaks as only idols can.
>
> Perhaps she learned the truth when Time
>   was young,
>   And comes again with Heaven-songs of
>   mirth;
> And leaves her god and goddesses alone,
>   To live with us a little while on earth.

Dressler loved this poem so much that she had it engraved and carried it in her purse. The engraving had been placed beside her body in the closed casket. Caroline Lewis, a musician friend of Dressler's, played the organ. Marie's neighbor, soprano Jeanette MacDonald, sang "Abide with Me," though she was "grief-stricken, tearful and on the verge of collapse."[23]

The pallbearers rose and carried the casket into the morning sunlight and to the mausoleum. At the Sanctuary of Benediction, Dodd held a brief Episcopal service of commitment: "May she rest in peace and may light perpetual shine upon her." Mamie and Jerry were closest to the coffin during interment. Their $6.50 floral piece was the only one laid on the coffin, which was opened only once to place the bouquet in as Dressler had instructed.[24] Her remains were then interred in Crypt 5415 in the Great Mausoleum. The service was over and the mourners shuffled away.

At the gates of Forest Lawn, thousands of fans had collected hoping for a glimpse of anyone famous, but guards kept celebrities and gawkers separate.[25] When the gates were opened, they swarmed toward the church and collected many of the flowers left behind. Some stood quietly with bowed heads, some wept. The bouquets and wreaths that were undamaged were sent to the children's ward of a nearby hospital.

When eyes were dry, the business began. Benjamin J. Bradner, Dressler's attorney, filed her will for probate on August 2 in Los Angeles.[26] As many had suspected, she had given away much of her fortune before she died. In her will she gave away an additional $77,000 in cash, with specific stocks, bonds, jewels, and furs going to close friends. In "appreciation of their service, loyalty and devotion," Dressler left Mamie the largest single cash bequest of $35,000 and her entire silverware collection "as a remembrance for [Mamie and Jerry's] silver wedding anniversary."[27] Mamie also received most of Dressler's wardrobe. To Jerry, she left $15,000 and her 1929 Lincoln Berline and 1931 Ford Tudor sedan. "We are overcome by Miss Dressler's generosity," said Jerry.[28] "But we are too saddened by her recent death to even think of our future plans."

Other specific bequests[29] were $10,000 to the American Women's Association and stocks, bonds, and a mink coat to Allen and Katherine Walker. Five thousand dollars went to Nella Webb, the astrologer who had predicted Dressler's comeback. Two other friends had their loans canceled. Hallie Phillips received a large diamond bracelet. She willed Frances a pin of pearls and diamonds. All the equipment and belongings used in Santa Barbara went to Grace Annable, including a hospital bed and several bed jackets.[30] According to her will, the movie projector on loan to the children's wing of General Hospital was to remain there.[31] Frances agreed to pay for film rentals and projectionists' salaries.

The rest of her property was to be sold by the executor of the estate, Allen Walker, with the proceeds to go to Dressler's 70-year-old sister Bonita Ganthony, still living in Richmond, Surrey, England. Marie also stipulated that any contests or claims against her estate by "pretended heirs" would be cut off with no more than one dollar each.[32]

The Walkers and the Coxes, still on Marie's payroll, stayed at Loafhaven while the estate was settled. On August 6, Dressler's home was put up for sale. Only legitimate buyers, not the "morbidly curious," would be permitted to go inside.[33] On September 20, Loafhaven was bought by Robert Mandel, a wealthy department-store merchant from Chicago, for a paltry $31,500.[34]

By September 15, the entire estate was appraised at $280,847.17, including $101,093 in cash, $67,303 in bonds, and $11,505 in personal effects.[35] Bonita was shocked at the amount of her inherited fortune.[36] She had lived in a one-room apartment in Richmond for 20 years with her adopted bachelor son Peter. "The newspaper here said that Marie had died penniless, and I cannot believe that she left so much after all her generosity," said her sister. "I am Marie's only relative left in the world and I haven't an old friend left alive. ... What shall I do with the money? Well, I am too old to let people fool me. I shall just go on living in luxury in my little flat." The windfall was little comfort to an old woman who lost her last close link to the past. "They should have taken me instead of her," she said. "Her work was not done."[37]

In keeping with her wishes, Dressler's household belongings that had not been listed in her will were sold to an auction house under the supervision of Allen Walker. Rugs, paintings, etchings, bric-a-brac accumulated over the years, a portrait of Dressler by Carl Brooks, drawings, drapes, books, letters, phonograph recordings, photos, bulging theatrical trunks, furniture, and little items such as jigsaw puzzles, dolls, jade figurines, costume jewelry, lipsticks, and ivory dice were included in a 30-page inventory. Pasadena Galleries bought the cache for $5,500, moved it to Pasadena, and arranged it so as to duplicate rooms in Marie's home.[38] On sale was the album of 8,000 signatures of well-wishers for Marie's last birthday. MGM, the studio that ensured that Marie remained indentured even on her deathbed, took no interest in her personal treasures when she was gone.

The auction of Dressler's possessions began on October 9 and was attended by 2,000 people.[39] Buyers came from all over the world. "The most spirited bidding was for Miss Dressler's more personal belongings. Her lipstick and compact brought $60 and three small dolls she cherished, worth a few cents, were sold for $10."[40] Polly Moran was seen wandering through the crowd and bought a few mementos. The auction continued for a week.

In March 1935, before final settlement, Claire DuBrey sued Marie's estate.[41] Ever the grudge holder, Marie left her nothing and she was among three claimants who petitioned for their piece of the money. The other two were rejected. Claire was seeking $25,000 for her "secretarial, personal and nursing services" and to help her finish her memoirs of recollections of Marie. To her disappointment, she was awarded just $3,000,[42] which may have been hush money. Claire told the press of her intentions to write a tell-all only after Marie died and two years after they parted company. Her gossipy manuscript survives and it does not flatter Marie.

Before the estate was fully distributed, Bonita formally objected[43] to the Probate Court, complaining that the funeral bills in excess of $10,000 would deplete her inheritance. Bills paid from the estate checkbook by Allen Walker were endless — more than $600 in phone bills, plus staff salaries and ongoing maintenance costs for the Beverly Hills home. Claire's settlement also made her nervous as she watched her share dwindle. Bonita's complaint went nowhere and more than $25,000 was given to her at the final distribution. When all the accounting was settled, Mamie and Jerry were the most lavishly bequeathed individuals of the estate.

The world was soon given *My Own Story*, Dressler's posthumously published memoirs, rather than Claire's spin on Marie's last few years. First excerpted in *Redbook* magazine and with a foreword by Will Rogers and "told" to Mildred Harrington, the $2.50 book from Little, Brown and Company earned warm reviews on its publication late in 1934. The book is "alive with humor and courage and common sense" though "there is very little in the narrative about Miss Dressler's personal life," announced the *New York Times Book Review*.[44] "These armies of her admirers will find in the book all they need to know in order to appreciate fully the remarkable artist and still more remarkable woman she was." The *San Francisco Chronicle*[45] declared that "this story of her life, taken down in natural, easy style from her own lips ... is a vastly human affair, a tale of tragedy and comedy that will amuse you and make you sigh and make you like Marie Dressler more than you ever did."

As Dressler's memoirs were published, and her personal effects were being cannibalized to the highest bidder, the people from her comedy-drama lived out their lives. Some of the key players:

WALLACE BEERY[46] worked steadily and remained popular after Marie's death, though the quality of productions offered slowly declined. Producer Harry Rapf made several movies with Beery in lovable guzzler character roles, such as *Old Hutch*, *The Good Old Soak*, and *The Bad Man of Brimstone*. "My father was always on the look-out for Beery 'slob' stories," noted Rapf's son, screenwriter Maurice Rapf.[47] His screen partnership with Marjorie Main in *Barnacle Bill* was a pale attempt to reignite the Dressler-Beery chemistry. On April 16, 1949, after dining alone at Romanoff's Restaurant, Beery returned to his Beverly Hills home and suffered a fatal heart attack. He was 64. Beery's service was a huge affair attended by more than 2,000 mourners.[48] In contrast to Marie, Beery was careful with his money and left an estate in excess of $2 million.[49]

CORNELIUS K. BILLINGS, who once hosted a dinner party on horseback and later housed Marie and her entourage during her dying days, was ill for the last ten years of his life and died on May 6, 1937, at the age of 75.[50]

MAMIE AND JERRY COX took their $50,000 cash inheritance and moved to Savannah, Mamie's hometown, where they opened "a night club and tourist camp for Negroes." Jerry was no stranger to nightclubs, having worked in Harlem at a lodge of "Negro Elks" before working as butler for Marie. The Coxes's new club, the Cocoanut Grove, opened in 1936 along highway 17, the main north-south route between New York and Florida. The Grove, with its friendly proprietors and huge ballroom, became a major stopover destination for blacks in the deep South. Jerry continued to drive the 1931 model Ford given to him by Marie. He converted it into a hearse, and mourners paid $100 extra to let their departed loved ones take a final ride in a car once owned by Marie Dressler. He and Mamie remained sensible about finances, having seen Marie broke all too often. "I know how hard Miss Dressler worked for her money," declared Mamie. "I'm not going to be foolish with what she left us." As owners of the ever popular Grove, Mamie and Jerry remained socially prominent for 30 years. Well into their eighties, Jerry died on April 23, 1965, and Mamie died on January 6, 1967. At Mamie's request, various memorabilia from Marie, including her silver, clothing, and portrait, were given to the Kiah Museum in Savannah by Mamie's niece, Sadie Davis Steele.[51]

LEW FIELDS, after the *March of Times* debacle, appeared in *The Story of Vernon and Irene Castle* without JOE WEBER. With vaudeville long since dead, neither Weber nor Fields made any major stage appearances after 1933. Fields appeared on screen with his old partner in *Blossoms on Broadway* and *Lillian Russell* before dying in 1941. Joe Weber, the pickle baron of *Higgledy-Piggledy*, died in 1942.

BONITA GANTHONY remained true to her word and lived the quiet life in England until she died at the age of 76 on September 20, 1939.

FRANCES MARION grieved repeatedly in 1934. George Hill, her fourth husband, committed suicide by gunshot on August 10, less than two weeks after Marie's death. Frances never remarried.

Professionally, she moved from screenplays to books. She wrote *How to Write and Sell Film Stories* and several novels, including *Valley People* and *The Powder Keg*. *Molly, Bless Her* of 1937 was a heartfelt novelized tribute to Marie in which down-on-her-luck actress Molly Drexel enlivens the constipated home of a wealthy gentleman when she assumes duties there as his maid. It became *Molly and Me,* a 1945 movie with Gracie Fields. In 1946, discouraged by both the production code's iron-fisted control of movie scripts and MGM's expanding patriarchy, Frances left the studio. She devoted herself to family life, enjoyed the company of grandchildren, and learned how to sculpt. She continued to venture out to the movies, and in her eighties judged *Midnight Cowboy* and *Five Easy Pieces* as "excellent." In a 1972 ceremony, Frances was given a plaque by the Los Angeles City Council. "Marion is one of the really great ladies of the motion picture industry," declared a council member.[52] "She contributed greatly to the growth and vitality of the industry and of Los Angeles." Later that year, Frances won a Lifetime Achievement Award from the Writers Guild of America.[53] That same year, at the age of 84, she published her memoirs, *Off with Their Heads!*

Frances checked into the Good Samaritan Hospital to have a malignant tumor removed, but died there on May 12, 1973, of an aneurism. As she wished, there was no service. Her remains were cremated and scattered over family property in Aetna Springs, California. She was survived by two sons from her marriage to Fred Thomson and four grandchildren.[54]

HOWARD STRICKLING, the well-liked publicity man at MGM, lived in Encino during his long tenure at the studio. As he neared retirement, he spent more time at his 90-acre ranch in the California desert. An avid outdoorsman, Strickling raised Hereford cattle and at one point kept Elvis Presley's pony. After his retirement from the studio in 1969, he and his wife Gail moved to the ranch permanently, where Marie's *Min and Bill* Academy Award stood on the living room mantel for many years.[55]

In 1974, the ever-modest Strickling submitted to a lavish dinner tribute. His predecessor as studio publicity chief, Pete

Smith, was there to proclaim that Strickling was "the man they should have placed in permanent charge of the whole damn studio." After Howard's death in 1982, Marie's Academy Award was acquired by his niece Marilyn Strickling Read, who is its current owner.

LOUIS B. MAYER, at one time the highest-paid person in the United States, kept churning out impeccably produced popular entertainments at MGM through the 1930s and 1940s. He was always misty-eyed when discussing Marie and publicly admitted that she was paid less than she was worth. In a palace coup involving Dore Schary and Nicholas Schenck, Mayer resigned from MGM in 1951 and died of leukemia on October 29, 1957. He was 72. For his epic tenure as MGM publicist, and for their enduring friendship, Mayer left Howard Strickling $50,000 in his will.

POLLY MORAN, like Wallace Beery, seemed to wander through the rest of her career looking for a suitable substitute for Marie. MGM did not renew her contract and by 1936 she was making two-reelers at Columbia. Republic paired her with Alison Skipworth for *Two Wise Maids* and *Ladies in Distress*, but with so-so results. She retired from the screen in 1940. She married attorney Martin T. Malone, who once held her at gunpoint after a party guest had called him "Mr. Moran." Polly's practical jokes became somewhat pathological. At a party given by Fanny Brice, Polly appeared without her dentures, heavily lipsticked and rouged, and served soup in a maid's uniform. Her candidacy for Laguna Beach City Council on a "Pro-Dogs" platform was a thorough failure. She made a minor movie comeback with tiny and indifferent roles in *Adam's Rib* in 1949 and *The Yellow Cab Man* in 1950. Of her performance in the former she said, "I worked in the picture two days before I got a real look at myself. After that I never went back." She died of heart failure on January 25, 1952, at the age of 66.[56]

MACK SENNETT, the young upstart who made history by moving Marie's Tillie from stage to film, saw his studio close in 1928 and his corporation go bankrupt in 1933. Keystone comedy died and slapstick became a memory. "We never [made] sport of religion, politics, race or mothers," Sennett said of his work. "A mother never gets hit with a custard pie. Mothers-in-law — yes. But mothers — never." With his movie fortunes dwindling, Mack Sennett died in the Motion Picture Country Home at the age of 76 on November 6, 1960.[57]

ALLEN WALKER, Marie's trusted friend and executor to her will, left Santa Barbara and La Quinta after the death of his wife Katherine in 1951. He died of a stroke in 1970 at 83 in his home in Cuernavaca, Mexico.

NELLA WEBB, Marie's astrologist-savior, died on December 1, 1954, in New York at the age of 78. She never returned to her earlier career as an actress but remained committed to astrology.

CLAIRE DUBREY went back to movie acting after leaving Marie but she never achieved prominence. She was once again doing low-grade programmers or bit parts in high-quality productions such as *Gabriel Over the White House*, *Blossoms on Broadway*, and *The Story of Alexander Graham Bell*. After World War II, she spent less time making movies and more time operating a small antiques business. She made her last appearances in *Escort West* and *Frontier Gun* in 1959.

Actor John Phillip Law was just 10 when Claire moved in down the street from him. She never remarried or had children, so Law became her surrogate son and caretaker when she lost much of her sight and hearing. "She was a good money manager and believed everyone should be self-sufficient," he says. "Claire had some amazing contradictions. She was a Victorian woman, full of discretion and privacy, but she also loved nature and was sometimes half in and half out of her clothes." A mastectomy of questionable necessity in the 1970s left her pained and bitter, but she was proud to have kept all her teeth. She died on August 1, 1993, just 30 days shy of her 101st birthday.[58]

COBOURG, ONTARIO, with a population hovering at 15,000, maintains dozens of its nineteenth-century buildings, including the imposing Victoria Hall. Walking in the old part of town, it is possible to imagine the community as the Koerbers saw it in the 1860s and 1870s. And Cobourg never forgot Leila. In 1934 the John Fields family owned the little brick house on King Street where she was born. The Fieldses were living there but by 1937 had converted it into a restaurant. "Dressler House" became a popular eatery as steamers from Rochester brought tourists and summer residents to Cobourg.[59] In 1970 a plaque commemorating it as Dressler's birthplace was unveiled in the front yard by the Archaeological and Historic Sites Board of Ontario.

After going through more owners, Dressler House grew into a restaurant of international repute and was reviewed in a 1988 issue of *Epicure* magazine as having "excellent duck/hazelnut pâté, silky-cool cucumber soup, ratatouille, local rainbow trout, pink lamb medallions as tender as can be, grilled-to-succulence chicken breast treated to a tangy basil/orange butter. ... Rooms furnished 1860s style." The restaurant was something of a local institution and stayed in business for more than 50 years. An oil portrait of Dressler greeted customers like some silent goddess of gastronomy.

On January 14, 1989, Dressler House was gutted by fire.[60] The portrait survived the blaze, but most other souvenirs and memorabilia were destroyed. Damage came to $250,000. In a great show of civic solidarity, the Chamber of Commerce purchased the building for its office. While the Canadian birthplaces of Norma Shearer and Mary Pickford had long since been reduced to rubble, the newly formed Marie Dressler Foundation spearheaded fundraising for the purchase of the home for $201,000, with restoration costing an additional $290,000. The Chamber negotiated a contract to repay the town over several years for the restoration and aggressively went after private contributions. The Grand Opening of the new Marie Dressler House took place on November 18, 1990, and the building became a visitors information center with a permanent display of Marie memorabilia.[61]

The Marie Dressler Foundation has made great effort to collect souvenirs of Dressler for their permanent display. Led by Cobourg businessman Ed Haynes, the call has gone out worldwide and the Foundation has been rewarded. They have received autographed portraits, an Adrian gown she owned, her six-page will, five wax cylinder voice recordings with a 1902 Edison gramophone, and the scrapbook of Norman Reilly Raine, author of *Tugboat Annie*. They also received several production stills; her two autobiographies; lobby cards of *Min and Bill*, *Emma*, and *Dinner at Eight*; a seven-minute video on Marie's life; and original sheet music from *Tillie's Nightmare*, *The Boy and the Girl*, and other stage shows. Most prominent in the two-room display is a complete setting and figures of Marie and Wallace Beery as *Min and Bill*, courtesy of the Movieland Wax Museum in Buena Park, California.

On July 1, 1996, the Foundation received a small tinted photograph etching on porcelain of Dressler postmarked Roseburg, Oregon. The accompanying letter ended with "I was given this [etching] by her, this little portrait, and I am delighted that it will find a home. I never had children, so I have often wondered what to do with it. Do take it and give it a place of honor — as I got to love her very much." The sender was Marie's last nurse, 89-year-old Grace Annable Ruthrruff.

What of Dressler's memory in the larger world? It has faded, to be sure, but bits of remembrance are passed down. The Grauman's Chinese Theater box office was on top of her footprints in 1935. In 1937, when actress Madge Evans's MGM dressing room was being stripped of its wallpaper, a message to previous tenant Joan Crawford was found one stratum below: "To Joan, a swell kid, I know you'll reach the top, Marie Dressler."[62] In 1939 the *Cavalcade of America* radio program dramatized portions of Marie's life with Agnes Moorehead narrating.[63] In 1960 Dressler was given a star on Hollywood's Walk of Fame. Just before her death in 1962, Marilyn Monroe told *Redbook* magazine that she looked forward to

A 1950s postcard of the fine Cobourg restaurant Dressler House. (Courtesy of the Marie Dressler Foundation.)

becoming a "marvelous" character actress like Marie when she grew old.[64]

Overall, there has been an amazing lack of attention paid to her career. In 1996 an inventory at the Library of Congress revealed 133 listings on Charlie Chaplin, 40 on Greta Garbo, 9 on Mary Pickford, and 0 on Marie Dressler. Marcella Rabwin offers an observation on Dressler's forgotten legacy.[65] "She was not a Joan Crawford or somebody who was invited to everyone's party. Everyone adored her, but she was not a peer. She was so much older than everyone else. She did not make such an impression in Hollywood, she made an impression on the American public."

Her surviving family was far-flung and no one took on the task of preserving her memory. The actress Jessica James, who died in 1990, claimed to be related to Dressler on her father's side.[66] Her brother, real-estate financier Arthur James, kept a genealogy, letters, clippings, diaries, photos, and movies of Marie in his Malibu home, but everything was destroyed in a late 1960s fire. Marie's cousins have long since died.

Dressler did not seem particularly interested in enshrining herself beyond her celluloid image and memoirs. As written and spoken memories attest to her old-fashioned privacy and ladylike manner, she might be misinterpreted as a relic with nothing to offer modern audiences. Her extraordinary career alone makes her fascinating historically, and her surviving performances remain lively, fresh, funny, and poignant today. And so many years later, she remains one of the movies' all-time great anomalies. America's cult of youth and beauty was thriving in the 1930s, but there have been no stars to fill the "antiglamour" niche once occupied so supremely by Marie.

In the intervening decades, there have been wisps of interest, a play here, a short retrospective there. *O Evening Star* was a fictional play by Zoë Akins that opened at the Empire Theater in New York on January 8, 1936.[67] Jobyna Howland, who appeared with Marie in *Miss Prinnt* in 1900, played Amy Bellaire, a thinly disguised character based on Marie. *O Evening Star* was produced twice again at the Pasadena Playhouse with Florence Bates,[68] the character actress who began acting at 47 and made a strong showing on screen in 1940 with *Rebecca*.

Dressler is often forgotten in comedy retrospectives. One exception is *MGM: The Big Parade of Comedy* produced in 1963. Included footage is the scene from *Reducing* when she is trying to get her enormous mass onto the upper berth of a train. Some rather gauche original lyrics were included in her tribute: "Fat and baggy, funny and saggy, that was Marie. She would twist your heart or make you shake with laughter, that was Marie. Everybody's grandma, everybody's pal, that was Marie." More recently, she was given brief but respectful homage in Turner Broadcasting System's 1992 documentary *MGM: When the Lion Roars*.

Dressler has been portrayed in a major movie only once, in the disastrous 1965 production of *Harlow* starring Carol Lynley. British actress Hermione Baddeley played Marie. In 1993 Toronto's Sharon Dyer mounted her one-woman stage show called *Sweet Marie*.

Although Dressler's fame fell sharply after her death, friends who lived on spoke of her with a lump in the throat. As recently as 1978, Adela Rogers St. Johns recalled Queen Marie:[69]

> I miss Marie more than anybody except Clark. I didn't really have her that much *in* my life, even when Talkies came and she rented my house and I moved permanently to live in the Malibu Colony. We used to gather there—Frances Marion, the scenarist, and Hedda Hopper, sometimes Margaret Mayer [Mrs. Louis B.] ... Occasionally Mary Pickford made a queenly appearance. And Joan Crawford ... and Jean Harlow. And, when Marie was alone, even Miss Greta Garbo. For once, since my emotions are sometimes mysterious even to me, I can tell you utterly and completely why I and everybody who knew her missed Marie Dressler more than anybody. ... Confidence. Full trust. Belief in the trustworthiness, reliability and ability of a person or thing or yourself. Marie, whether or no it was actually her conscious slogan, made you believe it could and should be yours. *Get on with it*. It's worth doing—she injected that into you. And when she prayed you felt that she spoke with a Higher Power face to face. Even a little or professional disappointment was something you took to Marie. ... The Greatest Lady of Hollywood. ... Marie Dressler did more than survive. She wallowed through each trough of the waves so gallantly, came rumbling to the crest again with such zest, that she *inspired*. She made everyone who knew her feel they could go and do likewise. ... I have to award top billing to Marie—who overcame, and overcame, and *overcame*. ... Let this tired old world borrow its mirth from her great heart. ... Somewhere along in here she invaded enemy territory when she broke through the barrier which decreed that *actresses* were not and could not be *ladies*, hence were socially unacceptable. ... It is impossible, always was, to give Marie a passing mention. Some folks you can fragment, write separately of their love life, their talent, politics, philosophy, isolate a moment of tragedy, of passion, of triumph. When Marie Dressler comes *in*—whether into your life, or your consciousness, or your book—she comes total and whole. There's no way to leave any of her *out*. So here she is. At sixty Marie Dressler was living poetry, perhaps to Browning. "Grow old along with me!" she seemed to encourage. "The best is yet to be/The last of life, for which the first was made." Wherever she went now it was like a royal progress, adoring fans pressed near to look into the ugly-beautiful, tough-tender, old-forever-young face of a great and famous lady, the face of age as age should be—not faltering, fretful, regretful, but dynamic, fearless, laughing and triumphant.

Amidst all the hyperbole and salty tears at her death came a singularly level-headed tribute that rings true so many decades later. Quick to remind readers of Dressler's failures, and of the ironies of her success, an anonymous writer from the *Commonweal* came to understand Marie's strange and wonderful allure:[70]

> The very sincere sorrow which is felt throughout the movie-going world at the death of Marie Dressler suggests two separate ideas. A sterling actress and an

unusually generous and human individual, she also owed part of her triumph to strange and unpredictable chance. She succeeded in films only after the stage had finished with her, after she had failed to make a go of modest non-theatrical ventures, after she had grown old. And the fact of success in these circumstances undoubtedly added to her legend. Not only did people prefer her to many young and beautiful stars. It tickled them to prefer her; and it even tickled Hollywood to see her preferred. It was a piquant departure from the usual Hollywood formula, and Hollywood must be credited with the intelligence of realizing its value. But the deeper fact about the phenomenon of Marie Dressler's friendly and affectionate public is one that Hollywood has not always been so prompt to see. She played many roles, but she was not remembered in many roles, but as one personality — wholesome, genial, direct, a creature in a different world from the exotic and neurotic or erotic types which so often pass as Hollywood staples. Whatever aberrations of public taste may have encouraged or condoned these latter it is not they whom people in their hearts truly remember, or to whom they instinctively turn. It is rather to the simple and universal and healthy types. The great comedians, led by Chaplin, have proved this again and again. Marie Dressler, with her own sound comedy often broadening into farce, her own often true and touching pathos, her suggestion of almost homespun humanity, had a modest but real share in proving it also.

Put in this light, her amazing late-life popularity is not so hard to grasp after all. After years of indifference, her newly adoring Depression-battered public understood what a previous generation had forgotten. They knew that Marie was beautiful.

Appendix 1

Major Stage Appearances

Cast members and theaters given are from original productions unless otherwise noted. Date is New York opening; most often out-of-town tryouts preceded. Production descriptions (vaudeville, comic opera, etc.) are taken from original wording used in marketing or reviews. Songs given were sung by Dressler or used prominently in the production. In addition to the oeuvre listed below, Dressler appeared in other vaudeville shows, revues, benefits, assemblies, and parties and on radio.

1883–1894

Comic opera with road companies including Nevada Stock Company, Starr Opera Company, Camille D'Arville and Company, and Bennett-Moulton Opera Company. Repertory included *Under Two Flags, The Mikado, Boccaccio, Said Pasha, Three Black Cloaks, Fatinitza, Nanon, Bohemian Girl, The Black Hussars, The Beggar Student, Grand Duchess, Chimes of Normandy, Olivette, Erminie, Mascot, Fra Diavolo, La Périchole,* and *Madame Favart.*

The Robber of the Rhine (comic opera)
Music by Charles Puerner, lyrics by Maurice Barrymore. Opened in New York May 28, 1892, at the Fifth Avenue Theater.
Cast: C. Hayden Coffin (Waldemar), Marie Dressler (Cunigonde), Edith Kenward (Flip), Henry C. Perkins (Klootz).

Princess Nicotine (comic opera)
Music by William Furst, lyrics by Charles Alfred Byrne and Louis Harrison. Opened in New York November 20, 1893, at the Casino; subsequent tour.
Cast: Lillian Russell (Rosa), Perry Averill (Chicos), Digby Bell (Don Pedro), Marie Dressler (the Duchess).

Giroflé-Girofla (comic opera)
Music by Charles Lecocq, lyrics and text by Eugène Leterrier. Premiered at the 1893 World's Fair in Chicago.
Production featuring Marie opened in New York March 30, 1894, at the Casino; subsequent tour.
Cast: Lillian Russell (Giroflé and Girofla), Signor Perugini (Marasquin), Digby Bell (Don Bolero), Marie Dressler (Aurora).

Madeleine; Or, the Magic Kiss (comic opera)
Music by Julian Edwards, lyrics and book by Stanislaus Stange and Julian Edwards. Opened in New York February 25, 1895, at the Bijou.
Cast: Aubrey Boucicault (Baron de Grimm), Camille D'Arville (Madeleine), Marie Dressler (Mary Doodle).

Little Robinson Crusoe (operatic burlesque)
Music by W. H. Bachelor and Gustav Luders, lyrics by Harry B. Smith. Opened in Chicago June 21, 1895, at the Schiller Theater.
Cast: Eddie Foy (Dare Devil Willie), Adele Farrington (Robinson Crusoe), Sadie MacDonald (Polly Perkins), Marie Dressler (Ophelia Crusoe), Douglas Flint (Tuffenuff), Daisy Gehrue (Algernon de Hatchway), Charles T. Crawford (Snowflake).

A Stag Party, or A Hero in Spite of Himself (musical travesty)
Music by Herman Perlet, lyrics by Paul Potter and Edgar Nye. Opened in New York December 17, 1895, at the Garden Theater.
Cast: Louis Harrison (Cuyler Van Tassell), Leo Dietrichstein (Count Otto Witzky), Sadie McDonald (Magdalen Witzky), Bessie Abbott (Freddy Van Tassell), Marie Dressler (Georgia Vest).

The Lady Slavey (musical)
Music by Gustave Kerker, book by George Dance. Opened in New York February 3, 1896, at the Casino; subsequent tours and revivals in 1898 and 1900.
Cast: Dan Daly (William Endymion Sykes), Henry Norman (Major Tolliver), Virginia Earle (Phyllis), Charles Dickson (Vincent Evelyn), Charles Danby (Roberts), Richard Carle (Lord Lavender), Marie Dressler (Flo Honeydew).

The Rivals (comedy)
By Richard Brinsley Sheridan. Opened in New York May 28, 1896 at the Hearld Square Theater.
Cast: William Collier (Bob Acres), Henry V. Donnelly (Sir Anthony Absolute), Andrew Mack (Sir Lucius O'Trigger), Marie Dressler (Mrs Malaprop).

Tess of the Vaudevilles (burlesque/vaudeville)
Book by A. R. Phillips. Opened in New York February 15, 1897, at Proctor's Pleasure Palace.
Cast: Marie Dressler (Sally/Tess), Frederick Backus (Mr. Smith), Frederick Clifton (Mr. Brown).

Courted into Court (musical farce)
Music, book and lyrics by John J. McNally. Tour included Cleveland and San Francisco, early 1898, subsequently opened in New York with May Irwin replacing Marie Dressler.
Songs included "Cake Walk," "Ram-a-Jam, I Want That Man" and "Susie, Dis Coon Has Got de Blues."
Cast: Marie Dressler, May Duryea, John J. Rice.

Hotel Topsy Turvey (vaudeville operetta)
Music and lyrics by Arthur Sturgess, Edgar Smith, and Lionel Monckton; adapted from *L'Auberge Tohu Bohu* by Maurice Ordonneau. Opened in New York October 3, 1898, at the Herald Square Theater; subsequent tour.
Cast: Eddie Foy (Labeau), Aubrey Boucicault (Paul Blanchard), Marie Dressler (Flora).

The Man in the Moon (extravaganza)
Music by Gustave Kerker, Ludwig Englander, and Reginald De Koven; book and lyrics by Louis Harrison and Stanislaus Stange. Opened in New York April 24, 1899, at the New York Theater.
Cast: Sam Bernard (Conan Doyle), Marie Dressler (Viola Alum), Christie MacDonald (Diana).

Miss Prinnt (farce-musical-comedy)
Music and lyrics by John Golden, book by George V. Hobart. Opened in New York December 25, 1900, at the Victoria Theater; subsequent tour.
Songs included "I'm Lookin' for an Angel (Without Wings)."
Cast: Marie Dressler (Helen Prinnt), Jobyna Howland (Mrs. Van Asteroid), Theodore Babcock (Richmond Blackstone).

The King's Carnival (burlesque revue)
Music by A. Baldwin Sloane, book and lyrics by Sydney Rosenfeld and George V. Hobart. Opened in New York May 13, 1901, at the New York Theater; subsequent tour.
Songs included "Ragtime Will Be Mah Finish."
Cast: Marie Dressler (Queen Anne of Spain), Louis Harrison (King Philip of Spain), Dan McAvoy (Bombastes Furloso), Emma Carcus (Lady Jane Bollingsbroke), Amelia Summerville (Inez).

The Hall of Fame (musical)
Music by A. Baldwin Sloane and Mae Anwerda Sloane, lyrics by George V. Hobart, book by Sydney Rosenfeld, George V. Hobart, and A. Baldwin Sloane. Opened in New York February 3, 1902, at the New York Theater.
Songs included "When Charlie Plays the Slide Trombone" and "Nancy."
Cast: Marie Dressler (Lady Oblivion), Amelia Summerville (Goddess Fame), Louis Harrison (Fame-Starved Actor).

King High Ball (comic opera)
Music by Frederick Bowers, lyrics by Charles Horwitz; based on *The Understudy* by Rupert Hughes. Opened in New York September 6, 1902, at the New York Theater; subsequent tour.
Cast: Marie Dressler (Ex-Queen Tarantula), Will H. Sloan (Diedrich Von Stumph), Charles Guyer (Booster).

Sweet Kitty Swellairs (burlesque/vaudeville)

Opened in New York March 1, 1904, at the Circle Theater.
Cast: Marie Dressler.

Higgledy-Piggledy (musical)
Music by Maurice Levi, book and lyrics by Edgar Smith. Opened in New York October 20, 1904, at the Weber Music Hall; subsequent tour.
Songs included "A Great Big Girl Like Me" and "The Game of Love."
Cast: Joe Weber (Adolph Schnitz), Anna Held (Mimi De Chartreuse), Marie Dressler (Philopoena Schnitz), Harry Morris (Gottlieb Gesler), Charles Bigelow (Sandy Walker).

The College Widower (burlesque)
Music by Maurice Levi, book and lyrics by Edgar Smith. Opened in New York January 5, 1905, at the Weber Music Hall; subsequent tour.
Cast: Marie Dressler (Tillie Buttin).

Twiddle-Twaddle (revue)
Music by Maurice Levi, book and lyrics by Edgar Smith. Opened in New York January 1, 1906, at the Weber Music Hall; subsequent tour.
Songs included "It's Hard to Be a Lady in a Case Like That," "Hats," and "Hard Luck Stories of the Stage."
Cast: Joe Weber (Philip Grabfelder), Marie Dressler (Matilda Grabfelder), Charles Bigelow (Ebenezer Dodge), Trixie Friganza (Mrs. "Jack" Van Shaik).

The Squaw Man's Girl of the Golden West (burlesque)
Music by Maurice Levi, book and lyrics by Edgar Smith. Opened in New York February 26, 1906, at the Weber Music Hall; subsequent tour.
Cast: Marie Dressler (The Girl), Joe Weber (Rash Tawkins), Charles Bigelow (Topictowna).

Oh! Mr. Belasco (vaudeville)
Book by John Golden. Opened in New York December 31, 1906, at the Colonial Theater; subsequent tour.
Cast: Marie Dressler.

Vaudeville/Revue
"Topical" lyrics by Eustace Baynes. Opened in London October 28, 1907, at the Palace Theater.
Songs included "Why Adam Sinned" and "The Glove."
Cast: Marie Dressler, Anne Dancrey, Margaret Cooper, Marcel and Rene Philippart.

Vaudeville
Opened in New York April 26, 1908, at the Colonial Theater.
Cast: Marie Dressler

Vaudeville
Opened in London October 1908, at the Palace Theater.
Cast: Marie Dressler, Ernest Lambart, Mabel Redfern, The Palace Girls.

Philopoena and the Collegettes (musical)
Music by Maurice Levi, lyrics by Edgar Smith. Opened in London February 27, 1909, at the Aldwych Theater.
Cast: Marie Dressler, Frank Bernard, Mrs. Lesemoir-Gordon, Lucy Kipling, Stanley Cooke.

The Boy and the Girl (musical)
Music by Richard Carle and H. L. Heartz, lyrics by M. E. Rourke. Opened in New York May 31, 1909, at the New Amsterdam Theater.
Songs included "Seductive Caroline," "A Poor Working Girl," and "Yoo-La (The Irish Spanish 'Sit Down!' Song)."
Cast: Marie Dressler (Gladys De Vine), Marion Garson (Avita), Toby Lyons (Professor Zero).

Tillie's Nightmare (musical)
Music by A. Baldwin Sloane, book and lyrics by Edgar Smith. Opened in New York May 5, 1910, at the Herald Square Theater; subsequent tours and revival in 1919.
Songs included "Heaven Will Protect the Working Girl" and "Life Is What We Make It, After All."
Cast: Marie Dressler (Tillie Blobbs), May Montford (Peroxia Snow), Octavia Broske (Maude Blobbs), Horace Newman (Sim Pettingill).

Roly-Poly and ***Without the Law*** (burlesque)
Music by A. Baldwin Sloane, book and lyrics by Edgar Smith. Opened in New York November 21, 1912, at Weber & Fields' New Music Hall.
Cast: Lew Fields, Joe Weber, Marie Dressler, Nora Bayes, Bessie Clayton.

All Star Gambol (also known as *The Marie Dressler Players, The Banqueteers,* or *Merry Gambol*) (revue)
Music by A. Baldwin Sloane, lyrics by Marie Dressler. Opened in New York March 10, 1913, at Weber & Fields' New Music Hall; subsequent tour.
Cast: Marie Dressler, Jefferson De Angelis, Madame Yorska.

A Mix Up (farce)
Book by Parker A. Hord. Opened in New York December 28, 1914, at the 39th Street Theater; subsequent tour.
Songs included "Sister Susie's Sewing Shirts for Soldiers."
Cast: Marie Dressler (Gladys Lorraine), Bert Lytell (Robert Hickman), Evelyn Vaughan (Angelica Hickman), John P. Dougherty (Sam Landman).

The Century Girl (revue)

Music and lyrics by Irving Berlin and Victor Herbert. Opened in New York November 6, 1916, at the Century Theater.

Songs included "The Balle Loose" and "You Belong to Me."

Cast: Sam Bernard, Hazel Dawn, Doyle & Dixon, Marie Dressler, Elsie Janis.

Vaudeville

Opened in New York March 31, 1919, at the Palace Theater.

Cast: Marie Dressler.

Cinderella on Broadway (revue)

Music by Bert Grand and Al Goodman, book and lyrics by Harold Atteridge. Opened in New York June 24, 1920, at the Winter Garden Theater; subsequent tour.

Cast: Al Brendel, Flo Burt, Eileen Van Biene, John T. Murray, Marie Dressler.

The Passing Show of 1921 (revue)

Music by Jean Schwartz, book and lyrics by Harold Atteridge. Opened in New York December 29, 1920, at the Winter Garden Theater.

Songs included "In Little Old New York."

Cast: Willie and Eugene Howard, Harry Watson, Marie Dressler.

Moments from the Winter Garden (vaudeville)

Tour included Cleveland, Chicago, St. Louis, and Milwaukee, November 1921.

Songs included "Lionel and Ethel and John."

Cast: Marie Dressler, John T. Murray, Arthur Geary, Francis Renault, Ethel Davis, Liora Hoffman.

The Dancing Girl (musical)

Music by Sigmund Romberg and Jay Gorney, lyrics and book by Harold Atteridge and Irving Caesar. Opened in New York January 24, 1923, at the Winter Garden Theater.

Songs included "I've Been Waiting for You" and "The Perfect Fool."

Cast: Kitty Doner, Ted Doner, Marie Dressler, Jack Pearl, Trini, Tom Burke.

Old Timers' Week (vaudeville)

Opened in New York October 19, 1925, at the Palace Theater.

Cast: Marie Dressler, Cissie Loftus, May Irwin, Marie Cahill.

Appendix 2

Filmography

Films are listed in order of release date. In addition to the films listed below, Marie appeared in newsreels, shorts, and public-service announcements and was animated at least twice in cartoon form. Following title, studio, release date, personnel, plot summary, and running time is information on the whereabouts of each film and where the author viewed them. Some are available on commercial video, but many more are housed in archives around the United States or are periodically shown on Turner Classic Movies cable television station. Those without an abbreviation after their entry in the filmography have evaded rediscovery. Missing films may be in private collections, but they are not housed at major archives and are most likely lost.

Abbreviations:

CR Cinémathèque Royale, Brussels
GEH George Eastman House, Rochester
LOC Library of Congress, Washington
MOMA Museum of Modern Art, New York
Roxie Roxie Theater, San Francisco
TCM Turner Classic Movies cable television station
UCLA University of California, Los Angeles, Film and Television Archive

Tillie's Punctured Romance (Keystone, November 14, 1914)

Alternate titles: *Tillie's Millions* and *For the Love of Tillie*.

Directed by Mack Sennett. Scenario by Hampton Del Ruth, based on the play *Tillie's Nightmare*. Slapstick comedy of a naive country maid taken in by a city swindler.

Cast: Marie Dressler (Tillie Banks), Charlie Chaplin (The City Guy, aka Charlie), Mabel Normand (The Other Girl, aka Mabel), Mack Swain (John Banks), Charles Bennett (Uncle Douglas Banks), Charles Murray (detective), Chester Conklin (guest), Minta Durfee (maid), Milton Berle (newspaper seller). 73 minutes; available on video.

Note: *Tillie's Punctured Romance* was remade in 1928 with Louise Fazenda and W. C. Fields.

Tillie's Tomato Surprise (Lubin, September 27, 1915)

Directed by Howell Hansel. Screenplay by Acton Davies. Slapstick physical comedy involving inheritance, a monkey, and modern inventions.

Cast: Marie Dressler (Tillie Todd), Tom McNaughton (Percy Jitney), Colin Campbell (The Bat, a flying Scotchman), Eleanor Fairbanks (Amber Gris), Sarah McVickar (Aunt Sally), Clara Lambert (Tillie's mother), Jim, the monkey (Jim, the monkey). Six reels; screened at LOC (incomplete surviving footage).

Tillie's Day Off (Marie Dressler Motion Picture Company/Mutual, 1916)

Cast: Marie Dressler. Two reels.

Tillie's Divorce Case (Marie Dressler Motion Picture Company/Mutual, 1916)

Cast: Marie Dressler. Two reels.

Elopement (Marie Dressler Motion Picture Company/Mutual, 1916)

Cast: Marie Dressler. Two reels.

Tillie Wakes Up (Peerless/World, January 29, 1917)

Alternate title: *Tillie's Night Out*.

Directed by Harry Davenport. Scenario by Frances Marion from an idea by Mark Swan. Farce of two hapless souls who live it up at Coney Island until their respective spouses appreciate them.

Cast: Marie Dressler (Tillie Tinkelpaw), Johnny Hines (J. Mortimer Pipkins), Frank Beamish (Henry Tinkelpaw), Rubye de Remer (Mrs. Luella Pipkins), Ruth Barrett (Mrs. Nosey), Jack Brown (Mr. Nosey). Five reels; screened at UCLA, also listed at MOMA and CR.

The Scrublady (Marie Dressler Motion Picture Company/Goldwyn/World, 1917)

Cast: Marie Dressler (Scrublady). Two reels; screened at LOC (only second reel survives).

Fired (Marie Dressler Motion Picture Company/Goldwyn/World, 1917)

Scenario by Marie Dressler.
Cast: Marie Dressler. Two reels.

The Agonies of Agnes (Marie Dressler Motion Picture Company/World, 1918)

Burlesque treatment of the *Perils of Pauline*.
Cast: Marie Dressler (Agnes). Two reels.

The Cross Red Nurse (Marie Dressler Motion Picture Company/World, 1918)

Wartime patriotic comedy.
Cast: Marie Dressler. Two reels.

The Callahans and the Murphys (MGM, June 16, 1927)

Directed by George Hill. Scenario by Frances Marion from a novel by Kathleen Norris, titles by Ralph Spence. Slapstick comedy of two warring Irish families.

Cast: Marie Dressler (Mrs. Callahan), Polly Moran (Mrs. Murphy), Sally O'Neil (Ellen Callahan), Lawrence Gray (Dan Murphy), Frank Currier (Grandpa Callahan), Eddie Gribbon (Jim Callahan), Gertrude Olmstead (Monica Murphy), Turner Savage (Timmy Callahan), Jackie Coombs (Terrance Callahan), Dawn O'Day (Mary Callahan). Seven reels.

The Joy Girl (Fox, September 3, 1927)

Directed by Allan Dwan. Screenplay by Frances Agnew, adapted by Adele Comandini from a *Saturday Evening Post* serial by May Edington. Complication in balmy Florida involving young lovers.

Cast: Olive Borden (Jewel Courage), Neil Hamilton (John Jeffrey Fleet), Mary Alden (Mrs. Courage), William Norris (Herbert Courage), Helen Chandler (Flora), Jerry Miley (Vicary), Frank Walsh (Hugh Sandman), Clarence J. Elmer (valet), Peggy Kelly (Isolde), Marie Dressler (Mrs. Heath). Seven reels; color sequences by Technicolor; screened at MOMA.

Breakfast at Sunrise (First National, October 23, 1927)

Directed by Malcolm St. Clair. Screenplay by Gladys Unger, adapted from the French play *Le Déjeuner au Soleil* by André Birabeau. Romantic comedy of lovers attempting to incite jealousy.

Cast: Constance Talmadge (Madeleine), Alice White (Loulou), Bryant Washburn (Marquis de Cerisey), Paulette Duval (Georgiana), Albert Gran (Champignol), Marie Dressler (Queen Sophia), David Mir (Prince Cyril Nitwitz). Seven reels; screened at GEH, master copy at LOC.

Bringing Up Father (MGM/Cosmopolitan, March 17, 1928)

Directed by Jack Conway. Scenario by Frances Marion, story by George McManus, titles by Ralph Spence. Comedy based on characters from the popular comic strip.

Cast: J. Farrell MacDonald (Jiggs), Jules Cowles (Dinty Moore), Polly Moran (Maggie), Marie Dressler (Annie Moore), Gertrude Olmstead (Ellen), Grant Withers (Dennis), Andre de Segurola (The Count), Rose Dione (Mrs. Smith), David Mir (Oswald), Toto (the dog). Seven reels; master copy at LOC.

The Patsy (MGM, April 21, 1928)

Alternate title: *The Political Flapper*.

Directed by King Vidor. Screenplay by Agnes Christine Johnstone, from a play by Barry Connors. Light romantic comedy of a neglected woman who seeks revenge on those who underestimate her.

Cast: Marion Davies (Patricia Harrington), Orvil Caldwell (Tony Anderson), Marie Dressler (Ma Harrington), Dell Henderson (Pa Harrington), Lawrence Gray (Bill), Jane Winton (Grace Harrington). 64 minutes; screened at UCLA.

The Divine Lady (First National, March 22, 1929)
Directed by Frank Lloyd. Screenplay by Agnes Christine Johnstone, titles by Harry Carr and Edwin Justus Mayer, adapted from the novel of E. Barrington by Forrest Halsey. Singing sequences by Vitaphone. Historical epic of Lord Nelson and Lady Hamilton.

Cast: Corinne Griffith (Lady Hamilton), Victor Varconi (Lord Nelson), H. B. Warner (Lord Hamilton), Ian Keith (Charles Grenville), William Conklin (George Romney), Marie Dressler (Mrs. Hart), Michael Vavitch (King Ferdinand). 105 minutes; screened at UCLA.

Hollywood Revue of 1929 (MGM, June 20, 1929)
Directed by Charles Reisner. Dialogue by Al Boasberg and Robert E. Hopkins. Musical revue introducing MGM roster of stars to sound through skits, songs, and dance.

Songs include "Singin' in the Rain," "You Were Meant for Me," "Strolling Through the Park One Day," "For I'm the Queen" (Marie), "Marie, Polly and Bess" (Marie Dressler, Polly Moran and Bessie Love), "Gotta Feelin' for You," and "Lon Chaney Will Get You If You Don't Watch Out."

Cast: Revue players include Conrad Nagel and Jack Benny (hosts), John Gilbert, Norma Shearer, William Haines, Joan Crawford, Anita Page, Marie Dressler, Polly Moran, Lionel Barrymore, Bessie Love, Nils Asther, the Brox Sisters, Charles King, Marion Davies, Buster Keaton, Charles King, Cliff Edwards, Gus Edwards, Karl Dane, George K. Arthur, Ann Dvorak, Gwen Lee, Laurel and Hardy, Albertina Rasch Ballet, Natacha Natova and Company, the Rounders, the Biltmore Quartet, Ernest Belcher's Dancing Tots. 130 minutes, color sequences by Technicolor; available on laser disc.

The Vagabond Lover (RKO, December 1, 1929)
Directed by Marshall Neilan. Screenplay by James Ashmore Creelman. A young orchestra conductor falls for the niece of a dotty society matron.

Songs include "The Vagabond Lover" (Vallee), "Heigh-Ho Everybody," "I Love You Believe Me I Love You."

Cast: Rudy Vallee (Rudy Bronson), Sally Blane (Jean), Marie Dressler (Ethel Whitehall), Charles Sellon (Officer Tuttle), Norman Peck (Swiftie), Danny O'Shea (Sam), Eddie Nugent (Sport), Nella Walker (Mrs. Tod Hunter), Malcolm Waite (Ted Grant), Alan Roscoe (manager), the Connecticut Yankees. 69 minutes; available on video.

Dangerous Females (Paramount, 1929)
Directed by William Watson. Screenplay by Florence Ryerson and Colin Clements. Two women mistake a preacher for a murderer, and vice-versa.

Cast: Marie Dressler (Sarah Bascom), Polly Moran (Tilly Cram). Two reels, screened at the Marie Dressler Foundation, Cobourg, Ontario.

Chasing Rainbows (MGM, January 10, 1930)
Alternate title: *The Road Show.*
Directed by Charles Reisner. Screenplay by Bess Meredyth, adapted by Wells Root, dialogue by Charles Reisner, Robert E. Hopkins, Kenyon Nicholson, and Al Boasberg. The backstage travails of a traveling theater troupe.

Songs include "Happy Days Are Here Again," "Poor But Honest" (solo for Marie), and "My Dynamic Personality" (solo for Marie).

Cast: Bessie Love (Carlie), Charles King (Terry), Jack Benny (Eddie), George K. Arthur (Loster), Marie Dressler (Bonnie), Polly Moran (Polly), Gwen Lee (Peggy), Nita Martan (Daphne), Eddie Phillips (Cordova), Youcca Troubertzkoy (Lanning). Eleven reels, color sequences by Technicolor (lost); viewed on TCM.

Anna Christie (MGM, March 14, 1930)
Directed by Clarence Brown. Screenplay by Frances Marion, based on the play by Eugene O'Neill. A somber drama of a prostitute who returns to her father and attempts to begin anew.

Cast: Greta Garbo (Anna Christie), Charles Bickford (Matt Burke), George Marion (Chris), Marie Dressler (Marthy Owens), James T. Mack (Johnny), Lee Phelps (Larry). 74 minutes; available on video, also listed at MOMA and GEH.

Note: *Anna Christie* was filmed as a silent movie in 1923 with Blanche Sweet at First National and in 1930 in German with Garbo at MGM. The English version was Garbo's first talkie.

The Girl Said No (MGM, April 4, 1930)
Directed by Sam Wood. Screenplay by Sarah Y. Mason, story by A. P. Younger, dialogue by Charles MacArthur. An irresponsible young playboy settles down with the right woman.

Cast: William Haines (Tom Ward), Leila Hyams (Mary Howe), Polly Moran (Polly), Marie Dressler (Hettie Brown), Francis X. Bushman, Jr. (McAndrews), Clara Blandick (Mrs. Ward), William Janney (Jimmy Ward), Frank "Junior" Coghlan (Eddie Ward). 90 minutes, viewed on commercial television.

The March of Time (MGM, 1930)
Directed by Charles Reisner. Revue featuring veterans and newcomers in song and dance.

Songs include "Ballet for Marie Dressler," "That's How It's Done on Stage," and "But Father Mustn't Know I'm Going on the Stage — He Thinks I'm a Shop Lifter," all sung by Marie.

Cast: Revue players include Marie Dressler, Joe Weber, Lew Fields, Polly Moran, Ramon Novarro, Bing Crosby, William Collier, Sr., Fay Templeton, Louis Mann, De Wolf Hopper, Charles King, the Duncan Sisters, Cliff Edwards, Karl Dane, Josephine Sabel, Barney Fagan.

Note: *The March of Time* was never released; some sequences were inserted into later productions.

One Romantic Night (United Artists, May 3, 1930)
Alternate title: *The Swan.*

Directed by Paul Stein. Screenplay by Melville Baker, adapted from the play *The Swan* by Ferenc Molnár. A princess falls for an astronomer rather than a prince.

Cast: Lillian Gish (Alexandra), Rod La Rocque (Prince Albert), Conrad Nagel (Dr. Nicholas Haller), Marie Dressler (Beatrice), O. P. Heggie (Father Benedict), Albert Conti (Count Lutzen), Edgar Norton (Colonel Wunderlich), Billie Bennett (Symphorosa), Philippe de Lacy (George), Byron Sage (Arsene), Barbara Leonard (Mitzi). Eight reels; screened at GEH.

Note: *One Romantic Night* was Gish's first talkie and Dressler's last feature made outside MGM. *The Swan* was filmed as a silent movie by Paramount in 1925 and remade by MGM in 1956.

Caught Short (MGM/Cosmopolitan, June 20, 1930)
Directed by Charles Reisner. Screenplay by Willard Mack and Joseph H. Johnson based on a gag story by Eddie Cantor. Comedy has Marie and Polly playing the stock market, losing big and then winning big.

Songs include "Going Spanish."

Cast: Marie Dressler (Marie Jones), Polly Moran (Polly Smith), Anita Page (Genevieve Jones), Charles Morton (William Smith), Thomas Conlin (Frankie), Douglas Haig (Johnny), Nanci Price (Priscilla), Greta Mann (Sophy), Herbert Prior (Mr. Frisby). 75 minutes; heard soundtrack only through private collector.

Note: A silent version of *Caught Short* was filmed to accommodate theaters not yet equipped for sound.

Let Us Be Gay (MGM, July 11, 1930)
Directed by Robert Z. Leonard. Screenplay by Frances Marion, based on the play by Rachel Crothers. A wife, with the help of a society dowager, plots to win back an erstwhile husband.

Cast: Norma Shearer (Kitty Brown), Rod La Rocque (Bob Brown), Marie Dressler (Mrs. Boucicault), Gilbert Emery (Townley), Hedda Hopper (Madge Livingston), Raymond Hackett (Bruce), Sally Eilers (Diane), Tyrrell Davis (Wallace), Wilfred Noy (Whitman). Eight reels; screened at the Roxie Theater, also listed at GEH.

Min and Bill (MGM, November 21, 1930)
Directed by George Hill. Screenplay by Frances Marion and Marion Jackson; based on the novel *Dark Star* by Lorna Moon. Comedy-drama of a proprietress of a seedy waterfront hotel who must give up the young woman she considers her daughter.

Cast: Marie Dressler (Min Divot), Wallace Beery (Bill), Marjorie Rambeau (Bella Pringle), Dorothy Jordan (Nancy Smith), Donald Dillaway (Dick Cameron), DeWitt Jennings (Groot), Russell Hopton (Alec Johnson). 69 minutes; available on video.

Note: Dressler won the 1930-31 Best Actress Academy Award for *Min and Bill.*

Reducing (MGM, January 16, 1931)
Directed by Charles Reisner. Screenplay by Willard Mack and Beatrice Banyard, with additional dialogue by Robert E. Hopkins and Zelda Sears. Country bumpkins invade the home and lives of their city relatives, with farce and romance ensuing.

Cast: Marie Dressler (Marie Truffle), Polly Moran (Polly Rochay), Anita Page (Vivian Truffle), William "Buster" Collier, Jr. (Johnnie Beasley), Lucien Littlefield (Elmer Truffle), Sally Eilers (Joyce Rochay), William Bakewell (Tommy Haverly), Billy Naylor (Jerry Truffle). 77 minutes; viewed on TCM.

Politics (MGM, July 31, 1931)
Directed by Charles Reisner. Screenplay by Wells Root, story by Robert E. Hopkins, dialogue by Zelda Sears and Malcolm Stuart Boylan. An inexperienced woman runs for mayor and wins on an anticorruption platform.

Cast: Marie Dressler (Hattie Burns), Polly Moran (Ivy), Roscoe Ates (Peter), Karen Morley (Myrtle), William Bakewell (Benny), John Miljan (Curango), Joan Marsh (Daisy), Tom McGuire (mayor), Kane Richmond (Nifty), Claire DuBrey (rally leader). 73 minutes, viewed on TCM.

Emma (MGM, January 2, 1932)
Directed by Clarence Brown. Screenplay by Leonard Praskins and Zelda Sears, story by Frances Marion. A faithful housekeeper marries her employer and must face his ungrateful children.

Cast: Marie Dressler (Emma Thatcher Smith), Jean Hersholt (Mr. Smith), Richard Cromwell (Ronnie Smith), Myrna Loy (Isabelle), John Miljan (district attorney), Purnell B. Pratt (Haskins), Leila Bennett (Matilda), Barbara Kent (gypsy), Kathryn

Crawford (Sue), George Meeker (Bill). 73 minutes; screened at Roxie.

Note: Dressler was nominated for the 1931-32 Best Actress Academy Award for *Emma*.

Prosperity (MGM, November 1, 1932)

Directed by Sam Wood. Screenplay by Zelda Sears and Eve Greene, story by Frank Butler and Sylvia Thalberg. A widowed bank president fights Depression panic to keep her family and community intact.

Cast: Marie Dressler (Maggie Warren), Polly Moran (Lizzie Praskins), Anita Page (Helen Praskins), Norman Foster (John Warren), Jacquie Lyn (Cissy), Jerry Tucker (Buster), Charles Giblyn (mayor), Frank Darien (Ezra Higgins), Henry Armetta (barber). 87 minutes; viewed on TCM.

The Christmas Party (MGM, 1932)

Directed by Charles Reisner. A lad uses an MGM soundstage to have a huge party.

Cast: As themselves — Jackie Cooper, Norma Shearer, Wallace Beery, Lionel Barrymore, Marie Dressler, Polly Moran, Marion Davies, Clark Gable, Anita Page, Leila Hyams. 12 minutes, screened at Roxie.

Tugboat Annie (MGM, July 28, 1933)

Directed by Mervyn LeRoy. Screenplay by Zelda Sears and Eve Greene, based on stories from the *Saturday Evening Post* by Norman Reilly Raine. A salty tugboat captain overcomes the heartache of filial misunderstanding and a dipsomaniacal husband.

Cast: Marie Dressler (Annie Brennan), Wallace Beery (Terry Brennan), Robert Young (Alec Brennan), Maureen O'Sullivan (Pat Severn), Willard Robertson (Red Severn), Tammany Young (Shif'-less), Frankie Darro (Alec as a boy), Jack Pennick (Pete), Willie Fung (Chow, the cook). 87 minutes; screened at UCLA.

Dinner at Eight (MGM, August 23, 1933)

Directed by George Cukor. Screenplay by Frances Marion, Herman Mankiewicz, and Donald Ogden Stewart, based on the play by George S. Kaufman and Edna Ferber. A New York society hostess plans a dinner party for guests preoccupied with intrigue and deceit.

Cast: Marie Dressler (Carlotta Vance), John Barrymore (Larry Renault), Wallace Beery (Dan Packard), Jean Harlow (Kitty Packard), Lionel Barrymore (Oliver Jordan), Lee Tracy (Max Kane), Edmund Lowe (Dr. Wayne Talbot), Billie Burke (Millicent Jordan), Madge Evans (Paula Jordan), Jean Hersholt (Jo Stengel), Karen Morley (Lucy Talbot), Louise Closser Hale (Hattie Loomis), Phillips Holmes (Ernest De Graff), May Robson (Mrs. Wendel), Ed Loomis (Grant Mitchell), Hilda Vaughn (Tina), Elizabeth Patterson (Miss Copeland). 113 minutes; available on video.

Note: *Dinner at Eight* was remade in 1989 for Turner Network Television with Lauren Bacall as Carlotta Vance.

Christopher Bean (MGM, November 17, 1933)

Alternate titles: *The Late Christopher Bean* and *Her Sweetheart.*

Directed by Sam Wood. Screenplay by Sylvia Thalberg and Laurence E. Johnson, based on the play *The Late Christopher Bean*, adapted by Sidney Howard from the French play *Prenez Garde à la Peinture* by René Fauchois. An artist's paintings become valuable after his death and his widow must protect his memory from greedy investors.

Cast: Marie Dressler (Abby), Lionel Barrymore (doctor), Beulah Bondi (wife), Helen Mack (Susan), Russell Hardie (Warren Creamer), Jean Hersholt (Rosen), H. B. Warner (Davenport), Helen Shipman (Ada). 90 minutes; screened at GEH.

(Some sources incorrectly list Dressler among the cast of the 1930 film *Call of the Flesh* with Ramon Novarro and Renee Adoree. She may have been assigned a supporting role in that film, most likely Mother Superior played by Nance O'Neil, but she was reassigned to other roles when *Anna Christie* became a hit.)

Appendix 3

Discography

All known recordings of songs from Marie Dressler's stage career are on Thomas Edison cylinders.

"Rastus Take Me Back" (coon song), recorded December 1909.

"I'm A-Goin' to Change My Man" (coon song), recorded March 1910.

"He's My Soft-Shelled Crab on Toast" (coon song), recorded May 1910.

"I'm Lookin' for an Angel (Without Wings)" from *Miss Prinnt*, recorded June 1910.

"Heaven Will Protect the Working Girl" from *Tillie's Nightmare*, recorded September 1910.

Notes

Abbreviations

AMPAS	The Margaret Herrick Library of the Center for Motion Picture Study at the Academy of Motion Picture Arts and Sciences, Beverly Hills, California.
DuBrey ms.	Unpublished memoirs of Claire DuBrey.
Duckling	*The Life Story of an Ugly Duckling*, by Marie Dressler, 1924.
LOC	Motion Picture, Broadcasting and Recorded Sound Division, Library of Congress.
Locke	Robinson Locke Scrapbook Collection, New York Public Library of the Performing Arts; vols. 163 and 164 are devoted to Marie Dressler.
Marion ms.	Frances Marion, "Hollywood," unpublished manuscript at the Frances Marion Collection, University of Southern California Cinema-Television Library.
MCNY	Museum of the City of New York.
MOS	*My Own Story*, by Marie Dressler, 1934.
"Private"	Adela Rogers St. Johns, "The Private Life of Marie Dressler," *Liberty*, May 13, 20, and 27 and June 3, 1933 (4 parts).
Raider	Roberta Raider (Sloan), "A Descriptive Study of the Acting of Marie Dressler," unpublished Ph.D. dissertation, University of Michigan, 1970.

Introduction

1. Marie Dressler file, Cleveland Public Library, Mar. 27, 1913.
2. *Cleveland News*, Mar. 4, 1907.
3. *Boston Herald*, Nov. 6, 1932.
4. *Theatre*, Oct. 1933, p. 39.
5. *Cincinnati Commercial*, Mar. 4, 1911.
6. Marie Dressler file, Free Library of Philadelphia, Feb. 1933.
7. Interview with author, Jan. 26, 1996.
8. Marie Dressler file, MCNY, Mar. 24, 1932.

9. Interview with author, Jan. 26, 1996.
10. *New York Post*, Marie Dressler file, MCNY.
11. Mayer to Gitta Parker and William Woodfield, *American Weekly* (date unknown).
12. *Los Angeles Post-Record*, Nov. 18, 1933.
13. Letter from Maureen O'Sullivan to the author, Jan. 1996.
14. Interview with author, Jan. 3, 1996.
15. Letter from Joseph Newman to the author, Mar. 14, 1996.
16. Interview with author, Jan. 26, 1996.
17. James Robert Parrish and Robert T. Leonard, *The Funsters*, p. 228.
18. Letter from Joan Marsh Morrill to the author, Jan. 28, 1996.
19. *New Movie Magazine*, Nov. 1932.
20. *Hollywood Spectator*, Aug. 29, 1931.
21. Interview with author, Jan. 3, 1996.
22. "Private," May 20, 1933, p. 11.

Chapter 1, The Koerbers

1. MOS, p. 11.
2. Letter from Mrs. Roy Sanford Powell to Roberta Raider, Nov. 1, 1969.
3. "Private," May 13, 1933, p. 22.
4. Ibid.
5. MOS, p. 24.
6. Ibid., p. 11.
7. "Private," May 13, 1933, p. 21.
8. Letter from Mrs. Roy Sanford Powell to Roberta Raider, Nov. 18, 1969.
9. Family History Center, Church of Jesus Christ of Latter-Day Saints.
10. Letter from Bruce C. Stinson to Edward R. Haynes, Dec. 7, 1992 (Marie Dressler Foundation, Cobourg); *Little Tales of Old Port Hope*, Marie Dressler Foundation, Cobourg, pp. 34–36.
11. Marie Dressler file, MCNY.
12. "Private," May 13, 1933, p. 23.
13. MOS, pp. 13–14.
14. *Duckling*, p. 10.
15. *Saturday Evening Post*, Sept. 10, 1932.
16. MOS, p. 3.
17. *Duckling*, p. 4.
18. "Private," May 13, 1933, p. 23.
19. MOS, p. 3.
20. "Private," May 13, 1933, p. 23.
21. Ibid.
22. MOS, p. 17.
23. "Private," May 13, 1933, p. 24.
24. *Cleveland Plain Dealer*, July 10, 1934.
25. *Bay City Times*, July 29, 1934.
26. News clipping, Hoyt Public Library, Saginaw, Michigan, as cited in Raider, p. 22.
27. "Private," May 13, 1933, p. 24; MOS, pp. 32–33.
28. MOS, pp. 33–34.

29. Letter from Mrs. Roy Sanford Powell to Roberta Raider, Jan. 6, 1969.
30. MOS, p. 37.

Chapter 2, The Apprentice

1. MOS, p. 60.
2. *Duckling*, p. 14.
3. *New York Telegraph*, June 8, 1909.
4. MOS, p. 40.
5. *Duckling*, p. 17.
6. Ouida, *Under Two Flags*, pp. 268–69.
7. "Private," May 20, 1933, p. 11.
8. "Private," May 20, 1933, p. 12.
9. Raider, p. 38.
10. MOS, p. 79.
11. Marie Dressler file, Free Library of Philadelphia.
12. Marie Dressler file, MCNY.
13. MOS, pp. 48–49.
14. Ibid., pp. 41–46.
15. *Hollywood Citizen News*, July 28, 1934.
16. *Duckling*, p. 15.
17. Ibid., p. 17.
18. MOS, p. 53.
19. Ibid.
20. Ibid., p. 57.
21. *New York Evening Post*, Aug. 2, 1934.
22. "Private," May 20, 1933, pp. 13–14; MOS, pp. 57–58.
23. "Private," May 20, 1933, p. 14.
24. Marie Dressler file, Free Library of Philadelphia.
25. MOS, pp. 53–54.
26. Ibid., pp. 54–55.
27. "Private," May 20, 1933, p. 14.
28. *Duckling*, pp. 33–34.
29. Ibid., p. 39.
30. "Private," May 20, 1933, p. 14.
31. *Duckling*, p. 42.
32. MOS, p. 68.
33. Theater Special Collection, Cleveland Public Library.
34. *Playbill*, Euclid Avenue Opera House, Theater Special Collection, Cleveland Public Library.
35. *Duckling*, p. 44.
36. Lewis C. Strang, *Celebrated Comedians*, p. 268.
37. Lewis C. Strang, *Prima Donnas and Soubrettes of Light Opera and Musical Comedy in America*, p. 181.
38. *Duckling*, p. 43.
39. Ibid., p. 25.
40. MOS, pp. 74–76.
41. *New York Dramatic Mirror*, June 4, 1892.
42. "Private," May 20, 1933, p. 15.
43. *Cleveland News Leader*, May 25, 1919.
44. *Duckling*, p. 101.

45. Marie Dressler file, Harvard Theater Collection.
46. *New York Dramatic Mirror*, Dec. 1898.
47. Foster Rhea Dulles, *America Learns to Play*, pp. 260–62.
48. *Duckling*, pp. 44–45.
49. MOS, p. 77; Linda Martin and Kerry Segrave, *Women in Comedy*, p. 49.
50. Douglas Gilbert, *American Vaudeville*, pp. 188–89.
51. *Duckling*, p. 52.
52. Ibid., p. 66.
53. MOS, p. 104, and *Long Island Daily Star*, Nov. 13, 1933.
54. MOS, p. 102.
55. Ibid., p. 108.
56. "Private," May 20, 1933, p. 15.
57. Ibid.
58. Strang, *Prima Donnas*, p. 31.
59. *Cosmopolitan*, Apr. 1922.
60. *Cleveland Plain Dealer*, July 29, 1934.
61. MOS, p. 84.
62. Lucius Beebe, *The Big Spenders*, p. 78; letter from Joseph J. O'Donohue IV to the author, Dec. 3, 1996.
63. *Liberty*, Nov. 9, 1929.
64. Beebe, *Spenders*, p. xiii.
65. *Star Weekly*, Dec. 5, 1914.
66. MOS, p. 87.
67. MOS, pp. 89–91; "Private," May 20, 1933, p. 15; John Burke, *Duet in Diamonds*, pp. 90–91; Parker Morell, *Lillian Russell: The Era of Plush*, pp. 146–47.
68. *Duckling*, p. 58.
69. Burke, *Duet*, p. 93.
70. *Los Angeles Evening Herald Express*, July 30, 1934.
71. *New York Dramatic Mirror*, Apr. 7, 1894.
72. Burke, *Duet*, p. 97.
73. Morell, *Lillian Russell*, pp. 152–53.

Chapter 3,
"Nothing to It but Dressler"

1. "Private," May 20, 1933, p. 15.
2. Ibid.
3. Adela Rogers St. Johns, *Some Are Born Great*, pp. 291–92.
4. Marriage certificate, New Jersey State Bureau of Vital Statistics.
5. *New York Clipper*, June 29, 1895.
6. *Duckling*, p. 47.
7. *New York Dramatic Mirror*, Feb. 8, 1896.
8. *New York Times*, Dec. 18, 1895.
9. Ibid.
10. *New York Dramatic Mirror*, Dec. 28, 1895.
11. Ibid.
12. "Private," May 20, 1933, p. 15.
13. MOS, p. 137.
14. Marie Dressler file, MCNY.
15. "Private," May 20, 1933, p. 15.
16. *New York Times*, Feb. 4, 1896.
17. Strang, *Prima Donnas*, p. 183.
18. Locke, vol. 163.
19. MOS, pp. 94–99.
20. *Duckling*, p. 64.
21. *New York Times*, Feb. 9, 1896.
22. MOS, pp. 107–8.
23. Ibid., pp. 108–9.
24. Ibid., pp. 97–98.
25. Ibid., pp. 114–15.
26. *New York Post*, Marie Dressler file, MCNY, 1934.
27. Marie Dressler file, MCNY, 1934.
28. Strang, *Prima Donnas*, pp. 182–83.
29. David Robinson, *The History of World Cinema*, p. 22; *New York Dramatic Mirror*, Mar. 13, 1897.
30. *Duckling*, pp. 88–90.
31. Beebe, *Spenders*, p. 108; letter from Joseph J. O'Donohue IV to the author, Dec. 3, 1996.
32. Beebe, *Spenders*, p. 108.
33. Benjamin McArthur, *Actors and American Culture 1880–1920*, p. 140.
34. *Duckling*, p. 152.
35. Locke vol. 163, Jan. 7, 1906.
36. Adela Rogers St. Johns, "The Irreplaceable Marie," *American Weekly*, p. 15 (Museum of Modern Art Library, New York).
37. Alfred L. Bernheim, *The Business of the Theater*, p. 59.
38. "Private," May 20, 1933, p. 15.
39. St. Johns, *Born Great*, p. 293.
40. *Shadowplay*, Jan. 1934, p. 76.
41. Edmond M. Gagey, *The San Francisco Stage*, p. 197.
42. *New York Times*, Apr. 26, 1898.
43. *New York Times*, Oct. 4, 1898.
44. *New York Telegraph*, Oct. 29, 1898.
45. *New York Sunday Telegraph*, May 11, 1902.
46. *Cleveland Plain Dealer*, Nov. 8, 1914.
47. Gerald Bordman, *American Musical Theater — A Chronicle*, pp. 165–66.
48. *New York Dramatic Mirror*, Dec. 29, 1900.
49. Locke, vol. 163.
50. Locke, vol. 163, Apr. 6, 1899.
51. Locke, vol. 163, May 22, 1899.
52. Locke, vol. 163, Aug. 1899.
53. Anthony Slide, *The Vaudevillians*, p. 39.
54. Letter from Joseph J. O'Donohue IV to the author, Dec. 3, 1996.
55. Anthony Slide, *The Encyclopedia of Vaudeville*, p. 115.
56. Locke, vol. 163.
57. Marie Dressler file, Harvard Theater Collection, 1906.

58. Locke, vol. 163.
59. *New York Journal*, Dec. 18, 1900.
60. Locke, vol. 163, Nov. 13, 1900.
61. *Cleveland Plain Dealer*, July 10, 1934.
62. *The Billboard*, Oct. 26, 1901.
63. Bordman, *Musical Theater*, p. 176.
64. *Duckling*, p. 76.
65. Locke, vol. 163.
66. Bordman, *Musical Theater*, p. 180.
67. Locke, vol. 163, Feb. 6, 1902.
68. Bordman, *Musical Theater*, p. 185.
69. *New York Dramatic Mirror*, Sept. 13, 1902.
70. *New York Times*, Sept. 7, 1902.
71. Locke, vol. 163, May 11, 1902.
72. Locke, vol. 163, Apr. 1902.
73. Locke, vol. 163, Apr. 1902.
74. Raider, p. 30.
75. Locke, vol. 163.
76. Locke, vol. 163, Oct. 24, 1902; *New York Dramatic Mirror*, Nov. 1, 1902.
77. Locke, vol. 163, Dec. 18, 1902.
78. *New York Dramatic Mirror*, Jan. 10, 1903.
79. Locke, vol. 163, Jan. 5, 1903.
80. Locke, vol. 163, Jan. 16, 1903.
81. Locke, vol. 163, Jan. 16, 1903.

Chapter 4, The London Ache

1. Locke, vol. 163, Jan. 17, 1903.
2. St. Johns, *Born Great*, p. 288.
3. Gilbert, *American Vaudeville*, pp. 216–17.
4. *Duckling*, p. 87.
5. *Morning Telegraph*, Apr. 19, 1903; letter from Moss MacWhirter to Roberta Raider, Oct. 3, 1969.
6. David Ewen, *Complete Book of the American Musical Theater*, p. 163.
7. *New York Telegraph*, May 13, 1903.
8. Locke, vol. 163, Mar. 27, 1904.
9. Locke, vol. 163, Mar. 1, 1904.
10. Locke, vol. 163.
11. Locke, vol. 163.
12. *New York Times*, Apr. 17, 1904.
13. Locke, vol. 163, June 18, 1904.
14. Lewis Strang, *Celebrated Comedians*, p. 117.
15. Ibid., p. 106.
16. Felix Isman, *Weber and Fields*, p. 180.
17. Ibid., p. 104.
18. *New York Dramatic Mirror*, Oct. 15, 1904.
19. "Private," May 27, 1933, p. 34.
20. Locke, vol. 163.
21. Daniel Blum, *Great Stars of the American Stage*, p. 76.
22. *New York Telegraph*, Oct. 21, 1904.
23. Locke, vol. 163, Oct. 21, 1904.
24. *The World*, Oct. 21, 1904.
25. *Saturday Evening Post*, Aug. 2, 1934.
26. *Chicago News*, Apr. 1905.
27. MOS, pp. 123–25.
28. *Toledo Blade*, Apr. 27, 1905.
29. *Chicago News*, May 16, 1905.
30. Locke, vol. 163.
31. "Private," May 20, 1933, p. 13.
32. Locke, vol. 163, Apr. 30, 1905.
33. Locke, vol. 163, Jan. 5, 1906.
34. *New York Post*, Dec. 31, 1905.
35. *Theatre*, Feb. 1906.
36. *New York American*, Jan. 3, 1906.
37. Locke, vol. 163, Jan. 21, 1906.
38. *Philadelphia Telegraph*, Oct. 16, 1906.
39. *New York American*, Jan. 3, 1906.
40. *New York Post*, Feb. 17, 1906.
41. Marie Dressler file, Harvard Theater Collection, 1906.
42. *New York World*, May 28, 1906.
43. *New York Times*, Mar. 4, 1906.
44. Locke, vol. 163, Mar. 3, 1906.
45. Locke, vol. 163.
46. *Cosmopolitan*, July 1922.
47. *New York Dramatic Mirror*, May 19, 1906.
48. *New York Telegraph*, May 10, 1906.
49. *New York Mail*, May 28, 1906.
50. *New York Telegraph*, May 25, 1906.
51. Locke, vol. 481.
52. Marie Dressler file, Harvard Theater Collection, 1906.
53. *New York American*, July 20, 1906.
54. Locke, vol. 163, Feb. 12, 1907.
55. Locke, vol. 163, Apr. 1, 1907.
56. *Corning Evening Leader*, Dec. 1, 1921.
57. Church records, Corning–Painted Post Roman Catholic Community.
58. Marie Dressler file, Harvard Theater Collection, 1911.
59. *New York Times*, Dec. 2, 1921.
60. Marie Dressler file, Harvard Theater Collection, 1911.
61. Mack Sennett, *King of Comedy*, p. 188.
62. Ibid.
63. MOS, pp. 177–78.
64. *New York Telegraph*, Sept. 17, 1907.
65. *New York Herald*, Oct. 30, 1907.
66. *Cleveland Plain Dealer*, Aug. 31, 1913.
67. Locke, vol. 163.
68. Locke, vol. 163, Nov. 24, 1907.
69. Marie Dressler file, Harvard Theater Collection, Oct. 29, 1907.
70. *New York Telegraph*, Nov. 10, 1907.
71. Locke, vol. 163, Apr. 19, 1908.
72. Locke, vol. 163.
73. *Times* (London), Nov. 3, 1907.
74. *New York Herald*, Mar. 5, 1908.
75. Locke, vol. 163, Mar 15, 1908.
76. *Philadelphia Times*, Sept. 9, 1909.
77. *New York Times*, Aug. 11, 1908.
78. *Variety*, Apr. 26, 1908.

79. *New York Telegraph*, Apr. 24, 1908.
80. *New York Dramatic Mirror*, May 2, 1908.
81. *New York Telegraph*, Dec. 10, 1907.
82. *Corning Evening Leader*, Dec. 3, 1921.
83. U.S. census records.
84. Locke, vol. 163.
85. Locke, vol. 163, Nov. 16, 1908.
86. *Duckling*, pp. 170–71.
87. Locke, vol. 163, Mar. 13, 1909.
88. Locke, vol. 163.
89. Ibid.
90. Ibid.
91. *New York Times*, Mar. 16, 1909.
92. Locke, vol. 163.
93. Locke, vol. 163, Mar. 30, 1909.
94. *New York Times*, Apr. 9, 1909.
95. *Duckling*, p. 103.
96. *New York Times*, Aug. 22, 1909.
97. Locke, vol. 163, May 20, 1909.
98. *Duckling*, pp. 98–99.
99. Bordman, *Musical Theater*, p. 250.
100. Locke, vol. 163, June 5, 1909.
101. *New York Star*, June 19, 1909.
102. *Variety*, July 17, 1909.
103. *Duckling*, p. 103; *New York Times*, Jan. 27, 1910.
104. *New York Times*, Sept. 27, 1923.
105. *San Francisco Call*, Sept. 4, 1909; *Philadelphia Times*, Sept. 9, 1909.
106. Marie Dressler file, Free Library of Philadelphia, Nov. 27, 1932.
107. Marie Dressler file, MCNY.
108. Ibid.
109. Shubert Archive.

Chapter 5, A Wretch Named Tillie

1. Shubert Archive.
2. Ibid.
3. *Cosmopolitan*, July 1922.
4. Nine frames of a paper print from LOC. The details of the making of this film are lost. There is no script for "Marie Dressler" at the Edison Collection of the Museum of Modern Art.
5. Charles W. Stein, *American Vaudeville as Seen by Its Contemporaries*, pp. 343–44.
6. *Edison Phonograph Monthly*, Jan., Feb., Apr., and July 1910.
7. *New York Times*, Dec. 25, 1909.
8. Shubert Archive.
9. *Chicago Tribune*, Jan. 3, 1910.
10. Locke, vol. 164, Jan. 8, 1910.
11. *Chicago Record*, Jan. 4, 1910.
12. Shubert Archive, Jan. 4, 1910.
13. MOS, pp. 152–53.
14. Locke, vol. 164, Mar. 10, 1912, and MOS, pp. 162–63.
15. Charles Neilson Gattey, *Luisa Tetrazzini: The Florentine Nightingale*, pp. 134–35.
16. Shubert Archive, Jan. 25, 1910.
17. Shubert Archive, Jan. 26, 1910.
18. Shubert Archive, Feb. 1, 1910.
19. Shubert Archive, Feb. 10, 1910.
20. Shubert Archive, Feb. 5, 1910.
21. Shubert Archive, Feb. 10, 1910.
22. Shubert Archive, Mar. 11, 1910.
23. Locke, vol. 164.
24. Shubert Archive, Mar. 11, 1910.
25. Shubert Archive, Feb. 22, 1910.
26. Ibid.
27. Ibid.
28. *Pittsburgh Leader*, Locke, vol. 164.
29. MOS, p. 153.
30. Shubert Archive, Mar. 11, 1910.
31. Locke, vol. 164.
32. *Chicago Journal*, May 10, 1910.
33. *New York Times*, May 6, 1910.
34. *Duckling*, pp. 113–14.
35. Ibid., p. 116
36. Ibid.
37. *New York Post*, Aug. 3, 1934.
38. *San Francisco Chronicle*, Apr. 2, 1911.
39. *Toledo News Beacon*, Feb. 17, 1911.
40. *Cincinnati Commercial*, Mar. 10, 1912.
41. *Theatre*, Locke, vol. 164.
42. MOS, p. 116.
43. LOC, Aug. 19, 1910.
44. *New York Review*, Nov. 5, 1910.
45. *Duckling*, p. 122.
46. *San Francisco Chronicle*, Apr. 2, 1911.
47. Frances Marion, *Off with Their Heads!* pp. 17–19.
48. Marion ms., p. 26.
49. Ibid., p. 27.
50. Ibid., p. 28.
51. MOS, p. 231.
52. *Duckling*, p. 117.
53. *New York Telegraph*, June 4, 1913; *Washington Star*, Oct. 12, 1913.
54. Marion ms., p. 101.
55. MOS, pp. 156–57.
56. *Duckling*, pp. 121–22.
57. *Duckling*, p. 119.
58. Marie Dressler file, Harvard Theater Collection, 1912.
59. Ibid.
60. Shubert Archive, July 25, 1911.
61. Shubert Archive.
62. Ibid., Oct. 19, 1911.
63. Ibid., Oct. 20, 1911.
64. *Toledo Blade*, Dec. 21, 1911.
65. *Variety*, Feb. 3, 1912.
66. *Columbus Journal*, Mar. 17, 1912.
67. Locke, vol. 164.
68. Armond Fields and L. Marc Fields, *From the Bowery to Broadway*, p. 321.

69. MOS, pp. 129–30.
70. *New York Times*, Nov. 22, 1912.
71. Locke, vol. 164, Nov. 1912.
72. *Duckling*, pp. 80–81.
73. Ibid., p. 82.
74. Ibid., p. 83.
75. *New York Telegraph*, Jan. 3, 1913.
76. *New York Telegraph*, Apr. 22, 1913.
77. *New York Dramatic Mirror*, Feb. 26, 1913.
78. Ibid.
79. Marie Dressler file, Cleveland Public Library, Mar. 27, 1913.
80. Locke, vol. 164, June 17, 1913.
81. *Chicago Tribune*, June 19, 1913.
82. Locke, vol. 164, July 16, 1913.
83. MOS, p. 158; *Duckling*, p. 118.
84. Locke, vol. 164.
85. *Philadelphia Record*, Oct. 5, 1913.
86. *San Francisco Examiner*, Nov. 23, 1913.

Chapter 6,
Mack Sennett's Grand Idea

1. Locke, vol. 164; Shubert Archive.
2. *San Francisco Examiner*, Jan. 27, 1914.
3. Ibid.
4. *San Francisco Examiner*, Jan. 28, 1914.
5. *New York Dramatic Mirror*, Feb. 11, 1914.
6. Cecil Smith, *Musical Comedy in America*, p. 195.
7. *San Francisco Examiner*, Feb. 10, 11, and 17, 1914.
8. *San Francisco Examiner*, Mar. 9, 1914; Shubert Archive.
9. *San Francisco Daily News*, Mar. 10, 1914; *Variety*, Mar. 11, 1914; Geoffrey Bell, *The Golden Gate and the Silver Screen*, p. 59.
10. *San Francisco Examiner*, Mar. 11, 1914.
11. *Los Angeles Times*, Mar. 12, 1914.
12. *San Francisco News*, Mar. 10, 1914.
13. Ibid.
14. Sennett, *King of Comedy*, pp. 21–24.
15. Charles Chaplin, *My Autobiography*, p. 138.
16. Frank Magill, ed., *Magill's Survey of Cinema*, vol. 1, 1982; Sennett, *King of Comedy*, pp. 183–88. The 1974 Broadway musical *Mack and Mabel* is based on the relationship of Sennett and Normand.
17. Marion, *Off with Their Heads!* pp. 3–4.
18. *Duckling*, p. 125.
19. Marion ms., pp. 33–38.
20. Sennett, *King of Comedy*, p. 187.
21. Andy Edmonds, *The Untold Story of Roscoe "Fatty" Arbuckle*, p. 77.
22. Leonard Maltin, *The Great Movie Comedians*, pp. 92–93.
23. *Collier's*, Nov. 1, 1930, p. 66.
24. Gary Carey, *All the Stars in Heaven — Louis B. Mayer's MGM*, p. 27.

25. *Vancouver World*, May 11, 1915.
26. *New York Dramatic Mirror*, Nov. 4, 1914.
27. *Variety*, Jan. 1, 1915.
28. *New York Telegraph*, Jan. 13, 1915.
29. Shubert Archive, Nov. 2, 1914.
30. Locke, vol. 164.
31. *Philadelphia Telegraph*, Mar. 20, 1915.
32. *New York Herald*, Dec. 29, 1914.
33. *New York Review*, Jan. 16, 1915.
34. Locke, vol. 164.
35. *New York Review*, Jan. 16, 1915.
36. Marie Dressler file, Cleveland Public Library, July 26, 1915.
37. Warner Bros. production files, USC Cinema-Television Library.
38. Letter from Marie Dressler to Sigmund Lubin, Dec. 22, 1915 (Warner Bros. production files, USC Cinema-Television Library).
39. *American Film Institute Catalog:* Feature Films, 1911–1920, p. 934.
40. Lubin scrapbook (Free Library of Philadelphia).
41. *Pittsburgh Leader*, Oct. 10, 1915.
42. *New York Telegraph*, Sept. 6, 1915.
43. *New York Dramatic Mirror*, Feb. 6, 1915.
44. Marion ms., pp. 80–82.
45. *Motion Picture World*, Oct. 16, 1915.
46. *New York Dramatic Mirror*, Oct. 16, 1915.
47. Lubin scrapbook (Free Library of Philadelphia).
48. *Variety*, Oct. 1, 1915.
49. *New York Times*, May 13 and Aug. 7, 1915; Locke, vol. 164; Kalton C. Lahue and Terry Brewer, *Kops and Custards*, pp. 65–69.
50. *New York Clipper*, Dec. 6, 1916.
51. *New York Times*, Aug. 15, 1916.
52. *American Film Institute Catalog:* Feature Films, 1911–1920, p. 934.
53. *New York Post*, Marie Dressler file, MCNY, 1934.
54. "Private," June 3, 1933, p. 35; Cari Beauchamp, *Without Lying Down*, p. 63.
55. Marion ms., p. 103.
56. Ibid., pp. 102–3.
57. Ibid., p. 171.
58. *New York Times*, July 29, 1934.
59. *Variety*, Nov. 10, 1916.
60. MOS, p. 171.
61. Letter from Frances Marion to Hedda Hopper (AMPAS Special Collections).
62. *New York Dramatic Mirror*, Jan. 27, 1917.
63. *New York Dramatic Mirror*, Feb. 6, 1915.
64. Stephan Thernstrom, *A History of the American People, Vol. 2: Since 1865*, p. 546.
65. Ibid.
66. *The Public Papers of Woodrow Wilson*, vol. 5, p. 22.
67. MOS, p. 172.

Chapter 7, Give Till It Hurts

1. *New York Telegraph*, Locke, vol. 164.
2. *New York Times*, June 26, 1916.
3. *New York Telegraph*, May 14, 1917; *New York Times*, May 24, 1917.
4. *New York Times*, May 25, 1919.
5. Ibid.
6. *New York Times*, Dec. 19, 1914.
7. Hedda Hopper, *From Under My Hat*, pp. 86–87; Marie Dressler file, MCNY.
8. Marion, *Off with Their Heads!* pp. 45–46.
9. Marion, *Off with Their Heads!* p. 155.
10. Marion ms., p. 298.
11. Marie Dressler file, Cleveland Public Library, Mar. 27, 1913.
12. "Private," May 27, 1933, p. 36.
13. Locke, vol. 164.
14. *The New Yorker*, Sept. 6, 1996, p. 84. According to writer Barbara Probst Solomon (personal communication), primary sources say the Lewis party took place in June 1917.
15. "Private," June 3, 1933, p. 38.
16. *Los Angeles Record*, Oct. 7, 1933.
17. "Private," May 27, 1933, p. 36.
18. MOS, pp. 173–74.
19. *New York Telegraph*, Nov. 25, 1917.
20. *Moving Picture World*, Dec. 29, 1917.
21. *New York Times*, Feb. 19, 1918.
22. *Pittsburgh Leader*, Oct. 10, 1915.
23. McAdoo press statement, Apr. 28, 1917, LOC.
24. William McAdoo, *The Crowded Years*, p. 374.
25. Ibid., pp. 378–79.
26. Ibid., p. 386.
27. David M. Kennedy, *Over There*, p. 106.
28. MOS, p. 178.
29. *Duckling*, p. 142.
30. *San Antonio Light*, Oct. 7, 1917.
31. David Robinson, *Chaplin: His Life and Art*, p. 237.
32. *Duckling*, p. 142.
33. Hopper, *My Hat*, p. 86.
34. Locke, vol. 164.
35. *Duckling*, pp. 141–42.
36. *Toledo Times*, Feb. 21, 1918.
37. *Duckling*, p. 144.
38. Ibid., p. 143.
39. Locke, vol. 164, Oct. 5, 1918.
40. "Private," May 27, 1933, p. 36; Locke, vol. 164.
41. *Kansas City Star*, Apr. 9, 1918.
42. *Los Angeles Times*, June 5, 1918.
43. Elinar Lauritzen and Gunnar Lundquist, *American Film Index 1916–1920*, p. 87; *Moving Picture World*, Aug. 11, 1917.
44. *Duckling*, pp. 145–47; *Variety*, Apr. 4, 1919; *New York Clipper*, Apr. 23, 1919.
45. *New York Dramatic Mirror*, Apr. 18, 1919.
46. *Cleveland News Leader*, May 25, 1919.
47. *New York Times*, Feb. 24, 1919.
48. MOS, pp. 183–84.
49. "Private," May 13, 1933, p. 24.
50. MOS, p. 184.
51. MOS, p. 118.
52. Alfred Harding, *The Revolt of the Actors*, p. 3.
53. Ibid., pp. 3–9.
54. Brooks Atkinson, *Broadway*, pp. 183–84.
55. *New York Post*, Marie Dressler file, MCNY.
56. Abel Green and Joe Laurie, Jr., *Show Biz from Vaude to Video*, p. 284.
57. Locke, vol. 164, Sept. 9, 1919.
58. Harding, *Revolt*, p. 116.
59. *Screenland*, Marie Dressler file, Free Library of Philadelphia.
60. Harding, *Revolt*, p. 208.
61. *Duckling*, p. 145.
62. Harding, *Revolt*, pp. 116–17.
63. *Cleveland Plain Dealer*, Oct. 19, 1919.
64. Harding, *Revolt*, pp. 150–52.
65. Locke, vol. 164, Aug. 13, 1919.
66. *New York Times*, Sept. 9, 1919.
67. "Private," May 27, 1933, p. 33.
68. John McCabe, *George M. Cohan*, pp. 149–50.
69. Green and Laurie, *Show Biz*, p. 334.
70. Locke, vol. 164.
71. *New York Times*, Aug. 27, 1919.
72. *Cleveland Plain Dealer*, Oct. 19, 1919.
73. Harding, *Revolt*, p. 557.
74. Harding, *Revolt*, p. 235, and *New York Times*, Sept. 9, 1919.
75. Green and Laurie, *Show Biz*, p. 334, and *New York Dramatic Mirror*, Sept. 11, 1919.
76. Atkinson, *Broadway*, p. 184.

Chapter 8, Ghosts

1. Bernheim, *Business*, pp. 75–84.
2. *New York Times*, Sept. 9, 1919; *New York Dramatic Mirror*, Sept. 18, 1919.
3. Harding, *Revolt*, p. 283.
4. Ibid., p. 284.
5. Ibid.; *Variety*, Nov. 14, 1919.
6. *Variety*, Apr. 23, 1920.
7. Marion ms., pp. 170–73.
8. Marion, *Off with Their Heads!* p. 155.
9. Ibid.; Hopper, *My Hat*, p. 88.
10. *Focus on Film*, Spring 1976, p. 24.
11. Marion ms., p. 299.
12. "Private," June 3, 1933, p. 33.
13. MOS, p. 181.
14. "Private," June 3, 1933, p. 33.
15. MOS, p. 188.

16. Marion ms., p. 299.
17. Marie Dressler file, Free Library of Philadelphia.
18. Stanley Green, *The Great Clowns of Broadway*, pp. 85–88; Bordman, *Musical Theater*, p. 357.
19. Ewen, *Complete Book*, p. 301.
20. Fields and Fields, *Bowery to Broadway*, p. 399.
21. Marie Dressler file, Free Library of Philadelphia.
22. *Cleveland Plain Dealer*, Nov. 6, 1921.
23. Letter from Marie Dressler to Archie Bell (Theater Special Collections, Cleveland Public Library).
24. *Variety*, Dec. 2, 1921; Cook County, Ill., Vital Records.
25. Marie Dressler file, Harvard Theater Collection.
26. Ibid.
27. *Corning* (New York) *Evening Leader*, Dec. 3, 1921.
28. Ibid.
29. *San Francisco Examiner*, Mar. 11, 1914.
30. *New York Post*, Marie Dressler file, MCNY, 1934.
31. MOS, p. 137.
32. Marie Dressler file, New York Public Library of the Performing Arts.
33. Marie Dressler file, MCNY.
34. Ibid.
35. MOS, p. 178.
36. MOS, p. 94; *Liberty*, Nov. 23, 1929.
37. Letter from Joseph J. O'Donohue IV to the author, Dec. 3, 1996.
38. "Private," May 13, 1933, p. 22.
39. Ibid.
40. *Duckling*, p. 186.
41. MOS, p. 150.
42. Ibid., pp. 200–201.
43. "Private," June 3, 1933, p. 36; MOS, pp. 205–6.
44. Adela Rogers St. Johns, *Love, Laughter and Tears*, p. 38.
45. *Duckling*, p. 193.
46. *New York Review*, Feb. 24, 1923.
47. Marion, *Off with Their Heads!* p. 127.
48. *New York Times*, Jan. 25, 1923.
49. Shubert Archive.
50. Bordman, *Musical Theater*, p. 377.
51. "Private," May 20, 1933, p. 12.
52. Marion, *Off with Their Heads!* pp. 127–30; Marion ms., p. 251.
53. *New York Times*, July 29, 1934.
54. *New York Times*, Sept. 27 and Oct. 7, 1923.
55. Lionel Barrymore, *We Barrymores*, p. 219.
56. Robert McAlmon and Kay Boyle, *Being Geniuses Together*, p. 146.
57. *Time*, July 28, 1930.
58. *New York Times*, Nov. 28, 1923.
59. *Los Angeles Evening Herald Express*, July 4, 1934.
60. Marie Dressler file, Free Library of Philadelphia, Dec. 11, 1932.
61. Marie Dressler file, Free Library of Philadelphia.
62. *New York Times*, July 29, 1934.
63. MOS, pp. 209–10.
64. "Private," May 27, 1933, p. 37.
65. *New York Telegraph*, Sept. 2, 1926; "Private," June 3, 1933, p. 32.
66. *New York Times*, Sept. 10, 1925.
67. *New York Times*, Marie Dressler file, New York Public Library of the Performing Arts.
68. MOS, p. 213.
69. *New York Times*, Oct. 20, 1925.
70. Gilbert, *American Vaudeville*, pp. 96–97.
71. Ibid., p. 354; *Variety*, Oct. 21, 1925.
72. Green and Laurie, *Show Biz*, p. 278.
73. *Boston Transcript*, May 11, 1926.
74. *Duckling*, p. 147.
75. Ibid., p. 231.
76. Ibid., p. 209.
77. "Private," May 27, 1933, p. 37.

Chapter 9, The Undying Affection of Friends

1. Maltin, *Comedians*, p. 93.
2. *Classic Film Collectors #35*; Peter Bogdanovich, *Allan Dwan—The Last Pioneer*, pp. 81–82.
3. "Private," May 27, 1933, p. 37, and MOS, pp. 223–24.
4. "Private," June 3, 1933, p. 32.
5. MOS, p. 221.
6. "Private," June 3, 1933, p. 32.
7. *Collier's*, Nov. 1, 1930.
8. Shubert Archive, Oct. 15, 1928.
9. St. Johns, *Love*, p. 40.
10. Marion ms., p. 295.
11. "Private," June 3, 1933, p. 35.
12. Marie Dressler file, Free Library of Philadelphia.
13. Marion ms., p. 297.
14. Ibid., p. 330.
15. MOS, p. 234.
16. "Private," June 3, 1933, p. 36.
17. Print ads, *The Callahans and the Murphys*, June 1927.
18. *New York Times*, July 12, 1927.
19. *Variety*, July 13, 1927.
20. Marion ms., p. 300.
21. MGM Collection, USC Cinema-Television Library.
22. AMPAS Special Collections and *Historical Journal of Film, Radio and Television* 10, no. 1 (1990): p. 41.

23. *Irish World*, Aug. 13, 1927.
24. Marion ms., p. 302. After it was withdrawn from circulation, *The Callahans and the Murphys* was "tossed into the discard," according to Frances. It is absent from the MGM/Turner film inventory and all other major archives, and it is widely assumed to be destroyed.
25. *Los Angeles Times*, Jan. 17, 1928.
26. Marie Dressler file, Free Library of Philadelphia.
27. "Private," June 3, 1933, p. 36.
28. Letter from Edward Everett Horton to Roberta Raider, Dec. 30, 1969; Parish and Leonard, *Funsters*, p. 224.
29. MOS, p. 245.
30. AMPAS Special Collections.
31. *Variety*, Mar. 21, 1928.
32. Richard Schickel, *The Men Who Made the Movies*, pp. 145–46.
33. *Photoplay*, Mar. 1930.
34. John Douglas Eames, *The MGM Story*, p. 44.
35. *New York Times*, Apr. 23, 1928.
36. Marion, *Off with Their Heads!* p. 175; King Vidor, *A Tree Is a Tree*, pp. 159–60; Fred Lawrence Guiles, *Marion Davies*, p. 187.
37. Hopper, *My Hat*, p. 87. William Randolph Hearst adored Dressler. At a party he gave at the Cocoanut Grove for returning aviator Charles Lindbergh, protocol dictated that Hearst dance first with hostess Marion Davies. Out of the huge gathering, Hearst reportedly chose Dressler as his first partner.
38. Warner Bros. production files, USC Cinema-Television Library.
39. *New York Times*, Mar. 23, 1929.
40. Mason Wiley and Damien Bona, *Inside Oscar: The Unofficial History of the Academy Awards*, p. 45. Lloyd was also cited by the Academy for his direction of *Weary River* and *Drag*, two other 1929 releases from First National.
41. *New Movie Magazine*, Jul. 1931.

Chapter 10, The Raspberry Season

1. David Robinson, *The History of World Cinema*, pp. 155–63; Marion ms., pp. 332b–34 and 353–54.
2. MOS, p. 246.
3. Hopper, *My Hat*, p. 190.
4. Marion ms., p. 331e.
5. Hopper, *My Hat*, pp. 190–91.
6. Ibid., p. 193.
7. *Los Angeles Times*, Aug. 5, 1929.
8. Harding, *Revolt*, pp. 418–19.
9. *Los Angeles Times*, June 12, 1929.
10. Harding, *Revolt*, p. 533.
11. Tino Balio, ed., *The American Film Industry*, p. 311.
12. Beth Day, *This Was Hollywood*, p. 81.
13. Letter from "Major" Carl Roup to the author, Jan. 28, 1996.
14. Marion, *Off with Their Heads!* p. 99.
15. Charles Higham, *Louis B. Mayer: Merchant of Dreams*, p. 170.
16. Ethan Mordden, *Movie Star*, p. 126.
17. Elinor Hughes, *Famous Stars of Filmdom*, p. 176.
18. *New York Times*, Aug. 15, 1929.
19. *Photoplay*, Sept. 1929.
20. *Brooklyn Times*, Aug. 15, 1929.
21. MGM Collection, USC Cinema-Television Library.
22. Marie Dressler file, Harvard Theater Collection.
23. Letter from Marie Dressler to Florence Ryerson and Colin Clements, Feb. 9, 1930 (Princeton University Library Collection).
24. Marion ms., pp. 345–46.
25. *New York Times*, Feb. 22, 1930.
26. Richard Barrios, *A Song in the Dark*, p. 326.
27. Rudy Vallee, *Let the Chips Fall*, pp. 34–35.
28. Ibid., p. 39.
29. George Eells, *Hedda and Louella*, p. 345.
30. Vallee, *Chips*, pp. 38–40.
31. Ibid., pp. 39–43.
32. Interview with author, Nov. 12, 1996.
33. Ibid.
34. *Variety*, Dec. 4, 1929.
35. *Ladies Home Journal*, Aug. 1929.
36. AMPAS Special Collections; *Architectural Digest*, Apr. 1996.
37. Marie Dressler file, Free Library of Philadelphia.
38. *Los Angeles Evening Herald Express*, July 7, 1930.
39. *Classic Images*, Dec. 1993 and Jan. 1994; *Motion Picture Studio Directory*, Oct. 1916.
40. Marie Dressler file, Free Library of Philadelphia.
41. Letter from Sierra Pecheur to the author, Aug. 14, 1996.
42. Letter from Sierra Pecheur to the author, Jan. 24, 1997; DuBrey ms.
43. "La Quinta and Club History," *La Quinta Historical Society*, p. 8.
44. Letter from Fred Rice to the author, Sept. 2, 1996.
45. AMPAS Special Collections; the Montecito History Committee of the Montecito Library and Hall; DuBrey ms.
46. Letter from Sierra Pecheur to the author, Jan. 24, 1997.

Chapter 11, Anna Christie

1. Alexander Walker, *Garbo: A Portrait*, p. 109. Walker dates this memo Oct. 24, 1930. An

error occurred somewhere. *Anna Christie*, Garbo's debut on sound, opened in March 1930.
   2. Robert Payne, *The Great Garbo*, p. 175; Marion ms., pp. 361–62.
   3. Peter Harry Brown and Pamela Ann Brown, *The MGM Girls*, pp. 112–13.
   4. AMPAS Special Collections.
   5. Marion ms., p. 361–362.
   6. Payne, *Garbo*, p. 175.
   7. Brown and Brown, *MGM Girls*, p. 113.
   8. Letter from Joseph J. O'Donohue IV to the author, Nov. 13, 1996.
   9. Antoni Gronowicz, *Garbo: Her Story*, p. 311.
   10. Payne, *Garbo*, p. 176.
   11. *Hollywood Citizen News*, Apr. 5, 1932.
   12. Barry Paris, *Garbo*, p. 218.
   13. Ibid., p. 289.
   14. Clarence Brown interview in Turner Entertainment Company, *The MGM Story: When the Lion Roars*.
   15. *Screenland*, June 1931, pp. 19–20.
   16. Mercedes de Acosta, *Here Lies the Heart*, p. 234.
   17. Pare Lorentz, *Lorentz on Film*, p. 40.
   18. MOS, pp. 251–52.
   19. AMPAS Special Collections.
   20. MOS, p. 249.
   21. *Time*, Aug. 7, 1933.
   22. AMPAS Special Collections.
   23. Ibid.
   24. Vidor, *Tree*, pp. 190–91; Bob Thomas, *Thalberg—Life and Legend*, p. 223.
   25. *Los Angeles Times*, Jan. 21, 1930.
   26. Marion, *Off with Their Heads!* p. 199.
   27. Day, *Hollywood*, p. 100.
   28. AMPAS Special Collections.
   29. Richard Schickel, *The Stars*, p. 134.
   30. *Film Spectator*, Jan. 18, 1930.
   31. *Life*, Mar. 21, 1930, p. 20.
   32. *Variety*, Mar. 19, 1930.
   33. Mordden, *Star*, p. 127.
   34. Payne, *Garbo*, p. 176.
   35. Ibid., pp. 168–69.
   36. AMPAS Special Collections.
   37. *New York Herald Tribune*, Mar. 15, 1930.
   38. *Nation*, Apr. 2, 1930.
   39. *Magill's Survey of Cinema*, p. 94.
   40. Ibid.
   41. Paris, *Garbo*, p. 570.
   42. AMPAS Special Collections.
   43. Ibid.
   44. *Shadowplay*, Jan. 1934.
   45. MOS, p. 251.
   46. Marie Dressler file, Theater Research Library, University of Wisconsin, Madison, as cited in Raider, p. 228.
   47. MOS, pp. 248–49.
   48. MOS, p. 152.
   49. *New York Times*, June 22, 1930.
   50. Ibid.
   51. *Hollywood Daily Citizen*, Apr. 7, 1930.

Chapter 12, Working

   1. *New York Times*, July 29, 1934.
   2. *Boston Herald*, Nov. 6, 1932.
   3. Day, *Hollywood*, pp. 100–101.
   4. Interview with author, Feb. 8, 1996.
   5. *New Movie Magazine*, Apr. 1930.
   6. Interview with author, Feb. 8, 1996.
   7. MGM accounting ledger, AMPAS Special Collections.
   8. Barrios, *Song in the Dark*, pp. 323–41; Eames, *MGM*, pp. 72, 95; Fields and Fields, *Bowery to Broadway*, pp. 495–98; MGM Collection, USC Cinema-Television Library.
   9. Letter from Marie Dressler to William Wolff, Dec. 16, 1929.
   10. Marie Dressler file, New York Public Library of the Performing Arts.
   11. Interview with author, Feb. 24, 1997.
   12. *Los Angeles Times*, Feb. 2, 1930.
   13. *Variety*, June 4, 1930.
   14. *Life*, June 27, 1930.
   15. *New York Times*, June 29, 1930.
   16. *Los Angeles Examiner*, Jan. 15, 1930.
   17. Day, *Hollywood*, p. 44.
   18. *New York Times*, June 21, 1930.
   19. *Life*, July 18, 1930.
   20. Day, *Hollywood*, p. 72.
   21. MOS, p. 253.
   22. *Los Angeles Times*, Sept. 14, 1930.
   23. Interview with author, Jan. 3, 1996.
   24. Frank "Junior" Coghlan, *They Still Call Me Junior*, p. 111.
   25. Martin and Segrave, *Women in Comedy*, pp. 97–99.
   26. *Los Angeles Record*, May 1, 1930.
   27. Polly Moran, "Marie Dressler," as cited in Raider, p. 27.
   28. Marie Dressler file, Free Library of Philadelphia.
   29. MOS, p. 258.
   30. Marion ms., p. 359.
   31. Ibid.
   32. Lawrence J. Quirk, *Norma—The Story of Norma Shearer*, p. 117.
   33. Marion ms., p. 360.
   34. Hopper, *Hat*, p. 89.
   35. *Variety*, July 16, 1930.
   36. *Los Angeles Times*, Sept. 14, 1930.
   37. *Theatre*, Oct. 1930.
   38. *New York Times*, May 10, 1930.
   39. *New York Times*, June 22, 1930.
   40. *New York World*, Sept. 13, 1930.

41. *Time*, July 28, 1930.
42. *Los Angeles Evening Herald Express*, July 28, 1930.
43. AMPAS Special Collections.
44. *Boston Herald*, Nov. 6, 1932.
45. Higham, *Mayer*, pp. 190–91.
46. Ibid.; Gloria Swanson, *Swanson on Swanson*, pp. 55–63.
47. Marion, *Off with Their Heads!* p. 207; AMPAS Special Collections.
48. Marion ms., p. 375.
49. Interview with author, Apr. 9, 1996.
50. *Variety*, May 7, 1930.
51. MOS, pp. 253–54.
52. Letter from Joseph Newman to the author, Mar. 14, 1996.
53. *Los Angeles Evening Herald Express*, Sept. 13, 1930.
54. MGM Collection, USC Cinema-Television Library.
55. *New York Times*, Nov. 24, 1930.
56. *Movie Classics*, Dec. 1933.
57. Letter from Mrs. Roy Sanford Powell (Marie's cousin) to Roberta Raider, Nov. 1, 1969.
58. Letter from Joseph Newman to the author, Mar. 14, 1996.
59. Interview with author, Jan. 28, 1996.
60. *Variety*, Nov. 26, 1930.
61. Day, *Hollywood*, pp. 42–43; *Los Angeles Evening Herald Express*, Nov. 21, 1930.
62. *Los Angeles Evening Herald Express*, Nov. 21, 1930.
63. *Los Angeles Examiner*, Nov. 22, 1930.
64. MGM accounting ledger, AMPAS Special Collections.
65. *Los Angeles Record*, Nov. 11, 1930.
66. *Los Angeles Evening Herald Express*, Nov. 25, 1930.
67. *Los Angeles Evening Herald Express*, Nov. 28, 1930.
68. *Los Angeles Evening Herald Express*, Nov. 15, 1930.
69. *Los Angeles Evening Herald Express*, Dec. 15, 1930.
70. *San Diego Union*, Aug. 27, 1933.
71. *New York Times*, Apr. 11, 1936.
72. Norman Zierold, *The Moguls*, p. 303.
73. Interview with author, Apr. 9, 1996.
74. *Los Angeles Record*, Nov. 10, 1930.

Chapter 13, Queen Marie of Hollywood

1. Frances Marion file, AMPAS Special Collections.
2. *Motion Picture Magazine*, Apr. 1931.
3. *Los Angeles Times*, Jan. 4, 1931.
4. Eells, *Hedda and Louella*, p. 152; *Los Angeles Evening Herald Express*, Apr. 16, 1931.
5. Hopper, *Hat*, p. 90.
6. Whitney Stine, *The Hurrell Style*, pp. 26–27.
7. *New York Times*, Jan. 17, 1931.
8. *Los Angeles Times*, Jan. 4, 1931.
9. *Variety*, Jan. 21, 1931.
10. *San Francisco News*, Jan. 24, 1931.
11. *Photoplay*, Feb. 1931.
12. *Los Angeles Examiner*, Dec. 26, 1930.
13. James Robert Parish and Ronald L. Bowers, *The MGM Stock Company*, p. 192.
14. *San Francisco Chronicle*, May 31, 1931; *Photoplay*, Sept. 1931; Anita Page author interview, Jan. 3, 1996.
15. Letter from Joanna Rapf to the author, July 1, 1997.
16. *New York Times*, Aug. 1, 1931.
17. *Los Angeles Examiner*, Aug. 6, 1931.
18. *Los Angeles Times*, Aug. 7, 1931.
19. *New York Times*, Aug. 1, 1931.
20. MGM accounting ledger, AMPAS Special Collections.
21. *Los Angeles Times*, June 7, 1931.
22. Marie Dressler file, Free Library of Philadelphia.
23. Ibid.
24. *New York Times*, July 24, 1931.
25. *Los Angeles Times*, July 29, 1931.
26. *Los Angeles Evening Herald Express*, Sept. 12, 1931.
27. "Private," June 3, 1933, p. 38.
28. Ibid.
29. *Los Angeles Times*, Nov. 29, 1931.
30. Interview with author, Apr. 9, 1996.
31. *Los Angeles Record*, Jan. 9, 1932.
32. Marion ms., p. 381.
33. AMPAS Special Collections.
34. Jackie Cooper interview in Turner, *MGM Story*, 1992.
35. Marion, *Off with Their Heads!* p. 210.
36. *Hearst Metrotone News*, vol. 3, no. 215 (UCLA Film and Television Archive).
37. MOS, pp. 254–55.
38. Parish and Leonard, *Funsters*, p. 226.
39. Marie Dressler file, Free Library of Philadelphia.
40. Wiley and Bona, *Inside Oscar*, p. 34.
41. Ibid.
42. MOS, p. 255.
43. Ibid., p. 256. Marie holds the dubious distinction of being the first major Academy Award winner to die. She preceded George Arliss (Best Actor of 1929/30 for *Disraeli*) by 14 years. She remained the oldest Best Actress winner for 50 years, until 74-year-old Katharine Hepburn won it for *On Golden Pond* in 1982.
44. LOC.

45. Marion, *Off with Their Heads!* p. 232.
46. MGM accounting ledger, AMPAS Special Collections.
47. James Kotsilibas-Davis and Myrna Loy, *Myrna Loy — Being and Becoming*, pp. 71–72.
48. *Variety*, Feb. 9, 1932.
49. *New York Times*, Feb. 6, 1932.
50. *Liberty*, Feb. 6, 1932.
51. *Los Angeles Evening Herald Express*, Oct. 23, 1931.
52. MGM Collection, USC Cinema-Television Library.
53. MOS, pp. 274–75.
54. Marie Dressler file, Free Library of Philadelphia.
55. Ibid.
56. Marie Dressler file, MCNY.
57. *Los Angeles Times*, reprinted in *Glow International*, May 1984.
58. C. B. Purdom, *The Perfect Master*, p. 1661.
59. MOS, pp. 278–79.
60. Ibid., pp. 277–78.
61. Marie Dressler file, Free Library of Philadelphia.
62. "Private," June 3, 1933, p. 38; *Architectural Digest*, Apr. 1996; AMPAS Special Collections.
63. *Los Angeles Times*, June 7, 1931.
64. Interview with author, Apr. 9, 1996.
65. *Los Angeles Evening Herald Express*, Oct. 4, 1932.
66. Interview with author, Apr. 9, 1996.
67. Interview with author, Jan. 28, 1996.
68. *Los Angeles Examiner*, May 29, 1931.
69. AMPAS Photo Collection.
70. *Los Angeles Record*, Aug. 18, 1933.
71. *Hollywood Citizen News*, June 15, 1933.
72. *Los Angeles Times*, June 7, 1931.
73. Ibid.
74. Marie Dressler file, MCNY.
75. AMPAS Photo Collection.
76. *Los Angeles Post-Record*, Nov. 18, 1933.

Chapter 14, "Careless Rapture"

1. Marion ms., p. 427.
2. *Classic Film Collector*, #35, p. 20.
3. Ibid.
4. Marie Dressler file, Free Library of Philadelphia.
5. Ibid.
6. *Variety*, Dec. 15, 1948.
7. MGM Collection, USC Cinema-Television Library.
8. AMPAS Photo Collection.
9. Interview with author, Jan. 3, 1996.
10. Ibid.
11. Ibid.
12. MGM accounting ledger, AMPAS Special Collections.
13. MGM Collection, USC Cinema–Television Library.
14. *Motion Picture Herald*, Nov. 5, 1932.
15. *Hollywood Reporter*, Nov. 1, 1932.
16. MGM Collection, USC Cinema–Television Library.
17. AMPAS Special Collections.
18. Interview with author, Jan. 26, 1996.
19. *New York Times*, Nov. 26, 1932.
20. MGM accounting ledger, AMPAS Special Collections.
21. *Time*, Dec. 5, 1932.
22. *Hollywood Citizen News*, June 6, 1932.
23. *Boston Herald*, Nov. 19, 1932.
24. Marie Dressler death certificate.
25. *Los Angeles Times Sunday Magazine*, Aug. 7, 1932.
26. *Los Angeles Evening Herald Express*, Sept. 17, 1932.
27. *Los Angeles Evening Herald Express*, Oct. 26, 1932.
28. "Private," May 20, 1933, p. 10.
29. Ibid., p. 12.
30. "Private," May 13, 1933, pp. 20, 21.
31. Wiley and Bona, *Inside Oscar*, p. 41.
32. Ibid.
33. Higham, *Mayer*, p. 219.
34. Dore Schary, *Heyday*, pp. 61–62.
35. Marie Dressler file, Cleveland Public Library, Dec. 22, 1932.
36. Marie Dressler file, Free Library of Philadelphia; letter from Sierra Pecheur to the author, Aug. 14, 1996.
37. Ibid.
38. *Los Angeles Times*, Mar. 31, 1933.
39. Marie Dressler ledger, Eric D. Bernhoft Collection.
40. *Photoplay*, Sept. 1932.
41. Ibid.
42. *Saturday Evening Post Movie Book*, p. 37.
43. Marie Dressler file, Free Library of Philadelphia.
44. Mervyn LeRoy, *Mervyn LeRoy: Take One*, pp. 119–21.
45. MOS, p. 279.
46. Ibid.
47. *Tugboat Annie* scrapbook (Marie Dressler Foundation).
48. LeRoy, *Take One*, p. 119.
49. Ibid., p. 120.
50. Ibid.
51. *Los Angeles Times*, Aug. 13, 1933.
52. AMPAS Special Collections.
53. *Los Angeles Evening Herald Express*, July 4, 1933.
54. MGM accounting ledger, AMPAS Special Collections; *Variety*, Aug. 15, 1933.

55. AMPAS Special Collections.
56. *Variety*, Aug. 15, 1933.
57. *Newsweek*, Aug. 19, 1933.
58. *Rob Wagner's Script*, Aug. 19, 1933.
59. AMPAS Special Collections.
60. Interview with Marcella Rabwin and author, Jan. 26, 1996.
61. Jay Robert Nash and Stanley Ralph Ross, *The Motion Picture Guide, 1927–1983*, p. 660.
62. AMPAS Special Collections.
63. Marion ms., p. 414.
64. Letter from George Cukor to David Chierichetti, AMPAS Special Collections.
65. Emanuel Levy, *George Cukor*, p. 72.
66. Ibid., p. 74.
67. AMPAS Special Collections.
68. Ibid.
69. Irving Shulman notes, AMPAS.
70. *Kansas City Star*, June 21, 1933.
71. MOS, p. 259.
72. Interview with author, Jan. 24, 1996.
73. Letter from Dora Eastman to the author, Mar. 14, 1996.
74. *New York Evening Post*, Aug. 19, 1933.
75. Letter from Joseph Newman to the author, Mar. 14, 1996.
76. George Cukor Collection, AMPAS.
77. Ibid., May 8, 1933.
78. *New York Times*, Aug. 24, 1933.
79. Ibid.
80. MGM accounting ledger, AMPAS Special Collections.
81. Nash and Ross, *Motion Picture Guide*, p. 660.
82. *Los Angeles Evening Herald Express*, Aug. 23, 1933.
83. *Time*, Aug. 7, 1933.
84. Marie Dressler file, AMPAS.
85. Marie Dressler file, MCNY.
86. *New York Times*, Oct. 8, 1933.
87. MOS, pp. 270–71.
88. *Los Angeles Evening Herald Express*, Feb. 6, 1932.
89. Ibid.
90. *Los Angeles Evening Herald Express*, Aug. 12, 1933.
91. *New York Times*, Sept. 21, 1933.
92. *New York Times*, Sept. 29, 1933.
93. *Los Angeles Examiner*, June 30, 1934.
94. MOS, p. 180.
95. *New York Times*, Oct. 11, 1933.
96. *New York Times*, Oct. 8, 1933.
97. *New York Times*, Sept. 21, 1933.

Chapter 15, Pacific

1. *Los Angeles Times*, Oct. 18, 1933.
2. *Tugboat Annie* scrapbook (Marie Dressler Foundation).
3. AMPAS Special Collections, Nov. 22, 1933.
4. *Marie Dressler Foundation*, vol. 1, no. 1 (July 1994).
5. Ibid.
6. Marie Dressler file, New York Public Library of the Performing Arts.
7. Ibid.
8. *Photoplay*, Oct. 1934.
9. *New York Times*, Nov. 10, 1933.
10. *Photoplay*, Oct. 1934.
11. *New York Times*, Nov. 10, 1933.
12. *Los Angeles Times*, Nov. 11, 1933.
13. *Los Angeles Evening Herald Express*, July 30, 1934.
14. *Hearst Metrotone News*, vol. 5, no. 215 (UCLA Film and Television Archive).
15. *Photoplay*, Oct. 1934.
16. *Los Angeles Times*, Nov. 10, 1933.
17. Ibid.
18. *Los Angeles Times*, Nov. 11, 1933.
19. *Los Angeles Times*, Nov. 12, 1933.
20. Ibid.
21. *Photoplay*, Oct. 1934.
22. *Motion Picture Herald*, Nov. 18, 1933. *Christopher Bean* is rarely seen today. Several movies have similar plots, including *His Double Life* (1933), *Woman in Distress* (1936) with May Robson, and *Holy Matrimony* (1943). *Christopher Bean* was taped three times as a television movie, with Abby played by Lillian Gish in 1949, Helen Hayes in 1950, and Thelma Ritter in 1955.
23. *Film Daily*, Nov. 22, 1933.
24. *Los Angeles Evening Herald Express*, Aug. 12, 1933.
25. Interview with author, Jan. 28, 1996.
26. *New York Times*, Nov. 13, 1933.
27. *Los Angeles Evening Herald Express*, Jan. 5, 1934.
28. *Los Angeles Examiner*, Jan. 16, 1934.
29. *Los Angeles Times*, Nov. 28 and 30, 1933.
30. Marion ms., pp. 427–29.
31. David F. Myrick, *Montecito and Santa Barbara*, p. 331.
32. Affidavit of Mamie Cox in the estate of Marie Dressler.
33. Interview with author, Apr. 9, 1996.
34. Mordden, *Star*, p. 128; Marie Dressler file, Free Library of Philadelphia; Higham, Mayer, p. 254.
35. Schickel, *Men Who Made*, p. 70.
36. Mordden, *Star*, p. 128.
37. Interview with "Major" Carl Roup and author, Jan. 28, 1996.
38. Strickling retirement tribute, AMPAS, Sept. 14, 1974.
39. Interview with author, Feb. 25, 1996.
40. Marion ms., pp. 429–30.
41. *Los Angeles Times*, Aug. 15, 1934.

42. *New York Times*, Aug. 15, 1934.
43. *Hollywood Citizen News*, Aug. 14, 1934.
44. Interview with author, Apr. 9, 1996.
45. *Los Angeles Times*, July 29, 1934; Eames, *MGM*, p. 176. The proposed Marie Dressler movies met different fates. *Tish* was filmed at MGM in 1942 with Marjorie Main in the title role. *Living in a Big Way* was doomed with the deaths of Irving Thalberg in 1936 and Jean Harlow in 1937. Gene Kelly starred in a 1947 release called *Living in a Big Way*, but it had no other resemblance to the original project.
46. Ronald J. Fields, *Fields on Fields*, p. 124.
47. MOS, pp. 289–90.
48. Letters from Grace A. Ruthrruff to the author, Sept. 1 and 2, 1996; letter from Ruthrruff to Marie Dressler Foundation, June 10, 1996; *Cobourg Daily Star*, Aug. 9, 1996.
49. *Santa Barbara Sunday Daily News*, July 29, 1934.
50. Marie Dressler file, MCNY.
51. Marion ms., p. 430.
52. Ibid.
53. Ibid.
54. MOS, p. 220.
55. Marie Dressler death certificate, Marie Dressler Foundation.

Epilogue

1. *Los Angeles Times*, July 29, 1934.
2. Ibid.
3. *Los Angeles Times*, July 30, 1934.
4. *Los Angeles Times*, July 29, 1934.
5. Ibid.
6. *Los Angeles Times*, July 31, 1934.
7. *Los Angeles Times*, July 29, 1934.
8. Ibid.
9. Ibid.
10. Marie Dressler file, New York Public Library of the Performing Arts.
11. *Los Angeles Times*, July 29, 1934.
12. Ibid.
13. *Los Angeles Times*, Aug. 1, 1934.
14. *Los Angeles Times*, July 30 and 31, 1934.
15. *New York Times*, July 31, 1934.
16. *Los Angeles Times*, Aug. 1, 1934; DuBrey ms.
17. *San Francisco Chronicle*, July 30, 1934.
18. Marie Dressler file, Free Library of Philadelphia; DuBrey ms.
19. Letter from Grace Annable Ruthrruff to Marie Dressler Foundation, June 10, 1996.
20. *Los Angeles Times*, Aug. 1, 1934; DuBrey ms.
21. Letter from Cari Beauchamp to the author, Oct. 31, 1995.
22. MOS, p. 276; DuBrey ms.
23. *Los Angeles Times*, Aug. 1, 1934.
24. Marie Dressler file, MCNY.
25. Marion, *Off with Their Heads!* p. 246.
26. *New York Times*, Aug. 2, 1934.
27. *New York Times*, Aug. 3, 1934.
28. Marie Dressler file, Cleveland Public Library, Aug. 3, 1934.
29. *Los Angeles Times*, Aug. 3, 1934.
30. Letter from Grace Annable Ruthrruff to Marie Dressler Foundation, June 10, 1996.
31. Marie Dressler file, MCNY, Dec. 2, 1934.
32. *New York Times*, Aug. 6, 1934.
33. *Los Angeles Times*, Aug. 7, 1934.
34. *Los Angeles Times*, Sept. 20, 1934.
35. *Los Angeles Times*, Sept. 15, 1934.
36. *New York Times*, Aug. 3, 1934.
37. Marie Dressler file, Cleveland Public Library.
38. *Los Angeles Times*, Oct. 7, 1934.
39. *New York Times*, Oct. 9, 1934.
40. *Los Angeles Times*, Oct. 9, 1934.
41. *New York Times*, Mar. 1, 1935.
42. *Los Angeles Times*, May 6, 1935.
43. *Los Angeles Times*, May 6, 1935; *New York Times*, Mar. 23, 1935.
44. *New York Times Book Review*, Nov. 25, 1934.
45. *San Francisco Chronicle*, Dec. 11, 1934.
46. *New York Times*, Apr. 17, 1949.
47. Interview with author, June 25, 1996.
48. *New York Times*, Apr. 20, 1949.
49. *New York Times*, Aug. 16, 1949.
50. Montecito History Committee.
51. *New York Times*, Apr. 11, 1936; Hopper, *Hat*, p. 91.
52. *Los Angeles Herald-Examiner*, Aug. 30, 1972.
53. *Variety*, Nov. 22, 1972.
54. Frances Marion file, AMPAS Special Collections.
55. Interview with author, Feb. 24, 1996.
56. *New York Times*, Jan. 26, 1952; Parrish and Leonard, *Funsters*, p. 480.
57. *New York Times*, Nov. 6, 1960.
58. Interview with John Phillip Law and author, Mar. 4, 1997; *Classic Images*, Dec. 1993.
59. Marie Dressler Foundation, "Marie" (July 1994).
60. *Cobourg Daily Star*, Jan. 16, 1989.
61. Marie Dressler Foundation, "Marie" (July 1994).
62. *Los Angeles Evening Herald Express*, Apr. 2, 1937.
63. *Variety*, Mar. 15, 1939.
64. *Redbook*, Aug. 1962, p. 40.
65. Interview with author, Jan. 26, 1996.
66. *Variety*, May 16, 1990; letter from Arthur James to the author, Jan. 31, 1997.
67. Diane Alexander, *Playhouse*, p. 72.
68. Ibid.; *Films in Review*, Dec. 1966.
69. St. Johns, *Love*, pp. 33–42.
70. *Commonweal*, Aug. 10, 1934.

Bibliography

Books

Acosta, Mercedes de. *Here Lies the Heart*. New York: Reynal, 1960.
Alexander, Diane. *Playhouse*. Los Angeles: Dorleac-MacLeish, 1984.
Atkinson, Brooks. *Broadway*. New York: Macmillan, 1970.
Balio, Tino, editor. *The American Film Industry*. Madison: University of Wisconsin Press, 1975.
Barrios, Richard. *A Song in the Dark*. New York: Oxford University Press, 1994.
Barrymore, Lionel. *We Barrymores*. New York: Appleton-Century-Crofts, 1951.
Beauchamp, Cari. *Without Lying Down: Frances Marion and the Powerful Women of Early Hollywood*. New York: Scribner, 1997.
Beebe, Lucius. *The Big Spenders*. New York: Doubleday, 1966.
Bell, Geoffrey. *The Golden Gate and the Silver Screen*. New York: Cornwall Books, 1984.
Bernheim, Alfred L. *The Business of the Theatre*. New York: Actors' Equity Association, 1932.
Bliss, Michael. *The Discovery of Insulin*. University of Chicago Press, 1982.
Blum, Daniel. *Great Stars of the American Stage*. New York: Greenberg, 1952.
_____. *A Pictorial History of the American Theatre 1860–1970*. New York: Crown, 1971.
Bogdanovich, Peter. *Allan Dwan — The Last Pioneer*. New York: Praeger Publishers, Inc., 1971.
Bordman, Gerald. *American Musical Theater — A Chronicle*. New York: Oxford University Press, 1992.
_____. *The Concise Oxford Companion to American Theatre*. New York: Oxford University Press, 1987.
Brown, Peter Harry, and Pamela Ann Brown. *The MGM Girls: Behind the Velvet Curtain*. New York: St. Martin's, 1983.
Burk, Margaret Tante. *Are the Stars Out Tonight?* Los Angeles: Round Table West, 1980.
Burke, John. *Duet in Diamonds: The Flamboyant Saga of Lillian Russell and Diamond Jim Brady in America's Gilded Age*. New York: G.P. Putnam's Sons, 1972.
Carey, Gary. *All the Stars in Heaven — Louis B. Mayer's MGM*. New York: E.P. Dutton and Company, 1981.
Chaplin, Charles. *My Autobiography*. New York: Simon and Schuster, 1964.
Coghlan, Frank "Junior." *They Still Call Me Junior*. Jefferson, N.C.: McFarland, 1993.
Crowther, Bosley. *The Lion's Share*. New York: E.P. Dutton, 1957.
_____. *Vintage Films*. New York: G.P. Putnam's Sons, 1977.
Davies, Marion. *The Times We Had*. New York: Bobbs-Merrill, 1975.
Day, Beth. *This Was Hollywood*. London: Sidgwick & Jackson, 1960.

Dressler, Marie. *The Life Story of an Ugly Duckling.* New York: Robert M. McBride, 1924.
_____. *My Own Story,* as told to Mildred Harrington. Boston: Little, Brown, 1934.
Dulles, Foster Rhea. *America Learns to Play.* New York: D. Appleton-Century, 1940.
Eames, John Douglas. *The MGM Story.* New York: Crown, 1975.
Edmonds, Andy. *Frame-Up: The Untold Story of Roscoe "Fatty" Arbuckle.* New York: Morrow, 1991.
Eells, George. *Hedda and Louella.* New York: Warner Paperback Library, 1973.
Ewen, David. *Complete Book of the American Musical Theatre.* New York: Henry Holt, 1958.
Fields, Armond, and L. Marc Fields. *From the Bowery to Broadway: Lew Fields and the Roots of American Popular Theater.* New York: Oxford University Press, 1993.
Fields, Ronald J. *W. C. Fields: A Life on Film.* New York: St. Martin's, 1984.
Flythe, Starkey, Jr., editor. *The Saturday Evening Post Movie Book.* New York: Curtis, 1977.
Foy, Eddie, and Alvin F. Harlow. *Clowning Through Life.* New York: E. P. Dutton, 1928.
Gagey, Edmond M. *The San Francisco Stage.* New York: Columbia University Press, 1950.
Gänzl, Kurt. *The Encyclopedia of Musical Theatre.* New York: Schirmer Books, 1994.
Gattey, Charles Nielson. *Luisa Tetrazzini: The Florentine Nightingale.* Portland, Ore.: Amadeus, 1995.
Gilbert, Douglas. *American Vaudeville.* New York: Dover, 1940.
Gish, Lillian. *Lillian Gish: The Movies, Mr. Griffith and Me.* Englewood Cliffs, N.J.: Prentice-Hall, 1969.
Green, Abel, and Joe Laurie, Jr. *Show Biz from Vaude to Video.* New York: Henry Holt, 1951.
Green, Stanley. *The Great Clowns of Broadway.* New York: Oxford University Press, 1984.
Gronowicz, Antoni. *Garbo: Her Story.* New York: Simon and Schuster, 1990.
Guiles, Fred Lawrence. *Marion Davies.* New York: McGraw-Hill, 1972.
Hamann, Gary D., editor. *Marie Dressler in the '30s.* Hollywood: Filming Today, 1996.
Harding, Alfred. *The Revolt of the Actors.* New York: William Morrow, 1929.
Higham, Charles. *Louis B. Mayer: Merchant of Dreams.* New York: Laurel, 1993.
Hofstadter, Richard. *The Age of Reform.* New York: Vintage Books, 1955.
Hopper, Hedda. *From Under My Hat.* Garden City, N.Y.: Doubleday, 1952.
Hughes, Elinor. *Famous Stars of Filmdom.* Boston: L. C. Page, 1931.
Isman, Felix. *Weber and Fields.* New York: Boni and Liveright, 1924.
Katz, Ephraim. *The Film Encyclopedia.* New York: Harper Perennial, 1994.
Kauffman, Stanley, editor. *American Film Criticism.* New York: Liveright, 1972.
Kennedy, David M. *Over There: The First World War and American Society.* New York: Oxford University Press, 1980.
Kotsilibas-Davis, James, and Myrna Loy. *Myrna Loy — Being and Becoming.* New York: Alfred A. Knopf, 1987.
Lahue, Kalton C., and Terry Brewer. *Kops and Custards.* Norman: University of Oklahoma Press, 1968.
Laurie, Joseph, Jr. *Vaudeville: From the Honky-Tonks to the Palace.* New York: Henry Holt, 1953.
Lauritzen, Einar, and Gunnar Lundquist. *American Film-Index 1916–1920.* Stockholm: Film-Index, 1984.
LeRoy, Mervyn. *Mervyn LeRoy: Take One.* New York: Hawthorn Books, 1974.
Levy, Emanuel. *George Cukor, Master of Elegance.* New York: William Morrow, 1994.
Lorentz, Pare. *Lorentz on Film — Movies 1927 to 1941.* New York: Hopkinson and Blake, 1975.
Lubbock, Mark. *The Complete Book of Light Opera.* New York: Appleton-Century-Crofts, 1962.
Magill, Frank M., editor. *Magill's Survey of Cinema,* vol. one essays. Englewood Cliffs, N.J.: Salem, 1982.
Maltin, Leonard. *The Great Movie Comedians.* New York: Harmony Books, 1978.
_____. *The Great Movie Shorts.* New York: Bonanza Books, 1972.
Marion, Frances. *Molly, Bless Her.* New York: Harper & Brothers, 1937.
_____. *Off with Their Heads! A Serio-Comic Tale of Hollywood.* New York: Macmillan, 1972.
Martin, Linda, and Kerry Segrave. *Women in Comedy.* Secaucus, N.J.: Citadel, 1986.
McAdoo, William Gibbs. *The Crowded Years.* Boston: Houghton Mifflin, 1931.
McAlmon, Robert, and Kay Boyle. *Being Geniuses Together.* Garden City, N.Y.: Doubleday, 1968.
McArthur, Benjamin. *Actors and American Culture, 1880–1920.* Philadelphia: Temple University Press, 1984.
McCabe, John. *Charlie Chaplin.* New York: Doubleday, 1978.
_____. *George M. Cohan: The Man Who Owned Broadway.* New York: Da Capo, 1973.
Michael, Paul, editor. *The Great American Movie Book.* Englewood Cliffs, N.J.: Prentice-Hall, 1980.
Moon, Lorna. *Dark Star.* Indianapolis: Bobbs-Merrill, 1929.
Mordden, Ethan. *Movie Star: A Look at the Women Who Made Hollywood.* New York: St. Martin's, 1983.
Morell, Parker. *Lillian Russell: The Era of Plush.* Garden City, N.Y.: Garden City, 1943.
Myrick, David F. *Montecito and Santa Barbara,* vol. 2. Glendale, Calif.: Trans-Anglo Books, 1991.
Nash, Jay Robert, and Stanley Ralph Ross. *The Motion Picture Guide, 1927–1983.* Chicago: Cinebooks, 1985.
Norris, Kathleen. *The Callahans and the Murphys.* New York: A. L. Burt, 1922.

Ouida. *Under Two Flags.* Philadelphia: J.B. Lippincott, 1898.
Paris, Barry. *Garbo.* New York: Alfred A. Knopf, 1995.
Parish, James Robert, and Ronald L. Bowers. *The MGM Stock Company.* New Rochelle, N.Y.: Arlington House, 1973.
Parish, James Robert, and William T. Leonard. *The Funsters.* New Rochelle, N.Y.: Arlington House, 1979.
Payne, Robert. *The Great Garbo.* New York: Praeger, 1976.
Pudovkin, V. I. *Film Technique and Film Acting.* London: Mayflower, 1937.
Purdom, C. B. *The Perfect Master.* North Myrtle Beach, S.C.: Sheriar, 1976.
Quirk, Lawrence J. *Norma — The Story of Norma Shearer.* New York: St. Martin's, 1988.
Raider, Roberta (Sloan). *A Descriptive Study of the Acting of Marie Dressler.* Ann Arbor: University of Michigan Ph.D. dissertation (unpublished), 1970.
Robinson, David. *The History of World Cinema.* New York: Stein and Day, 1973.
_____. *Chaplin: His Life and Art.* New York: Da Capo, 1994.
St. Johns, Adela Rogers. *Love, Laughter and Tears.* New York: Doubleday, 1978.
_____. *Some Are Born Great.* Garden City, N.Y.: Doubleday, 1974.
Schary, Dore. *Heyday.* Boston: Little, Brown, 1979.
Schickel, Richard. *The Men Who Made the Movies.* New York: Atheneum, 1975.
_____. *The Stars.* New York: Bonanza Books, 1962.
Sennett, Mack. *King of Comedy.* San Francisco: Mercury House, 1954.
Shipman, David. *The Great Movie Stars.* New York: Crown, 1970.
Slide, Anthony. *The Encyclopedia of Vaudeville.* Westport, Conn.: Greenwood, 1994.
_____, editor. *Selected Film Criticism.* London: Scarecrow, 1982.
_____. *The Vaudevillians.* Westport, Conn.: Arlington House, 1981.
Smith, Cecil. *Musical Comedy in America.* New York: Theatre Arts Books, 1950.
Springer, John. *All Talking! All Singing! All Dancing!* Secaucus, N.J.: Citadel, 1966.
Stenn, David. *Bombshell, The Life and Death of Jean Harlow.* New York: Doubleday, 1993.
Stine, Whitney. *The Hurrell Style.* New York: John Day, 1976.
Strang, Lewis C. *Celebrated Comedians.* Boston: L.C. Page, 1900.
_____. *Prima Donnas and Soubrettes of Light Opera and Musical Comedy in America.* Boston: L.C. Page, 1900.
Swanson, Gloria. *Swanson on Swanson.* New York: Random House, 1980.
Thernstrom, Stephan. *A History of the American People,* vol. 2: *Since 1865.* New York: Harcourt Brace Jovanovich, 1984.
Thomas, Bob. *Thalberg — Life and Legend.* Garden City, N.Y.: Doubleday, 1969.
Thomas, Nicholas. *International Dictionary of Film and Filmmakers,* vols. 1, 2 and 3. Chicago and London: St. James, 1990.
Thomson, David. *A Biographical Dictionary of Film.* New York: Alfred A. Knopf, 1994.
Vallee, Rudy. *Let the Chips Fall.* Harrisburg, Penn.: Stackpole, 1975.
Vidor, King. *A Tree Is a Tree.* New York: Harcourt, Brace, 1952.
Walker, Alexander. *Garbo: A Portrait.* New York: Macmillan, 1980.
Walsh, Frank. *Sin and Censorship: The Catholic Church and the Motion Picture Industry.* New Haven, Conn.: Yale University Press, 1996.
Wiley, Mason, and Damien Bona. *Inside Oscar: An Unofficial History of the Academy Awards.* New York: Ballantine, 1986.
Zierold, Norman. *The Moguls.* New York: Coward-McCann, 1969.

Major Articles

Bodeen, DeWitt. "The Four Dowagers of MGM." *Focus on Film,* Spring 1976, pp. 20–26.
Bram, Christopher. "Marie Dressler: The Popular Star of *Min and Bill* on Alpine Drive." *Architectural Digest,* Apr. 1996, pp. 186–189, 288.
Dressler, Marie. "The Chorus Girls' Rebellion." *San Francisco Chronicle,* Oct. 5, 1919.
DuBrey, Claire. "The Last Dark Days of Marie Dressler." Unattributed clip, Free Library of Philadelphia.
"Les Immortels du Cinéma: Marie Dressler." *Ciné Review,* Dec. 11, 1980, p. 23.
Kennedy, John B. "Working Girl." *Collier's,* Nov. 1930, pp. 16, 89–90.
North, Jeanne. "Don't Expect Too Much." *Photoplay,* Sept. 1931, pp. 45, 117.
Packer, Eleanor. "She Was the Noblest Lady of Them All." *Photoplay,* Oct. 1934, pp. 28–29, 102–103.

Rapf, Joanna. "Queen of the Movies: Marie Dressler and 'Politics,'" in *The Life of the Party: Comediennes and Hollywood*. Kristine Brunovska, editor. Forthcoming.
Ruth, Jay W. "A Great Actress Who Found New Success in the Pictures." *Theatre*, Oct. 1930, pp. 39, 62.
St. Johns, Adela Rogers. "The Private Life of Marie Dressler." *Liberty*, May 13, 1933, pp. 20–25; May 20, 1933, pp. 10–15; May 27, 1933, pp. 32–37, and June 3, 1933, pp. 32–38.
Thayer, John E. "The Most Beloved Crook." *Classic Film Collector*, Summer 1978, pp. 16, 37.
"Tugboat Annie." *Time*, Aug. 7, 1933, pp. 23–24.
Turner, Zan. "Marie Dressler, 1869–1934." *Films in Review*, Aug.-Sept. 1975, pp. 419–22.
Walsh, Frank. "*The Callahans and the Murphys* (MGM, 1927): A Case Study of Irish-American and Catholic Church Censorship." *Historical Journal of Film, Radio and Television* 10, 1 (1990): 33–45.

Source Institutions

Libraries, Museums, and Archives

Academy of Motion Picture Arts and Sciences, Margaret Herrick Library, Beverly Hills
American Film Institute, Louis B. Mayer Library, Los Angeles
Bay City Times Library, Bay City, Michigan
California State Library, Sacramento
California State Library, Sutro Library Genealogy and Local History, San Francisco
Cleveland Public Library
Corning Area Public Library, Corning, New York
Detroit Public Library
Free Library of Philadelphia
Harvard University Archives, Cambridge
Harvard University Pusey Library Theater Collection, Cambridge
Kansas City Public Library
Library of Congress, Washington, D.C.
Los Angeles Public Library, Main Branch
Los Angeles Public Library, Hollywood Branch
Museum of the City of New York
New York Public Library of the Performing Arts
Princeton University Library
San Francisco Performing Arts Library and Museum
San Francisco Public Library
Santa Barbara Cottage Hospital, Daniel L. Reeves Library
The Shubert Archive, New York
University of California, Berkeley, Northern Regional Library Facility
University of California, Los Angeles, Film and Television Archive Research and Study Center
University of California, Los Angeles, Southern Regional Library Facility
University of Southern California, Cinema-Television Library, Los Angeles
Variety Arts Theater Library, Los Angeles
Woodrow Wilson House, Washington, D.C.

Film and Sound Recording Archives/Services

American Film Institute, National Center for Film and Video Preservation, Washington, D.C.
George Eastman House, Rochester
Harvard University Film Archive, Cambridge
Internet Movie Database
Library of Congress Motion Picture, Broadcasting and Recorded Sound Division, Washington, D.C.
Museum of Modern Art Film Library, New York
Národni Filmovy Archiv, Praha, Czech Republic
National Archives of Canada, Ottawa
National Film Archive of the British Film Institute, London
Syracuse University, Belfer Audio Laboratory and Archive

Turner Entertainment Company, Entertainment Film and Tape Services, Los Angeles
University of California, Berkeley, Pacific Film Archive
University of California, Los Angeles, Film and Television Archive
Wisconsin Center for Film and Theater Research, Madison

Associations, Churches, Historical Societies, Government Agencies, School Administrations, and Cemeteries

American Medical Association
Church of Jesus Christ of Latter Day Saints, Family History Center
Cook County Vital Records, Chicago
Corning–Painted Post Historical Society
Corning–Painted Post Roman Catholic Community
Forest Lawn Memorial Park, Glendale
Harvard University Law School Alumni Records, Cambridge
Hearst San Simeon State Historic Monument
Hollywood Cemetery
La Quinta Historical Society
La Quinta Hotel
Marie Dressler Foundation, Cobourg, Ontario
Montecito History Committee
New Jersey State Bureau of Vital Statistics
New Jersey Superior Court
New York City Municipal Archives
Office of Vital Records, Department of Health Services, Sacramento
Office of Vital Records, Essex County, Elizabeth, New Jersey
Santa Barbara County Hall of Records
Santa Barbara Historical Society
Steuben County Historical Society
University of Michigan, Dissertation Services, Ann Arbor
Whitley Heights Civic Association

Index

Numbers in **boldface** refer to pages with photographs and illustrations.

Abbey Theater Players 191
Academy Awards 1, 133, 139, 154, 164, 176–178, 188, 191–192
Academy of Motion Picture Arts and Sciences 133, 137, 146, 179*n*, 219
Actors' Club 205, 206–207
Actors' Equity Association (AEA) 6, 101–105, 107; founding of 101; in Hollywood 137–138; 1919 strike 102–105, 137
"Actors Fund/Field Day at the Polo Grounds" 66
Adrian 162, 179, 196
AEA *see* Actors' Equity Association
The Agonies of Agnes 96
Ah, Wilderness! (O'Neill) 212
Akins, Zoë 225
Alco 82, 82*n*, 88
Aldwych Theater (London) 55
All Quiet on the Western Front 154
All Star Gambol 73–74, 76; reworked as *Merry Gambol* 76–77, **77**
Allen, Irene 169, 185
Allen, Louise 42
Ambassador Hotel (Los Angeles) 129, 176, 192
American Federation of Labor 104–105
American Federation of Musicians 102, 104
American Women's Association (AWA) 117–118, 220
Amos and Andy 215

Anderson, Earl 3
Anderson, Gilbert ("Bronco Billy") 6, 76–77
Anna Christie 2, 3, 147–155, **156, 157**, 163, 169, 179, 181; alcoholic character in 146, 152–153, 158, 195, 209; censorship of 148, 150, 151, 154; Dressler's breakthrough in 151–153; Garbo's first talkie 147–148, 151, 159; German version 148, 164; success of 154–155, 164
Anna Christie (O'Neill) 147
Annable, Grace (Ruthrruff) 217, 219, 220, 224; service to Dressler 213–215
Arbuckle, Roscoe "Fatty" 81, 82
Arliss, George 108, **177**
Ashurst, Henry F. 207
Astor Theater (New York) 200
Ates, Roscoe 5, 174
Atlantic Garden on the Bowery (New York) 22, 27
Atteridge, Harold 109
Averill, Perry 23
AWA *see* American Women's Association

Baddeley, Hermione 226
Baer, Max 200, 208
Baker, George A. 18
"Ballet for Marie Dressler" 158
"Ballet Russe" 93
Bara, Theda 109
Barker, Richard 20, 28

Barnacle Bill 196
Barrett, Louise 108, 116, 122
Barrymore, Ethel 102, 104, 109
Barrymore, John 1, 109, 149, **196**, 197
Barrymore, Lionel 1, 5, 102, 108, 109, 116, 139, 177, 178, 188, **196**, 207, 218; *Christopher Bean* 203, 209; *Dinner at Eight* 197, 199
Barrymore, Maurice 19–20
Barthelmess, Richard 200
Bates, Blanche 52
Bates, Florence 225
Bauman, Charles 79, 80, 82, 88
Beery, Wallace 1, 5, 138, **167**, 178, 185, 188, 192, **196**, 210, 218, 219; background of 164; career of 164; difficulty with 164, 167, 194; *Dinner at Eight* 197–198; later years and death of 221; *Min and Bill* 164–168; partner to Dressler 164, 167–168, 171–172, 203; *Tugboat Annie* 193–196, 210
The Beggar Student 18, 19, 21
Belasco, David 52, 79
"Believe Me, If All Those Endearing Young Charms" 31
Bell, Archie 2, 21, 53–54, 74, 86, 100, 109, 111, 192
Bell, Digby 23
Belmont, Alva E. 93–94, 117
Belmont, Oliver Hazard Perry 33, 94
Bennett, Constance 219
Bennett-Moulton Opera Company 18–19, 20–21
Benny, Jack 138, 139, 140, 200
Berlin, Irving 3, 90, 191
Bern, Paul 198
Bernard, Sam 38, 45, 102, 119
Bernhardt, Sarah 35, 42
Bickford, Charles 149, 150, 151, 152–154
The Big House 164
Bigelow, Charley 50, 51
Billings, Cornelius K. 32, 33, 219; death of, 221; Santa Barbara estate of 145, 210–211
The Black Hussars 18, 19, 21, 27
Blair, Eugenie 148
Blane, Sally 141–143
Block, Al 154
Boccaccio 18, 19, 27
Bohemian Girl 18, 19
Boland, Mary 212
Bondi, Beulah 203
"The Bonnet Store-y" 54
Borden, Olive 123
Borzage, Frank 192
The Boy and the Girl 57–58, 224
Boylan, Malcolm Stuart 174
Bradner, Benjamin J. 220
Brady, Alice 219
Brady, Diamond Jim 25, 72
Brady, William A. 89
Braham, Harry 25

Breakfast at Sunrise 130
Breen, Joseph 154, 212
Bringing Up Father 130–131, **131**, 160
Broadway to Hollywood 158
Brogdin, George 10
Brooks, Carl 220
Broones, Martin 139
Broske, Octavia 65
Brown, Clarence 4, 154, 209, 219; *Anna Christie* 146, 148–149, 152; *Emma* 179, 181n
Brox Sisters 139
Bryant, Dorothy 106–107
Bulger, Harry 42
Bull, Clarence Sinclair 172
Burke, Billie 178, **196**, 199
"But Father Musn't Know I'm Going on the Stage—He Thinks I'm a Shop Lifter" 158
Butler, Frank 189

Cahill, Marie 118
Caine, Georgia 44
The Callahans and the Murphys 123–124, **126**, 142, 148, 154, 157, 158, 160, 164, 165; Irish revolt over 127–129, 130; making of 125–127; withdrawal from circulation of 128–129
The Callahans and the Murphys (Norris) 123, 127
Camille (Dumas *fils*) 73, 76
Campbell, Mrs. Patrick 199
Canary, Thomas 23
Cantor, Eddie 102, 160
Capitol Theater (New York) 164, 168, 215
Capra, Frank 145, 211
Captain Tugboat Annie 196
Carmen (Bizet) 91
Carnegie, Hattie 182
Carter, Mrs. Leslie 52
Carthay Circle Theater (Los Angeles) 168
Caruso, Enrico 3, 35, 91, 113, 119
Casino Theater (New York) 23, 26, 30, 36, 59
Caught Short 3, 5, 159–160, **161**, 163, 168, 169, 188, 189, 190; box-office success of 160, 164, 195; Dressler's opinion of 160
Cavalcade of America 224
Cawthorne, Joseph 42
The Century Girl 90–91, 92
The Champ 192
Chaney, Lon 218
Chaplin, Charlie 1, 5, 81, **83**, 89, **97**, 127, 132, 150, 219, 225; early career of 79, 88, 90; Liberty loan drives and 98–99; *Tillie's Punctured Romance* 82–84
Chasing Rainbows 140, 160, 169
Chestnut Street Opera House (Philadelphia) 17, 31, 40, 119
Child, Richard Washburn 113
Chimes of Normandy 19, 21, 27
Chipman, Sam 129
Chonynski, Robert 78

Chorus Equity Association 102–105, 137; Dressler elected president of 102–103, 106–107; Dressler resignation from 107; founding of 102–103
Christie, Al 140
The Christmas Party 188
Christopher Bean 4, 5, 203–204, 206, 208–209, 212
Churchill, Winston 69
Cimarron 176, 178
Cinderella on Broadway 109
Clamille 73
Clements, Colin 140
Cleveland, Grover 23, 31
Cobb, Irwin 119
Cobourg, Ontario 9, 206, 218, 224
Cochran, Charles 102
Cody, Buffalo Bill 31
Cody, Lew 150
Coghlan, Frank "Junior" 157
Cohan, George M. 35, 92, 103, 104
Cole, Robert 39
Colebrooke, Lady Alice 113, 116
The Collegettes 55–56
The College Widow (Ade) 48
The College Widower 48, **49**, 60
Collidge, Beulah 38
Collier, Constance 199
Collier, William 42, 158
Colonial Theater (New York) 52, 54–55
Conklin, Chester 80, 81, 150
Conway, Jack **131**, 219
Coolidge, Calvin 79
"Coon songs" 39
Cooper, Gary 169
Cooper, Jackie 177–178, 188, 212
Corbaley, Kate 165
Cosmopolitan Productions 130–132, 160
Courted into Court 36, 68, 71
Cowl, Jane 191
Cowle, Richard 36
Cox, Jerry 143, 144, 170, 176, **183**, 210–211, 217, 219; inheritance of 220; later years and death of 221; service to Dressler of 117, 124, 184–185, 213
Cox, Mamie (Steele) 66, 86, 143, 144, 145–146, 159, 169–170, **183**, 204, 210, 215, 217, 219; inheritance of 220; later years and death of 221; Dressler's health and 175–176, 182, 192, 211; service to Dressler of 117, 124, 184–185, 213
Crawford, Joan 3, 138, 185, 191, 224, 226
Cromwell, Richard 179
Crosby, Bing 157, 212
The Cross Red Nurse 99–100
Crothers, Rachel 162
Cukor, George 4, 184, 209, 219; *Dinner at Eight* 196–200
Curtis, Charles 176, 178
Curtis, M. B. 28

D'Abbadie D'Arrast, Harry 159
Dale, Alan 40, 50
Dalton, Benjamin 42
Dalton, Christopher 55, 111
Dalton, Dorothy 55
Dalton, Elizabeth 55, 57, 94, 108, 111
Dalton, Hannah 52, 111
Dalton, James H. (Jim) 6, **53**, 54, 58, 72, 74–75, 89, 92, 93, 102, 125, 144, 193; background of 52; bigamy charges of 78; death of 111; diabetes of 108–109; Dressler "married" to 57, 63, 70, 86, 94–95, 111; drinking of 53, 62; management of Dressler by 57, 76–79, 86, 88, 89, 94–96, 100, 107–108; meeting Dressler 52; relationship with Dressler 52–53, 55, 61–62, 68, 78, 98, 108, 111–112, 204; *Tillie's Nightmare* 63–64, 70–71, 107
Daly, Augustin 37, 74
Daly, Dan 30, **31**, 36
Daly, Peter F. 42
Dance, George 30
The Dancing Girl 115–116
Dangerfield, Major 33
Dangerous Females 140, **141**, 195
Dark Star (Moon) 165
Darling, Edward 118
Darnton, Charles 72
D'Arville, Camille 27
Darwell, Jane 196
Davies, Acton 88
Davies, Marion 1, 131–132, **133**, 138, 144, 169, 188, 212, 219
Davis, Bessie McCoy 111
Davis, Henry 111
Dayton, Helena 108, 116, 122
De Angelis, Jefferson 73, 76, 77
de Beauvoir, Simone 153
Delanty, J. P. 206
de Lappe, Marion *see* Marion, Frances
de Lappe, Wesley 68
Del Ruth, Hampton 80
DeMille, Cecil B. 207
Depew, Chauncey 31
Depression of 1929 143, 146, 160, 189–191, 199
Deshon, Frank 17
Dietrich, Marlene 169, 176
di Frasso, Countess Dorothy 132
Dillingham, Charles 35, 90–91, 102
Dinner at Eight 1, 3, 4, **196**–200, **197**, **200**, 209, 212, 224; final scene of 198, 212; rewrites of 198; success of 199, 200
Dinner at Eight (Kaufman and Ferber) 196, 198
The Divine Lady 132–134, 139
The Divorcée 154
Dodd, Neal 219
Doner, Kitty 115
Dressler, Marie (Leila Marie Koerber), **ii**, 20, 21, 31, 33, 39, 46, 47, 48, 49, 53, 56, 57, 65, 66, 83,

86, 97, 113, 126, 131, 133, 141, 145, 153, 161, 166, 167, 168, 169, 173, 177, 179, 180, 196, 201, 202, 208; Academy Awards and 176–178, 178*n*, 191–192; Actors' Equity Association in Hollywood and 137–138; American patriotism of, 92, 98, 99; animals and 10–11, 23, 30, 51, 68, 70, 74, 89–90, 95, 129, 183; appetite of 17, 38; astrology and 6, 123, 129, 140; bankruptcy of 56, 58; benefits and charities of 50, 66, 93–104, 113–114, 117–118, 207, 209–210, 215; birth of 9, 9*n*; birthday party of (1933) 206–208; broken contracts of 28, 51, 72–73, 86, 130; burlesque performances of 32, 40, 44, 50, 72, 73; cancer of 175, 182, 187–188, 191, 192, 194, 204–205, 209, 213–216; career of 75, 146, 150, 209, 213, 226–227; career decline of 91, 92, 106, 108–109, 111, 115–116, 118–120; characters of, 5, 148, 209; childhood of 9–13, 14; Chorus Equity Association and 6, 102–104, 106–107; colleagues opinions of 4, 17, 24–25, 35, 42, 46–47, 49, 115, 162, 177–178, 180, 226; comic opera and 16–21, 22; cooking of 3, 132, 185; dancing of 28, 30, 36, 50, 77, 83, 96, 114; death of 216, 217; direction taken by 4, 25, 63, 81–82, 96, 172, 190; early movies and 32, 79; estate of 220–221; Europe and 95, 107–108, 112–114, 116, 117, 118, 119–120, 122, 130, 163; family history of 9, 10, 112–113; father disliked by 6; film stardom of 1, 2–4, 146, 155, 203; finances of 3, 30, 41, 58, 100, 107–108, 146, 182; friendships of 4, 23–26, 33, 123, 125, 129, 136, 162; funeral service of 218–220; generosity of 17, 22, 42, 68, 74, 81, 89, 103, 205, 220; haughtiness of 14, 107, 158–159, 162, 170; homes of 23, 38, 40, 98, 116–117, 129, 143, **175**, 176, 182–186; icon status of 3, 146, 172, 181, 190–191, 200–201, 203; ill health of 41–42, 43, 44, 52, 54, 55, 57, 66, 75, 158, 166, 169, 204, 209, 213–216; investments and businesses of 44–45, 49, 51, 57–58, 118; Italian Fascism and 113, 137; Liberty Loan drives and 96–98; likes and dislikes of 3, 5; litigation and 73, 78, 88, 93–94, 100; mellowing of 92, 156; mother loved by 10, 18; physical description of 2, 11, 14, 119, 124; piano playing of 3, 10, 23, 31, 40, 53–54, 84; popularity of 3, 4, 5, 41, 155, 156, 163, 170, 185–186, 188, 200, 203, 212, 227; posthumous neglect of 224–226; producing of 40, 55–56, 76–78, 89; radio appearances of 172, 178, 204, 209; romances of 5, 6, 15–16, 27, 29, 58, 94–95, 111–112, 143–144; salaries in film of 80, 124, 133, 163, 174, 193; salaries on stage of 14, 16, 18, 23–24, 28, 43, 46, 51, 55, 58, 61, 71, 100, 130; screen acting qualities of 1, 3–5, 81, 83–84, 91, 96, 127, 132, 140, 142–143, 150, 151–153, 155, 163, 166–167, 181, 189, 199, 209, 226–227; sexuality of 5, 29, 112, 144, 149; singing of 3, 17, 18, 22, 28, 31, 40, 48, 53, 54, 101; social climbing of 32, 33–35, 144–146, 182; sound movies and 134, 135–136, 139; speaking voice of 74, 136, 139; stage acting qualities of 2–3, 17, 19, 24, 25, 28, 30, 32, 35, 36, 48, 54, 63–64, 65–66; stage fright of 3, 15, 72, 115, 172; strength and agility of 11, 30, 87, 88; suffrage struggle of 75, 87; temper of 10, 26, 38, 49, 60–61, 69, 156–157; *Time* magazine cover story on 150, 200, **201**, 203; vaudeville and 36, 52, 54–55, 57, 58, 74, 100, 169; Vermont farm of 69–70, 74, 85, 89, **90**, 94–95; vocal recordings of 60; World War I and 93–101; writing of 5, 114, 116, 175, 212–213, 221

Dressler Foundation (Cobourg, Ontario) 224
Dressler House (Cobourg, Ontario) 224, **225**
DuBrey, Claire (Clara Violet Dubreyvich) 5, **144**, 149, 156, 159, 169, 174, 184, 219; acting career of 143–144, 223; background of 143–144; Dressler's estrangement from 192–193, 212, 213; Dressler's health and 175–176, 182; later years and death of 223; sues Dressler's estate 221; travels with Dressler 163, 175, 182, 187, 191
The Duncan Sisters 157
Dunne, Irene 176
Durante, Jimmy 200, 207
Duryea, May 17, 38
Dwan, Allan 121–122, 123
Dyer, Sharon 226

Earle, Virginia 30
Eddy, Nelson 207
Edison, Thomas 60
Edward VII, King of England 54
Edwardes, George 50–55, 119
Edwards, Gus 157
Elopement 89
Emma 3, 5, 179–182, **179**, 188, 190, 203–204, 206, 208, 209, 224; best actress Academy Award nomination for 191–192; success of 181
The Enchantress 101
Erlanger, Abe 6, 35–36, 59, 103–104, 156
Erminine 21
Ernest Belcher's Dancing Tots 139
Essanay Studios 88
Euclid Opera House (Cleveland) 18–19, 31
Evans, Edith 203
Evans, Madge 197, 199, 200, 207, 224
"Every Race Has a Flag but the Coon!" 39

Fairbanks, Douglas **97**, 99
Fatinitza 18, 19, 21
Fenwick, Irene 197*n*
Ferber, Edna 191, 196
Fercke 212
Feyder, Jacques 148
Fields, Gracie 222
Fields, John 224
Fields, Lew 2, 45–46, 51, 58, 59, 72, **73**, 74, 104,

119, 157–158; artistry of 60; later years and death of 222; problems with Dalton 70–71, 109; problems with Dressler 72–73, 156; *Tillie's Nightmare* 60–62, 64, 70–71; *see also* Weber and Fields
Fields, W. C. 174, 212
Fifth Avenue Theater (New York) 20
Fired 96
First National of Beverly Hills 191*n*
First National Studio 130, 132–133, 147
Fish, Marion (Mamie) 32, 33, 37, 72, 119
Fisherman's Paradise 168
Fiske, Mrs. (Minnie Maddern) 32, 35
Fitzmaurice, George 159
Fletcher, Horace 93
Fontanne, Lynn 191–192
"For I'm the Queen" 139, 158
Forbes, James 89, 122, 127, 191
Forest Lawn Memorial Park (Glendale) 218–220
1492 28
Foy, Eddie 28, 36, 42, 60, 102
Fra Diavolo 19
Franklin, Irene 207
Frauenthal, Henry 42
A Free Soul 176, 177
Friganza, Trixie 48

Gable, Clark 1, 3, 185, 188, 207, 226
Gaiety Theater (San Francisco) 76–78, 111
Gann, Dolly 176, 178
Ganthony, Bonita (Koerber) (sister) 14, 15, 16, 43, 52, 95, 119, 163, 167, 174; childhood of 9, 10, 11, 12–13; death of 222; inheritance of 220, 221
Ganthony, Peter (nephew) 220
Ganthony, Richard (brother-in-law) 15, 16, 27, 43, 52, 95, 119
Garbo, Greta 1, 3, 4, 138, 185, 219, 225, 226; *Anna Christie* 147–155; relationship with Dressler 149, 154; screen acting of 149, 153
Garbo: Her Story (Gronowicz) 149
Gaynor, Janet 178*n*, 185
Geary, Arthur 109
Gebhard, Freddy 33
Gentleman Joe 28–29
Gershwin, George 3, 107
Gerson, Sam P. 61–64
Gibbons, Cedric 196
Gibson, Hoot 200
Gilbert, John 132, 138–139
Gillette, King Camp 182
Gillman, Rita 168
Gillmore, Frank 104
The Girl of the Golden West (Belasco) 50
The Girl Said No 157, 158, 169, 195
"Girls, Keep Your Figure" 54
Giroflé-Girofla 26, 27, 29
Gish, Lillian 1, 159

Glover, Thomas J. 188
Glyn, Elinor 132
Godowsky, Leopold 35
Going Hollywood 212
Golden, George Fuller 42
Golden, Martha 77–78
Gordon, Kitty 101
Gorman, William M. 78
"Gotta Feelin' for You" 138
Grand Duchess 19, 21
Grand Hotel 1, 149, 196
Grant, Julia Dent 32
Grau, Jules 17
Grau, Robert 60
Grau Opera Company 16
Grauman, Sid 207, 219
Grauman's Chinese Theater (Hollywood) 139, 171, 195, 224
Graves, Ralph 189
Gray, Gilda 114
Gray, Lawrence 127, 128
Gray, Martha **202**
"A Great Big Girl Like Me" 47, 52, 54
Greene, Eve 193
Greene, Milton **202**
Griffith, Corinne 133
Griffith, David Wark (D. W.) 79
Gronowicz, Antoni 149
The Guardsman 191

Haines, William 125, 157, 176, 177, 183, 184
Hale, Louise Closser 197
Hall, Mordaunt 132, 133, 200
The Hall of Fame 41, 60, 63
Halleck, Agnes 16, 17
Hamilton, Neil 123
Hammerstein, Arthur 104
Hammerstein, Oscar 40, 42, 119
Hangen, Emile 210
Hansel, Howell **86**
Hapgood, Norman 69
Happy Days 102
"Happy Days Are Here Again" 140, 188
Harding, Ann 176
Harding, Warren G. 98, 112
Hardwicke, Cedric 203
Harlow 226
Harlow, Jean 1, 3, 172, **196**, 212, 226; *Dinner at Eight* 1, 197–199
Harlow, Richard 28
Harrington, Mildred 213, 221
Harris, Henry B. 71
Harrison, Louis 40, 41
"Hats" 50
Hayes, Helen 191–192
Haynes, Ed 224
Hays, Will 130, 137, 148, 176
Hearst, William Randolph 6, 68–69, 72, 81, 132,

144, 219; Cosmopolitan Productions and 130–132, 160
"Heaven Will Protect the Working Girl" 65, 75, 88
Heiskell, J. N. 176
Held, Anna 47, 48
Henderson, Dell **133**
Henderson, Thomas 10
Herald Square Theater (New York) 31, 36, 64
Herbert, Victor 60
Hersholt, Jean 5, 179, 179*n*, 181–182, 197, 200, 203, 218, 219
Higgledy-Piggledy 2, **46**, 46–49, **47**, 51, 55, 149*n*
Hill, George **169**, 171, 176, 207, 209, 219, 222; *The Callahans and the Murphys* 127, 128; on Dressler's acting 4, 172; marries Marion 150–151; *Min and Bill* 163, 166, 167
Hines, Johnny 89, 91
Hippodrome Theater (New York) 102, 104
Hobart, George 40
Holiday 176
Hollywood on Parade, Number Thirteen 210
Hollywood Party 212
Hollywood Revue of 1929 3, 138–140, 147, 152, 158; sound introduction for Dressler 139; success of 139–140
Holmes, Phillips 197
Hoover, Herbert 178
Hopkins, Robert 160
Hopper, De Wolf 45, 157
Hopper, Hedda 99, 107, 125, 129, 132, 136, 142*n*, 172, 176, 226; *Let Us Be Gay* 162
Hoppert, George (husband) 6, 27, 29, 144
Hord, Parker A. 84
Horton, Edward Everett 130, 140
Hotel Topsy Turvey 36
Howard, Sidney 203
Howard, William K. 219
Howard, Willie and Eugene 109
Howland, Jobyna 225
"The Human Fly" 30
Hurrell, George 172, **173**
Huston, Walter 200
Hutchison, Craig 80

"I Could Never Do a Thing Like That" 139
"I'm a Devil with the Ladies" 115
"I'm a Respectable Working Girl" 65
"I'm in a Position to Know" 57
"I'm Lookin' for an Angel (Without Wings)" 40, 41, 60
Immerman, Joseph 40, 41–42, 46, 50, 51, 52
In the Chorus 58
International Alliance of Stagehands 104
International Alliance of Theatrical Stage Employees 102, 104
Irwin, May 36, 42, 118, 119
"It's Hard to Be a Lady in a Case Like That" 50
Itzel, Adam, Jr. 22

Jackson, Marion 165
Jacobs, J. W. 70
Jake 12, 40
James, Arthur 225
James, Jessica 225
Jennings, De Witt C. 104
Jenny 31, 36, 38, 58, 66
Johnstone, Earl G. 212
Jones, Edward B. 182, 187
Jordan, Dorothy 165, 167
Joy, Jason S. 128, 130, 148, 150, 151
The Joy Girl 121, 122–123, 124, 129

Kaufman, George S. 196
Keaton, Buster 132, 138, 139, 150
Keith, Benjamin Franklin 43, 100
Keith, Joel 219
Keller, Albert 117
Kelly, Mildred 169, 185
Kendall, Kuy 103
Kern, Jerome 44, 191
Kessel, Adam 79, 82, 88
Keystone Film Company 79–81, 84, 86, 88, 164
Keystone Kops 80, 83
King, Charles 140, 157
King High Ball 41
The King's Carnival 40–41, 60
Klaw, Marc 35, 59
Klein, William 71
Koerber, Alexander (father) 9, 12, 14, 23, 27, 40, 42, 43, 44, 48, 53, 112; temper of 9–10, 11, 12
Koerber, Annie (Henderson) (mother) 9, 10, 11, 12–13, 14, 23, 27, 30, 40; death of 42, 68
Koerber, Bonita (sister) *see* Ganthony, Bonita
Koerber, Leila Marie *see* Dressler, Marie
Koster and Bial's Music Hall (New York) 22, 119
Koverman, Ida 182
Kreisler, Fritz 3, 35

Lady for a Day 211
The Lady Slavey 2, 29–32, **31**, 35, 36, 40, 79
Lambs Club 76
Landau, Arthur 198
Langdon, Harry 150
La Rocque, Rod 159
The Late Christopher Bean (Howard) 203
Laurel and Hardy 139
Law, John Phillip 223
Laykin, Sol 170
Lederer, George 6, 20, 23–24, 25, 27, 29, 30, 35, 38, 109
Lehr, Harry 33
Leno, Dan 56
Leonard, Robert Z. 162
LeRoy, Mervyn 193, 195, 219; Dressler on *Tugboat Annie* set 194
Leslie, Amy 61
Let Us Be Gay 162–163, 164, 168, 169, 176

Levi, Maurice, 32, 43, 50, 55, 119
Levin, Albert 148
Lewis, Caroline 219
Lewis, Frederick E. 95
Lexington Avenue Opera House (New York) 103, 104
Liberty Loan drives 96–100, **97**
Lichtman, Alexander 82
The Life Story of an Ugly Duckling (Dressler) 5, 116, 212
Little, Brown and Company (publisher) 212–213, 221
Little Minna 55
Little Robinson Crusoe 28, 36
Living in a Big Way 212
Lloyd, Frank 132
Lloyd, Harold 127, 218, 219
Loew, Marcus 128, 128n
Loew's State Theater (Los Angeles) 174–175, 194, 195
Loftus, Cecilia 118
Lord, Pauline 203
Lorentz, Pare 149
Louise, Ruth Harriet ii, 172
Love, Bessie 139, 140
Lowe, Edmund **196**, 197
Loy, Myrna 1, **179**, 179–180
Lubin, Sigmund 86
Lumière Cinematograph 32
Lynley, Carol 226
Lyric Theater (Cincinnati) 62, 71

MacDonald, J. Farrell 130, **131**
MacDonald, Jeanette 207, 219
Mack, Willard 188
Madame Favart 19
Maddern, Minnie *see* Fiske, Mrs.
Madeleine; Or, the Magic Kiss 27
The Maid in the Moon 38
Main, Marjorie 196
Majestic Theater (Brooklyn) 68, 74
The Man in the Moon 2, 37–38, **39**
Mandel, Robert 220
Mankiewicz, Herman J. 197
Mann, Louis 157–158
Mannix, Eddie 128, 130, 150, 168, 219
Marbury, Elisabeth 123, 124, 193
The March of Time 157–158, 170
Marie Dressler Motion Picture Company 89, 96, 99–100
Marie Dressler Players 73, 76; *see also All Star Gambol*
"Marie, Polly and Bess" 139
Marion, Frances 5–6, **87**, 89, 94, 107, 108, 114–116, **125**, 129, 132, 140, 141–142, 142n, 159, **166**, 171, 176, 187, 192, 207, 210, 219, 220, 226; *Anna Christie* 147, 148, 151; *The Callahans and the Murphy* 123–125, 127–128; career of 87–88, 94, 115, 123; *Dinner at Eight* 197; Dressler cared for 89, 141; Dressler cared for by 211, 213, 215–216; *Emma* 178–179; friendship with Dressler 87–88, 94, 144; later years and death of 222; *Let Us Be Gay* 162; meeting Dressler 68–69; *Min and Bill* 163, 164–165; screenwriting for Dressler 6, 130, 154, 165, 178, 209; Thomson's death and 136, 141; *Tillie Wakes Up* 89
Marion, George 149, 149n, 150, 153
Marsh, Joan (Morrill) 4, 174, 185, 209
Marshall, James 111
Martin, Freddy Townsend 33
Mascot 21
Maugham, Somerset 115
Maxwell, Elsa 93
Mayer, Adolphe 62–63
Mayer, Louis B. 4, 82, 140, 159, 170, 207, **208**, 209, 212, 219; *Anna Christie* 146, 147–148, 151; *Dinner at Eight* 197; Dressler's health and 176, 182, 186, 187–188, 192, 206, 214; later years and death of 223; manipulation of people by 137, 192–193, 211; *Min and Bill* 168; *Prosperity* 189, 191; relationship with Dressler 144, 154, 157, 217–218; studio chief at MGM 123, 138; *Tugboat Annie* 193, 194–195
Mayer, Margaret 182, 226
McAdoo, William Gibbs 96, 98, 207
McAvoy, Dan 40, 42
McCarey, Leo 188–189, 203
McCoy, "Kid" 40
McCron, Mrs. 12
McManus, George 130, 131
Meadows, Jean 170
Meher Baba 182–183
Melinda and Her Sisters 93
Merkel, Una 200
Merrick, Mollie 24
Merry Gambol see All Star Gambol
Mervyn LeRoy: Take One (LeRoy) 194
Metro-Goldwyn-Mayer *see* MGM
MGM 4, 5, 123, 127, 130–131, 140, 154, 165, 170, 171–172, 189, 207, 219; Dressler and 154–155, 157, 159, 170, 212, 220; early years of 138; origins of 82
MGM: The Big Parade of Comedy 226
MGM: When the Lion Roars 226
Mickey Mouse 3
Mickey's Gala Premiere 203
The Mikado 16–17, 19, 21
Miles Stavordale Quintette 38
Milestown, Lewis 154
Milliken, Carl E. 128
Min and Bill 1, 3, 4, 5, 164–169, **166**, **167**, **168**, 181, 190, 193, 195, 209, 215, 224; best actress Academy Award for 176–178, 222–223; production meeting of 165; shooting of 165–166; success of 168–169, 171

Miss Prinnt 2, 40, 41, 60, 225
A Mix Up 2, 84–85, **85**, 86
Molly and Me 222
Molly, Bless Her (Marion) 222
Moments from the Winter Garden 109, 111
Monroe, Marilyn 224–225
Montford, May 17, 49, 60
Moon, Lorna 165, 178
Moorehead, Agnes 224
Moran, Polly 5, 125, **126**, 130, 140, **141**, 157, **161**, 188, 200, 207, 218, 219, 221; *The Callahans and the Murphys* 123, 125, 127, 128; *Caught Short* 159–160; comedy style of 160, 162; *Hollywood Revue of 1929* 139; later years and death of 223; partner to Dressler 140, 160, 162; *Politics* 174–175; *Prosperity* 188–191; *Reducing* 172–174
Mordden, Ethan 152
Morgan, Anne 95, 117, 118, 123, 144, 191
Morley, Karen 174, 197
Morocco 169, 176
Morosco, Oliver 79, 80, 86
Morris, Harry **46**
Morton, Charles **161**
Motion Picture Producers and Distributors of America (MPPDA) 128, 129, 130, 137, 148, 150, 194–195; *see also* specific movies
Mrs. Van Kleek 212
Murdock, John J. 144, 187–188
Murphy, Timothy 111
Murray, John T. 109
Music Hall (Brighton Beach) 58
Music Hall (New York, Weber & Fields) 45–46, 71–73, 157
Music Hall (New York, Weber and Ziegfeld) 46–52
Music in the Air (Kern) 191
Mutual Film Corporation 89, 96
My Autobiography (Chaplin) 79
"My Dynamic Personality" 140
My Own Story (Dressler) 5, 121, 125, 130, 155, 212–213, 216, 221

Nagel, Conrad 138, 139, 159
Nanon 19
National League of Women's Service 95, 100
National Recovery Administration (NRA) 204, 210
National Women's Party 94
Nazimova, Alla 132
Neiland, Marshall 141–143, 150
Nevada Stock Company 12, 14–16
New Amsterdam Opera House (New York) 58, 102
Newman, Joseph 4; *Dinner at Eight* 199; *Min and Bill* 165–166, 167
Nixon, Doris 175
Nordica, Lillian 33
Normand, Mabel 79, 80, 81, **83**, 88; problems and death of 150; *Tillie's Punctured Romance* 82–84

Norris, Kathleen 123, 127, 128
Novarro, Ramon 1, 138, 156–157, 184, 188
NRA *see* National Recovery Administration
Nuzum, Franklin 210, 213, 217; health reports of Dressler by 214–216

O Evening Star 225–226
Ochs, Adolph 144, 219
O'Day, Thomas 84
O'Donohue, Joseph J., IV 39, 112
Off with Their Heads! (Marion) 222
Oh! Mr. Belasco 52
Old Timers' Week 118, 119, 158
Olivette 19
One Romantic Night 159, 169
O'Neil, Sally **126**, 127, 128
O'Neill, Eugene 147
Orpheum Vaudeville Circuit 42
Osterman, Katherine 76
O'Sullivan, Maureen 4, 193, 195
Ouida 15
"Over There" 103

Page, Anita 4, 5, 139, 160, **161**, 188, 191
Paid to Laugh 212
Palace Theater (New York) 39, 100, 118
Palace Theater (London) 53–54, 55
Palmer, Albert 28, 119
Parade of the Award Nominees 191–192
Paramount Pictures 82, 140, 210
Paris, Barry 149
Parsons, Louella 159, 172, 174
The Passing Show of 1921 109, **110**
Pastor, Tony 23, 44
The Patsy 130–132, **133**, 152, 157
Patterson, Elizabeth 199
Payne, Robert 149, 152
PCA *see* Production Code Administration
Pearl, Jack 115, 172, 185, 191, 200
Peggy Ann 119
La Périchole 21
Perils of Pauline 96
Pershing, John Joseph 98
Perugini, Signor (Chatterton) 25–26, 29
Phillips, A. R. 32
Phillips, Hallie 95, 176, **202**, 220; travels with Dressler 112, 204
Phillips, Robert 95
Philopoena 55–57, 107, 116
Pickford, Mary 1, 89, **97**, 99, 178n, 207, 215, 225, 226
Pike, Robert 80, 107
Pius XI, Pope 113
PMA *see* Producing Managers' Association
Politics 4, 5, 174–175, 176, 185, 189, 209
Pope, Alexander (epigram) 1
Potter, Paul 29
Preston, John 78

Princess Nicotine 23, 25–26, 29
Proctor's Pleasure Palace (New York) 32, 34, 52
Production Code Administration (PCA) 212
Producing Managers' Association (PMA) 104
Prohibition 101, 114, 145, 195
Prosperity 5, 188–191, 195, 203, 209; marketing and rewrites of 188–189; success of 190

Queen Christina 149
La Quinta Resort 144–145, 169, 170, 193, 210–211

Rabwin, Marcella 4, 190, 198, 225
Radio-Keith-Orpheum *see* RKO
"Ragtime Will Be Mah Finish" 40
Rain (Maugham) 115
Raine, Norman Reilly 224
Rambeau, Marjorie 165, **166**, 196
Rankin, Doris 197*n*
Rapf, Harry 157–158, 164, 165, 193, 219
Rapf, Maurice 221
"Rastus Take Me Back" 60
Read, Marilyn Strickling 211, 223
Red-Headed Woman 172
Reducing 5, 172–174, 176, 188, 189, 209, 226; success of 174
Rehan, Ada 37, 37*n*
Reichenbach, Harry 117
Reisner, Charles 140, 157–158, **169**, 172–173, 174, 219; on Dressler's acting 171–172
Renault, Francis 109
"Rhapsody in Blue" (Gershwin) 107
Rice, Andrew 139, 158
Rice, Edward E. 28, 119
Richardson, Anna Steese 117, 118
Ring, Blanche 64, 107
The Rivals (Sheridan) 31
RKO 140–141, 142
Robber of the Rhine 20
Robert M. McBride and Company (publisher) 116
Robinson, Edward G. 218
Robson, May 95, 163, 185, 197, 207, 211*n*, 218, 219
Roche, John **202**
Rockefeller, Mrs. John D., Jr. 103
Rogers, Will 117, 178, 185, 207, 212, 221; radio tribute to Dressler 214
Rolph, James, Jr. 176, 207, **208**
Roly-Poly 2, 72–73
Romance 154
Roosevelt, Eleanor 204, 207, 214, 215
Roosevelt, Franklin D. 5, 97, 98, 189, 204, 207, 210, 215
Roosevelt, Theodore 53
Root, Wells 174
The Rose of Algeria 62
Rosenthal, J. J. 76, 78
Ross, Charles 42
"Rough Perfect" 100–101

Roup, "Major" Carl 167
Roycroft, Ida May 169
Russell, Lillian 2, 23–26, **24**, 28, 36, 45, 47, 51, 102, 104, 108, 209; background of 23; beauty of 24; later years and death of 112; friendship with Dressler 23–26; marriages of 25, 26, 29
Ryerson, Florence 140

Said Pasha 18, 21
St. Clair, Malcolm 130
St. Johns, Adela Rogers 112, 123, 165, 176, 193; written tribute to Dressler 226
St. Johns, Elaine 165, 170, 176, 184, 185, 211, 212
Samuel Goldwyn Company 96
Sanders, Marion B. 212
Savoy Theater (San Francisco) 68, 77
Schaeffer, Chester 198
Schalenburg, Harold 214, 217
Schary, Dore 192
Schenck, Nicholas 219
Screen Actors' Guild 209–210, 219
The Scrublady 96
Sears, Zelda 174, 174*n* 188, 193
"Seductive Caroline" 57
Selznick, David O. 4, 192, 196, 197–198, 200, 207
Sennett, Mack 6, 53, 79, 88, 150, 156, 160, 164; career of 79; later years and death of 223; *Tillie's Punctured Romance* 80–82, 84
Shaw, George Bernard 193, 199
Shay, Charles 104
Shearer, Norma 1, 132, 138–139, 154, 176, **177**, 178n, 185, 207, 218, 219; Academy Award presented to Dressler by 177–178; *Let Us Be Gay* 162–163, 164
Shilling, Marion 158
Shippey, Lee 208
Shubert, Jake 59, 61–64, 104, 108, 109, 114, 117; business of 70–71, 74, 84
Shubert, Lee 59–63, 74, 104, 114, 117; business of 61, 70–71, 84
Shubert, Sam 59
Silverman, Sime 90
The Sin of Madeline Claudet 191–192
"Singin' in the Rain" 139
Sire Brothers 40–41
"Sister Susie's Sewing Shirts for Soldiers" 84
Skippy 177
Sloane, A. Baldwin 60, 64–65, 70, 119
Smith, Edgar 36, 44, 55, 56, 60, 61, 62, 64, 70, 72
Smith, Harry B. 22, 28, 59
Solomon, Edward "Teddy" 25
A Son Comes Home 212
"Spanish Love" 109
The Squaw Man (Royle) 50
The Squaw Man's Girl of the Golden West 50
A Stag Party 28–29
Stage Women's War Relief 100
Starr Opera Company 17, 60

Stavordale, Jack 38
Steele, Mamie *see* Cox, Mamie
Stein, Paul 159
Stewart, Donald Ogden 198
Strang, Louis 19, 23, 30, 32
Strickling, Howard 151, 176, 193, 215; friendship with Dressler 211, 212; later years and death of 222–223
"Strolling Through the Park" 139
Stromberg, Hunt 165
Summerville, Amelia 41
Swain, Mack 80, 84, 150
The Swan (Molnár) 130, 140, 158
Swanson, Gloria 164
Sweet, Blanche 147
Sweet Genevieve 88–89, 92
Sweet Kitty Bellairs 44
Sweet Kitty Swellairs 44
Sweet Marie 226
"Symposium of Terpsichore" 77

Talmadge, Constance 130
The Tar and the Tartar 22
Temple, Shirley 3
Templeton, Fay 42, 45, 119, 157
Terrence 15–16
Tess of the D'Ubervilles 32
Tess of the Vaudevilles 32, **33**, **34**
Tetrazzini, Luisa 3, 62, 112, 113
Thalberg, Irving J. 132, 140, 162, 196, 212, 218, 219; *Anna Christie* 146, 147–148, 151; *Caught Short* 159–160; Dressler's health and 179, 194, 215; head of production at MGM 123–124, 138, 209; *Min and Bill* 168; *Prosperity* 188–189, 191
Thalberg, Irving J., Jr. 164
Thalberg, Sylvia 170, 189, 203
"That's How It's Done on Stage" 158
Theatrical Women's Athletic Club 36–37
Thistlewaite, Jennie 12
Thomson, Fred 107, 114, 115, 124–125; illness and death of 136
Thomson, Fred, Jr. 125, 136
Thomson, Richard 136
Three Black Cloaks 18, 19, 21
Tillie Wakes Up 89–91, 92, 96
Tillie's Day Off 89
Tillie's Divorce Case 89
Tillie's Nightmare 2, 59, 60–71, **65**, **66**, **67**, 80, 85, 119, 224; early performances of 60–64; New York opening of 64–65; 1919 revival of 106–107; success of 66, 84
Tillie's Punctured Romance 1, 5, **83**, 86, 129, 150, 154, 164; development of 79–80; distribution and financing of 82; lawsuit and 88; shooting of 80–82
Tillie's Tomato Surprise **86**, 86–88
Tish (Rinehart) 212
Titanic 71

Tod, Quentin 182
Toland, Gregg 196
Tracy, Lee **196**, 197
Tracy, Spencer 4
Traffic in Souls 77
Travelaffs 117
La Traviata (Verdi) 62
Trini 115
The Trust (Theatrical Syndicate) 35–36
Tuchock, Wanda 188
Tugboat Annie 1, 4, 5, 193, **195**, **201**, 209, 210, 212; Dressler ill during 193–194; shooting of 193–194, 200; success of 195–196
Tugboat Annie Sails Again 196
Turpin, Ben 150
Twiddle-Twaddle 49–50, 51, 52

Under Two Flags 14–15
Under Two Flags (Ouida) 15
United Artists 158
Universal Studios 164
Urecal, Minerva 196

The Vagabond Lover 141–143, 152
"The Vagabond Lover" 141
Valentino, Rudolph 114, 218
Vallee, Rudy 1, 141–142, 172
Valley Club of Montecito 145
Vanderbilt, Anne 144, 191
Vanderbilt, William K. 94
Van Derhoef, Newell 182, **202**
Van Dyke, W. S. 219
Vaudeville Managers' Association 43
Veiller, Bayard 72
Victoria Theater (New York) 40, 42
Vidor, King 132, 150
Viertel, Salka 154, 164
Vitagraph Production Company 44, 66
Vitaphone 133–134

Walker, Allen Breed 144–145, 187, 193, 195, **202**, 210, 215, 217–218, 219; death of 223; executor to Dressler's will 211–212, 220, 221
Walker, Katherine Frisbee 144–145, 187, 193, 195, **202**, 215, 217–218, 220, 223
Wall, E. Berry 33
Walsh, Raoul 182
Warfield, David 45
Warner, Jack 219
Water Rats of America 101
Water Rats of London 101
Watson, Martha 218
Wayburn, Ned 63–64
Webb, Faye 142
Webb, Nella 108, 117, 124, 127, 220; astrology of 121–122, 129, 140; death of 223; friendship with Dressler 121
Weber, Joe 2, 27, 45, **46**, **47**, 52, 72, **73**, 104;

Higgledy-Piggledy 46–49; later years and death of 222; *The March of Time* 157–158; problems with Dressler 49, 51, 72–73; *Twiddle-Twaddle* 49–50; *see also* Weber and Fields
Weber and Fields 45–46, 71–72, **73**, 118, 158, 209
Weingarten, Lawrence 169–170, 188
Weissmuller, Johnny 172
West, Mae 218
Wheatley, Louise 129
"When Baby Souls Sail Away" 74
"When Charlie Plays the Slide Trombone" 41
Whitbeck, Frank 151, 151*n*, 159–160, 168
White, Pearl 96
White, Stanford 33
White City (Cleveland) 49, 51
"Why Adam Sinned" 54
Williams, Percy 43, 44, 52, 54–55, 119
Willis, W. F. 150
Wilson, Lois 130
Wilson, Woodrow 69, 74, 80, 91–92, 96, 98, 100
Wilton, Alf 100
Winchell, Henry 61–62
Wingate, James 194–195

Winslow, Jack 184, 191, **202**
Winter Garden Theater (New York) 109, 115
Wise, Thomas A. 61
Within the Law (Veiller) 72
Without the Law 72
Women's Christian Temperance Union 53, 101
Women's Trade Union League 106
Woolf, Edgar Allan 207
Wood, Sam 189, 203, 207
World Pictures 87, 89, 96, 100
World War I 80, 91–92, 93–101
Wynn, Ed 102, 104

Yankee Girl 64
"Yoo-La (The Irish Spanish 'Sit Down!' Song)" 57
Yorska, Madame 74
"You Were Meant for Me" 139
Young, Robert 193, 195
Young's Pier (Atlantic City) 58
Yulida Copper Company 75, 93

Zanft, Major John 182
Ziegfeld, Florenz 35, 46, 47, 48, 90, 109, 218
Zukor, Adolph 82

www.ingramcontent.com/pod-product-compliance
Ingram Content Group UK Ltd.
Pitfield, Milton Keynes, MK11 3LW, UK
UKHW050539150426
5217IPUK00026B/1993

9 780786 428441